C0-GIK-780

PHILOSOPHY AND POWER IN THE GRAECO-ROMAN WORLD

Miriam Griffin (Bob Brown, N.E.A.C.).

Philosophy and Power in the Graeco-Roman World

Essays in Honour of Miriam Griffin

EDITED BY
GILLIAN CLARK AND TESSA RAJAK

OXFORD
UNIVERSITY PRESS

OXFORD
UNIVERSITY PRESS

Great Clarendon Street, Oxford OX2 6DP

Oxford University Press is a department of the University of Oxford.
It furthers the University's objective of excellence in research, scholarship,
and education by publishing worldwide in

Oxford New York

Auckland Bangkok Buenos Aires Cape Town Chennai
Dar es Salaam Delhi Hong Kong Istanbul Karachi Kolkata
Kuala Lumpur Madrid Melbourne Mexico City Mumbai Nairobi
São Paulo Shanghai Singapore Taipei Tokyo Toronto

with an associated company in Berlin

Oxford is a registered trade mark of Oxford University Press
in the UK and certain other countries

Published in the United States
by Oxford University Press Inc., New York

© Oxford University Press 2002

The moral rights of the authors have been asserted

Database right Oxford University Press (maker)

First published 2002

All rights reserved. No part of this publication may be reproduced,
stored in a retrieval system, or transmitted, in any form or by any means,
without the prior permission in writing of Oxford University Press,
or as expressly permitted by law, or under terms agreed with the appropriate
reprographics rights organization. Enquiries concerning reproduction
outside the scope of the above should be sent to the Rights Department,
Oxford University Press, at the address above

You must not circulate this book in any other binding or cover
and you must impose this same condition on any acquirer

British Library Cataloguing in Publication Data
Data available

Library of Congress Cataloging in Publication Data
Philosophy and power in the Graeco-Roman world: essays in honour of
Miriam Griffin / edited by Gillian Clark and Tessa Rajak.
p. cm.
Include bibliographical references.
1. Philosophy, Ancient. 2. Power (Philosophy)–History.
I. Griffin, Miriam T. (Miriam Tamara). II. Clark, Gillian. III. Rajak, Tessa, 1946–
B162.9 P452002
180–dc21 2001059303

ISBN 0-19-829990-7

1 3 5 7 9 10 8 6 4 2

Typeset in Ehrhardt
by Regent Typesetting, London
Printed in Great Britain
on acid-free paper by
Biddles Ltd., Guildford and King's Lynn

PREFACE

Miriam Griffin's tutorial fellowship in ancient history at Somerville College, Oxford, began in 1967, when the second part of 'Greats' (Literae Humaniores, Oxford's version of Classics until this year) consisted of ancient history and philosophy. Her teaching and research have always and uniquely connected the two. This book began with a conversation among some of her many devoted students. The two editors were (GC) in the first year she taught at Somerville and (TR) in the first year she taught for all of Greats. We invited contributions from those of Miriam's students, colleagues, and friends who were, we thought, particularly interested in the subject of this book. Their immediate and warm response was a delight, though not a surprise: she has that effect on people. We know there are many others who would willingly have contributed. We are deeply indebted to Jasper Griffin for keeping a secret for just the right length of time, and for finding our expert research assistant Claire Phillpotts, without whom this book would never have kept on schedule and might well have remained without an Index. We also thank Jill Harries and Fergus Millar for their wise advice; the Jowett Copyright Fund, University of Oxford, and the Faculty of Arts Research Fund, University of Bristol, for financial support in editing the book; and Leofranc Holford-Strevens, Lucy Qureshi, Jane Robson, Jenny Wagstaffe, and, especially, Hilary O'Shea of Oxford University Press.

CONTENTS

BIBLIOGRAPHY OF WORKS BY MIRIAM T. GRIFFIN

1962 '*De Brevitate Vitae*', *JRS* 52: 104–14.

1965 Review of J. Brisset, *Les Idées politiques de Lucain* (1964), *JRS* 55: 304–5.

1968 'Seneca on Cato's Politics: *Epistle* 14. 12–13', *CQ* 18: 373–5.

1971 Review of G. W. Bowersock, *Greek Sophists in the Roman Empire* (1969), *JRS* 61: 278–80.

1972 'The Elder Seneca and Spain', *JRS* 62: 1–19.
Review of E. Meise, *Untersuchungen zur Geschichte der Julisch-Claudischen Dynastie* (1969), *JRS* 62: 184–5.

1973 'The "Leges Iudiciariae" of the Pre-Sullan Era', *CQ* 23: 108–26.
'The Tribune C. Cornelius', *JRS* 63: 196–213.

1974 'Imago Vitae Suae', in C. D. M. Costa (ed.), *Seneca* (London), 1–38.
Review of R. Seager, *Tiberius* (1972), *JRS* 64: 226–9.

1976 *Seneca: A Philosopher in Politics* (Oxford; reissued with corrections and a Postscript, 1992).
'Nero's Recall of Suetonius Paullinus', *Scripta Classica Israelica* 3: 138–52.
Review of E. Cizek, *L'Époque de Néron et ses controverses idéologiques* (1972), *JRS* 66: 229–30.

1977 Review of F. M. Ahl, *Lucan* (1976), *Notes and Queries*, 24: 368–70.

1979 'Lucan and Neronian Rome.' Review of W. D. Lebek, *Lucans Pharsalia* (1976), *CR* 29: 44–6.

1980 'Seneca on the Couch.' Review of M. Rozelaar, *Seneca. Eine Gesamtdarstellung* (1976), *CR* 30: 28–31.
Review of P. V. Cova, *Lo Stoico imperfetto* (1978), *CR* 30: 288–9.

1981 'Demetrius the Cynic.' Review of M. Billerbeck, *Der Kyniker Demetrium: Ein Beitrag zur Geschichte der frühkaiserzeitlichen Popularphilosophie* (1979), *CR* 31: 58–60.

1982 'The Lyons Tablet and Tacitean Hindsight', *CQ* 32: 404–18.
The Roman World in the Age of Pliny and Tacitus, Broadsheet of the JACT Ancient History Bureau 21.
Review of A. De Vivo, *Tacito e Claudio* (1980), *JRS* 72: 188–9.
Review of J. Ginsburg, *Tradition and Theme in the* Annals *of Tacitus* (1981), *JRS* 72: 215–16.

1983 Review of E. Fantham, *Seneca's Troades* (1982), *TLS* 82: 1285.

Review of L. Moscadi et al. (eds.), *Cultura e ideologia da Cicerone a Seneca* (1981), *CR* 33: 138–9.

Review of P. Kragelund, *Prophecy, Populism and Propaganda in the 'Octavia'* (1982), *CR* 33: 321–2.

Review of J. M. Alonso-Núñez, *The Ages of Rome* (1982), *CR* 33: 351.

1984 *Nero: The End of a Dynasty* (London and New York; revised edns. 1987, 1996 with corrections and supplementary bibliography).

1985 Review of Y. Grisé, *Le Suicide dans la Rome antique* (1982), *Gnomon*, 57: 437–40.

Review of J. Malitz, *Die Historien des Poseidonios* (1983), *Gnomon*, 57: 568–70.

Review of W. Heilmann, *Ethische Reflexion und römische Lebenswirklichkeit in Ciceros Schrift De Officiis* (1982), *JRS* 75: 311–13.

1986 'Cicero and Rome', in J. Boardman, J. Griffin, and O. Murray (eds.), *The Oxford History of the Classical World* (Oxford), 454–78.

'Philosophy, Cato, and Roman Suicide: I and II', *G&R* 33: 64–77; 192–202. Modified repr. in M. Fulford, G. Gillett, and J. Soskice (eds.), *Medicine and Moral Reasoning* (Cambridge, 1994), 106–30.

'Ephemeral Rome.' Review of M. Beard and M. Crawford, *Rome in the Late Republic* (1985), *CR* 36: 270–3.

1987 Review of B. Maier, *Philosophie und römisches Kaisertum* (1985), *Gnomon*, 59: 369–70.

'A Commentary on Asconius.' Review of B. A. Marshall, *A Historical Commentary on Asconius* (1986), *CR* 37: 187–90.

1988 'Philosophy for Statesmen: Cicero and Seneca', in H. W. Schmidt and P. Wülfing (eds.), *Antikes Denken—moderne Schule: Beiträge zu den antiken Grundlagen unseres Denkens* (Gymnasium Beih. 9; Heidelberg and Zurich), 133–50.

'Un frammento del libro XI di Tito Livio?' (with B. Bravo), *Athenaeum*, 66: 447–521.

'Gallic Elegance.' Review of P. Grimal, *Rome: La Littérature et l'histoire* (1986), *CR* 38: 379–80.

1989 *Philosophia Togata: Essays on Philosophy and Roman Society*, with Jonathan Barnes (eds.) (Oxford; paperback corrected edn. 1997, retitled *Philosophia Togata*, i).

'Philosophy, Politics and Politicians at Rome', in M. T. Griffin and J. Barnes (eds.), *Philosophia Togata* (Oxford), 1–37.

'The Legendary Cato.' Review of R. J. Goar, *The Legend of Cato*

Uticensis from the First Century BC to the Fifth Century AD (1987), *CR* 39: 247–8.

1990 'Claudius in Tacitus', *CQ* 40: 482–501.

Obituary of Sir Ronald Syme, *JRS* 80: xi–xiv.

'Of Clients and Patrons.' Review of A. Wallace-Hadrill (ed.), *Patronage in Ancient Society* (1989), *CR* 40: 399–403.

Review of T. F. Scanlon, *Spes Frustrata: A Reading of Sallust* (1987) and G. Cipriani, *Sallustio e l'immaginario: per una biografia eroica di Giugurta* (1988), *JRS* 80: 205–6.

1991 *Cicero: On Duties,* with Margaret Atkins (eds.) (Cambridge).

'Urbs Roma, Plebs and Princeps', in L. C. A. Alexander (ed.), *Images of Empire* (Sheffield), 19–46.

'The Stoical Emperor.' Review of R. B. Rutherford, *The* Meditations *of Marcus Aurelius: A Study* (1989) and *The* Meditations *of Marcus Aurelius Antoninus* (World's Classics translation, 1989), *CR* 41: 42–4.

Review of P. MacKendrick, *The Philosophical Books of Cicero* (1989), *JRS* 81: 196–7.

1992 'Nero', in D. N. Freedman (ed.), *The Anchor Bible Dictionary* (New York), iv. 1075–81.

'Ancestors.' Review of T. Mitchell, *Cicero the Senior Statesman* (1991) and C. Habicht, *Cicero the Politician* (1990), *London Review of Books* (13 Feb 1992), 17–18.

'Ancient Attitudes to Suicide.' Review of A. J. L. van Hooff, *From Autothanasia to Suicide: Self-Killing in Classical Antiquity* (1990), *CR* 42: 130–2.

1993 'Le Mouvement cynique et les Romains: attraction et répulsion', in M.-O. Goulet-Cazé and R. Goulet (eds.), *Le Cynisme ancient et ses prolongements* (Paris), 241–58.

'The Unlikeable Emperor.' Review of B. W. Jones, *The Emperor Domitian* (1992), *CR* 43: 113–16.

Review of A. Giovannini (ed.), *Nourrir la plèbe: Actes du colloque tenu a Genève les 28 et 29 IX, 1989* (1991), *JRS* 83: 225–6.

1994 'The Intellectual Developments of the Ciceronian Age', in *Cambridge Ancient History,* ix (2nd edn. Cambridge), 689–728.

'Roman Suicide', in M. Fulford, G. Gillett, and J. Soskice (eds.), *Medicine and Moral Reasoning* (Cambridge), 106–30.

'Claudius in the Judgement of the Next Half-Century', in V. M. Strocka (ed.), *Die Regierungszeit des Kaisers Claudius (41–54 n.Chr.): Umbruch oder Episode?* (Mainz), 307–16.

Review of C. Edwards, *The Politics of Immorality* (1993), *JRS* 84: 186–9.

1995 'Tacitus, Tiberius and the Principate', in I. Malkin and Z. W. Rubinsohn (eds.), *Leaders and Masses in the Roman World: Studies in Honour of Zvi Yavetz* (Leiden), 33–57.

'Philosophical Badinage in Cicero's Letters to his Friends', in J. G. F. Powell (ed.), *Cicero the Philosopher* (Oxford), 325–46.

'Emperor of Experiment.' Review of J. Elsner and J. Masters (eds.), *Reflections of Nero* (1995), *TLS* 3 March 1995: 25.

Review of C. Lévy, *Cicero Academicus* (1992), *ECM* NS 14: 306–10.

Review of M. C. Nussbaum, *The Therapy of Desire: Theory and Practice in Hellenistic Ethics* (1994), *JRS* 85: 280–1.

1996 'Cynicism and the Romans: Attraction and Repulsion', in R. B. Branham and M.-O. Goulet-Cazé (eds.), *The Cynics: The Cynic Movement in Antiquity and its Legacy* (Berkeley, Calif.), 190–204.

'When is Thought Political?' Review Article of A. Laks and M. Schofield (eds.), *Justice and Generosity* (1995), *Apeiron*, 29: 269–82.

1997 *Philosophia Togata*, ii. *Plato and Aristotle at Rome*, with Jonathan Barnes (eds.) (Oxford; paperback edn. 1999).

'Aristotle to Atticus: Cicero and Matius on Friendship', in M. T. Griffin and J. Barnes (eds.), *Philosophia Togata*, ii. *Plato and Aristotle at Rome* (Oxford), 86–109.

'The Composition of the *Academica:* Motives and Versions', in B. Inwood and J. Mansfeld (eds.). *Assent and Argument: Studies in Cicero's* Academic Books (Leiden), 1–35.

'Show Us You Care, Ma'am' (with Jasper Griffin), *New York Review of Books* (9 October 1997): 29.

'The Senate's Story', Review article of W. Eck, A. Caballos, and F. Fernández (eds.), *Das Senatus Consultum de Cn. Pisone Patre* (1996), *JRS* 87: 249–63.

'Roman History Now and Then.' Review of A. K. Bowman, E. Champlin, and A. Lintott (eds.), *Cambridge Ancient History, x. The Augustan Empire 43 BC–AD 69* (1996); D. Braund, *Ruling Roman Britain* (1996); and A. A. Barrett, *Agrippina* (1996), *History Today*, 47/8: 56–7.

1998 'Sallust on Catiline.' Review of A. Drummond, *Law, Politics and Power: Sallust and the Execution of the Catilinarian Conspirators* (1995), *CR* 48: 48–9.

Review of R. Oniga, *Sallustio e l'etnografia* (1995), *CR* 48: 201–2.

Review of D. Shotter, *Nero* (1996), *CR* 48: 224–5.

1999 'Pliny and Tacitus', *Scripta Classica Israelica*, 18: 139–58.

2000 'Seneca and Pliny', in C. Rowe and M. Schofield (eds.), *Cambridge History of Greek and Roman Political Thought* (Cambridge), 532–58.

'The Flavians', in *The Cambridge Ancient History*, xi (2nd edn. Cambridge), 1–83.

'Nerva to Hadrian', in *The Cambridge Ancient History*, xi (2nd edn. Cambridge), 84–131.

'Piso, Cicero and their Audience', in C. Auvray-Assayas and D. Delattre (eds.), *Les Polémiques philosophiques à Rome à la fin de la République: Cicéron et Philodème de Gadara* (Paris), 85–99.

Review of R. Dobbin, *Epictetus* Discourses *Book I* (1998), *Ancient Philosophy* 20: 255–9.

Review of P. Plass, *The Game of Death in Ancient Rome: Arena Sport and Political Suicide* (1995), *JRS* 90: 235–6.

Review of K. Abel, *Die Sinnfrage des Lebens* (1995), *CR* 50: 630–1.

Review of H. Botermann, *Das Judenedikt des Kaisers Claudius* (1996), *Latomus*, 59: 694–5.

2001 Review of S. E. Hoffer, *The Anxieties of Pliny the Younger* (1999), *JRS* 91: 253–4.

2002 'Seneca's Life and Works', review of G. Maurack, *Seneca: Leben and Werk* (2000), *CR* 52: 68–90.

Forthcoming

'Political Thought in the Age of Nero', in *Proceedings of Neronia VI Rome 1999* (Collection Latomus; Brussels), 325–37.

'Seneca as a Sociologist', in P. Fedeli and G. Cipriani, *Proceedings of Convegno Senecano of 1999* (Bari, 2002).

NOTES ON CONTRIBUTORS

LOVEDAY ALEXANDER is a Professor in Biblical Studies at the University of Sheffield and a priest of the Church of England. She is author of *The Preface to Luke's Gospel* (1993) and editor of *Images of Empire* (1991). She also contributed to *Paul and his Hellenistic Context* (1993). She is currently writing a commentary on the Acts of the Apostles and completing a research project on Acts and ancient literary genre.

POLYMNIA ATHANASSIADI is Professor of Late Antique History at the University of Athens. Recent publications include Damascius, *The Philosophical History: Text with Translation and Notes* (Athens, 1999) and *Julian: A Biography*, a new version in Greek (Athens, 2001). Together with Michael Frede she has edited *Pagan Monotheism in Late Antiquity* (Oxford, 1999).

MARGARET ATKINS is Lecturer in Theology at Trinity and All Saints College, Leeds. She collaborated with Miriam Griffin in translating and editing *Cicero: On Duties* (1990). Recent publications include *Augustine: Selected Political Writings* (2001) with R. J. Dodaro and 'Cicero' in Malcolm Schofield and Christopher Rowe (eds.), *The Cambridge History of Greek and Roman Political Thought*.

JONATHAN BARNES taught philosophy at Oxford for thirty years, first at Oriel and then at Balliol. He is now at the University of Geneva. He has published widely on ancient philosophy. Miriam Griffin and he edited the two volumes of *Philosophia Togata*.

MARY BEAGON is Lecturer in Ancient History at the University of Manchester. Her recent publications include *Roman Nature* (1992). She is presently writing a commentary on Pliny, *Natural History Book VII*.

GLEN BOWERSOCK was Professor at Harvard University in the Departments of Classics and History from 1962 until 1980, when he accepted an invitation to become Professor of Ancient History at the Institute for Advanced Study in Princeton. He has published numerous works on the classical world, with particular reference to Eastern Mediterranean cultures under Roman and Byzantine rule.

LESLEY BROWN is Centenary Fellow in Philosophy at Somerville College, Oxford. She is the author of articles on Plato and Aristotle, and is preparing a commentary on Plato's *Sophist*.

GILLIAN CLARK is Professor of Ancient History at the University of Bristol. Her recent publications include *Porphyry: On Abstinence from Killing Animals* (2000). She is co-editing a commentary on Augustine, *City of God*.

HANNAH COTTON is Professor of Classics and Ancient History at the Hebrew University of Jerusalem. Her recent publications include *Aramaic, Hebrew and Greek Texts from Nahal Hever and Other Sites (The Seîyal Collection II)* (Discoveries in the Judaean Desert, 27; 1997), with A. Yardeni. She is editor of *Scripta Classica Israelica* and coordinator of the project *Corpus Inscriptionum Iudaeae/Palaestinae*.

WERNER ECK is Professor of Ancient History at the University of Cologne. The main focus of his work has been Roman imperial history, especially the Empire's developing administration and social history, and the early Christian era as well as Roman epigraphy. Recent publications include 'Die Stellung Italiens in Traians Reichspolitik', in *Traian in Germanien—Traian im Reich* (1999) and 'Traian: Der Weg zum Kaisertum', in *Antike Welt* (2001).

JILL HARRIES is Professor of Ancient History at the University of St Andrews. Her recent publications include *Law and Empire in Late Antiquity* (1999).

BARBARA LEVICK's recent publications include *Vespasian* (London, 1999) and second editions of *Tiberius the Politician* (London, 1999) and *The Government of the Roman Empire* (London, 2000). She is currently working on Lactor 18: *The High Tide of Empire, Financing the Roman Empire*, and is a contributor both to a new edition of *Historicum Romanorum Reliquiae* and to *The Customs Law of Asia*.

FERGUS MILLAR has been Camden Professor of Ancient History at Oxford since 1984. His most recent books are *The Roman Near East* (1993), *The Crowd in Rome in the Late Republic* (1998), and *The Roman Republic in Political Thought* (2002), as well as the first of three volumes of his collected papers, *The Roman Republic and the Augustan Revolution*, ed. H. M. Cotton and G. M. Rogers (2002).

MARTHA NUSSBAUM is Ernst Freund Distinguished Service Professor of Law and Ethics at the University of Chicago. She is an Associate in the Classics Department, an Affiliate of the Committee on Southern Asian Studies, and a member of the Board of the Centre for Gender Studies. Her most recent books are *Women and Human Development: The Capabilities Approach* (2000) and *Upheavals of Thought: The Intelligence of Emotions* (2001).

TESSA RAJAK is Professor of Ancient History at the University of Reading where she directs an AHRB project on *The Greek Bible in the Greco-Roman World*. In 2000–1 she was a Fellow of the Institute for Advanced Studies in the Hebrew University of Jerusalem. Her recent publications include a revised edition of *Josephus: The Historian and His Society* (2002) and *The Jewish Dialogue with Greece and Rome* (2001).

MALCOLM SCHOFIELD is Professor of Ancient Philosophy at the University of Cambridge. His publications include *The Stoic Idea of the City* (1991, expanded 1999) and *Saving the City* (1999). He has edited a large number of works, including most recently *The Cambridge History of Greek and Roman Political Thought* (2001) with Christopher Rowe. He has been Secretary to the Council of the Classical Association since 1989.

DAVID WARDLE is Associate Professor and Head of the Department of Modern and Classical Languages at the University of South Africa. He is the author of *Valerius Maximus: Memorable Deeds and Sayings*, i (1998).

ALEXANDER YAKOBSON is Senior Lecturer in History at the Hebrew University of Jerusalem. He has published a book on elections and electioneering in the late Roman Republic in *Historia Einzelschriften*, 128 (1999). He is currently working on the Augustan Principate.

ZVI YAVETZ is Fred and Helen Lessing Professor Emeritus in Ancient History at Tel-Aviv University and Distinguished Professor of Ancient History at Queens College and the Center for Graduate Studies in the City University of New York. His books include *Plebs and Princeps* (1969) and a number of other works on Roman imperial history.

Introduction: Philosophy and Power

GILLIAN CLARK AND TESSA RAJAK

Unless either philosophers become kings in our states or those whom we now call kings and rulers take to the pursuit of philosophy seriously and adequately, and there is a conjunction of these two things, political power and philosophical intelligence, there can be no end of troubles for our states, or, I think, for the human race. (Plato, *Republic* 473c–d)

With this quotation Miriam Griffin began a paper on 'Philosophy, Politics and Politicians at Rome' (Griffin 1989), adding, characteristically, 'No profession has ever devised a piece of self-advertisement more blatant or more successful.' But was it always and everywhere successful in the classical world? Philosophy is, literally, the love of wisdom, the need to understand what the world is like and how human beings should live. In its classical context, it is familiar as a consolation for those who have lost power, or else as an intellectual and rhetorical exercise for the young who have no power yet and for their teachers who never will have any. It could be a relaxation, or even a spiritual resource, for working politicians; it could provide them with symbolic capital, by displaying them as thoughtful and cultured human beings. But did it have any effect on the way people behaved when they had political power and wanted to keep it, or when they feared the consequences for themselves and others if they lost it? Miriam Griffin's fundamental study *Seneca: A Philosopher in Politics* (1976) raises the question whether there ever was a philosopher in the politics of classical Greece or of Republican and Imperial Rome: that is, whether anyone ever managed to integrate philosophical belief and political responsibility.

All the contributors to this collection agree on one thing, that philosophy played a significant and distinctive role in Graeco-Roman culture. The claims of philosophy were great: the processes of government, the essence of education, the art of living, ideals of conduct, definitions of the transcendental—philosophy was the underpinning for all these. The belief of philosophers and their pupils in their subject far exceeded the wildest dreams of academics today. Although philosophy, then as now, was a tradition of scholarship, some of whose branches were technical and even abstruse, what philosophers did and said in classical societies laid claim to relevance far beyond their own kind. They could justly argue that they assisted in the mental formation of ruling elites, advised the most influential people, and contributed directly and indirectly to all genres of literature. Some of them took their questions and their models of human behaviour out of the lecture-room or their patron's villa and into the street. Moreover, as Miriam Griffin (1989: 37) wrote, philosophy provided ethical concepts and a language for making moral decisions, even for 'those who neither knew nor cared much about the philosophical sects'. For Jewish and Christian self-definition too, philosophy was vital.

Yet there are marked differences in the meaning given to this large phenomenon by the various contributors to this collection. These differences arise not merely because of the wide range of their concerns across geography and time and disciplinary boundaries, but more importantly because the role of philosophy is elusive and its influence hard to pin down. Was philosophy really essential to the power structure, to public policy, to political life? What difference did it make? If ancient philosophers are the equivalent in their societies of modern intellectuals, how does that comparison help us to understand their role or their effectiveness? The two most constant presences in this collection are Socrates and Cicero. Socrates had no more political power than any other citizen of late fifth-century Athens: he became the role-model for the philosopher who fearlessly challenges power-holders to examine their beliefs, and who faces menace and death with the serenity of one who knows what really matters. Cicero, for a year, held the highest political office of Republican Rome, and believed that his philosophical writings were part of his service to the state: he has been blamed for failing to live up to his principles.

Ancient philosophical schools assisted the powerful, as instructor or instrument: their investigations of truth and reality also assisted the non-powerful in the face of power. Greek and Roman philosophy approached some of the key problems of power directly. Plato and Diogenes, Stoics and Academic Sceptics, even Epicureans who believed in living unnoticed, offered reflections on the exercise of power, on reasons for obedience to the ruling power, on routes to practical or moral independence from the ruling power: in other words, on the kinds of choice that confronted the elite men who studied philosophy as part of their education. Should they seek power, renounce it, accept it, resist it, or regard it as indifferent? Should a philosopher try to educate and challenge those in power, or simply avoid them? A philosophically trained man might follow Epicurus and live unnoticed, dismissing the pursuit of power as a dangerous delusion, and avoiding politics except on those rare occasions when avoidance was more damaging than participation. Or he might be inspired by the radical Cynics to think there was nothing the power-holders could do for him, and that, as a citizen of the world, he was under no obligation to follow local rules; so he should make a political statement by staying out of politics. Yet Plato's Socrates advanced the argument that a citizen has tacitly agreed to obey the laws of the city in which he lives, and Plato's *Republic* offered the ideal of philosophers in power. Should he then accept the Stoic call to do his duty in the place where divine providence had put him? That would mean exercising power, if he had it, for the general benefit, and advising those in power, if he had access to them, without fear of the consequences; but, in the end, he would have to recognize that nothing is really within the power of human beings, except the choice to do what is right.

If the choice to do right is all that we have in our power, then power itself must be reassessed. People who are apparently powerless, in that they have lost political power or have never had it, may be more in control of their lives, and better able to benefit others, than kings or emperors whose power seems overwhelming. 'History to the defeated may say Alas, but cannot help or pardon.' Auden's memorable observation declares history powerless in its inability to undo what has been done; though historians may still reply that it is better for the defeated to be remembered, and to some extent understood, than to be obliterated or reinterpreted by a conqueror whose version of events is never challenged. At any rate Auden could not have said the same of philosophy, which declares to the apparently defeated 'you are defeated only if you accept defeat and surrender your moral independence, whether to a human enemy, to fortune or to desire'.

So philosophy, in the classical tradition, had the power to moderate passion, both in the sense of strong emotion and in the sense of suffering what is done to us. It could therefore console people for the loss or the absence of political power, and could inspire both the powerful and the powerless with the desire to reorder their lives. Recent scholarship (for instance, Nussbaum 1994; Sorabji 2000) has argued that some of its techniques are still therapeutic, both in extreme situations and in dealing with the ordinary crises and confusions of life. But that raises another question about the power of philosophy: in Graeco-Roman culture, was the therapy put to work, and how many people could use it?

Whatever the space it occupied, whether in the thick of things or on the margins, philosophy never lost its prevailing concern with the relation between the individual and government. As a consequence, philosophy played a major part in the evolution of political thought on law and the state, on how political systems can best enable human flourishing and how legal systems can best embody natural law. This evolution is observed here over a wide span of time. The story begins with Socrates, facing execution on a political charge in Athens of the late fifth century BC. In Plato's dialogue *Crito*, Socrates argues that he must accept death, rather than the escape his friends have organized, because he has agreed to obey the laws of Athens. He has not made a formal public undertaking, but he has accepted the benefits of life under Athenian law, and has chosen to bring up his own children in Athens, though he was free to leave. He can present his case, but if he cannot persuade the Athenians that he is innocent, he must accept their sentence. From antiquity through Hume to modern interpreters, the *Crito* has been taken as the fundamental formulation of a citizen's agreement to obey the law of the state. It has often been understood as arguing for an obligation to absolute obedience, and as grounding that obligation in a particular kind of promise. Lesley Brown engages in Socratic examination of 'agreement' and its implications, arguing that Plato has conflated agreement about what one really believes with agreement that generates an obligation to do something. She uses Cicero to make an important contrast. *Crito* takes the supposed agreement of the citizens as the ground for their obedience, but not (as in later contractual theorists) as the ground for the legitimacy of the state to which they owe obedience. Citizens obey the state as children obey the parents to whom they are born. But Cicero, in his *Republic*, envisages a state that belongs to the people, who have agreed to entrust it to its leaders.

Martha Nussbaum's paper addresses another fundamental question about the power of the state. Many philosophers argued that virtue alone is necessary for human flourishing: but is that true? Can we expect people to achieve virtue without education, or to flourish without health care and a basic standard of living? When Alexander said to Diogenes 'Ask me for anything you want', surely Diogenes should have replied not 'Get out of my light' but 'Give me health care and welfare provision for all your subjects' (even though that request would have amazed any Greek or Roman government). But the problem is that once we acknowledge need of some external goods, we also acknowledge the power of those who may be able and willing to provide them, and we diminish our human dignity by accepting the status of victim. Nussbaum contrasts two extreme cases. Diogenes, the Cynic drop-out who called himself a citizen of the world, rejected all dependence on political power. Marcus Aurelius, the Roman emperor who was also a Stoic philosopher, had the highest political power and tried to exercise it rightly. Cynics and Stoics had much in common. They shared the philosophical belief that nothing in human life matters, other than making the right moral choices, and they also believed that emotional attachments disrupt the making of moral choices. Diogenes sought to achieve human dignity and independence from power-holders and from fortune; Marcus Aurelius sought to avoid the satisfactions of power and to disengage from emotional entanglement in transient human concerns. But this detachment implies that it does not really matter whether people have food or peace or health care. How can virtue alone, without emotional attachment, motivate anyone to make even basic provision for the other citizens of the world?

The two other papers in this section move to *philosophia togata*, philosophy in the formal Roman dress of public officials and lawyers. Jill Harries reflects on the role of Greek thought in Roman definitions of law and its authority. She takes Cicero as representative of Roman legal culture in the late Republic, and of its reception by the people who sat as jurors or listened to oratory. There is some disjunction between Cicero writing philosophical works for the Roman elite who might also preside over legal cases, and Cicero speaking in the lawcourt or the Forum to persuade an audience. Nevertheless, orators could successfully deploy techniques of definition sharpened by Greek philosophy, and could appeal to popular audiences with arguments about natural law, unwritten law, moral law, or equity. Harries emphasizes Cicero's concern for communication and consensus. He recognized the political role of juries and of popular assemblies, and his *Republic*, unlike Plato's, did not create a special role for a philosophical elite who monopolized the power of knowledge.

Fergus Millar considers a legal expert in another context, 300 years later. Cicero made no claim to be a jurist, an expert interpreter of law, but Ulpian made a major contribution to juristic writing under the Severan emperors. Ulpian, Millar suggests, is immediately recognizable from his writings as an intellectual, an unmistakable academic who researches and compares texts, pursues minutiae, analyses concepts, and develops explanations. Like many of his fellow-jurists, he also had a political career; indeed, he apparently exercised great power as praetorian prefect, and died as a result, killed in a mutiny of the praetorian guard. Ulpian claimed, at least in the preface to his *Institutes*, that law is philosophy: but did that claim apply beyond the preface? Harries and Millar both point to the fluidity of law and the constant need for interpretation. Late republican law was administered by amateurs, themselves members of the philosophically trained elite, and was modified by lawmaking in political assemblies. The surge of juristic writing in the third century was an attempt to engage with new sources of law, typically case-law rulings from a local official or from the emperor. Techniques of analysis and definition, ideas of consistency and equity, recognition of legitimate authority, all had a part to play in the juristic interpretation that could directly affect the well-being of a Roman citizen and the exercise of imperial power. But Millar leaves us with the question whether Ulpian, the intellectual in politics, really was a philosopher in politics.

The second of our four sections begins with the resounding voice of Epicurus, quoted by Malcolm Schofield: 'empty is that philosopher's discourse that offers no therapy for human passion'. Schofield's paper starts from a tradition of philosophical therapy that has not yet been discussed, that of the Academic Sceptics, especially Philo of Larissa who had so strong an influence on Cicero. Philo developed the analogy between philosophical therapy for the soul and medical therapy for the body: both require persuasion to accept treatment, restoration and maintenance of health, and prescriptions for the individual and the community. Schofield argues that Philo's therapeutic conception of philosophy is essentially Socratic, and that Cicero's own account of his philosophical writings reveals a similar understanding of philosophy as an ethical project. Cicero gave pride of place to his *Tusculan Disputations* because, in his view, they were of practical help to people in difficulty. Schofield observes that modern readers do not generally find them helpful, though Cicero no doubt found it therapeutic to write them. This, he suggests, is because the *Tusculans* are mostly not practical ethics: they are self-reflexive, much more concerned with setting out debates and communicating philosophy in elegant Latin than with analysing our responses to pain and grief and helping us to think differently. So Cicero's therapy is all too academic, and does too little to restore or maintain the health of the soul.

Mary Beagon's paper begins from physical health and from the attitudes to deformity and disability that helped to make an *exemplum* of Roman virtue fighting off the challenges of fortune. M. Sergius Silvus, repeatedly disabled in the wars against Hannibal, fought on without reward: his bravery was exercised in defeats and he won no honours. He achieved political office as praetor, but now fortune took a political form. Opponents tried to exclude him from his religious role because his disability made him unacceptable to the gods. Cicero, in forensic mode, chose not to evoke this hero as a challenge to his degenerate grandson, the Catiline who, according to Cicero, threatened to bring down the Roman Republic. This Catiline was not a descendant but a *monstrum*, a malignant growth. The elder Pliny, by contrast, provides us with an excellent instance of the power of philosophy in a subsequent generation to tease *exempla* out of history (or tradition). He made Sergius' apparent loss of power and potential into a paradigm of moral as opposed to worldly success, internal excellence opposed to fortune.

Barbara Levick challenges those claims of philosophy to change the powerful and empower the powerless. Philosophy, she argues, failed half the human race. She raises the possibility that philosophy was thought to be too exalted, or too disruptive, for study by anyone except the elite male. On the other hand, she questions whether it was in any way truly subversive or made people reassess the system in which they lived; whether its effect was ever more than patchy; whether philosophy ever caused anyone to act differently, and whether it ever told anyone what to do. She surveys the effect of philosophy on Greek and Roman women, who were excluded both from the high ground of intellectual debate and from official power, and finds among women perhaps one philosopher, but no historians. Some women got some education, within limits and despite social constraints on learning and discussion; some were even described as philosophers: but overall, 'ancient philosophy and philosophers failed women'.

Glen Bowersock explores the extraordinary power of philosophy in the second century, when (as Miriam Griffin put it) Roman emperors had stopped sneering at philosophy, and intellectuals were high fashion. Philostratus labelled this period the Second Sophistic, because, as in Athens at the time of Socrates, intellectuals who could give a good performance were admired and highly paid. Bowersock traces the changing reception in modern scholarship of this 'performance philosophy' and its startling reversals. Philosophers who were (on principle) shabby and hairy had makeovers and presented themselves as the media stars they were, so that nobody knew what an intellectual looked like any more. Philosophers seek knowledge, sophists boldly claim to have it: but now a philosopher with sufficient rhetorical brilliance might achieve the status of sophist. Philosophy brought worldly success.

Our third section shows how the ideologies that determined and defined power could be formulated at Rome without the visible input of any brand of philosophy, at points where some might have been expected. If Miriam Griffin was right in suggesting that philosophy provided, in the late Republic, above all a language in which the dilemmas of power could be expressed (Griffin 1989: 36), then we might be tempted to conclude that the Principate was not prey to such dilemmas and could do without the language. The subjects of the *princeps* of course saw things differently, but close to the heart of power, we often look in vain for philosophy. Once more Cicero provides a starting-point. In recent years his philosophical work has gained in status, where once it was valued only when he transmitted fragments of serious philosophers. Judgements of his political activity have also become more charitable, where once he was despised as a politician who had poor judgement and did not stick to his principles. Zvi Yavetz points out that Cicero, so immediately recognizable as a human being, has carried the burden of unreasonable expectations. Yavetz evokes, with firmness and sympathy, the pressures on a power-holder who must make political judgements without time for philosophical reflection. Cicero, for him, is not a philosopher or even an intellectual in politics: he is an intellectual politician, a man of letters.

Three papers trace the increasing power and acceptability of the Roman emperor. David Wardle examines the choice of *divus* as the title of the deified Caesar. He finds no connection with traditional Roman religious terminology, as examined by the philosophical Varro, or with Cicero's philosophical speculations on the afterlife of great statesmen. Instead, he argues, tradition was invented, and was given credibility by using the vocabulary of archaic Roman religious law. Hannah Cotton and Alex Yakobson reassess the very careful formulation of Augustus' imperial powers and his repeated formal refusals of power. Here too, what matters is political tradition and the acceptable representation of untraditional power. Modern debate has moved from 'what exactly was the content of imperial power?' to 'what was imperial power meant to look like?' Ronald Syme famously interpreted the rise of Augustus to power in terms of 1930s Fascism; Cotton and Yakobson use Stalin to illuminate praise of the established emperor. Imperial power does not require debate on forms of government, or on whether the good man must accept political office for the good of the community, though both debates could be invoked to make a point. As Cotton and Yakobson point out, Tiberius could, in one and the same speech, reaffirm dynastic claims and gesture towards an alternative form of government or towards release from the burdens of office.

A century later, imperial power and its refusal have become standardized. Werner Eck decodes Trajan's accession in terms of political deals and putting the chosen candidate in charge of the nearest army. On the evidence of prosopography, Trajan's military and political career was much less distinguished than the official story suggests. He was not the obvious best man for the job. Pliny, in the *Panegyricus*, does what he can, and affirms that Trajan was persuaded to take supreme power only because his country so urgently needed him. Eck's own silences are eloquent. If anyone was engaged in discussing government by 'adoptive' monarchy, as a way of combining dynastic stability with the choice of the most appropriate successor, such discussions had no effect on the accession of Trajan. Even his formal adoption by Nerva was minimized, for he kept his biological father's name.

But beyond the decision-making and the definition and presentation of power, philosophy was pervasive. Loveday Alexander shows how Jews and Christians used Graeco-Roman philosophy to explain their own beliefs. In the first century, Philo and Josephus presented the Jews as a philosophic people, who meet on the Sabbath to discuss philosophy and can choose among different schools of thought. The Christian mission of Paul, a Jew by birth and a Pharisee by choice, began in synagogues, or else in modest private houses. He rarely had access, as some philosophers did, to the houses of the powerful or to the public spaces of the cities he visited. But the book of Acts portrays him as following a philosophical model at Athens, in Socratic engagement with the council of the Areopagus; and when he is arrested and brought before magistrates, he has the chance to speak out like a philosopher on trial. Paul works with the culture, but does not collude with power. Philosophers were expected to manifest *parrhesia*, free and open speech, towards those in power. Anecdotes of philosophers brought before tyrants helped to construct a paradigm of spectacular confrontation with those in power, and provided a model for constructing Jewish and Christian martyrdom.

Margaret Atkins takes us three centuries on, to a Roman world in which Christianity is the religion supported by the structures of power. She begins with the image of Cicero's *Republic* scraped off a parchment to make room for a sermon by Augustine. Yet it is Augustine who makes serious philosophical use of the *Republic* in this transformed political and legal setting. His correspondent Nectarius, who seeks to mitigate the impact of imperial law on local custom, does no more than deploy half-remembered philosophical tags and platitudes in an attempt to evoke a shared literary culture. Augustine, unlike Cicero, does not show a disjunction between philosophical treatises and popular sermons: he adapts his style to his audience, but uses the same arguments and interpretations. This is a world in which Christian preaching takes accessible philosophy to anyone who will come and listen, and Christian charity works to provide health care and basic welfare.

Polymnia Athanassiadi considers traffic in the other direction, and envisages Hellenic philosophers absorbing from Judaism and Christianity only intolerance and the wish to exclude. Right belief hardens into orthodoxy; a choice among philosophical options, *haireseis*, narrows to the choice between right and wrong, orthodoxy and heresy. Julian, the only emperor after Constantine to renounce Christianity, begins the 'intellectual protectionism' that finds its full force in his sixth-century successor, the orthodox Justinian. Philosophers who seek the true interpretation of Plato, or of the benign and social Iamblichus, disqualify each other from the true succession to Plato's chair; but that chair is now 'a post which combined academic and spiritual duties with a heavy administrative load'. In the fourth and fifth centuries these Platonist philosophers are increasingly marginalized, and too often use their remaining power, their intellectual and spiritual authority, to marginalize their colleagues. The result is a diminishing number of people, all impressive characters of formidable intelligence and austerity, doing extremely difficult intellectual work that they cannot communicate to each other, let alone to a wider community. Eventually Damascius, after long struggles to make language express the ineffable, departs from the Roman world.

Even though these Platonists had a profound and exceptional concern for the relationship of human beings to the cosmic powers, Neoplatonism is widely perceived as the classic case of philosophy far beyond the general reach. Our collection ends with a quite different perspective on the role of philosophy in Graeco-Roman culture. Jonathan Barnes goes back to basics and asks what it meant to be called, or to call oneself, *philosophos*. This is a good question, for almost every paper has made us aware of the problems of definition in different contexts. Barnes, at the conclusion of our quest, offers reassurance and an unexpectedly simple answer. To call oneself, or to be called, *philosophos* is to declare a love of wisdom, a readiness to study things divine and human. A philosopher in this sense might be a man or a woman, a Christian or a pagan. He or she need not be a professional or an intellectual high-flyer or a person of political importance. There were many philosophical choices, including strict asceticism, but a philosopher need not be ascetic; Christians called themselves philosophers, but there is no specifically Christian meaning of philosophy. Philosophy, as it was widely understood, was familiar, popular, and part of the general culture: 'the Empire teemed with such people'.

Part I
Philosophy and the State

Did Socrates Agree to Obey the Laws of Athens?

Lesley Brown

Plato's *Crito* contains a justly famous discussion of what has come to be known as the problem of political obligation, of what obligations a citizen has to the government, and what are the grounds of those obligations. To many, the most surprising aspect of the work is that it appears to argue, on many grounds, that a citizen owes absolute obedience to the laws; a position scarcely to be credited to Socrates of all people. But one argument in particular caught the attention of David Hume. His essay 'Of the Original Contract' is an attack on political theories such as Locke's which held, in Hume's words, that men 'owe allegiance to no prince or government unless bound by the obligation and sanction of a promise' (1985: 469). Hume thought this an absurd theory, and concludes his attack on it by remarking that it was a view not found in ancient writers, with the one exception of the *Crito* where Socrates 'refuses to escape from prison because he had tacitly promised to obey the laws'. 'New discoveries are not to be expected in these matters. If scarce any man, till very lately, ever imagined that government was founded on compact, it is certain, that it cannot, in general, have any such foundation.'

In this paper I explore the *Crito*'s argument from agreement, paying particular attention to the arguments *for* agreement, that is, to the arguments which purport to show that Socrates has made an agreement of the appropriate kind. I am convinced that the arguments on this point in the *Crito* are unsuccessful.[1] But they have a tremendous appeal. I find that most of those with whom I discuss these issues believe that they themselves have (in one way or another) agreed to obey the laws, and that this agreement is the (or one) ground of their obligation to obey. I shall suggest that the (erroneous) claim that Socrates, or a present-day citizen, has agreed to obey the law is made plausible in part due to a conflation of different notions of

I am very grateful to the editors for the opportunity to offer this small tribute to Miriam Griffin: scholar, teacher, and colleague nonpareil.

[1] Below I consider the views of those who claim that Socrates (in the *Crito*) does not endorse the arguments put in the mouth of the personified Laws.

agreement, a conflation to which Plato was especially prone thanks to his interest in another kind of agreement, that involved in Socrates' examination of the beliefs of another, the *elenchus*. These different kinds of agreement are set out in the next section and explored further in what follows. First, some scene-setting.

I

It is simplest to read the development of the arguments in the *Crito* as follows.[2] To counter Crito's insistence that, for the sake of his friends, his children and himself, Socrates ought to escape from prison and avoid his sentence, Socrates proceeds by first securing Crito's agreement that living well is the aim, and that to live well one should never act unjustly (*adikein*). Next he gets Crito to agree to the following: one shouldn't do harm of any kind, including returning harm for harm, or retaliating (*antikakourgein*, *antadikein*), and one shouldn't break just agreements. What follows is put into the mouth of the personified Laws of Athens, with a few interjections and replies from Socrates. The Laws set out to show that Socrates' conduct in escaping would contravene both these principles, for in breaking the law which enjoins that verdicts be carried out he would be attempting to destroy the city (that is, to harm it), and he would be breaking an agreement he had entered into with the laws. And they add a new argument, comparing Socrates' obligation to the laws with that of offspring to father. Arguing from the benefits they have provided and from their superior status, they insist that a citizen, and hence Socrates, must obey them in whatever they command, and that not to do so would again be to *adikein*.

There is a well-known problem that the Laws' arguments seem to aim for a conclusion that is both far stronger than is needed and unacceptable. All that needs to be established (to counter Crito) is that it would be wrong for Socrates to escape, that is, to disobey the law which holds that verdicts be carried out. But the arguments used by the Laws, and in particular the last mentioned, seem to argue that it would be wrong for Socrates to disobey any law at all. As well as being undesirably authoritarian, this would seem to conflict with the guiding principle of the dialogue, that one should never *adikein*. For might a law not command one to *adikein*, and how could Socrates possibly regard himself bound, in that case, to obey it?

Though my aim is not to offer a solution to this problem, I mention here two recent, independent, attempts to solve it by finding indications from

[2] See the analysis and discussion of Bostock (1990) who defends the 'three arguments' interpretation.

Plato to the reader that Socrates does not endorse the arguments used by the Laws, and so does not endorse their apparently authoritarian stance. They are those of Roslyn Weiss (1998) and Verity Harte (1999). Though they argue the case in very different ways, both read the Laws as using arguments which are directed principally at Crito, and each discerns Socrates' views only in what he says *propria voce*.[3] I am not persuaded by either of these subtle and careful treatments, but, though important for our overall understanding of the *Crito*, the issue is to some extent irrelevant to my purpose here. First, the arguments deserve scrutiny, whether or not Socrates is presented as endorsing them, and whether or not we suppose Plato endorsed them. Second, my interest in the stretches of argument concerning agreement focuses mainly on the claim that Socrates *did make an agreement* with the Laws to obey them. And Socrates does twice *in propria persona* interrupt the flow of the Laws' speech to concede that he has made an agreement with them (52a6–9 and 52d3–6).[4]

The next preliminary is to look closely at kinds of agreement. There are two distinctions that must be drawn, the first between different kinds of agreement, agreeing to do something, and agreeing that something is so. Borrowing the labels from Raz (1986: 80–1), let us call agreement to do something a *performative agreement*, and agreement that something is the case *cognitive agreement*. The second distinction concerns the public and the private, and I illustrate it first in connection with cognitive agreement. 'She agreed that p' can describe either public assent or private belief. One who publicly *asserts* that p (agrees that p) may or may not *believe* that p (may or may not agree—inwardly—that p), though in asserting that p you present yourself as believing that p, and the assertion (agreement) is insincere if you don't believe it. So cognitive agreement can be either public or private, and, if public, either sincere or insincere.

But agreement to do something must be public, as the label 'performative agreement' signals. As such it must be sharply distinguished from an intention to do the thing in question, and from approval or other pro-attitudes. One who agrees with someone to do something undertakes an obligation to that person, and in making the agreement performs an action which, in Raz's formulation, 'changes the normative situation of another'.

[3] R. Weiss (1998) holds that Socrates gives a full account of his reasons for not escaping before the speech of the Laws begins. One surprising feature of her case is to understand Socrates' appeal to the principle of keeping just agreements at 49e5–7 in such a way that it has no connection with the Laws' subsequent claim (endorsed by Socrates) that Socrates has agreed to obey them. See n. 8.

[4] I do not find a satisfactory account, in either Harte or Weiss, of Socrates' repeated assertions, in his own voice, that he did make an agreement.

In other words, it gives the person with whom the agreement was made rights they did not have before, namely, the right to require that I do the thing I promised, unless they release me from my agreement. For me to agree with you to do something, it is irrelevant whether I actually intend to do it, or whether I have one or another pro-attitude towards it. I may have these without agreeing (performative) to do the thing in question, and conversely I may agree without having the pro-attitudes. In the former case I have not bound myself, and in the latter I have. So performative agreement is always public, and as such can be sincere or insincere. And, as the dialogue reminds us, it can be made verbally or non-verbally. The Laws claim that it is by what he did, not by what he said, that Socrates agreed to obey them.

Both kinds of agreement figure prominently in the *Crito*, and we shall shortly trace them.[5] The focus of this paper is the argument from agreement to obey: you agreed to obey, and you ought to keep your agreements, so you must obey. This is of course a performative agreement, an agreement to do something. Before moving on, a word about the relation between performative agreement, consent, and promising. All of these are public acts, which generate obligations. Both consent and agreement may be to the actions of others—such as permitting or authorizing. But one can promise only one's own actions. Since the kind of agreements we are interested in (from the *Crito*) are agreements to do something, they are more akin to promises than to authorizations. Locke's tacit consent—which, in a manner highly reminiscent of the *Crito*, he held to be given by anyone who resides in the country or uses the highway—is at once a promise to obey and an authorization which legitimates the government's authority. Significantly, only the former aspect is prominent in the *Crito*'s argument, a topic to which I return in the conclusion. Remembering that we must be clear in all cases which kind of agreement is in question, we can safely continue to use the word agreement, which, fortunately, has just the same range of uses as Greek *homologia* and the cognate verbs *homologein* and compounds.

[5] A distinction between what she labels 'agreement in argument' and 'agreement in act' forms the heart of Lane's paper (1998). But the contrast as she draws it is misconceived. The crucial point about the agreement which Socrates is said to have made 'by what he did' is not that it was made by an action (remaining in Athens) but that it was an agreement to do something. Such an agreement could as well have been made by words as by an action. There is no suggestion that it is less binding because it has been made by an action, not by a verbal promise.

II

Before any mention of agreements to act, we find, as in so many dialogues, much play with the language of cognitive agreement. Socrates reminds Crito of what they had agreed before Crito's urgent plea that Socrates should let him arrange an escape (48b11, 49a7–8: the second passage refers to 'all those former agreements of ours'). In an important exchange at 49d, Socrates urges Crito that in agreeing these things he should be sure not to agree them contrary to his belief; for no common counsel, no *koine boule*, can obtain between those who do and those who don't accept these principles. The political metaphor 'no common counsel' is striking. Socrates emphasizes that Crito's beliefs are what matter to Socrates, not (or not merely) his assent. This is an important theme to which I return. Pressed on whether he abides by these principles, Crito replies that he does, and that he shares Socrates' beliefs (49e2–4).

At this point Socrates introduces a new principle, this time that one should do what one has agreed with someone to do, provided they (the agreements) are just.

> (T1) Should one do whatever one has agreed upon with someone, providing that it is just, or should one play false?
>
> πότερον ἃ ἄν τις ὁμολογήσῃ τῳ δίκαια ὄντα ποιητέον ἢ ἐξαπατητέον; (49e6–7)

Pace some commentators[6] it is clear that a new kind of agreement is under discussion: an agreement made *with someone* to *do* something. This ethical principle, that one should do what one has agreed with someone (promised someone) to do, and not play false, is a commonplace which Crito naturally accepts, especially with the qualification, 'provided it is just', which evidently is equivalent to 'provided it (the action promised) is not unjust'. We may think of the familiar exchange in *Republic* 1. Returning a sword, something you have promised to do when borrowing it, should be done—the agreement should be kept—unless (say) the owner has become a lunatic, for to return his sword would then be unjust. Unlike the earlier principle forbidding *antadikein*, which Socrates acknowledges as controversial, this new

[6] Surprisingly, and surely incorrectly, Adam takes this to involve an agreement 'that such-and-such'. He glosses the sentence 'it is our duty to carry out in practice that which we have in theory admitted to be right' (1938: 56) and he glosses ἐξαπατητέον thus: 'to believe a theory and not to carry it into practice is a living lie' (p. 60). Lane (1998: 321) seems to share Adam's view, as she glosses the question 'Should we do the things we've agreed definitionally to be just?'

one, the principle that just agreements should be kept, is one on which they swiftly agree.[7]

Armed with this principle, together with the earlier ones to which Crito has assented, Socrates begins a line of argument which will only be completed during the speech of the personified Laws. He asks Crito whether by escaping

> (T2) we are (*a*) treating badly those whom we should least treat badly and (*b*) abiding by those things we have agreed, they being just, or not?
>
> *πότερον κακῶς τινας ποιοῦμεν καὶ ταῦτα οὓς ἥκιστα δεῖ, ἢ οὔ; καὶ ἐμμένομεν οἷς ὡμολογήσαμεν δικαίοις οὖσιν, ἢ οὔ;* (49e–50a)

Crito is at a loss how to reply: he doesn't understand. What the reader can already guess, and what the Laws will spell out with relish in their speech, is that the minor premiss is about to be established. In escaping from prison Socrates would be acting in a way which contravenes both principles: he will be treating badly those he least should, and he will not be abiding by, but breaking, agreements which were just. In other words, Socrates is here continuing the theme he has just introduced, that of agreements to do something (again with the proviso *dikaia onta*), to prepare for the demonstration that he *did make* such an agreement, so that in escaping he would be breaking an agreement—contravening this newly enunciated principle. Note the language used: would we (if we escaped) be abiding by (*emmenein*) our agreements? Here to abide by an agreement is to keep a promise, whereas in the earlier passage it was to stick to—to continue to believe—the things one agreed and so assented to.[8] Crito, not surprisingly, cannot yet see how Socrates' conduct counts as (*a)* and (*b*) above. And that is where the Laws come in.

[7] R. Weiss (1998: 73) accepts that here Socrates is discussing agreeing with someone to do something. But she disputes the standard interpretation which takes this to be the enunciation of a general principle whose application to the case in hand will be explained in the lines that follow: in Socrates' question at 50a2–3, and in the Laws' speech, when it is argued that in escaping Socrates would be breaking an agreement he had made. Instead she holds that this must rely on 'old ideas and events with which Crito is familiar', that here Socrates is referring to 'an actual agreement Crito has witnessed', which she locates in *Apology* 39b6, 'I will abide by my penalty'.

[8] R. Weiss (1998: 79) attempts a different interpretation of this sentence. Impressed by the verbal echo of 48b11–c1, where Socrates spoke of abiding by agreements that such and such, she says, 'what can he be asking but whether he and Crito remain true to the principles they have just agreed?' I cannot accept this. The logic of 49e–50a is clear: first Socrates gets Crito to accept a new principle, that agreements (to do something) should be kept, then at 50a he asks whether his conduct satisfies this principle about keeping (now called abiding by) agreements. Weiss's attempt to read 'agreeing' differently at 49e6 (agreeing to do) and at 50a1–2 (agreeing that certain principles hold) cannot succeed, as it destroys the logic of the passage.

Their arguments will be scrutinized in the next section. But first let's jump to the end of their speech, and note how they end by echoing Socrates' question (T2). After their lengthy rhetorical arguments, they have a final minatory flourish: not only we but our brothers in Hades will be angry with you,

> (T3) . . . if you depart having so shamefully retaliated and returned ill for ill, having broken your agreements and treaties that you made with us, and having treated badly those you should least so treat: yourself, friends, country and us.
>
> . . . ἐαν δὲ ἐξέλθῃς οὕτως αἰσχρῶς ἀνταδικήσας τε καὶ ἀντικακουργήσας, τὰς σαυτοῦ ὁμολογίας τε καὶ συνθήκας τὰς πρὸς ἡμᾶς παραβὰς καὶ κακὰ ἐργασάμενος τούτους οὓς ἥκιστα ἔδει, σαυτόν τε καὶ φίλους καὶ πατρίδα καὶ ἡμᾶς (54c2–5).

These closing lines, with their close echo of Socrates' words which puzzled Crito (T2), confirm two points. First, that T2 'are we abiding by what we agreed?' continues the theme of T1 'doing what one agreed with someone to do' of 49e6–7; this is indicated by the echo of T2 in T3 where the words are 'agreements and treaties you made with us'. In all three passages, agreeing is agreeing to act. Second, in making the Laws in T3 deliberately echo Socrates' phraseology in T2 just before their speech began, Plato indicates to the reader that the Laws are indeed to be seen as making Socrates' case for him, though no doubt in a more vulgarly rhetorical manner than had Socrates stuck to his own voice.[9]

Speaking in part through the medium of the personified Laws, and in part in his own voice, Socrates now embarks on the lengthy discourse designed to establish that, if he accepted Crito's proposal and escaped, he would be breaching the principles they previously affirmed. The charge of agreement-breaking is delayed while other issues are pursued, in the voice of the Laws. They claim that to escape would be to try to destroy the city

[9] This article does not attempt to defend at length the traditional view according to which Socrates should be read as endorsing the arguments he puts in the mouth of the Laws. The standard view involves discerning a division of labour between what Socrates does *in propria persona* (enunciate principles, and ask whether his conduct falls foul of them) and what the Laws do (demonstrate that Socrates' conduct does indeed fall foul of them). R. Weiss denies that reading, but at the cost of strained interpretations of T1–T3 cited above. Harte points out, correctly, that the principle accepted by Socrates about agreements contains the proviso 'provided the actions are just', while that enunciated by the Laws does not contain that vital qualification. But her view cannot explain satisfactorily the division of labour between Socrates, who argues for the major premiss, and the Laws who argue for the minor premiss. That being so, dissociating their arguments becomes problematic.

and the laws, laws which fathered, bred, and educated him and provided the legal setting for his parents to marry and rear him. They then move to the most menacing but also most puzzling part of their argument, where, comparing Socrates to their offspring or slave, they remind him that he does not meet them on equal terms, but must submit to them in whatever they (or, at one point, the *polis* and *patris*) command. Or rather, as they several times reiterate, Socrates must either persuade them or obey them.[10]

Commentators have regretted the stringency of this requirement 'you must do whatever we command', and have puzzled over the significance of the let-out clause 'or persuade us'. Since this oft-repeated phrase appears to offer some alternative to absolute obedience, and to do so where questions arise of what is just (51c1) or well done (51e7), these remarks have been scrutinized by recent writers in the hope of finding an interpretation which is consonant with Socrates' stance in the *Apology*, and with the overarching principle of the *Crito* that one must never do injustice. While the principle of keeping agreements stated by Socrates at 49e (T1) contains the proviso 'provided they are just', the thesis enunciated by the Laws, 'whatever your *polis* and your *patris* commands, you must obey us', seems to leave no such scope for principled disobedience. Hence an attempt to find some leeway in the alternatives of 'persuade or obey'.

How should we understand these alternatives? Without entering deeply into the controversy, I make a few points, and first agree with Kraut (1984: ch. 3) that it is wrong to see, as many commentators from Grote onwards have done, an allusion to the citizen's opportunities to participate in law-making in the *ekklesia*. The forum of persuasion envisaged is, as Kraut says, the lawcourts. But I disagree with the way Kraut pursues this insight. He has a highly nuanced interpretation, which reads the Laws—through their repeated alternative: persuade or obey—as envisaging various different scenarios in which disobedience would be justified. I am not persuaded that (in what the Laws say) justified disobedience is countenanced. It is far simpler to suppose that the alternative 'persuade it (the city) as to what is just' alludes to the obvious fact that a verdict and sentence (which must be *obeyed*) follow a trial, a forum where the accused has a chance to *persuade* the jury to acquit him or to impose a lighter sentence. Two other passages confirm this interpretation. Socrates' remark that, if he escaped, he would do so 'not having persuaded the city' (49e9), and the Laws' claim (51e7) that, were he to escape, he would be 'neither obeying us nor persuading us if we're doing something not well (*kalos*)', surely allude to Socrates' failure

[10] 51b3–4, 51c1 (do what the *polis* commands or persuade it as to what is just); the motif reappears in the section on agreement 51e7 and 52a2–3.

to secure an acquittal or a lighter sentence. The point is pressed home when the Laws remind him that, had he requested exile as his penalty, he would have secured legitimately an outcome which he would now be seizing illegitimately should he escape prison and the death sentence.

If I am right that references to persuading as an alternative to obeying are simply reminders that there is a trial before a sentence, then no room for principled disobedience is given by this alternative, nor does it remind the citizen of his democratic right to have a say in lawmaking. But as my aim is not to offer a solution to the problem of the apparently authoritarian line taken by the Laws, I pass on.

III

How do the Laws argue that Socrates did make an agreement with them? I discern two versions of (or stages in) their argument. In what I label the black-and-white version (51de) it is simply Socrates' remaining in Athens after the *dokimasia* (see below) which constitutes his agreeing to obey the Laws. What I call the full-colour version follows at 52a–e, where facts are adduced about Socrates' lifestyle and his alleged satisfaction with Athens and its laws. This complicates matters, and it will be of especial interest to my theme.

The black-and-white version starts with the Laws reminding Socrates how well they have treated him: 'we begat you, reared you, educated you and gave you and all your fellow citizens a share of all the good things we could'. They say that they permit anyone who so wishes, once they have undergone the *dokimasia* and seen the workings of the city and the laws to go to a colony or elsewhere, taking their property with them.

> But whichever of you remains, seeing how we judge lawsuits and manage things generally in the city: he, we say, has thereby agreed with us, by what he does, to do whatever we command.
>
> *ὃς δ' ἂν ὑμῶν παραμείνῃ ὁρῶν ὃν τρόπον ἡμεῖς τάς τε δίκας δικάζομεν καὶ τἆλλα τὴν πόλιν διοικοῦμεν, ἤδη φαμὲν τοῦτον ὡμολογηκέναι ἔργῳ ἡμῖν ἃ ἂν ἡμεῖς κελεύωμεν ποιήσειν ταῦτα.* (51e1–4)

This is the *ἤδη* of so-called logical proximity, and the passage is strikingly reminiscent of Locke's famous claim that 'every man that hath any possession or enjoyment of any part of the dominions of any government doth hereby give his tacit consent' (1988: ch. 8).

I said above that an agreement, to ground an obligation, must be a public act, either verbal or non-verbal. The Laws claim that the act of remaining in Athens after the *dokimasia* constitutes the making of an agreement by non-verbal means: ἔργῳ. The *dokimasia* was the procedure by which an Athenian male of 17 or 18 years was presented by his father or other male relative for membership of his *deme*, and thereby (if his claim was deemed legitimate, after scrutiny by the *deme*, and ratified by the *boule*) became enrolled in the citizen body (*Ath. Pol.* 42).[11] Though some scholars hold that the imposition of an oath of obedience on young men on this occasion, attested to in the fourth century, must date back to the fifth century,[12] it is plain that the Laws make no claim that Socrates took such an oath of allegiance, quite the reverse. The agreeing is done by deed, not words, and the deed cited is the remaining in Athens after the *dokimasia*, and after the chance to see how the city is ordered.

Could the Laws have made the more plausible claim that in applying for enrolment in the *deme* a young man thereby agreed to undertake the obligations of a citizen? Kraut thinks not, on the ground that the agreement is not alleged to be made until the newly enrolled citizen has had time to see how the city works. This may be right, but a further reason against citing the application to be enrolled as the act which constitutes agreeing may be that it was the father or male relative, rather than the youth himself, who took the initiative to get the enrolment made.

What is required for an action (or a remaining) to count as an agreement? The useful discussion by Simmons (1979: 80) of tacit consent can be adapted for this purpose. He requires the following conditions:

1. The situation must be such that it is clear that consent is appropriate and that the individual is aware of it.
2. There must be a definite period when objections or expressions of dissent are appropriate.
3. It must be clear to the potential consentor when this period is ended.
4. The means acceptable for indicating dissent must be reasonable and reasonably easily performed.
5. The consequences of dissent must not be extremely detrimental to the potential consentor.

Hume and others who criticize theories (such as Locke's) which ground political obligation in the supposed tacit consent given by remaining in the country tend to focus on its inability to meet conditions (4) and (5). So it is of great interest that the Laws try, as it were, to meet these points by show-

[11] Rhodes' commentary (1981) ad loc. opts for 18 as the crucial age.

[12] Rhodes (1981: 495): 'We should accept that the *dokimasia* of young citizens and the imposition of an oath on them were ancient institutions'.

ing that a citizen is free to leave (reasonable means of dissent) taking his property (consequences not too serious).

But these considerations are in vain if the first condition is not met. Simmons's version of condition (1) is that it must be clear that consent is appropriate and the individual is aware of this. To put it more plainly: if my conduct is to count as agreeing, I and those with whom I make the agreement must know this. Kraut disagrees. He writes 'one can discover that one's previous actions constituted an agreement, even though one did not at the time think of them in that light. Socrates is claiming <in the Laws' speech> to have discovered that his previous actions constituted an agreement, and it is irrelevant that neither he nor his fellow-citizens realised it at the time' (1984: 158). But this cannot be right. To repeat: for my conduct to count as an agreement given to X to do A, then I must be aware that this is so.

It may be objected that in some circumstances I can incur an obligation by what I do without knowing it. One who orders goods or a meal is committed to paying for them even if that individual is unaware of the conventions, provided they are generally known and understood. This is sometimes called an implied agreement. And it might be suggested that the Laws' use of the perfect tense, ὡμολογηκέναι, suggests that this is what should be said of Socrates. It is not that he has done anything which counts as agreeing; rather he is 'in a state of having agreed', so has incurred an obligation of the kind one incurs by agreeing, but without an act of agreeing.[13] But even if the Laws could be interpreted as making the weaker claim, that Socrates has unintentionally incurred this kind of commitment, this could not succeed either, since this can exist only against a background of general knowledge that such conduct creates obligations. There is nothing to suggest either that all citizens or that most apart from Socrates knew that to remain in Athens counted as agreeing to obey the laws, any more than there is general knowledge today that conduct such as voting in an election constitutes—as some contend—undertaking an obligation of political obedience. One reason why this is so, of course, is that most people believe they owe obedience independently of the act in question.

To sum up on the 'black-and-white' version of the argument for agreement. The Laws argue that public conduct, remaining in Athens after certain conditions were fulfilled, constituted an agreement made by

[13] This would be similar to the *Meno*'s use of the perfect to suggest that the soul is 'in a state of having learned' (e.g. 86a10) without there having actually been an episode of learning. But although the perfect is used (51e3, 52a9, 52d4), the aorist participle is also used, implying that there *was* an act of agreeing. And this is what the Laws are most plausibly taken as claiming, *passim*.

Socrates with them. The right sort of agreement—a public act—is argued for, and the Laws make important and relevant points about adequate time, fair terms, and available alternatives. But their argument falls at the first hurdle, I suggest, since they fail to show that a newly enrolled citizen knows that remaining in Athens constitutes agreeing to obey its laws.

I now turn to what I labelled the full-colour version. I shall argue that the sort of considerations adduced cannot help make the case for an agreement, because they appeal to the wrong sort of thing, Socrates' attitudes. But none the less such appeals have an air of plausibility, for reasons I shall explore.

From 52a–53a the Laws adduce arguments why Socrates in particular has made such an agreement, citing great proofs that 'we and the city pleased you'. He remained in Athens, bar his military service and one visit to the Isthmian festival; he had no desire for other cities or other laws. Indeed, he had children here; he refused to suggest exile at his trial, priding himself on his preferring death to exile. His agreement was neither forced nor hasty; he had seventy years to leave if the laws didn't please him and 'the agreements didn't seem just'. Despite his frequent praise for the government of Sparta and Crete, he chose neither them nor anywhere but Athens, spending more time in his native city than even the lame and poor. And so on.

This fascinating passage raises obvious problems. To account for the prima-facie conflict on when the agreement was made by Socrates (version one: at or soon after enrolment; version two: 'you had seventy years'), a number of solutions have been proposed. One is to say that the first version is definitive on when the agreement was made, while the second (mentioning Socrates' satisfaction with Athens, demonstrated by his fathering children and so on) gives reasons for honouring the agreement. But that doesn't fit the text, which adduces them as showing that he agreed, not as showing why he should stick to an earlier agreement.

A second solution, due to Woozley (1979: 78–9), can also be rejected. He proposed that the subsequent period is presented as a sort of 'cooling-off period' of the kind which allows gullible purchasers the right to revoke a hastily made agreement. But neither the text nor common sense allow this reading. An agreement with an indefinite 'cooling-off period' would be no agreement at all.

We must read the text as doing what it purports to do: offering further reasons for the claim that Socrates (in particular) did make the agreement in question. Though I believe these reasons are insufficient, I think the appeal to them is highly significant. The reasons adduced are Socrates' alleged satisfaction, with Athens and its laws, as evidenced by various things he did and did not do. An obvious difficulty is that, as I stressed above, a person's attitudes are strictly irrelevant to whether or not they made a public agreement. Recognizing this, Kraut insists that the appeal is not to Socrates' inner state, his attitudes, but to his public demonstration of these attitudes.[14] The appeal to these must show, he claims, that remaining in Athens was not put forward as establishing that an agreement was made. Rather, it is a citizen's continued residence plus his manifestations of satisfaction which constitute the agreement. But this is too strained an interpretation, in my view, and the suggestion that to complete an agreement one must demonstrate satisfaction is a very strange one.

A simpler reading seems correct: the new argument is simply gilding the lily, adding extra reasons for the claim that Socrates did agree. The argument from an accused's lifestyle—*ex anteacta vita*—is, after all, a familiar way of gilding the lily in forensic oratory, and this passage is an inversion of the usual appeals to the accused's lifestyle to show that he couldn't have done the act of which he stands accused.[15]

So, in adducing 'great proofs that we and the city pleased you', the Laws are—they suppose—adding to the case for saying that Socrates in particular did make an agreement with them to obey them, or, as they now put it, 'to live as a citizen (*politeuesthai*) according to us' (52c2). And they do so by conflating the attitudes they argue for with the agreement they are trying to pin on him. The conflation is clearest where the Laws sum up their proofs of Socrates' satisfaction as follows: 'So strongly did you choose us and agree to act as a citizen in obedience to us, that you begat children in the city: proving it really did satisfy you' (52c1–3).

Emboldened by their further 'proofs', the Laws proceed to describe the alleged agreement in thoroughly formal and political terms as 'compacts and agreements you compacted with us' (52d 2–3, repeated at 52d8–9 and 54c3–4), alleging that to escape prison would be acting contrary to them (52d2), contravening them (52e1, 54c4), not abiding by them (53a5). These further proofs—appeals to Socrates' attitudes—should not be, but are naturally seen as, salient to their case that he agreed. I explain in the next section why the mistake may have been an especially tempting one for Plato, given his interest in the other kind of agreement, cognitive agreement.

[14] 'Any reasonable thinker ought to realise that what counts in the making of agreements is observable behaviour rather than a person's inner satisfaction' (1984: 172). 'No-one can seriously believe that agreements are ratified by feelings of satisfaction rather than by behaviour' (1984: 176).

[15] I owe this point to Lucinda Coventry.

IV

Let us look in more detail at Plato's focus on agreement 'that such and such', the stuff of the Socratic method. We have already considered the important passage where Socrates both stresses to Crito the importance of sincerity, and characterizes the agreement between them (both of them accepting the ethical principles) in political terms: *koine boule* is possible only between those who accept these principles. Agreement—that is, public assent—without belief is what we find Thrasymachus manifesting at the end of *Republic* 1. Several times he concedes reluctantly and with bad grace theses whose opposites he had earlier maintained. To reinforce the readers' perception that no genuine change of heart has occurred in Thrasymachus, Plato makes Glaucon reopen the issue of whether justice is a good for the agent with the question: do you want to *seem* to have persuaded us, or really to have done so? (357a5–b1). Here, as elsewhere, Plato stresses that for agreement 'that such and such', belief, not outward assent, is what matters. A host of passages (collected by Vlastos 1983) emphasize this salient feature of Socratic method. We may think of Socrates' rebuke to Protagoras: I'm not examining *if you like* or *if you think so,* but you and me (*Prot.* 331c), or of the repeated injunction not to agree to something 'contrary to your beliefs' (*Rep.* 346a, *Crito* 49d, *Gorgias* 500b among others).[16]

That Plato saw many affinities between the two kinds of agreement is evident from the common vocabulary. The language of sticking to what has been agreed is used for agreements 'that such and such' as well as agreements to act. We saw this already at *Crito* 49e2. The term used in Socrates' question and in Crito's answer—*emmenein*—is that used in oaths to abide by treaties (for example, Thucydides 5. 18. 9), giving Crito's reply the air of an oath, though he is not talking about a promise, but about continuing to accept certain principles. *Republic* 345b combines an injunction to Thrasymachus to 'stick to what you've agreed' (where what is agreed is certain theses) with the request that, if he changes his opinions, he do so openly and not act deceitfully. The very same verb (*exapatan*) is used of making a false agreement/promise at *Crito* 49e7. In other words, the same

[16] At *Prot.* 333c6–9 Protagoras defends, at Socrates' request, a thesis he has already disavowed (the thesis that one who acts unjustly may be sensible in so acting). Taylor (1976) suggests ad loc. 'The rule of the game was presumably that anyone defending a thesis of his own must give only what he believed to be true answers, while anyone answering on behalf of someone else could give whatever answers he took to express the beliefs of the person whose views he was defending.' The passage is also noted by Vlastos (1983: 37–8) as an exception to what he calls the 'say what you believe' rule.

vocabulary of agreement, sticking to agreements, contrary to agreements, and acting deceitfully is used interchangeably where both types of agreement are involved.

My thesis is that the importance, for the Socratic *elenchus*, of people's souls, of what they really believed and not just what they were willing to assert, spills over, as it were, into the field of that other sort of agreement, the one which generates obligations to act or obey or permit. As a result, an appeal to the individual's attitudes may seem relevant to the claim that they agreed to do something, when strictly it is not. And indeed I have found many who believe that—given their willingness to obey the laws, their recognition of good reasons to do so, and their feeling of obligation to obey—they have agreed to obey, and that from this agreement stems their obligation.[17] In the next section I trace in Cicero signs of a tendency—similar to that found in the Laws' arguments—to mislocate the role of the 'inner' in agreements, oaths, and promises.

V

I have suggested that, though it is an error to conflate inner states such as attitudes or intentions with promises, or to cite them as evidence that promises were made, it is a fully understandable one. It was a hard-won insight that, where promising or contracting is involved, an actual intention (on the part of the promisor) to do the thing promised is neither necessary nor sufficient, and even less so are pro-attitudes such as approval.

Cicero's famous discussions in *de Officiis* of when promises do and don't obligate include the case of a promise given to a pirate (3. 107). Understandably Cicero wants to argue that one is not obligated to keep such a promise, but one of the grounds he cites is surely incorrect.

For if an oath is sworn in such a way that the mind grasps that this ought to be done, it should be kept; but if not, then there is no perjury if the thing is not done.

Quod enim ita iuratum est, ut mens conciperet fieri oportere, id servandum est; quod aliter, id si non fecerit, nullum est periurium.

This suggests that the salient question, determining whether you have a duty to keep the promise, is: when making it, 'did your mind grasp that it

[17] Raz (1986: 98–9) allows that very few citizens have actually consented to obey the laws, and that therefore obligation is only rarely grounded in consent. But, with the aim of establishing that political obligation is voluntarily assumed, he makes the puzzling suggestion that *attitudes of respect for the state* can ground obligation, in those who have them, in manner analogous to consent.

ought to be done?' If grasping that p is possible when p is false, this would be a shocking claim. Even if Cicero's language implies that one's beliefs on the matter are correct,[18] he still misstates the salient consideration. The explanation which follows is surely his considered argument why such a promise does not bind: a pirate, the common foe of all, is not someone with whom faith must be kept. None the less, he appears to endorse the earlier faulty formulation by adding that the oaths which bind are those which are sworn 'in accordance with your mind's opinion' (*ex animi tui sententia*), suggesting that it is the state of mind of the one who promises which determines whether the promise must be kept. And the impression that this is so is reinforced when he proceeds to quote Euripides' notorious line about keeping one's mind unsworn. Where the *Crito*'s line seemed to be: you approved, so you agreed; Cicero's suggests: if you didn't approve, you didn't agree (that is, promise).

A similar misformulation of the salient feature in promising is found at *Off.* 1. 40. Here Cicero is reproaching the behaviour of the Roman general whom Hannibal released after he had sworn to return to the enemy camp. 'For after leaving the camp with Hannibal's permission he returned a little later saying he had forgotten something or other. He then considered that he had released himself from his oath on leaving the camp, but he had done so only in word but not in fact'. So far so good, but Cicero goes on: 'For on the question of keeping faith, you must always think of what you meant, not of what you said' (semper autem in fide quid senseris, non quid dixeris, cogitandum). Once again Cicero incautiously suggests that what really counts is what you had in mind, not what you said. But this is not the salient feature. What matters is what you are publicly committing yourself to in promising; what you can expect others to understand by your words. The general did wrong not in saying one thing while meaning another; rather, he tried to maintain that a certain action (returning briefly before leaving again) counted as keeping the promise, when the normal understanding of the words of his promise committed him to something different. Of course, Cicero is not here claiming that what you have in mind to do when you promise is what you are committed to. None the less, in putting the point by saying that '*quid senseris*' rather than '*quid dixeris*' is crucial, he unhelpfully suggests that what binds is a matter of the promisor's inner state, rather than his public commitment.

[18] Griffin's note ad loc. exculpates Cicero from holding that one can break promises one did not really mean at the time. 'It would be perjury to break a solemn promise freely made to an appropriate person, such as a legitimate enemy; then the mind would "grasp that this ought to be done"' (Atkins and Griffin 1991: 142). But Cicero can hardly assume that, when and only when promises ought to be kept, the promisor will grasp this.

That concludes my discussion of the proper role of the public and the private in performative agreements. But a further reference to Cicero will help spotlight some concluding points about the *Crito*'s arguments. In an article on Cicero's *De Republica,* Malcolm Schofield (1995: 66) argued that Cicero raises 'firmly and explicitly a question about legitimacy that is never broached in Greek political philosophy, not even the *Crito*'. Schofield focuses on Cicero's concept of the *res publica* as the *res populi,* and on his notion that a free people has *entrusted itself* to its leaders. I believe that Schofield is right in playing down, in the *Crito*, an interest in political legitimacy. Its focus is on the citizen's obligations to the *polis* and its laws rather than on the legitimacy of the latter. In particular, the *Crito*'s argument from agreement cites the alleged agreement as grounding obligations to obey, but not as simultaneously grounding the legitimacy of the laws' authority over the citizen.

There are good reasons why this is so, which can be seen if we contrast the *Crito*'s arguments with those of Locke, for instance. For Locke, not only did the supposed consent ground both the citizen's obligation and the government's legitimacy, but it was a *necessary* condition of both. Without voluntary consent, no obligation, and no legitimacy. The *Crito*, by contrast, combines, in a rather unstable way, arguments for voluntary and for non-voluntary sources of obligation to obey the laws.[19] As well as the argument from an alleged agreement there are the other arguments which ground the citizen's obligations quite differently, and in considerations of a kind far more familiar in Greek political philosophy. The parent–city (or parent–laws) analogy is used to argue that citizens have obligations independently of any they have voluntarily incurred, ones which rest simply on the laws' status as authority figures and as bringers of benefits. And when the Laws contend that Socrates' whole being and formation is owed to them, through the framework for marriage, rearing, and education they provide, they reinforce a picture which leaves scant room for a freely chosen obligation to obey them. Since the arguments for an agreement, a freely chosen obligation, are faulty, it is as well to have recourse to others, which argue the

[19] Kraut (1984: 112) writes that neither the arguments from benefits received nor the argument from the parent–city analogy is strong enough to lead to the conclusion that the obedience owed by the citizen extends to requiring them to suffer any injustice the city might impose. Only voluntary agreements commit people to suffering injustice; hence the importance of the argument from agreement, he believes. But this relies on Kraut's reading of the parent–city analogy as figuring the citizen as owing what an *adult* offspring owes his parent, rather than what a *child* owes his parents. The latter analogy is less palatable, but is arguably what the language implies, especially, as Bostock (1990: 15) notes, the requirement to yield to the *polis* as to a parent.

case from the relevant considerations of the favourable conditions a *polis* provides for its citizens. These, and not any supposed voluntary act such as an agreement, are the best hope for grounding political obligation.[20]

[20] Thanks are due to all who made helpful comments when I aired these issues in various fora including the Oxford Philological Society, and to Christopher Taylor for comments on an earlier version.

The Worth of Human Dignity: Two Tensions in Stoic Cosmopolitanism

MARTHA C. NUSSBAUM

I

Asked where he came from, Diogenes the Cynic answered with a single word: *kosmopolitês*, meaning, 'a citizen of the world' (Diog. Laert. 6. 63). This moment, however fictive, might be said to inaugurate a long tradition of cosmopolitan political thought in the Western tradition. A Greek male refuses the invitation to define himself by lineage, city, social class, even free birth, even sex. He insists on defining himself in terms of a characteristic that he shares with all other human beings, male and female, Greek and non-Greek, slave and free. And by calling himself not simply a dweller in the world, but a citizen of the world, Diogenes suggests, as well, the possibility of a politics, or a moral approach to politics, that focuses on the humanity we share rather than the marks of local origin, status, class, and gender that divide us. It is the first step on the road that leads to Kant's idea of the kingdom of ends, a virtual polity of moral aspiration that unites all rational beings, and to Kant's vision of a cosmopolitan politics that will join all humanity under laws given not by convention and class but by free moral reason. Diogenes, they say, 'used to make fun of good birth and distinctions of rank and all that sort of thing, calling them decorations of vice. The only correct political order was, he said, that in the world (*kosmos*) as a whole' (6. 72).

Cynic/Stoic cosmopolitanism urges us to recognize the equal, and unconditional, worth of all human beings, a worth grounded in reason and moral capacity, rather than on traits that depend on fortuitous natural or social arrangements. The insight that politics ought to treat human beings both as equal and as having a worth beyond price is one of the deepest and most influential insights of Western thought; it is responsible for much that is fine in the modern political imagination. One day, Alexander came and stood over Diogenes, as he was sunning himself in the market-place. 'Ask me for anything you want', Alexander said. He said, 'Get out of my light'

(6. 38). This image of the dignity of humanity, which can shine forth in its nakedness unless shadowed by the false claims of rank and kingship, a dignity which only needs the removal of that shadow to be vigorous and free, is one endpoint of a line that leads to the modern human rights movement.

On the other hand, the founders of this tradition also introduce a problem with which the tradition has been wrestling ever since. For they think that, in order to treat people as having a dignity that life's accidents cannot erode, they must scoff at money, rank, and power, saying that they are unnecessary for human flourishing. The dignity of moral capacity is complete in itself. Diogenes doesn't need to ask Alexander for a decent living, citizenship, health care: all he needs to say is, 'Get out of my light.' Moral personality is complete, and completely beautiful, without any external aids. In this essay I investigate the roots and consequences of that idea.

First, I shall characterize the moral core of Cynic and Stoic cosmopolitanism, focusing on those features that most strongly influenced modern thinkers such as Pufendorf, Grotius, Smith, and Kant; second, I shall try to articulate the rationale for the Stoic position about the relationship between human dignity and the worth of external goods. Many subsequent thinkers simply reject the Stoic claim that externals make no contribution to the flourishing life. I shall argue that the Stoic position, while problematic, is deeper and more persuasive than it is usually taken to be; it confronts us with a problem about human dignity that is difficult to solve if we do not adopt their position on the worth of externals. Even if we do solve this problem, however, another rationale for Stoic detachment lurks in the wings, in their beliefs about partiality and the moral imagination. I argue that contemporary cosmopolitans must grapple, as well, with this line of thought.

I shall begin with the Cynics, who set the cosmopolitan tradition off on a course both radical and, in some ways, profoundly problematic. In discussing Stoic ideas, I shall focus on thinkers who are orthodox in their Stoicism, but shall draw on Seneca, Epictetus, and Marcus Aurelius to supplement the scanty Greek evidence.[1] It seems particularly fitting to investigate such Roman texts in a volume in honour of Miriam Griffin, whose work has been an inspiration to all of us who believe that Roman thought has a great deal to offer to the history of philosophy. Griffin's groundbreaking work shows how important it is not to treat these Roman figures simply as sources for an abstract picture of 'Hellenistic philosophy'.

[1] I do not focus on Cicero here, both because his views are eclectic and require separate treatment, and also because the longer project from which this essay is drawn devotes separate attention to Cicero: see Nussbaum 2000.

Thinkers in their own right, they are also creative participants in their political context. This essay, being that of a political philosopher, lacks the historical richness that distinguishes Griffin's work, and is in that sense an unworthy tribute. But it is offered, nonetheless, with the greatest gratitude for the illumination of her work, and the pleasure of her friendship.

II

The life of Diogenes the Cynic is a tissue of exemplary legends; but it is as such that they should hold our interest. What the historical figure actually said and did has, ultimately, less importance than what subsequent admirers constructed as an exemplary life. In its general outlines, however, the life reveals a historical figure who was a reflective social radical of some type, and who called his way of life philosophy. 'A Socrates gone mad' was Plato's description (6. 53), and a good one. A philosophical questioner, he gained adherents through his shocking counter-cultural life, far more unconventional than that of Socrates; like Socrates, he used his strangeness to call his society to account.

Born in 404 in the Greek city of Sinope, Diogenes was exiled for defacing the city's coinage—a crime we can think of as comparable to flag-burning in its symbolic shock value (6. 20; see Branham 1996). In later years 'defacing the coinage' became a metaphor in the Cynic school for their radical disdain for local belonging and wealth. 'He said that the love of money is the mother city (*mêtropolis*) of all evils' (Diog. Laert. 6. 50). Arriving in Athens, Diogenes set up in the market-place, making his home in a tub or large jar. (He said that he had learnt by watching a mouse that it was not necessary to have a fancy house, and one could sleep in any corner.) He cultivated a frugal lifestyle: 'One day he saw a child drinking out of its hands. He hurled away the cup from his purse, saying, "A little child has beaten me in simplicity of life"' (6. 37). He connected this life with dignity and independence. One day Diogenes was washing some lettuce. Plato came up to him and said quietly, 'If you had paid court to Dionysius [the childish and immoral tyrant of Syracuse, whom Plato tried to teach], you would not have been washing lettuce'. Diogenes replied, just as quietly: 'If you had washed lettuce, you would not have been paying court to Dionysius' (6. 58).

Especially notorious was Diogenes' deliberately shocking assault on conventional propriety. By evoking outrage and even disgust, he challenged observers to ask what is truly good or bad, and what is thought good or bad on the basis of habit only. Diogenes spits in a rich man's house, mocks religious rituals that have no relation to virtue, defies conventional norms about eating and sexual behaviour. 'He used to do everything in public', reports the biographer, 'the acts of both Demeter and Aphrodite' (6. 69). The appellation 'doggy' was given to Diogenes and his followers because they ate in public, tearing at their food like animals: 'He even attempted to eat meat raw, but he could not digest it' (6. 34). Today most people eat constantly in public, so we do not readily understand what the fuss was about. This, of course, proves Diogenes' point: we are dealing with a mere habit, unconnected to anything deep about character or virtue. 'Reproached for eating in the market-place, he said, "Well, it was in the market-place that I felt hungry"' (6. 58). As for sex, his followers Crates and Hipparchia famously copulated in the public square. Diogenes pursued a more radical self-sufficiency: 'And while he was masturbating in public he would continually say, "I wish it were possible to relieve hunger by rubbing one's guts"' (6. 69)

Is all this simply childish acting out? And where is there anything in it that we might call philosophy? Because no Cynic treatises survive, it is difficult to know what the positive content of their thought was, but it seems likely that the movement was not solely critical and negative (see also Branham 1996). Behind the shock tactics lay, it seems, a conviction that the worth of a human being consists in moral capacity, and that human flourishing consists in the development of those capacities towards virtue. Diogenes famously spent his life in search of a virtuous man; this positive search was the counterpart to his denunciation of rank and wealth. 'Asked where in Greece he saw good men, he said . . . that men compete in digging and kicking to outdo one another, but nobody competes over virtue and excellence' (6. 27). Another passage tells us that Diogenes believed education was of two kinds, mental and bodily. Both types are important, but bodily fitness is important only as a prerequisite for the development of the virtues (6. 70–2). So I think we may see the negative shock tactics as, indeed, a mad kind of Socratism, a kind that spits on the false images of goodness in order to draw attention to what is truly fine within. Diogenes appears to believe that all human beings are potentially fine within, and that this potential is a deep source of human equality.

Already in these anecdotes, however, we see the problem on which I want to focus in this essay. Why should the cosmopolitan life, so construed, also be a poor life, a life that proudly displays its homelessness and its lack of possessions? Shouldn't cosmopolitans be concerned about getting people the material things they need in order to live well?

One reason for Diogenes' dismissive attitude to material need is surely that he is more worried about the damage done to people by their excessive dependency on money and status than about the damage that can be done by hunger, illness, and exposure. So he pushes people to cultivate independence from externals, in order to correct the unbalanced worship of externals he observes. Perhaps he thinks that this will leave people in about the right place, wanting only what they really need. There is surely truth in this account. And yet we still want to know why, in his critique of the powerful, he did not stress the importance of material redistribution. Why didn't he say to Alexander, 'I want you to give all your subjects a decent minimum living standard, including adequate nutrition and basic health care'?

This imagined response, however, suggests a deeper reason for Diogenes' reticence. Picture him saying this to Alexander and you are picturing a needy man admitting that he needs what power can give. He would be saying, you have power over me, and he would be paying court to that power. We have difficulty imagining a Diogenes who behaved like that; he would not be the dignified scornful Diogenes we know.

To put the point more generally, when someone behaves like a victim, saying, 'These social arrangements damage me and I want you to rectify those damages,' he seems to be saying at the same time, 'I am damaged goods. I am vulnerable to what you have dished out.' Maybe he does not have to say that his human dignity itself is injured—maybe he can convince you that there is a sharp distinction to be drawn between human dignity and happiness, and that his worth is untouched, though his happiness is not. But to the extent that the damaged thing really matters, you are admitting that you lack what really matters for human life. And you are in effect flattering power, imploring it to bind up your wounds. I think this is how the Cynics saw things. For that reason they thought that the only way of showing that human dignity has full worth in itself, no matter what natural and social arrangements have done to it, is to show that they really don't need any of the things kings can give. So: life in a tub, marriage in the market-place. We are already on the road to a pernicious distinction between duties of respect and duties of material aid that has vexed cosmopolitan philosophy ever since: for Diogenes is happy to say 'give me respect', and most unwilling to say 'give me food and shelter'. Indeed, he appears to think that he can say 'give me respect', only if he totally refuses to lay claim to food and shelter. 'Asked what he had got out of philosophy, he said, "If nothing else, at least to be prepared for every fortune"' (6. 63).

III

The Stoics, both Greek and Roman, developed the image of the *kosmopolitês*, or world citizen, much more fully. They argued that each of us dwells, in effect, in two communities—the community of our birth, and the community of human aspiration that is, in Seneca's words, 'truly great and truly common, in which we look neither to this corner nor to that, but measure the boundaries of our nation by the sun' (*Ot.* 4.1, tr. Long and Sedley 1987: 431). The Stoics held that this community is the source of our most fundamental moral and social obligations:

> The much admired *Republic* of Zeno is aimed at this one main point, that we should not organize our daily lives around the city or the deme, divided from one another by local schemes of justice, but we should regard all human beings as our fellow demesmen and fellow citizens, and there should be one way of life and one order, just as a herd that feeds together shares a common nurturance and a common law. Zeno wrote this as a dream or image of a well-ordered and philosophical community. (Plut. *De Alex. fort.* 329a–b; see Long and Sedley 1987: 429–37)

Even in its Roman incarnation, where the Empire did make it plausible to think of an actual worldwide political community, the Stoic idea of world citizenship is not focused on the goal of creating a world state. Zeno did propose an ideal city, but we know very little about its institutional structure (Schofield 1991). More important by far is the Stoic insistence on a certain way of perceiving our standing in the moral and social world. We should view ourselves as fundamentally and deeply linked to the human kind as a whole, and take thought in our deliberations, both personal and political, for the good of the whole species. This idea is compatible with local forms of political organization; but it directs political, as well as moral, thought (Griffin 1976, 1989, on Cicero and Seneca; on Marcus Aurelius, Rutherford 1989).

The basis for the cosmopolitan community is the worth of reason in each and every human being (Nussbaum 1994: ch. 9). Reason is a portion of the divine in each of us. And each and every human being, just in virtue of being rational and moral (Stoic reason is above all a faculty of moral choice) has boundless worth. Male or female, slave or free, all are alike of boundless moral value, and the dignity of reason is worthy of respect wherever it is found. This reason makes us fellow citizens. Zeno, it would appear, spoke of rational humanity as grounding a common idea of law (see above with Schofield 1991). Cicero borrowed this idea in book 3 of the *De Officiis* to speak of a single law of nature, which commands us not to harm anyone (*Off.* 3. 21–2, 27). Marcus Aurelius carries it further: 'If reason is common, so too is law; and if this is common, then we are fellow citizens. If this is so, we share in a kind of organized polity. And if that is so, the world is as it were a city-state' (*Med.* 4. 4: see also 1. 14; 5. 16).

Under cosmopolitan law, all human beings are in a very deep sense worthy of equal respect and concern. The accident of where one is born is just that, an accident; any human being might have been born in any nation. Recognizing this, we should not allow differences of nationality or class or ethnic membership or even gender (for the Stoic attitude see Schofield 1991) to erect barriers between us and our fellow human beings. We should recognize humanity wherever it occurs, and give it our first allegiance and respect (Annas 1993). As Marcus Aurelius puts it: 'My city and my country, as I am Antoninus, is Rome; as I am a human being, it is the world' (6. 44). Seneca is especially eloquent in describing the beauty of humanity, and the attitude of quasi-religious awe with which he is inspired by his contemplation of a human being's rational and moral purpose, which he compares to the awe with which one might contemplate the sublime beauty of nature (*Ep.* 41). Respect for humanity is a regulative ideal, against which all actual earthly politics should be measured.[2]

Why does respect for humanity give rise to an idea of a city or community? Why not, instead, to rules governing human beings as creatures unconnected to one another? Stoic ethics held that our moral capacities are also fundamentally social: we are born to live and work together, and our dignity is the dignity of interacting and thoroughly interconnected beings. Language is the sign of this aspect of our nature. Thus to respect human reason is also to respect human sociability (Schofield 1991: ch. 3).

The Stoics stress that to be a world citizen one does not need to give up local identifications and affiliations. Hierocles argued that we should regard ourselves not as devoid of local affiliations, but as surrounded by a series of concentric circles. The first one is drawn around the self; the next takes in one's immediate family; then follows the extended family; then, in order, one's neighbours or local group, one's fellow city-dwellers, one's fellow countrymen. Outside all these circles is the largest one, that of humanity as a whole. Our task as citizens of the world will be to 'draw the circles somehow toward the centre', making all human beings more like our fellow city-dwellers, and so forth (Annas 1993: 267–8; Long and Sedley 1987: 349). In general, we should think of nobody as a stranger, outside our sphere of concern and obligation. Presumably the idea of concentric circles is a device of

[2] Kant's idea of the Kingdom of Ends plays a similar role, and he was almost certainly influenced by these Stoic ideas. See Nussbaum 1997.

moral education: in the end, human beings have fully equal worth, and the really wise person will see this. But one way to approach that difficult idea is to think of the circles, beginning from the connections one understands from experience (Annas 1993).

In practical terms, we may give what is near to us a special degree of attention and concern. But, first, we should always remember that these features of placement are incidental and that our most fundamental allegiance is to what is human. Second, we should consider that even the special measure of concern we give to our own is justified not by any intrinsic superiority in the local, but by the overall requirements of humanity. (We usually promote the goals of humanity best by doing our duty where life has placed us—raising our own children, for example, rather than trying vainly to care for all the world's children: see Nussbaum 2000.)

Seen in this way, respect for humanity has implications for social and educational reform. Thus Musonius Rufus uses Stoic cosmopolitanism to defend the equal education of boys and girls and the higher education of married women, arguing that rational and moral nature needs educational development. Marriage itself must be reformed so that it expresses mutual respect. The Cynics proposed doing away with marriage altogether: Diogenes said that anyone who persuaded the other person should have intercourse with that person, and the resulting children should be brought up communally (6. 72). Similarly, in the ideal city of the early Greek Stoics, marriage was ruled out on grounds that it would lead to jealousy and competition; a system of free consent to intercourse plus communal child-rearing was established. The Roman Stoics focused on reforming marriage rather than junking it; they proposed an equal partnership of male and female, in which both would freely exercise moral choice, albeit in different spheres. Musonius even proposed the abolition of the sexual double standard: if men expect their wives to be monogamous, they should make the same demand of themselves (see Nussbaum 2002).

So respect for humanity is not empty of consequences. But now we must turn to what is missing from the cosmic city: for, as we know, Stoic cosmopolitanism also involves the thought that the so-called 'external goods' are indifferent. They have no true worth, nor are they even necessary instruments of human flourishing. Money, honour, status, but also health, friendship, the lives of one's children and spouse—all these are things that should never be the objects of eager attachment. One should recognize that only virtue and moral capacity deserve our reverence. These externals may sensibly be pursued if nothing impedes us; in that way, the Stoics were much less antinomian than the Cynics, and they did not advocate a lifestyle of radical defiance of conventional attachments. But if the usual externals should fail us we are not to grieve. Paradigmatic is the Stoic father described by Cicero, who, being told of the death of his child, replied calmly, 'I was already aware that I had begotten a mortal.'

Why should the Stoics have taken such an extreme line? And why can't the modern cosmopolitan simply drop this aspect of their view, saying instead that some externals have a very high importance for human flourishing—though perhaps not all the externals people usually pursue, and not to the extent that they sometimes pursue them? Why didn't these sensitive and humane thinkers just say that of course people need food, and health care, and shelter, and they suffer in great and fundamental ways if they don't have these things in sufficient measure?

We have, really, two distinct questions. Why did the Stoics not grant that externals play a necessary role in the development of moral capacities? And why did they not grant that externals have a separate importance for human happiness, even if virtue is complete in itself?

I believe that the Stoics' reasons for making virtue radically self-sufficient in these two ways were in essence the reasons of Diogenes. They believe that in order to give human dignity its due reverence they had to show it to be radically independent of the accidents of fortune. If moral capacities are of equal and infinite worth, then they can't be the sort of thing that is tarnished or eclipsed by fortune: for otherwise the degree of people's human worth will be dependent on fortune, and the well-born and healthy will be worth more than the ill-born and hungry.

Suppose for a moment that we accept this move (though in fact we should not, as I shall later argue). We grant that moral capacities are sufficient for the development of virtue. Why, still, we might ask, could the Stoics not have taken Aristotle's line (and, later, Kant's), drawing a distinction between virtue and happiness? Moral capacities are necessary, but not sufficient, for the fullness of human flourishing, or *eudaimonia*? Here again, it appears that the Stoics go with Diogenes. Think of the person who suffers poverty or hardship. Now either this person has something that is beyond price, by comparison to which all the money and health care and shelter in the world is as nothing—or she does not have something that is beyond price, but virtue is just one piece of her happiness, a piece that can be victimized and held hostage to fortune, in such a way that she is needy and unhappy, even though she has virtue. That would mean that virtue is being put in the balance with other things and is not the thing of infinite worth that we took it to be.

Let's put it this way. A virtuous person is hit by the blows of fortune.

Now either he is lofty and beautiful, and at no time more beautiful than when he suffers the greatest loss (Seneca, *Ep. Mor.* 41)—or he is a pathetic victim, moaning and groaning, asking fate and his fellow men for help, childishly dependent. Like Diogenes, the Stoics don't want to depict virtue as flattering power. So they say the virtuous person is complete, even though he lacks the whole world.

Before we reject this move utterly, we should think about people who are victims in our own society: let's say, victims of inequality based on race or sex. There is a quite understandable tendency for such people to demand things from the powerful, saying, we need these things in order to live. But there is an equally understandable tendency for some members of that group to say: 'We have our pride and strength. We are complete in ourselves. No whining and complaining for us. We are more beautiful, ultimately, than those who oppress us.' Think of recent attacks on 'victim feminism' in the name of 'agency feminism'. Naomi Wolf, for example, decries a 'victim feminism' that '[c]harges women to identify with powerlessness'. I think we see here the basic intuition behind the negative side of Stoicism: to conceive of people as helpless is to denigrate them, to fail to respect their dignity as agents.

Most of the readers of this volume live in rich nations in relatively rich times; so it is easy for us to say, people need the things of chance, and without that they are sorry victims. It is less easy if you are one of the victims, and you want to hold up your head. Stoics were not unreasonable in their idea that our kinship in the cosmic city could not be based on a division into haves and have-nots, and the kind of condescension to the victim that so often accompanies such divisions. They are not unreasonable, therefore, in saying: nobody is ever a victim, for moral capacity is always enough.

So there is a deep problem here: how can we give sufficient respect to virtue, while still portraying both virtue and happiness as in need of external resources?

IV

We understand our problem better, and see its depth more clearly, if we now consider the psychology of the cosmopolitan, one of Stoicism's most fascinating topics. According to the Stoics, as we by now see, none of the passions will figure in the life of the good cosmopolitan, since all ascribe to people and things outside the agent's own moral powers an importance *vis-à-vis* her good that they do not really possess. To the person who sees the world aright, there is nothing to fear, because moral powers cannot be lost.

There is nothing to be angry at, because the things that can be damaged by other people's malice are just externals; damage never cuts to the core.

In one way this has to look like a very attractive proposal: for we are just as aware as were the Greeks and Romans that a lot of damage is done in the world by anxieties and angers that are the result of unwise attachments to externals, such as money, power, and status. When one walks out into that difficult world, it is not so bad to do so with the thoughts of Marcus Aurelius, as he prepares to greet the new day:

> Say to yourself in the morning: I shall meet people who are interfering, ungracious, insolent, full of guile, deceitful and antisocial. . . . But I . . . who know that the nature of the wrongdoer is of one kin with mine—not indeed of the same blood or seed but sharing the same kind, the same portion of the divine—I cannot be harmed by any one of them, and no one can involve me in shame. I cannot feel anger against him who is of my kin, nor hate him. We were born to labour together, like the feet, the hands, the eyes, and the rows of upper and lower teeth. To work against one another is therefore contrary to nature, and to be angry against a man or turn one's back on him is to work against him. (2.1, tr. Grube)[3]

Marcus speaks to himself as to a person very prone to anger and resentment. Here the cosmopolitan thought of respect for humanity and sociability steps in to give him a new view of his political enemies. This humane view, in turn, permits him to cultivate his own humanity towards them, and to persist in the goals of cosmopolitanism, rather than relapsing into the faction-ridden style of politics he has sought to avoid. Cosmopolitanism supports the removal of anger, because it tells him that connectedness is important and insults are unimportant. And the removal of anger further supports cosmopolitanism. Because he sees his enemies as fellow humans, sharing purposes and ends with him, he can treat them as ends, rather than merely as obstacles in the way of his policies.

The Stoics seem right to think that, if we are to produce a world in which respect for humanity governs actions and policies, we need to deploy at least some of these tactics. We can't pursue common goals well—especially when they involve personal sacrifice—if we are all the time worrying about our own standing towards external goods such as wealth and status. And they seem right to say that the radical programme of passion-extirpation they propose is sufficient for removing many problems that stand between human beings and the kingdom of ends. And yet, as we reflect, we sense that the life with which extirpation leaves us is not free from difficulty, even from the viewpoint of cosmopolitan goals.

[3] Cf. also 6. 6: 'The best method of defence is not to become like your enemy'.

First, we encounter a problem about moral development. For Stoics are deeply concerned about education, and, reformers in that area of social life, they clearly think that in giving everyone education (women, slaves, the poor) they are giving them not just a nice frill but something they need. They think that respect for humanity naturally expresses itself in the desire to educate people, as also in non-cruelty and sexual restraint. But why? Either these things are external goods or they aren't. If education is not external to virtue, but required for human flourishing, then the Stoics are just flatly inconsistent when they claim that we don't need anything beyond our power to flourish. But if it is an external good and not required for flourishing—if the Stoic idea is consistent—then it makes no sense to be upset if someone doesn't have it, any more than it makes sense to be upset if she doesn't have dinner, or a place to sleep. They are forced to admit that something politics can deliver or fail to deliver is of such great importance that it makes sense to be passionate about it. Or if they don't make this concession, they have difficulty explaining their own zeal for the broad dissemination of philosophical teaching.

Let us now look more deeply at this picture of a cosmopolitan moral life held together by respect and humane concern, without the taint of divisive passions. Even where consistent, how attractive is it? What, precisely, is the nature of the Stoic's concern for his fellow human beings? What does the good cosmopolitan feel when they are hungry or ill or burdened by aggressive warfare?

One thing that the texts make clear is that the cosmopolitan's attitude cannot be the emotion that we usually called pity or compassion, a painful emotion grounded in the belief that someone else is suffering in a serious way, and that this suffering is a bad thing—the emotion of the spectator at a tragic drama. The Stoics like compassion just as little as they like the tragic dramas that cultivate it. 'For what are tragedies', writes Epictetus, 'but the sufferings of people who have been wonderstruck by external things, set down and displayed in the customary metre?' (*Disc.* 1. 4. 6). Of course these wonderstruck people are just wrong, and we shouldn't weep with them. As Epictetus again says: 'Look how tragedy comes about: when chance events befall fools' (*Disc.* 2. 26. 31). If the person were not a fool he would not mind the chance event, any more than Socrates minded his death. And why should we moan and groan over the inflated sufferings of a fool?

If the attitude is not compassion, however, what is it? It is not indifference, clearly: for Stoics again and again commend their line on emotions by pointing to the way in which getting rid of emotions helps us cultivate a humane attitude of concern and benevolence towards our fellow citizens. Marcus Aurelius urges the cosmopolitan to be closely and keenly concerned with the interests of his fellow humans: 'Love the human kind', he writes (7. 31), using Aristotle's word for friendly love, *phileô*. Indeed, we are to see all other people's concerns as our own: 'That which is not in the interests of the hive cannot be in the interests of the bee' (6. 54).[4] This concern has to remain in a certain way provisional: for the minute a person becomes an obstacle to our concerns we must distance ourselves from thoughts that would lead to anger. Thus, Marcus makes the following interesting suggestion:

> Looking at things one way, human beings are the closest things in the world to us, insofar as we should do them good and stick to it through difficulty. But in so far as some of them pose an obstacle to the acts that most concern us, human beings become one of the things indifferent to me, no less indifferent than the sun or the wind or a wild beast. (5. 20)

We may wonder how close the closeness can really be, if it can so easily flip over into that cool detachment. Marcus is on sounder psychological ground in a later passage, when he suggests that the wrongdoer continues to be an object of intense concern, with the aim of reform and benefit:

> Kindliness is immovable, if it is genuine and not a pretend smile or a theatrical performance. For what can the most violent person do to you, if you persist in being kindly to him, and, if you have a chance, gently exhort him and teach him a better way at the very time when he is trying to damage you? No, child. We were born for something other than this. I won't be harmed, but you, my child, will harm yourself. (11. 18. 9)

Stoics are ambivalent, then, about how we are to regard difficult and unpredictable creatures of the human species. On balance, however, and not without vacillation, they think we should have a close and sympathetic concern, and try assiduously to benefit them, even when they are hostile. 'Your only joy, and your only rest, is to pass from one action performed in the service of the human community to another action performed in the service of the human community' (6. 7; P. Hadot 1998).

The problem I now want to raise is, how will this benefiting take place, against the background of a view that has leached all importance out of the things in life with respect to which people usually would like to be benefited? What, in short, is the point and purpose of the moral life? In one

[4] There are many similar images of connected purposes: see e.g. 6. 38, 11. 8, 2. 3, 3. 11, and discussion of Marcus' use of *sun*-compounds in Rutherford 1989: 21 n. 58.

mood, Marcus assures us that benevolence and good works will forward the purposes of cosmopolitan humanity, and that we will be all the more free to give such benefits when we are less hung up by personal anxiety. But if they are fools, we reply, why should we encourage them in foolishness by giving them the external things they need? Listen to Marcus talk about his own military enterprise, as he tries to repel the invading Sarmatians, who threaten the safety of his people: 'A spider prides itself on hunting down a fly, one man a hare, another a sardine, another wild boars, another bears, another Sarmatians' (10. 10). The defence of one's own is no more truly weighty, properly regarded, than some fishing for sport, or the reflexive movements of an insect. Can such attachments sustain a cosmopolitanism grounded in the defence of human beings against aggression, rape, and torture?

In response to this question, Stoics move in different directions. Seneca, I argue elsewhere (1994: chs. 11–12), moves, unsteadily, towards a more passionate engagement with at least some externals, such as the struggle for liberty and the defence of one's own against a tyrant's onslaught. Cicero too allows himself to become deeply upset over the fate of the Republic: there is no way in which that emotional man was going to assume a posture of passionless detachment about justice at least, although he does remain detached about material aid to people who live at a distance. Marcus, by contrast, remains consistent with the Stoic programme. He gives our problem the best solution it can be given within that framework.

Recall that in his little lecture to the evildoer he addressed him as 'child'. This is, in effect, his answer. 'If there is a shortage of things indifferent', he writes, 'do not imagine that there is any great evil present; for that is a bad habit. But still, as the old man in the play . . . gave his child back the little top, fully mindful that it was just a top, you too behave in a similar way' (5. 36). This image of parental concern for the distress of a child is his image for the Stoic cosmopolitan's benevolence. Do not think, yourself, that the externals around which the drama of the moral life revolves are of deep and abiding significance. But recognize that most people do care about them very intensely, like little children who have not yet developed a sense of true value. Because you care for those children, and those children are all wrought up over trivial things, you too have to take those trivial things seriously, in a way. You give them the things they need, but you never forget that they are childish things.

This is a very good attempt on our problem. For we know that parents can be genuinely and very actively concerned for the well-being of their children—without sharing these children's view of what constitutes real importance. But Marcus' idea is not altogether satisfactory. First, it seems insufficient to motivate the kind of aggressive concern with the redistribution of externals that a cosmopolitan life would appear to require. It is not surprising that thinkers who take such an attitude should fail to pursue material aid to people at a distance, or even the abolition of slavery: for as Seneca says in his letter on the latter topic, what harm does that institution do, if the soul is free within (*Ep.* 47)? That letter is a fascinating document, because it argues that the slave's humanity requires respect and some radical changes in treatment. Slaves are not to be beaten or terrorized or sexually used. And yet the institution of slavery is left intact, with explicit reference to the irrelevance of externals for true happiness. Don't we need to say that such material conditions are themselves an insult to humanity, and that changing them is an essential step in a cosmopolitan politics?

Second, Marcus Aurelius' view really leaves too little in human life to make it a life worth valuing at all. What we are left with, it would appear, is moral capacity, but nothing for which these capacities actually matter; the tendency to justice, but no urgent work for justice to accomplish. Marcus really does see life as a kind of dead procession of meaningless occurrences:

> The vain solemnity of a procession; dramas played out on the stage; troops of sheep or goats; fights with spears; a little bone thrown to dogs; a chunk of bread thrown into a fish-pond; the exhausting labor and heavy burdens under which ants must bear up; crazed mice running for shelter; puppets pulled by strings . . . (7. 3; P. Hadot 1998)

Nothing stands out above anything else; and everything looks equally devoid of value. Nor is this a momentary lapse, or a sign of personal depression. It is of the essence of Stoic cosmopolitanism that things should be seen this way, denuded of their ordinary human significances, since these significances are erroneous. Marcus does not come by his strange vision of the world naturally, or as the result of a lonely stress-filled life. It is through Stoic exercises that he strips the humanity from human things, rewriting his inner discourse to bring it into consistency with the doctrine that externals are indifferent. Consider the following extraordinary passage:

> How important it is to represent to oneself, when it comes to fancy dishes and other such foods: 'This is the corpse of a fish, this other thing the corpse of a bird or a pig.' Similarly: 'This Falernian wine is just some grape juice', and: 'This purple vestment is some sheep's hair moistened in the blood of some shellfish'. When it comes to sexual intercourse, we must say: 'This is the rubbing together of membranes, accompanied by the spasmodic ejaculation of a sticky liquid'. How important are these representations, which reach the thing itself and penetrate right through it, so that one can see what it is in reality. (7. 13; P. Hadot 1998, with modifications)

Well, yes. It is important to think this way, if what one wants is to escape from bondage to externals. But this detached way of viewing human events and actions, if applied to hunger, pain, and the horrors of war, will hardly prove sufficient to motivate energetic efforts of benevolence or, indeed, to make a world humanly worth dwelling in. Marcus suggests that we have two choices only: the world of real-life Rome, which is like a large gladiatorial contest (Sen. *Ir.* 2. 8), each person striving to outdo others in a vain competition for externals, a world exploding with rage and poisoned by malice; and the world of Marcus' lonely gentle sympathy, where kindliness to one's foolish children is mingled with thoughts of the emptiness and vanity of all human endeavours.

Not so, we might say. We have other options of a more hopeful, a more moderate, sort. On some points, we may accept Marcus' programme of revaluation. Distinctions of rank, for example, really are just silly fantasies, correctly dispelled (along with the passions to which they give rise) by a process of detached reflection. With other goods, such as money, health, shelter, and social honour, we should agree with Marcus that the excessive and idolatrous pursuit of them is both ridiculous and reprehensible—and that all the inflamed passions that go with them should be eliminated. We should still insist, however, that there is a certain level of these things that it is right to be concerned about, because a decent life for a human being is not possible without that; nor is it possible without political liberty, and education, confirming and mutually respectful relations with one's fellow citizens.

On the question of moral capacity and our respect for it, we can adopt a two-tiered solution that is more Aristotelian than Stoic. We can insist, that is, on a distinction between basic or innate capacities and trained or developed capacities, and on a further distinction between trained or developed capacities and the real opportunity to express these in a flourishing life. A moderate cosmopolitan can hold that the source of our infinite and equal worth as persons is the capacity for choice and moral living with which we come into the world. Those capacities, however, are as yet unformed. They require external support—love, health, food, shelter, education—to develop into mature moral virtue. But even complete virtue is not sufficient for human flourishing. Here we need externals once again: the conditions of action, citizenship, liberty, friendship—and, as before, health, food, shelter. If a person is denied that which transforms innate capacities into virtue, this is tragic. We cannot have for this victim of life the kind of awe we feel for Seneca's strong man who has survived nature's accidents; but we can and should still feel respect and awe for the human potentiality that has been tragically starved or deformed. If a mature developed person is denied the things of chance, then we should react as we do to the tragic hero: with respect and awe for the intact virtue that is manifest even in disaster, but also with real sorrow for the eclipse of human flourishing.

These suggestions need further development. But they give us hope, at any rate, that we can forge a moderate cosmopolitanism based on Stoic ideas without the deforming consequences to which the Stoic rejection of externals leads them.

V

When we have solved this problem, however, if we have, another one awaits us. For the Stoics believe that if we reintroduce even a limited attachment to externals, those attachments are likely to be partial and uneven, binding the mind to its immediate sphere, to friends, family, and loved ones. Such attachments are especially likely to be unstable, giving rise to vindictive anger should they be blocked. (Epictetus addresses Medea, saying: 'Stop wanting your husband, and there is not one of the things you want that will fail to happen', (*Disc.* 2. 17. 22). They are also likely to turn attention away from the legitimate claims of human beings in other places, giving rise to aggressive war and other crimes against humanity. Even Cicero, who deplores such crimes, still advocates giving one's material aid only to the near and dear, something that ought to be highly problematic from the point of view of a just cosmopolitanism (Nussbaum 2000). Thus even the most limited and reasonable reintroduction of emotional attachments—for example, Adam Smith's idea that we can have love and anger concerning members of our own family, provided that these are bounded by what a 'judicious spectator' will feel appropriate—leaves too much room for both malice and partiality.

The Stoics have identified a very serious problem for any moderate cosmopolitanism. A few rare human beings may be able to have intense love and concern that is truly cosmopolitan (compatible with due respect for all human life and due attention to the just claims of all) and to live their lives with an awareness of the equal worth and the equal needs of all. But once we let the passions back in, we will discover that they are not stably supportive of these ends. They take their nourishment from the soil of intense particular attachments, and in most people they wither in the absence of such attachments. Aristotle, criticizing Plato's fantasy of intense brotherly love uniting an entire city wrote: 'There are two things that make people love and care for something: the thought that it is all theirs, and the thought that it is the only one they have. Neither of these will be present in that city' (*Pol.* 1262^b22–3). Instead of intense brotherly love, Plato's city, lacking close erotic and family ties, will contain only a concern that is 'watery' all round (1262^b15).

Yes, Marcus will say, Aristotle is right. The roots of the strong passions are indeed particularistic. And there is no doubt that my even-handed cosmopolitan concern will, in consequence, strike some as watery. But watery even-handedness is the only real alternative to jealousy and competitive hate—just as sex as the rubbing of membranes is the only real alternative to sex as a source of fantasied delight and divisive jealousy. There is no happy moderate in-between. Because Medea loved her husband, she was 'transformed from a human being into a poisonous snake' (Epict. *Disc.* 1. 28. 8–9).

It is thus, I believe, in the Stoics' distrust of personal attachment, and their view that all strong attachment is at root non-cosmopolitanly personal, that we should find the deepest source of their rejection of externals. It is because they think that we must ultimately choose between a self that is respectful of the dignity of all humanity and a self that is devoured by erotic longing and jealousy that they persistently deny the importance of externals for flourishing, even when externals seem required for cosmopolitan politics itself. They have concluded, in effect, that we cannot have cosmopolitan politics without remaking humanity. Marcus' first lesson from his tutor was 'not to be a fan of the Greens or Blues at the races, or the light-armed or heavy-armed gladiators at the Circus' (1. 5). But we are all Bulls fans and Knicks fans, and our emotional life is radically partisan, revolving around the sharp imagining of the seen.

The Stoics show us a world of austere gentleness, of tender yet restrained sympathy—and they ask us to live in that world rather than in the world of tragic poetry. If we find it a barren and frightening world, as we probably will, we none the less have to take its challenge seriously. For their idea is supported not only by a powerful picture of dignity, but also by even deeper intuitive ideas about partisanship and the emotional conditions of world peace. If we reject the world of Marcus, we must try to say how else cosmopolitan morality, and a perpetual peace among nations, might be possible. How might we, remaining ourselves, still enter that kingdom of ends?

For Marcus, a passionate man for whom the question becomes a lifelong obsession, the answer remains dark: there is no alternative. We really have to give it all up in order to be just. Only in something like death, in effect, is moral rectitude possible. And the best consolation for that bleak conclusion comes also from the thought of death. I shall end this essay with a characteristic reflection on that theme, which I find both deeply moving and horribly unsatisfactory:

> Think all the time about how human beings of all sorts, and from all walks of life and all peoples, are dead. . . . We must arrive at the same condition where so many clever orators have ended up, so many grave philosophers, Heraclitus, Pythagoras, Socrates; so many heroes of the old days, so many recent generals and tyrants. And besides these, Eudoxus, Hipparchus, Archimedes, other highly intelligent minds, thinkers of large thoughts, hard workers, versatile in ability, daring people, even mockers of the perishable and transitory character of human life, like Menippus. Think about all of these that they are long since in the ground. . . . And what of those whose very names are forgotten? So: one thing is worth a lot, to live out one's life with truth and justice, and with kindliness toward liars and wrongdoers. (6. 47)

Because we shall die, we must recognize that everything particular about us will eventually be wiped out. Family, city, sex, children, all will pass into oblivion. So really, giving up those attachments is not such a big deal. What remains, and the only thing that remains, is truth and justice, the moral order of the world. In the face of the looming inevitability of our end, we should not mind being dead already. Only the true city should claim our allegiance.

If we feel that this cannot be right, that justice must be from and for the living, we cannot simply assert that Marcus is wrong. We must solve his problem, creating a convincing theory of cosmopolitan emotion and of the relationship between particular attachments and the love of humanity. We have yet to respond well to this challenge.

Cicero and the Defining of the *Ius Civile*

Jill Harries

Every definition in the civil law is risky; it is very unlikely that it cannot be undermined.

(Iavolenus Priscus, second century AD, at *Dig*. 50. 17. 202)

Law in the late Roman Republic was an exciting discipline, although Cicero in certain moods (as in *Pro Murena* 19–30) would have maintained that Roman jurists did their best to make it otherwise. Its expression took written and unwritten form. The Twelve Tables of *c*.450 BC were regarded as the beginning of written law, which was also represented by statutes, supported by the authority of the *populus*, decrees of the Senate or magistrates, or the responses and treatises of the jurists. Much, however, was unwritten, yet had, in certain circumstances, legal authority as great as, if not greater than, the written law. This was because the 'law of nature' (a concept open to various definitions), custom (see Schiller 1971), and equity, the main components of the 'unwritten' law, rested on either inbred 'force' (*Inv*. 2. 22. 65) or social consent (e.g. at *Tusc*. 1. 13. 30; and 1. 15. 35; also *Div*. 1. 1. 1 and 1. 6. 11).

This paper will argue that one of the less noticed conflicts of the late Roman Republic centred on who controlled ultimate legal authority, as exercised through its application in the courts. Such a conflict was possible because the written law was under pressure on two fronts. One was the contribution made by philosophical concepts, notably, but not exclusively, that of the (unwritten) *ius naturae*, based on Stoic ideas, along with new techniques of definition and the systematic arrangement of material which had a wide impact ranging from the structuring of forensic argument to the notional composition of law-codes, an idea briefly entertained by Cicero (Aulus Gellius, *NA* 1. 22. 7) and explored also by his 'Crassus' in the *De Oratore* (1. 42. 190).

The other source of pressure was the exploitation of unwritten law by advocates in the lawcourts. While it is not at all clear how, or if, court judgments actually affected the content of the *ius civile*, Cicero maintained (as we shall see in connection with Caecina) that *iudices* could make judgments

For Miriam's many *beneficia* I offer this small return with love and gratitude.

on points of law, with wider implications. Indeed, in the *De Oratore* (2. 130–45) he suggested that all cases could be reduced to debates on legal principles, regardless of the personalities involved (although, for the orator, personalities were of course fair game). Moreover, as we shall see, repeatedly the merits of the unwritten, based on concepts such as *aequitas*, proportional fairness, *consuetudo*, custom, and the *mos maiorum*, are trumpeted by Cicero. Such concepts had been refined by philosophers and latterly jurists over the centuries; however, the forensic advocate had to adapt to popular understanding of such terms, so that the *iudices*' idea of what was 'fair' might work in favour of his client and prevail over whatever alternative legal authority the opposition had available to them.

It should be acknowledged that to build a picture of an entire legal culture mainly on the basis of the witness of one source, Cicero, carries risks. However, surviving writings of jurists, assembled by Lenel (1889), such as Cicero's mentor, Q. Mucius Scaevola the Pontiff, known to juristic posterity as Q. Mucius, and his friends, Servius Sulpicius Rufus, consul in 51 (analysed by Bauman 1985: 15–24; Stein 1978), and the equestrian follower of Caesar, C. Trebatius Testa, provide an alternative commentary on one aspect of the evolving written law. Also, Cicero's writings were consciously geared to his audiences, ranging from the jurors in the popular courts to senators to other wealthy men with philosophical interests. Thus wider cultural assumptions can be inferred from both the speeches and Cicero's theoretical comments on how to influence audiences (cf. *Orator* 8. 24), while his philosophical treatises reflected the intellectual preoccupations of his narrower, elite readership, as well as his own concerns.

A further difficulty facing the analyst of Republican law in its social setting is that there appears little scholarly consensus on the nature and extent of the influence of Greek philosophy and Greek ideas in general on Roman law. It has been argued, notably by Alan Watson (1974), that, although some influence from the Greeks, particularly Stoic dialectic, might be conceded, the Romans were clever enough to think of such devices as definitions from etymology or the classification of things by *genera* and *species* (or, as Cicero would say, *forma*) for themselves. Moreover, there is little to no evidence that Roman jurists, who wrote distinctively Roman treatises, were influenced by Greek legal rules or philosophical concepts as the basis of rules. Finally, while the influence of Greek rhetorical theory was widespread, by the first century BC the role of the orator, it is argued, and that of the jurist were distinct.

These objections to the importance of Greek philosophy for Roman law are formidable. However, they are also open to question in their turn. First, the analysis is based on an unspoken assumption, that Roman law was jurists' law. In fact, as shall be shown below, 'ownership' of Roman law was disputed; it was open to the forensic advocate to suggest that *ius* had a broader meaning than what was acceptable to jurists. Secondly, although it is true that jurists were probably decisively involved at the first stage of the civil process, the praetor's issuing of his formula for the case (Ciferri 1991: 105–8), their authority could be cited at any stage; hence Cicero's appeal to the authority of C. Aquillius Gallus in the hearing of the Caecina case before the board of *recuperatores* in 69. Thirdly, jurists could act as orators, as did Q. Mucius Scaevola or Servius Sulpicius Rufus, even though they might not (in Cicero's view) be very good at it; Scaevola, for example, had to concede victory to L. Licinius Crassus in the 'causa Curiana' in 92 (see esp. *Brutus* 197–8), while Servius, as prosecutor of Murena in 63, was ridiculed for his pedantry by Murena's advocate, the consul Cicero. There was nothing formally to stop a jurist pleading in court and those with a taste for advocacy must frequently have done so. Finally, and more generally, the operation of cultural influence is a more complex process than the tracing of an idea or a set of ideas back to a single source or school of thought. For example, as we shall see, Romans might have thought of defining things for themselves, but their refinements on how to go about it might not have evolved as they did without a little extra help. Conversely, Greek theory might be deliberately modified in the light of experience; Cicero believed that the most effective way to evolve a theory of what he was doing as an orator was to combine the observations of the theorists with his practical experience (*usus*) of politics and the courts.

The issue of definition, which is the main focus of this paper, provides a number of useful routes into the maze that is Roman law in action in the late Republic. As Iavolenus observed, definitions were easily subverted. They are therefore symptomatic of two contradictory trends: one, the urge to clarify and systematize through definition; the other, to employ competing definitions to support arguments in disputed cases in court, or even in the more sheltered environment of the philosophical treatise. For jurists, the formulation of definitions was a means of imposing their individual and collective authority on legal thought; for forensic orators, the vulnerability of definitions offered scope to impose themselves on opponents and, by implication, on dissenting jurists as well. The beauty of law, then as now, was its uncertainty; because so much was disputed, the outcome, which could always be contested in theory if not in practice, was less significant than the means by which it was reached (cf. for ignoring of this principle today, Thomas 1998).

Cicero, the advocate who was also a philosopher, understood the importance of definitions for his trade. In the course of his life, he provided a number of definitions of the *ius civile*, most notably in the *De Legibus* in the late 50s BC, where he implicitly acknowledged the existence of competing definitions of *ius*, and in the *Topica*, of mid-44, where techniques of definition used by the orator are illustrated by reference to the legal examples likely to appeal to the jurist Trebatius, his addressee. He also knew from experience that, in practical terms, definition was often central to the advocate's argument in a trial. A man accused of that most political of crimes, *maiestas*, before a *maiestas* court, would get off, even if he had done what he was alleged to have done, if what he had done was not *maiestas*, an argument that Cicero used effectively in his defence of the ex-tribune Cornelius. Similarly, the halting of an attempt at repossession on the part of Aulus Caecina by the threat of violence was argued by Cicero in 69 to be subject to the interdict on armed violence, despite aspects of its wording which suggested the opposite (below, pp. 65–6); this line could only work if the adjudicator accepted Cicero's definition of what violence was.

DEFINITIONS I: LAW AND PHILOSOPHY

The latter part of the 50s was devoted by Cicero to a series of treatises, the *De Oratore, De Republica*, and, probably, the *De Legibus*, in which he incorporated his experience as a politician and orator into theoretical frameworks inspired by philosophers. While much has been written on the philosophers Cicero knew (for example, on his mentor, Antiochus of Ascalon, J. Barnes 1989 and Görler 1995), the following treatment of the first part of the *De Legibus* will be based on the assumption that, whatever Cicero's philosophical sources wrote (or were understood by Cicero to have written), the line of argument put forward was by Cicero's own choice. In addition, it will be suggested that he wrote in pursuit of an agenda which was at least as much political as it was philosophical.

Cicero's line in the early part of the work is that definitions of law should be based on philosophical principles. He therefore begins the discussion by rejecting the concept of law advocated by the jurists:

> I believe that there have been men of supreme importance in our state who made it their practice to interpret the law to the people and issue regular responses, but that although they made large claims, they in fact engaged in minor matters. For what could matter more than the law of the state? Yet what is so trivial as the pursuit on which they are engaged who act as jurisconsults? However, it is a necessity for the people. Now I do not believe that those who devote themselves to this career are

ignorant of universal law, but they have carried their practice of the *ius civile* only so far as it suits their aim of benefiting the people. So that line is lightweight as far as understanding goes, although essential in practical terms (*usu*). (Leg. 1. 4. 14)

In case the point of whose necessary but trivial labours were being rejected was missed, Cicero cites examples of discussions of law that would be inappropriate: eaves and house-walls; formulae for agreements and court trials. In other words, treatises by jurists were too 'humble' a subject to engage the legal philosopher.

However, this was not an attack on jurists *per se*. Cicero's object was simply to establish that his philosophical form of law was the 'real' one. Therefore other forms of law also were rejected, on Atticus' suggestion, as irrelevant to the true knowledge of law: 'So you think that the discipline of law is not to be drawn from the praetor's edict, as many think now, nor from the Twelve Tables, as our predecessors did, but from the very depths of philosophy?' (*Leg.* 1. 5. 17). The privilege granted to philosophy was absolute. So too was the implied rejection of the view of 'the many' who saw praetorian law as the main source of the discipline. Yet the praetor's edict and the *ius honorarium*, magistrates' law, which evolved round it, were regarded as reflecting custom, *consuetudo*, in written form, and therefore carried the popular authority of custom itself, the form of law that had superior legitimacy because based on popular consent.

Casual though Atticus' dismissal was, it is significant for what follows. Cicero, as we shall see, will argue that, properly understood, the 'natural law' of the *doctissimi*, the philosophers, had even greater popular legitimacy than what was perceived by the 'many' to be law. In other words, Cicero's extended definition of natural law aimed to 'popularize' or 'democratize' the right reason that formed the basis of law and justice. Moreover, as its exponent, Cicero would in turn identify himself with a definition of law that was more truly 'popular' than any other.

In brief, Cicero's argument ran that law is the highest reason, implanted in nature, which commands what should be done and forbids what should not be done. It followed, therefore, that the origin of justice was to be found in law, as law is a natural force. Man was created as uniquely endowed with reason by God and shares it with God. All men have this right reason in common and share it with the gods. As they share law, they must also share justice, and are united by natural feelings of kindness and goodwill and a partnership in justice. Conversely, wickedness was against nature, as is shown by the fact that wickedness is defined in relation to justice, not to the existence of a penalty for wrongdoing. Similarly, justice could not be defined only in terms of conformity to the laws; it was possible for injustice to be found in the laws of states. Justice and law (as opposed to the laws) were not matters of 'opinion' but fixed in nature and worth pursuing as an absolute good.

Cicero's emphasis in his view of natural law was on its universality. Although he conceded that the formulation of theories about it was due to a small elite of the learned, he also argued that 'right reason' was common to all and enabled mankind to live as one community with the gods. This emphasis is significant because it represented a choice among the various Stoic doctrines available. While there is controversy among modern interpreters about what lay behind Cicero's thinking, what is clear is that, if Cicero had read his Stoics, old and new, in detail, he would have realized that there was one strong school of thought among the Stoics which saw full understanding of right reason as the property only of a few sages, while everyone else had some share of right reason and did what was required of them without fully understanding why (Dyck 1996: 2–8; Kidd 1955). Had Cicero wanted to follow this more elitist route, and create in the process some special niche for philosophical (and political) *boni*, he could have done.

That he did not seems at first sight surprising. On a conventional reading of his career, Cicero had taken nearly forty-three years to penetrate the senatorial nobility, and spent the rest of his life trying (and failing) to be accepted by it. His political instincts were conservative, and philosophy itself was an elite pastime. The setting of *De Legibus* was designed to recall the rural context of Plato's *Laws* but it also conforms with Cicero's belief in intellectual exclusiveness; the garden of a rich man's villa was not a place the denizens of the cesspit of Romulus were likely to frequent and the participants in the conversation were two intelligent politicians, Cicero and his brother Quintus, along with the wealthy Atticus. Nor could philosophy ever translate to the Forum. In youth he had acknowledged that: 'the rights of nature are themselves less relevant to this controversy, because they are not implicated in the civil law and are somewhat removed from the perceptions of the crowd' (*Inv.* 2. 22. 67). At the other end of his life, too, Cicero continued to advance the view that, while orators owed a great debt to the Academy and Plato, their modes of thought were incompatible with forensic oratory, which was consigned to 'more rustic Muses' (*Orator* 12). Philosophers lacked *eloquentia popularis*, while orators (it was alleged) were not known for the refinement of their learning (*elegans doctrina*). Stoics, in Cicero's opinion, were especially bad orators, with the exception of the younger Cato.

However, what Cicero understood, although he might not have phrased it so, is that many cultural influences are invisible and unexpressed. Philosophy could not communicate, but it could, through its theoretical understanding of society, interact with society to influence how it worked. As we have seen, it was, in Cicero's view, jurists' responsiveness to the requirements of the *populus* which had dictated what form their shaping of law should take; it was socially necessary and required by *usus*, yet, as Cicero had shown in his demolition of Servius in 63, it was not 'popular'. For this reason some bridge-building was necessary:

since our whole discussion is set in the context of the reason of the people (*in populari ratione*), from time to time it will be necessary to speak in the popular manner (*populariter*) and to call that 'law' (*lex*) which decrees in written form what it wishes, by issuing either orders or prohibitions—as the common people call it (*ut vulgus appellat*). (*Leg.* 1. 6. 19; cf. *Off.* 2. 35, advocating the use of popular language, as the philosopher Panaetius had done)

This did not mean that he had reversed his view that arguments based on philosophy and natural law lacked popular appeal. What Cicero did acknowledge, as politicians with an interest in communication with their public have always done, was that the language used must be comprehensible—even when, as in the *De Legibus*, the *populus* was not physically present to hear the discussion.

Cicero also had the virtue of consistency. Although his version of natural law is not the one adopted by later jurists, it was present in the early influences which fed into the immature and perhaps derivative *De Inventione* (2. 22. 65–8), where he defined the *ius naturae* as being something implanted not by opinion but by a kind of innate instinct, and including religion, duty, gratitude, retaliation, reverence, and truth. This conflicted with the view espoused by the anonymous author of the *Rhetorica ad Herennium* (2. 19), also perhaps writing in the 80s, that the law of nature could be confined to feelings between parents and children. Then, as much later in the *De Officiis* (3. 6. 28), Cicero's natural law embraced social as well as kinship ties; it was nonsense, he said, that the law of nature should apply to parents and children but not to the rest of the citizen body. Given this consistent view of natural law, it followed that the concept of the state as developed in the *De Republica* was also based on a universal collective, the *societas humana*, and required some form of general consensus on 'Law' to establish its legitimacy (*Rep.* 1. 39: Schofield 1995; Coleman 2000: 275–84).

Finally, a reason for Cicero's advocacy of a universal and superior legal standard may be suggested which had more to do with politics than with philosophy. Cicero's identification of law and justice with the *summa ratio* of the natural law enabled him to create an independent standard against which the laws of real states could be assessed by privileged interpreters like himself. At the same time, because the *ius naturae* was universal, it had the legitimacy of being based on the 'consensus' of everyone. In other words, it was really *popularis*, even though the real *populus* could not be expected to appreciate it.

This was no abstract proposition. At a seminar in St Andrews in 1999, A. Dyck argued that Cicero's resentment against the tribunician laws of Clodius strongly influenced the content of his imaginary Roman constitution in book 3 of the *De Legibus*. Although Clodius is never named, the proposition, that the laws of states could be unjust, was set out in book 1, and illustrated by the Thirty Tyrants of Athens in 404–403 BC and, from more recent history, the empowerment of the dictator Sulla (unnamed) to put Roman citizens to death without trial (*Leg.* 1. 16. 42–4). Clearly Cicero's own exile by Clodius in 58 also came under this heading, and the notion that, if the state was controlled by those who passed unjust laws, then the state itself was no longer a functioning entity, had been advanced by Cicero in the *Pro Sestio*, aimed against Clodius, as recently as 56. If, then, the law and justice of the *ius naturae* were not only superior to the laws of states, but also more truly 'popular' than the unjust legislation of the kind passed by Clodius, then Cicero could claim (as in very different circumstances he had done over Rullus in 63) that he, and his system of legislation, were the real representatives of the popular will.

Although Cicero the rhetorical theorist and Cicero the philosopher had different perspectives on what 'law' was, Cicero's intellectual and practical preoccupations were not isolated from each other but, rather, reacted together. The philosophical idea, in rudimentary form, of the *ius naturae* starts life in Cicero's writing in the 80s in a work on rhetoric; only later does it develop more fully in the philosophical context of the *De Legibus*. The idea that dominated in Cicero's mind in the late 50s of a *res publica* that was indeed the property of a right-thinking *populus* was the product, both of long reflection on the nature of law and the state, and of personal circumstances, disillusionment, and, doubtless, resentment: if the Roman state was imperfect, what did the perfect *res publica* look like, how were its laws to be legitimized, and how could it be established that these laws had greater authority than the laws of Clodius' and the triumvirs' flawed state? The *De Legibus* provided answers to questions that were not abstract, but rooted in the realities of Roman political life.

Definitions II: Rhetoric and Law

Cicero's *Topica*, allegedly, but probably fallaciously, associated by him with a work of the same title by Aristotle (J. Barnes 1999: 55–7), was written for the young jurist and follower of Caesar, C. Trebatius Testa, in the troubled summer of 44, a matter of weeks before his more celebrated *De Officiis*. The subject was the invention of arguments (*Top.* 2) for use by orators. Obviously, the same techniques could be, and were, used by jurists, and Cicero's frequent use of legal examples to illustrate his technical points was designed not only as a compliment to the recipient but also a statement of the close relationship that existed—or could be made to exist—between rhetoric and law.

One of Cicero's two 'definitions' of law in the *Topica* is offered as an example of *partitio*, the splitting up of a topic into its component parts (*membra*): 'for example, if one should define the *ius civile* as consisting of statutes (*leges*), resolutions of the Senate (*senatus consulta*), judicial decisions (or, 'decided cases', *res iudicatae*), the authority (*auctoritas*) of jurists, the edicts of magistrates, custom (*mos*) and equity (*aequitas*)' (*Top.* 5. 28). If treated as an absolute definition of the *ius civile*, designed for lawyers, the dissonance of the component parts is startling. Statutes were binding on the whole state, and were permanent, unless revoked or abrogated in some way (see Richardson 1998 for complications of this); *senatusconsulta*, however, were, technically, advisory only, and the edicts of magistrates had effect, in theory, only for as long as the author was a magistrate (the *ius honorarium* is not mentioned). Jurists, whatever their standing, also did not have the same binding force as statutes, and the reference to their role in terms of *auctoritas*, rather than *responsa* or *opiniones*, suggests a nebulous, albeit powerful role. Custom and equity were, unlike the rest, not written down. *Res iudicatae* raises problems of interpretation to be discussed below; one aspect worth noting is that it drops out of a similar list offered by the jurist Gaius in the second century AD (*Inst.* 1. 2), an omission which may reflect the diminished standing of the courts under the Empire.

To further complicate matters, Cicero had already offered, in the same treatise but in a different context, another definition of the *ius civile*: this was the type of definition that consisted of unwrapping what was there already, and focused on equity, to the exclusion of other component parts: 'the *ius civile* is an established system of fairness (*aequitas constituta*) for those who are members of the same citizen body (*civitas*) for the purpose of securing to each his own; knowledge of this system of fairness is useful; therefore knowledge of the *ius civile* is useful' (*Top.* 2.9). This combination of two definitions with markedly different emphases should serve as a salutary warning against taking passages out of context. The *Topica* is a rhetorical manual, not a legal textbook. Were these two definitions in fact designed primarily by an orator for orators, or jurists aspiring to be orators? An orator in court was not bound by the technicalities of which form of legal authority had precedence; as every schoolboy knew (*De Oratore* 1. 244; 2. 100), advocates were trained in the merits of the written versus the unwritten, the letter of the law as opposed to equity, and literal interpretations as against intentions. By emphasizing equity in one definition, Cicero opened up wider opportunities for the orator to exploit the social assumptions of the adjudicators, whose verdicts were often determined by 'popular prejudice' (*Top.* 73). Similarly, in the other, by giving equal weight to the various *partitiones* of the *ius civile*, the orator could have discreetly reminded his jurist friend that the primacy of the written, including the writings of jurists, could not be taken for granted.

However, the *Topica* is not a work about confrontation. Nor was it only an exercise in flattery, although Cicero's repeated exploitation of legal illustrations was in compliment to his friend, whose legal services and personal friendship he valued highly (see letters to Trebatius, *Ad Fam.* 7. 10–21). The interest of the *Topica* is that it was a serious attempt to show how techniques of legal and of rhetorical argumentation could be one and the same thing, and should be used as a central text for anyone seeking to understand the connection of rhetoric and law, which survives, in numerous different forms, in the writings of the imperial jurists.

If we had more of Trebatius' writings, it might be possible to discern even closer links between Cicero's text and Trebatius' legal interests than those explicitly stated. On *genus* and *species*, which Cicero calls *forma*, for example, Cicero could have learned his precepts directly from their originators. His admired teacher, Q. Mucius Scaevola the Pontiff, systematized the *ius civile* in eighteen books, and had formulated five different *genera* of *tutela*, guardianship (reduced by Servius (*Dig.* 26. 1. 1) to three). Most known late Republican jurists had made some attempt at defining something: Q. Mucius Scaevola had written on the content of store cupboards, for purposes of wills (Gellius, *NA* 4. 1. 17), as also had Servius on felled timber (*Dig.* 50. 16. 30.pr.); Q. Mucius had also written on *vis* (*Dig.* 50. 17. 73. 2) and *gentiles* (*Top.* 6. 29) Servius had defined secretly (*Dig.* 43. 24. 4); C. Aquillius Gallus had produced a definition of shoreline (*litus*), for boundary purposes (*Top.* 7. 32), and of legal deception (*Nat. Deor.* 3. 30. 74); he had also advised on questions of violence over the Caecina case (*Caec.* 27. 77). Thus when Cicero used legal examples for different types of definition, he was doing nothing new, except that he was not doing it (he said) as a jurist but as an advocate. His aim was to illustrate, through use of legal examples, that methods of argument used by orators were shared by jurists. Despite the element of competition implicit in the privileging of *aequitas* noted above, the *Topica* is about the common ground shared by the advocate and the legal expert.

Cicero's sensitivity to legal niceties and his ability to use them in compliment to his friend are well illustrated in his handling of the question of rainwater damage, which is worth a short digression. This was a subject which had been discussed by Q. Mucius, whose influence on the *Topica* is revealed at several points, such as his definition of *gentiles* and his interpretation of the significance of 'post' for the definition of *postliminium*, on which he was contradicted by Servius (*Top.* 36–7). The *actio aquae pluviae arcendae* also was (or would be in the future) the subject of writings by Trebatius, who took a different line from Scaevola on some matters of definition. Evidence for these controversies comes, not from Cicero, but from later commentators, such as Ulpian, who provide speculative insights into what may underlie Cicero's interest in this perhaps surprising subject.

Problems of definition started with the most basic question of all: what was rain? Cicero began by quoting Q. Mucius' argument as an example of one based on etymology. If we understand rainwater (*aqua pluvia*) as being only that which we see is collected from rainwater (*imber*), then 'Mucius should be brought in, as he said that, because the words *pluvia* and *pluendo* (raining) are connected (or conjugate), all water should be subject to exclusion, which has been increased by rainfall' (*Top.* 39). However, the point of the action had to be defined more precisely in terms of whether the nature of the ground or human intervention was to blame; if the former, there was no case to answer; if the latter, it had to go to *arbitrium*, adjudication by formal means or an agreed arbitrator, whose decision would be binding. Continuing with the topic, but now on the subject of likenesses, Cicero observed that because boundary disputes in crowded urban areas are different in kind from those in the countryside, because *fines*, boundaries, are not marked in the same way, disputes over rainwater damage cannot be resolved by the *actio aquae pluviae arcendae*, although there were other actions available.

The author and dedicatee of the *Topica* both had access to texts of Q. Mucius and (perhaps) of Trebatius now lost. Their contents could have been the subject of multiple allusions now beyond recovery. But later writers, notably Ulpian, provided their own record of the ongoing argument about what rainwater was and where liability for damage should lie. Like

Q. Mucius and Cicero, with minor modifications, Ulpian defined rainwater as that which falls from the sky and/or combines with water already on the ground. But Ulpian also knew about another controversy about definition not covered by Cicero but present in Trebatius: were hot springs (*aquae callidae*), familiar to the holiday-makers of Baiae and Campania, to be classed as rainwater? Trebatius, who had a house in Rome and a villa, not in the holiday resorts but at Velia in Lucania, adjoining marshes and affected by the noise of frogs—who were alleged to be clients of Cicero procured by the absent Trebatius (*Ad Fam.* 7. 12)—thought they were; the non-Italian Ulpian, whose experience of volcanic springs may have been more limited, thought otherwise (*Dig.* 39. 9. 3. *pr.*).

Ulpian also recorded material from Scaevola and Trebatius, omitted by Cicero, on availability of actions, which shows the younger jurist asserting his independence of the elder. All agreed that the action was available if the water-damage was due to man-made constructions (*Dig.* 39. 3. 1. 1). But was this to include the effects of ploughing a field, if rainwater damage to a neighbour resulted? Q. Mucius, as Ulpian reported, thought not, but Trebatius modified his view and restricted its application; only ploughing with the intention of growing a crop was exempt from the action (*Dig.* 39. 3. 1. 3). If the offender dug ditches on his land, this was not likely to trigger the action, provided that he did not dig a single channel which directed the water onto his neighbour's land; again, the condition that the ditches should be necessary to cultivation was to apply (*Dig.* 39. 3. 1. 4–5).

Cicero's interest in rainwater, then, was not fortuitous; Q. Mucius and Trebatius both had (or were to have) their learned say on it, and Cicero joined in, reporting, but not creating, aspects of the problem which showed that he had sufficient grasp of legal modes of thought to have been a jurist if he tried. Perhaps, indeed, as an estate-owner himself, who moved between town and country, his interest was not only theoretical. Moreover, the question of rain impinged on all kinds of other issues affecting the land-owning elite of Rome. Boundaries in town and country were different, and Publius Mucius Scaevola had specified that the *ambitus*, space round about, a house is only that part covered by the roof put up to protect a party wall (*Top.* 4. 24). Therefore in towns the law was different too; in the town house roofs could overlap, as they did not in the countryside. Ploughing and digging had to be thought about, not only in relation to the estate cultivated, but the neighbours also; absentee or indifferent owners faced with complaints about rainwater damage needed a lawyer as well as an efficient estate-manager. And, given the restriction of application of the *actio aquae pluviae arcendae* to the countryside, it may be asked how much confirmed urban types would have cared; perhaps Trebatius, the *eques*, was a country boy at heart.

Yet, as has been said, the *Topica*, although full of law, and showing Cicero as one who understood its technicalities (cf. Costa 1927), is primarily about the rules of argument; law is used as the means by which the orator illustrates the connections between his favoured discipline and that of his friend. His 'definitions' of the *ius civile* should be seen as ones those orators would use and the number and range of the component parts played in favour of the orator's self-interested dilution of the power of the written and the technical. It was for this reason, the underlying rivalry between the orator and the jurist, that the 'otherness' of jurists is maintained throughout. *Similitudines*, resemblances, Cicero maintains, will be more useful to orators and philosophers than to 'you' jurisconsults (*Top*. 10. 41). Invented examples (*ficta exempla*) had more to do with rhetoric than 'what you do' (although jurists did also use fictitious cases). And when jurists argued cases in court, their approach was totally different from that of the orator or philosopher; in a case involving the transfer of a *res mancipi* by the process of *mancipium* by a person not empowered to do so, the jurist would ask technical questions about whether the recipient was still the owner or whether the seller was liable, while the orator (and philosopher) would play on emotions, make the dumb speak, raise the dead, and so on 'to stir things up' (*Top*. 45). Two years earlier, in the *Orator* (141), Cicero had declared that, in time of peace, eloquence held first place and *iuris scientia* the second. In the *Topica*, as Trebatius was a good friend, Cicero was too polite to specify which discipline he thought really counted.

Interpretation and Authority

Discussion of Cicero's views on *ius* and the *ius civile* thus far has had little to say on Cicero's view of written law. This was not because he had no time for statutes, praetorian formulae, or juristic writing. Where applicable, these were exploited in his speeches, sometimes, especially in civil cases, at perhaps excessive length. But, as the definitions offered to Trebatius illustrate, Cicero's bent as an orator was towards the more flexible concepts inherent in the unwritten law that derived from socially based but legally conceptualized concepts of custom and equity (see Ducos 1994: 5150–60). These contained assumptions about what ought to happen, because it always had, or because any other outcome would be 'unfair' (at least in the eyes of the jury). On the written law, therefore, he knew what he needed to know, but his real flair, as others also acknowledged, was in the extra-legal aspects of oratory as he had formulated them to Trebatius, the making the dumb speak and raising the dead.

For the forensic orator, flexibility of definition of what the law was could be the key to success, because it placed a premium on arts of persuasion, which appealed to the emotions and prejudices of the *iudices* as well as to their reason. Once in the public arena, it was also possible to formulate definitions of law that appealed to popular emotions, such as patriotism, as Cicero did for the benefit of Cluentius in 66:

> For this (Law) is the bond which guarantees this standing which we enjoy in the state, this is the foundation of freedom, this the source of justice (*aequitatis*); the mind and soul and judgement and decision of the state reside in its statutes (*legibus*). Just like bodies without a mind, so a state without law cannot make use of its parts, which are as nerves and blood and limbs. The servants of the law, the magistrates, the interpreters of law, the *iudices*, in short all of us are servants of the law that we can be free. (*Clu*. 53. 146)

This is the public face of legal definition, identifying the law as a necessary part of the *civitas*, and giving it a somewhat elitist spin: statutes preserve *dignitas* and the 'freedoms' of Cicero's and the jurors' class. But he also plays on the jury's sense of its own importance in a way more significant for its role in the making of law than might be expected; they, like jurists, are saluted as 'interpreters of law'. But did their interpretations really carry the same authority as did those of the jurists? The question, though lacking a definitive answer is important, because it affects what may be thought of the power of the courts to make law through its judgments (*res iudicatae*) and of forensic orators in influencing what law was made. And, to make the issue broader still, if *iudices* can be argued to be, to a limited extent, an extension of the *populus*, then the power of the *iudices* to 'make' law, and the emphasis put on it by Cicero, add a further dimension to the 'popularizing' of Roman public life, noted as a feature of the first century BC by historians from Tacitus to Fergus Millar (1998).

Writing as a rhetorical theorist, Cicero, as we have seen, cited *res iudicatae* as being one of the component parts of the *ius civile*. In the *De Inventione*, he defines *consuetudo*, customary law, as principles of law established by antiquity, without the benefit of written statute, 'voluntate omnium', by general consent. Among the ideas fixed by custom are agreements, equity, and *iudicatum*, which he defines as something established by the formal opinion (*sententia*) of someone or some people (*Inv*. 2. 22. 67–8 and 54. 162). He does not specify that the formulator of the *sententia* should be a *iudex* or *iudices*. Later, as we have seen, the continuing relevance of *iudicata* are confirmed in his list of *partitiones* of the *ius civile* offered to Trebatius, but no elaboration is forthcoming; Trebatius, presumably (unlike us), knew what he meant.

Despite Cicero's unhelpful vagueness, however, it appears that he did believe that *iudices* were empowered to take decisions that counted as *ius*. While the initial stage of a civil suit, the issuing of the formula, was the responsibility of the praetor, who decided on what the main legal issue was and what legal action could be made available, it did not follow from this that the hearing by the appointed adjudicator would deal only with matters of fact. Points of legal principle could be at stake at any stage, and the *iudices*' decisions on legal points determined the outcome of the case as a whole. Here, a brief treatment of the *Pro Caecina*, a civil case concerning possession but also revolving round the praetorian interdict on violence (Frier 1985: 171–83), will demonstrate what expectations of their role Cicero could impose on adjudicators, in this case, *recuperatores*.

Much of Cicero's argument revolves round the letter and the spirit of the wording of the praetorian interdict *de vi armata*. Cicero's opponents appear, from his representation, to have relied heavily on the letter—indeed, literally one letter (the 'r' or the 'd' of 'reieci' or 'deieci', *Caec*. 13. 38)—of the interdict. Cicero's response was to emphasize, repeatedly, the superiority of intention over exact wording. From the outset, there is introduced a concept of the application of force either in accordance with custom (*moribus*) or against both law and custom (*contra ius moremque*). Aebutius, the offender against whom the interdict was aimed, being an audacious villain, reasoned that, if his defence was compatible with 'more institutoque omnium', Caecina's case would benefit, whereas if he behaved badly, in violation of *consuetudo*, he would gain by it. The purpose of law, however, was to prevent force:

> since I must speak about the Law which applies to all, which was established by our ancestors and preserved to the present time, by the destruction of which, not only a part of our legal right is destroyed, but also that violence which is the absolute opposite of law may seem to be supported by your judgement (*iudicio confirmata*). (*Caec*. 2. 5)

This view of law was designed to prepare the ground for what followed, an analysis of the intention of the interdict. For if praetorian law was the expression of *consuetudo* in the written law (*Inv*. 2. 22. 67), then the principles of fairness grounded in *consuetudo* should apply. As it was manifestly unfair that the interdict, whatever its wording, should not supply a remedy for the kind of violence inflicted on Caecina, when he was frightened away from the farm he claimed by Aebutius' thugs, it followed that the interdict should apply.

Since our ancestors were men of hard work and wisdom so that they ordained and ensured legal rights not only in such great matters as these but also in the most trivial things, would they have omitted this one very important type of action (*genus*), that if a man forces me to leave my house by arms, I should have the action, whereas if he prevents me from entering it, I should not have it? (*Caec.* 12.34)

Intention, then, was paramount. If it were not, maintained the orator, society would break down; statutes, senatorial decrees, edicts of magistrates, treaties, wills, and all forms of agreement would no longer function and, in daily life, masters could no longer even give orders to their slaves, if they were only to be obeyed to the letter (*Caec.* 18. 51–2). All kinds of other statutes too would need to be recast; property in land was determined after two years and that principle now applied to buildings as well (cf. also *Top.* 4. 23), although not specified; a bequest to a ward would fail if the ward was now 20 years old, and out of pupillage; and the general permission granted drivers of beasts to go round any route, if a road was impassable, would be limited to permission for drivers in Bruttium to pass through the estate of M. Scaurus at Tusculum (*Caec.* 19. 54). Much of this was perhaps entertaining distraction but the principle behind it, which is sustained throughout the speech, is the overriding importance of custom and equity, as against legal technicality, and the orator's belief, which he counted on the jury to share, that *aequitas* and intention counted for more than the exact wording of the praetor's law (see, explicitly, *Caec.* 28. 80).

All cases, however, hinged on the advocate's and the adjudicators' reading of equity. Did it then follow from that that juries could, by their decisions, affect what the law was, as Cicero's references to *res iudicatae* as being parts of law, alongside statutes and equity would indicate? Some observations can perhaps be dismissed as flattery of the jury, through exaggeration of its powers. Early in the speech, for example, having deplored earlier evidence of indecision on the part of the judges, Cicero emphasized to them the impact that their decision could have on the legitimacy of force in society: 'consider . . . what law (*ius*) you wish for us, what situation for yourselves, what, in short, form of statute (*lex*) for the state' (*Caec.* 14. 40). Other, later, reflections offer greater depth. On the subject of the attempts of his opponents to subvert the authority of the jurist, C. Aquillius Gallus, who had pronounced in favour of Cicero's case, on grounds, apparently, of equity, Cicero reaches the core of what he thought of the *ius civile* in court. There were some, he said, even some rather clever people, who argued that jurisconsults should not be deferred to, nor should the *ius civile* invariably apply. This was acceptable, if it was argued that the jurist was wrong, or, as he explains later, if the *iudices* followed one jurist rather than another, opting, say, for Manilius rather than Q. Mucius. What was not acceptable was that, while it was conceded that the views of the jurists were right, the court should nevertheless decide against them; this was to advocate wrong judgments. '"But judgments have sometimes been made against them (the jurists)." First, rightly or wrongly? If rightly, then that was law which the judgment of the court laid down (*id fuit ius quod iudicatum est*). If otherwise, there is no doubt which is to blame, the jurists or the *iudices*' (*Caec*. 24. 69). What was right, Cicero argued, was based on the abstract and agreed notions of law and justice which he took as given, but which were also central to his case. Law was essential to the existence of community, or at least to the rights of the owners of property within the community. Without law, individuals cannot establish what belongs to them and what to other people. Questions of law cannot be changed by the courts and are invulnerable to corruption or bribery. Possession of property depends on the law of ownership, inheritance, and bequest; rights over property, such as boundaries, water, and roads, also depend on law. Therefore the adjudicators should uphold the 'publica patrimonia', the public heritage, of law, with the same care with which they safeguarded their personal property rights. This would not happen, he argued, if they as the 'vox iuris', the voice of law, decided in Aebutius' favour.

Cicero's argument to the *recuperatores*, then, included the suggestion that what they would decide would affect not only Caecina personally but also the content of the law itself, and would thus ultimately damage their self-interest, as property-owners whose rights depended on the laws. But, as is well known, Cicero liked to raise the stakes and exaggerate the importance of the case in hand. Although, in the passage cited above, Cicero stated explicitly that what was *iudicatum* counted as *ius*, was even this a polite exaggeration? If *iudicata* were indeed *ius*, would we not expect previous decided cases to be used as precedents?

The main difficulty for *iudicata* as *ius* is that Cicero hardly ever cited judicial decisions as legal precedents in court. This does not mean that he was ignorant of previous cases or that he did not cite them for other purposes, as is evidenced by his frequent reference to the 'causa Curiana' and other cases (for example, those collected at *De Or*. 1. 175–7) not, as a rule, for their outcome but for the methods of argument employed. It is possible, however, that if more speeches of Cicero from civil cases had survived, more use of *iudicata* as precedents might be in evidence. For, as it happens, the Caecina trial does contain use of a 'decided case' as a legal precedent. It involved citizenship and freedom and showed Cicero, as in the Roscius case, taking on the allies of Sulla:

> I established this point when I acted against Cotta, that most learned lawyer of our state. When I was defending the freedom of a woman of Arretium, and Cotta was pushing religious scruple down the throats of the decemviri, arguing that judgment could not be given in favour of our case, because the people of Arretium had lost their citizenship, I contended with passion that they could not lose their citizenship. The decemviri reached no verdict in the first hearing, but after investigating and debating the matter, they ruled that our case was justified. And this verdict was reached, even though Cotta spoke against it, and Sulla was still alive. (*Caec.* 33. 97)

While one exception does not prove the rule, Cicero's approach to custom, equity, and the powers of adjudicators in the *Pro Caecina* adds a public dimension to the philosophical and rhetorical approaches to defining law in general and the *ius civile* in particular, outlined above. Despite obvious differences of emphasis and levels of sophistication, they have much in common. Law was an ideal, and essential to the ordering of the community; man-made law could be fallible and could be shown to be so when set against the requirements of natural law, custom, or fairness. The *ius civile* had many facets when analysed; written law was open to challenge, using the resources of the unwritten, which, unlike the written, could be argued to be sanctioned by universal consent. Little was certain and much could be disputed; while the Republic lasted, neither the orator nor the jurist would find themselves redundant.

The uncertainties of law should not be overstated. Much of law was specific, detailed, and required hard work to learn. As Cicero observed in the *De Oratore* (1. 173; 184; 2. 110), disasters could happen if advocates were employed who got the law wrong. But round the hard core of written statutes and other legal materials, which could themselves be open to challenge, glosses, and alternative readings, was a growing accumulation of interpretations, based on writings of jurists, who frequently did not agree, but who influenced the creation of formulae and also could argue in court. Hardest to quantify, it has been argued, is the influence of advocates on the content of *ius*. Were Cicero's claims that 'res iudicatae' were a part of law no more than an attempt to ascribe greater importance to his favoured branch of legal activity than it, or he, deserved? Or did the decisions of *iudices*, and with them, the 'opinion of the crowd' (*Top.* 19. 73) have a direct input into the content of law, even if its route cannot yet be clearly mapped?

Government and Law: Ulpian, a Philosopher in Politics?

FERGUS MILLAR

In a well-known passage from the beginning of his *Institutes*, to which we will return later, Ulpian claims that the science of the law is the truest form of philosophy. Whether what we find when we read the extensive remains of his writings, reconstituted from Justinian's *Digest*, really justifies this bold claim, is another matter. What is certain, however, is, first, that the writings of Ulpian and the other jurists of the second and earlier third centuries represent both a very significant proportion of surviving classical Latin prose, and an intense intellectual activity conducted in extremely academic style, with constant explicit reference not merely to other jurists and their opinions, but to named works by them and even to book numbers within those works. But though the style was academic, and we must never forget in reading the *Digest* that the works excerpted in it were not themselves official publications, or still less 'law-codes', but private scholarly productions, the study of the law itself necessarily brought the jurists to make constant reference to the various forms in which the emperors of their time interpreted existing law or promulgated new laws. In that sense their works could not avoid being a commentary on contemporary government. But beyond that, as is well known, many of the juristic writers of the period not only sat as *assessores* in the courts of governors, Roman magistrates, and the emperors themselves, but held 'secretarial' positions at the side of the emperor, above all the post of *a libellis*, and even occupied major prefectures such as that of the vigiles or the praetorian cohorts. More even than their contemporaries, namely the sophists who often held the post of *ab epistulis Graecis*, the jurists must come in the category of 'intellectuals in politics'. But whether Ulpian in particular would deserve the further title of 'a philosopher in politics', which Miriam Griffin used as the subtitle of her fundamental study of Seneca (1976), remains to be seen.

Seneca's writings of course belong in that central period of Roman culture, and of Latin literature in prose and verse, which stretches from Cicero to Tacitus (or perhaps from Catullus to Martial). But, while we need not feel compelled to admire imperialism, we ought to be aware, when we look at the evolution of Roman culture, that the period of the greatest extension of the Empire was not the lifetime of Seneca or Tacitus, but precisely that of Ulpian, when no losses of territory had yet occurred in Europe, and in the East Septimius Severus conquered Mesopotamia and extended the boundaries of the Empire to the Tigris. The language which Senate and people used in dedicating an arch in the Forum to Septimius Severus and his son, M. Aurelius Antoninus ('Caracalla'), was entirely traditional: 'ob rem publicam restitutam imperiumque populi Romani propagatum'.[1] But the nature of the Empire had changed profoundly all the same. The Roman citizenship was already very widespread among the upper classes of the Greek East, and Greeks were common in all types of equestrian post, and in the Senate. Similarly, Septimius Severus gave the rank of *colonia* to a whole series of cities in the Near East — and, as it happens, our most detailed source for this is Ulpian himself, who records that one of them was his own native city of Tyre in Syria Phoenice.[2] But it is also Ulpian who, alone of all the jurists whose works survive, records explicitly that, thanks to the now sole Emperor, Antoninus ('Caracalla'), all were now Roman citizens: 'In orbe Romano qui sunt ex constitutione imperatoris Antonini cives Romani effecti sunt' (All those within the Roman world have been made Roman citizens under the constitution of the Emperor Antoninus). This brief phrase, plucked out of context and incorporated in the *Digest* (1. 5. 17), comes from book 22 of Ulpian's massive commentary *Ad Edictum*, which, like the vast bulk of his work, was written under Caracalla (AD 211–17) (Honoré 2002). Whether Ulpian consciously related his juristic writing to the now vastly extended field of application of Roman law can only be a matter of speculation.

What is certainly the case is that the major jurists writing between the middle of the second century and the third or fourth decade of the third represent a very distinctive phase in the history of Roman legal scholarship, both in the social and geographical origins of the individuals concerned and in the nature of the public positions which some of them came to occupy. Not all the details can be rehearsed here, and we are fortunate now to be able to rely on the masterly analysis of 'Jurisprudenz' by Detlef Liebs which is contained in the survey of Roman literature from AD 117 to 284 edited by Klaus Salmann (1997: 82–217). It is perhaps this chapter above all which

[1] *ILS* no. 425; see Steinby 1993: s.v. 'Arcus: Septimius Severus (Forum)'.
[2] Ulpian, *De Censibus* 1, quoted in *Digest* 50. 15. 1 *pr*. See Millar 1990: 34–7.

should serve to bring the juristic literature of the High Empire within the purview of Latinists and students of Roman culture. Along with juristic writing might come two other branches of academic or technical literature in Latin: medical writings, whose vocabulary is analysed by David Langslow (2000); and the remarkably varied and interesting works of the land-surveyors (*agrimensores*), newly presented and translated by Brian Campbell (2000).

To sum up the phase of Roman legal scholarship to which Ulpian belongs, after Salvius Julianus, a senator who on Hadrian's orders produced a definitive edition of the praetor's edict, the main juristic writers were characteristically no longer senators but (where their status is known at all) *equites*. Quite a number have Greek names (for instance Arrius Menander and Callistratus), which will not necessarily prove personal origins in a Greek environment. Others, like Iulius Paulus, have names which strongly suggest the acquisition of citizenship by the family in the early Empire. Others, like Ulpian himself, from Tyre (as we have seen), or Licinius Rufinus from Thyatira in Asia, we know to have come from Greek cities, even though their names would not suggest this (Millar 1999). As W. Kunkel's classic work on the origins of Roman jurists (1967) showed, there is no doubt, in a broad sense, that the study and practice of Roman law became an activity, even a career, taken up by young men from educated provincial families, including families from Greek cities. Given the generally limited currency of Latin literature in the Greek East, the fact that Roman law, as a field which by its nature was expressed and practised in Latin, was studied by Greeks is a very significant element in the culture of the Empire, and in the formation of a (partially) integrated Graeco-Roman governing class. It remains irritating that in the case of the one jurist of this period who wrote an entire work of Roman law in Greek, Herennius Modestinus, we cannot be sure whether his first language was Latin or Greek (Millar 1999: 102–3, 108).

It is also unfortunate that we can only in rare cases gain a sense of the social and family background of individual juristic writers, or of the complex educational processes which they must have gone through to be able to write extensive academic works with copious and detailed reference to the works of their predecessors and contemporaries. Given the nature of our evidence, we tend to see them only in the context of the specific public positions which some of them held. None the less, even the evidence for these public positions, taken with that for their writings, is very striking, and may be summarily presented here.

1. Ulpius Marcellus, the author of *Digesta* in thirty-one books, and several other works including *De Officio Consulis* (Lenel 1889: ii. 589–640), gives a detailed verbatim report of a trial before Marcus Aurelius in AD 166, evidently from personal observation as one of the *consilium* (*Dig*. 28. 4. 3). We cannot tell whether this was as an *amicus* or, like others, as a paid *consiliarius*.

2. L. Volusius Maecianus, the author of *Quaestiones de Fideicommissis* in sixteen books, and *De Iudiciis Publicis* in fourteen (Lenel 1889: i. 575–88), pursued a full equestrian career, from military posts upwards to being *a libellis* to Antoninus Pius at the end of Hadrian's reign, to *Praefectus vehiculorum*, *a studiis* and *procurator bibliothecarum*, *a libellis* and *a censibus* under Antoninus Pius, and then *Praefectus Annonae* and Prefect of Egypt (Pflaum 1960–1: no. 141). Significantly, one of the inscriptions from Ostia which records these details refers to him explicitly as a *iuris consultus* (*CIL* xiv, no. 5348: '[iuris cons]ulto'). It is Ulpian himself, in book 11 of his *Ad Legem Iuliam et Papiam*, who quotes the 'Divi Fratres' (Marcus Aurelius and Verus) for the report that Volusius had finally agreed in their presence to their view of a case under inheritance law (*Dig*. 37. 14. 17 *pr*.):

sed et Volusius Maecianus, amicus noster ut et iuris civilis praeter veterem et bene fundatam peritiam anxie diligens, religione rescripti nostri ductus sit ut coram nobis adfirmarit non arbitratum se aliter respondere debere.

But even our friend Volusius Maecianus, as a man conscientiously devoted to the civil law besides his long and well-established expertise in it, was brought by reverence for our rescript to acknowledge in our presence that he did not think he ought to give a different response.

It was a crucial feature of the period that jurists advised, but emperors decided. We need not speculate as to whether it was this complaisance which allowed him subsequently to ascend to senatorial rank (*AE* 1955: no. 179).

3. Q. Cervidius Scaevola, the author of *Digesta* in forty books, twenty books of *Quaestiones*, six of *Regulae* and of *Responsa*, and perhaps other works (Lenel 1889: ii. 215–322), is referred to by the *Historia Augusta* as a *iuris peritus* on whom Marcus Aurelius particularly relied, and perhaps also as one of the *Praefecti* whom he kept at his side (*v. Marci* 11. 10). Furthermore, it is once again Ulpian, in book 5 of his *Disputationes*, who records a judgment given by Marcus Aurelius *in auditorio*, of which the details were reported by Scaevola: 'Scaevola divum Marcum in auditorio de huismodi specie iudicasse refert' ('Scaevola reports that the deified Marcus decided a case of this type *in auditorio*': *Dig*. 36. 1. 23 (22) *pr*.). An

inscription from Ostia of AD 175 names Cervidius Scaevola as *Pr(aefectus)*, evidently of the vigiles (Pflaum 1960–1: no. 168*a*). Two years later, in AD 177, he is listed on the *Tabula Banasitana* as one of the *consilium* of Marcus Aurelius and Commodus when citizenship was granted to a leading family in Mauretania (*AE* 1971: no. 534).

4. P. Taruttienus Paternus, who appears with the correct form of his name for the first time on the same document, is known as the author of only one juristic work, *De Re Militari* in four books (Lenel 1889: ii. 335–6). He is recorded as *ab epistulis Latinis* in the early 170s, and as praetorian prefect in 179–80 (Pflaum 1960–1: no. 172).

5. Aemilius Papinianus, one of the major figures in the history of Roman legal scholarship, was the author of many works, including thirty-seven books of *Quaestiones* and nineteen of *Responsa* (Lenel 1889: i. 803–946). He himself records, in book 20 of his *Quaestiones* (*Dig.* 22. 1. 3. 3), that he persuaded ('suasi') the praetorian prefects to take a certain view of an inheritance case. The date seems uncertain. But Tryphoninus records a rescript given by the emperor, evidently Septimius Severus, 'when Papinian was handling the *libelli*' (*Dig.* 20. 5. 12. *pr.*): 'libellos agente Papiniano'. Papinian was thus *a libellis*, and with him we enter the territory of 'emperors and lawyers' brilliantly explored by Tony Honoré (1994: 76–81), who identifies him as 'secretary no. 1', in office from 194 to 202. He was later praetorian prefect, and was dismissed and then executed early in Caracalla's reign (see *PIR*² A 388). Iulius Paulus (no. 8 below) refers to a *cautio* read 'in auditorio Aemilii Papiani praefecti praetorio, iuris consulti' (*Dig.* 12. 1 40 pr.). The implication of a connection between the two roles is significant.

6. Arrius Menander, the author of a work *De Re Militari* in four books (Lenel 1889: i. 695–700), is mentioned in passing by Ulpian as a *consiliarius* who had been excused from *tutela* on the grounds of attendance on the emperor (*Dig.* 4. 4. 11. 2), and is speculatively identified by Honoré (1994: 88–91) as *a libellis* in 212–13.

7. Claudius Tryphoninus, the author of twenty-one books of *Disputationes*, written under Caracalla (Lenel 1889: ii. 351–78), records an opinion of his own given *in auditorio* (*Dig.* 23. 3. 78. 4), while Paulus in book 3 of his *Decreta* mentions a property case in which opinions were given by Papinian, Messius, and Tryphoninus (*Dig.* 49. 14–50). Since Paulus' *Decreta*, as it seems, dealt solely with cases in the emperor's court, both instances seem to relate to that context. In any case they both illustrate the involvement of juristic writers in actual cases.

8. Iulius Paulus, another of the leading figures in juristic scholarship

(Lenel 1889: i. 951–1308), was the author of a vast range of works, including *Ad Edictum* in eighty books as well as the above-mentioned *Decreta* in three books; whether these were the same as, or distinct from, the six books of *Imperiales Sententiae in Cognitionibus Prolatae* is obscure; but the content of both certainly relates to cases heard in person by Septimius Severus, in some of which Paulus' own opinions are recorded (for example, *Dig*. 4. 4. 38. *pr*.). Similarly, he records the opinion which he gave in a case before Papinian (no. 5 above), presumably as praetorian prefect (*Dig*. 29. 2. 97). Paulus certainly lived into the reign of Severus Alexander (AD 222–35), since he quotes a letter from Alexander to the *praefectus urbi* (*Dig*. 31. 87. 3). Whether he held any actual posts is very uncertain, since the evidence that he did comes from the *Historia Augusta*; Ronald Syme rightly saw these reports as prime examples of 'fiction about Roman jurists'.[3] But again an active role in court is attested, and in this instance certainly the imperial court.

9. Aelius Marcianus, the author of many works, including sixteen books of *Institutiones* and two *De Iudiciis Publicis* (Lenel 1889: i. 639–90), refers to his own opinion given *in auditorio publico*, without saying which (*Dig*. 40. 15. 1. 4), and is tentatively identified by Honoré (1994: 91–5) as the *a libellis* in office in 213–17.

10. M. Cn. Licinius Rufinus, from Thyatira in Asia, was the author of a single known juristic work, his *Regulae* in twelve books (Lenel 1889: i. 559–62). An inscription from Thessalonica characterizes him as a *iuris peritus* (ἐνπειρότατος νόμων, *IG* 10. 2. 1 (1), no. 142), but now a remarkable Greek inscription from near his native city reveals an extensive career, of which the first part, at equestrian level, was all spent in the immediate service of the emperor, while in the latter part he became a quite prominent senator (Millar 1999). He was first a *consiliarius*, then in charge of the Greek letters, and then of the 'general accounts', while his final 'secretarial' post was almost certainly *a libellis* (ἐπὶ τῶν ἀποκριμάτων). If so, he may possibly be identified with Honoré's 'secretary no. 7', in office from October 222 to October 223. In that case then he will have been responsible for the rescript of December 222 in which Severus Alexander lays down that a provincial governor should send certain defendants to the current praetorian prefect: 'Domitius Ulpianus, the *praefectus praetorio* and *parens meus*' (*Cod. Just*. 4. 65. 4. 1). Rufinus' *Regulae* had, it seems, been written under Caracalla, and by 238 he had entered on a senatorial career, and was one of the board of twenty *consulares* who opposed Maximinus.

[3] For the complex and uncertain evidence as to his career see *PIR*[2] i. 453. See Syme 1970 and 1980.

11. Herennius Modestinus, the author of a number of works, including nine books of *Differentiae*, twelve books of *Pandectae*, and nineteen of *Responsa* (Lenel 1889: i. 701–56), also wrote, as mentioned earlier, what was so far the only extended expression of Roman law in Greek, his *Παραίτησις Ἐπιτροπῆς καὶ Κουρατορίας* in six books, usually labelled *De excusationibus* (Lenel 1889: i. 707–18). Under Caracalla he is mentioned by Ulpian as 'studiosus meus' (*Dig.* 47. 2. 50. 20), but his only securely attested post is that of *praefectus vigilum* at some time between 226 and 244. Honoré (1994: 101–7), however, advances strong arguments for identifying him with 'secretary no. 8', who will thus have followed Rufinus as *a libellis* between October 223 and October 225.

These eleven examples of juristic writers of equestrian rank who performed significant public functions in the period between the 160s and the 220s are surely sufficient to make us see this as a distinctive phase in the history of Roman government, and thereby to put the role of Ulpian himself in context. The definition of the category of 'juristic writers' can be quite simple—anyone who is quoted as the author of at least one juristic work. The public functions attested are themselves of various types, from acting as a member of the *consilium* of a magistrate, governor, or emperor, to 'secretarial' functions with the emperor, as *ab epistulis* or more commonly *a libellis*, to being prefect of the vigiles, the Annona, or the praetorian cohorts.

We have, it is true, almost no evidence on the educational processes which led to recognition as a *iuris consultus*, and absolutely no reason to imagine any formal process of qualification. But, since our topic is 'intellectuals in politics', it is important to stress how profoundly intellectual, indeed how profoundly academic in style, the conduct of debate on points of Roman law was. 'Debate' in this context means two things. First, there is repeated reference in the juristic works of this period not just to earlier or contemporary authorities by name, but to the titles of their works and to book numbers within them. One example out of hundreds will have to suffice: in book 4 of his *Disputationes* Ulpian begins a discussion by saying 'Iulianus in book 26 of his *Digesta* wrote . . .', and continues by noting the contrary opinion of Marcellus (*Dig.* 29. 2. 43). But 'debate' also means actual oral debate over cases heard by magistrates, governors, or emperors, in which more than one *iuris consultus* might be involved (see above under 7, Tryphoninus). Alternatively, as we have seen in the case of Volusius Maecianus (no. 2 above), a jurist might feel constrained to yield to the opinion of the emperor. A similar relationship is revealed when Iulius Paulus reports an instance where a *pupilla* lost a case before the praetor, then (presumably on appeal) before the *praefectus urbi*, and finally appealed to the Emperor himself (*Dig*. 4. 4. 38):

> The *pupilla* sought *restitutio in integrum*. Having lost in the proceedings both before the praetor and the urban prefect, she had appealed. I was of the opinion that the judgment was correct. . . . However the Emperor was swayed by the fact . . . I argued that a better reason for granting *restitutio* would be . . . and that I was not moved by the consideration that . . . Nevertheless, because the *lex commissoria* displeased him, the Emperor awarded *restitutio in integrum*. He was also influenced by the fact that the former *tutores* who had not sought *restitutio* had been declared suspect.

Just as the dialogue with other jurists could be an academic one, conducted on paper, but also a literal one, conducted in court, so the confrontation of jurists with the imperial role could be in actual court settings, but could also take the form of citations of the wide variety of different vehicles through which emperors interpreted or modified the law, established new precedents, or explicitly promulgated new law: judgments (*decreta* or *sententiae*) in court; *mandata* issued to office-holders; replies to letters from office-holders, provincial leagues, or cities; rescripts (earlier called *subscriptiones*) in reply to petitions (*libelli*) submitted by private persons (and sometimes communities); *edicta*; *orationes* delivered in the Senate. The record of the jurists' citations of, and responses to, these very varied forms of imperial lawmaking fill the pages of the indispensable work by Gualandi (1963), and need not be repeated here. One example of how *ad hoc* promulgations of legal principles by emperors might enter the academic literature may suffice: Ulpian notes in his *Ad Edictum* that a rescript of Antoninus Pius to Cornelius Proculus was quoted by Pomponius in his *Liber Epistularum*; by Marcellus in book 3 of his *Digesta*; and by Papinian in book 3 of his *Quaestiones* (*Dig*. 2. 8. 7 pr.). But this was also, at least to some extent, a two-way exchange. For the jurists quite frequently note that principles expounded by earlier jurists had subsequently been incorporated in imperial pronouncements (Gualandi 1963: ii. 107–8). Explicit acknowledgement by emperors of the influence of jurists in general, or of named individual jurists, is rare, however, and should probably not be expected. But Severus Alexander records in a rescript that the principle on which he is basing his reply had been approved by the *prudentes* (*Cod. Just*. 6. 53. 6). Moreover, in the rescript in which Marcus Aurelius and Verus report that Volusius Maecianus had bowed to their opinion (p. 72 above) they also acknowledge that they had learnt that Proculus had shared the view in question, as had several other *iuris auctores*, as well as Sabinus Iulianus, *amicus noster, vir clarissimus* (*Dig*. 34. 14. 17 pr.). Alternatively, an emperor might state explicitly that his interpretation goes against that of the *iuris periti*, as Caracalla does in a private rescript of 212: 'Quamquam ita interpretentur iuris periti' ('Although those skilled in the laws have this opinion . . .') (*Cod. Just*. 9. 23. 1). Herennius Modestinus seems to be the only other jurist who is explicitly named as an authority in an imperial pronouncement of this period, in a private rescript of Gordian III dating to 239: 'The view that not only he who is in possession but also he who has used fraud so that he would not be liable is bound by an action *ad exhibendum* was the justified content of a reply to you by a *iurisconsultus* of no mean authority, Modestinus' (*Cod. Just*. 3. 42. 5).

The fact that the authors of legal works—from a single known monograph to a vast range of different works, some of very great length—were engaged in a constant debate, on paper and in real life (and if on paper with both predecessors and contemporaries), both with each other and also with the views of emperors, both dead and living, is the main reason for stressing what a significant case of 'intellectuals in politics' they represent. It is only in this context that we can attempt to understand the career and role of Ulpian.

But before we turn to that role it is necessary to sketch very briefly why there was so much scope in this period for juristic debate. The reason is the very high level of novelty and procedural indeterminancy which in the second and earlier third centuries characterized the day-to-day operation of the law (see now especially Peachin 1996: ch. 1). A substantial volume would hardly be sufficient to explore the novelty and fluidity of the system, so the crudest of outlines will have to suffice here.

Roman civil and criminal law, as studied by the writers of the Antonine and Severan period, was firmly rooted in the legislation and procedures of the Republic and early Empire: the passing of *leges* by the popular assemblies (*comitia*); the conduct of criminal trials before jury-courts (*iudicia publica* or *quaestiones*) which arrived at a verdict by majority vote; and the handling of civil suits by the two-stage, 'formulary' system, by which a procedure before a magistrate (*in iure*), to determine the grounds of the action, was followed by a hearing *apud iudicem*, before a single lay person appointed as *iudex*.

There are many fundamental uncertainties as to the stages by which all this changed, as regards both civil and criminal jurisdiction, to the arrangements which we can see in force between the lines of the juristic works and Imperial rescripts (above all as collected in the *Codex Justinianus*, but also frequently cited in juristic writings) of the Antonine–Severan period. But, first, while *leges* are still quoted (the latest being from the reign of Nerva), other sources of law have appeared (I define 'source of law' as anything cited by juristic writers as a precedent): *senatus consulta*, or imperial *orationes* in the Senate; imperial *edicta*; letters to officials; imperial judgments in court (*decreta* or *sententiae*); imperial private rescripts, and even *interlocutiones* not delivered formally from a tribunal (*de plano*) (see Nörr 1983).

As regards criminal jurisdiction, there seems to be no further evidence of jury-courts delivering verdicts in Rome, and it is obscure how far such a system had ever obtained in the provinces. Instead, the juristic writers, and the emperors whom they frequently cite, seem to assume that all verdicts are delivered by office-holders, on the advice of a *consilium*. As for the formulary system, it seems clear that it represented at least one possible form of procedure, in both Rome and the provinces, at any rate until the first half of the second century (see Hackl 1997 and Turpin 1999). But in the world of the jurists, in civil as in criminal jurisdiction, verdicts are characteristically delivered by office-holders in their own right.

Some entirely traditional elements none the less survive. The jurisdiction of the praetors (as of the aediles) in Rome continues, and would well deserve study from the ample empirical evidence available. But even in Rome there is a concurrent jurisdiction by new office-holders of the Imperial period, the prefects of the annona, the vigiles and the praetorian cohorts, the consular prefect of the city, and the emperor himself. In the provinces, equally, the governor in person delivers verdicts in both criminal and civil cases.

There were also many new elements, above all in criminal jurisdiction, which had arisen over the first two centuries: the claims of the imperial *fiscus* on *bona damnatorum*, and on *bona caduca* (Millar 1963: 34–7); the elaboration of new, or newly defined, penalties, *relegatio*, *deportatio*, condemnation *ad metallum* (Millar 1984), with very different effects on the civil status of the individual; the differentiation of criminal penalties in accordance with the social class of the individual, with the harsher and more physically degrading penalties being reserved for the lower classes (Garnsey 1970).

Complicating everything was the legislative-cum-judicial role of the emperor. It would not necessarily have been anticipated that, even if the Republican system were to give place to a single ruler, that ruler would not only legislate, in his own person or through the Senate or (in the earlier period) through the *comitia*, but would also sit in judgment himself, and moreover (what was possibly even more ubiquitously influential in establishing precedents which the jurists then quoted) would receive and reply to consultations from office-holders on points of law, procedure, or the penalties to be applied, and would also do the same for very considerable numbers of private parties who were embroiled in civil suits, faced threats to their civil status, or might be liable to criminal penalties. In effect, either a party to a case or the official conducting it might suspend proceedings by the dispatch of a petition (*libellus*) or a letter (*epistula*, sometimes called *consultatio*) to the emperor. Other cases might formally be brought to the emperor on appeal, to be heard by him with his advisers (as we have seen above, p. 76).

It was the vast area left to the discretion of the official giving jurisdiction, combined with the range of ways in which emperors might be brought into individual cases, which produced the 'formlessness' of jurisdiction in the Antonine–Severan period, and with it a juristic literature of vast proportions, built in part on actual legislation, but also on a complex and continually evolving 'case-law' of precedents, deriving in almost all instances from specific rulings by emperors.

It is this tension between the presumption that there are indeed fundamental principles, on the one hand, and the observable fact of constant evolution and variation in procedure on the other which, it may be suggested, gives the juristic writing of this period its distinctive flavour. Before we turn finally to a sketch of the place of Ulpian himself in all this, it may be useful to quote an extract from his work which illustrates these themes.

As good an example as any, illustrating the range of office-holders who could now exercise criminal jurisdiction, legal innovation by emperors at their discretion even as regards cases not heard by themselves, and the civil-law effects of the new criminal penalties which had come into use, is a passage from Ulpian's first book on *Fideicommissa* (*Dig.* 32. 1. 2–5). Strikingly, he begins his discussion of the effects of the severer form of exile (*deportatio*) by using the ancient terminology of *aquae et ignis interdictio*. But everything else in the passage bears the stamp of the Severan period:

Those who have been forbidden fire and water, and also those *deportati*, cannot leave *fideicommissa*, for they also do not have the right to make a will, since they are stateless [*he uses the Greek word* ἀπόλιδες]. We must consider as *deportati* (also) those to whom the Emperor has assigned islands or in regard to whom he has written that they should be deported; but before the Emperor has approved the decision of the governor, the person is to be regarded as not yet having lost his citizenship. Moreover, if he dies first, he is regarded as having died as a citizen, and the *fideicommissum* which he had left before he suffered condemnation will be valid. But even if after the verdict, but before the Emperor has approved it, whatever has been done will be valid, because he still retained a definite status. But as regards those *deportati* by the praetorian prefects or whoever gives judgment in place of the prefects on the basis of the Emperor's *mandata*, (and) equally by the praefectus urbis (for to him to the right of deportation has been given by a letter of the Deified Severus and our Emperor [Caracalla]), it is established that they lose their citizenship immediately, and hence do not have the right of making a will or giving a *fideicommissum*.

If someone who has unquestionably been deported to an island has written *codicilli* while there, and, having been restored by the *indulgentia* of the Emperor and, while the *codicilli* remained unaltered, has died, it can be maintained that the *codicilli* are valid, provided only that he persisted in the same intention.

The passage brings out, perhaps as clearly as any could, how the Roman law of the jurists, which had of course evolved in the 'classical' world described by Cicero and Livy, in fact now functioned in a context of wholly new institutions, new 'judges', new procedures in court, new penalties with new consequences for civil status—and under the all-embracing influence of the emperor. To repeat, it was this new world where everything was subject to a myriad of minor adjustments—and occasional formal acts of innovation, like the letter of Severus and Caracalla which Ulpian quotes—which the writings of the major Roman jurists reflected.

Of these jurists, the one whose works occupy by far the largest proportion of the *Digest* is Ulpian (some 300,000 out of some 1,000,000 words). If ever there was an 'intellectual in politics', it was he; and if we accepted his own claims, made in the first book of his *Institutes*, we would have to give him a yet higher status, as a philosopher (pp. 85–6 below). It will be worth reviewing briefly what we know of his origins and career, while recalling the public careers of the eleven other jurists which we saw earlier.

There is no detailed career-inscription for Ulpian, as there is now for M. Cn. Licinius Rufinus (no. 10 above), and it is perfectly possible that, like Licinius, he held a whole series of posts at the imperial court. But what we know of his career, partial as it is, is striking enough. Domitius Ulpianus, like Licinius, came from the Greek East, for he himself asserts with considerable pride that his *origo* was Tyre in Phoenicia (p. 70 above). Other Οὐλπιανοί from the town are known, and there is every reason to see him as the product of an established local family. 'Greek', however, is too simple a description. Phoenician lettering appears on the coinage of the city up to the moment in the 190s when Severus made it a *colonia*, and there is no doubt that even after that its Phoenician past was remembered and celebrated (Millar 1993: 285–95).

There is every reason to think that the first language of the family will have been Greek. But *origo* does not formally imply that someone was born and educated in the city in question; the greatest gap in our knowledge of Ulpian, as of the other jurists, is that we have no access to the successive stages of his upbringing and education. All that we can be certain of is that he must have been born before, and probably several decades before, Tyre became a *colonia*, perhaps in the 160s—and that the later stages of his education will have involved a vast range of reading in earlier juristic writings, which he refers to almost obsessively in his own works (Honoré 1982: 206–7; 2002, 126–57).

How Ulpian came to the notice of the emperors is thus wholly unknown, and nor do we when this took place. Indeed, for our conception of Ulpian as an Imperial 'secretary' we are wholly dependent on the linguistic detective work of Tony Honoré, in identifying Ulpian as the *a libellis* in office (in succession to Papinian) from April 203 to May 209, in the joint reign of Severus and Caracalla (Honoré 1994: 81–8). This proposition, which I accept, has two consequences. First, the already enormous volume of writing by Ulpian is significantly increased, by including over 100 private rescripts explicitly dated, or assigned by Honoré, to this period.[4] These identifications are achieved, as is well known, by comparing the marks of style in the private rescripts of successive periods with those to be found in the works of different juristic writers. In Ulpian's case this comparison takes on a distinctive form. For Honoré's own dating of Ulpian's massive output of juristic writings, based on allusions in it to the current or the previous emperors, shows that the vast bulk of it was written in the sole reign of Caracalla (211–17). On this hypothesis, therefore, Ulpian's style was formed, or at least is first attested, when he had the role of composing Imperial legal rulings in the form of private rescripts in AD 203–9, and found its full expression subsequently in an immense output of private legal, or academic, works, written in his own name, in the second decade of the century. In consequence, therefore, the general context, which is beyond question, of an intense 'dialogue' and mutual influence as between juristic writing and imperial law-creation in its highly varied forms, takes on a very particular character.

It remains quite uncertain whether Ulpian was holding any Imperial position in the period of his concentrated output of scholarly works. We next hear of him in April 222, when Severus Alexander refers a petitioner to 'the *responsum* of Domitius Ulpianus, Praefectus Annonae, *iuris consultus*, *amicus meus*' (*Cod. Just.* 8. 37. 4). The explicit Imperial reference to his

[4] The rescripts attributed to Ulpian, as of any others of the *a libellis* concerned, reassembled in chronological order from the *Codex Justinianus*, can be printed out from the disk supplied with Honoré 1994.

status as a jurist is of course very significant, as it is in other cases noted earlier. By the end of the same year he had been appointed praetorian prefect, since the emperor refers to him in December as 'Praetorian Prefect and *parens meus*' (*Cod. Just.* 4. 65. 4. 1, see p. 74 above). Cassius Dio, a direct contemporary, and consul in 229, records his important role, and then his death in a mutiny by the praetorians (80. 2. 2–4). Whether this took place almost immediately, in 223, as new documentary evidence suggests, or not long before Dio's consulate in 229, is much debated, but need not be discussed here.[5]

It is striking that evidence of various very different kinds confirms the lasting public status of Ulpian as a juristic writer. In a rescript of 290 Diocletian, nominally with Maximian, refers to a principle which 'the *vir prudentissimus*, Domitius Ulpianus, established in his books of *Publicae Disputationes* for the permanent record of *scientia*' (*Cod. Just.* 9. 41. 11). In his *Divine Institutes* Lactantius makes an even more precise reference: 'Domitius in *De Officio Proconsulis*, book 7, collected the impious rescripts of Emperors, in order to make clear to which punishment those who confessed themselves worshippers of God should be subjected' (*Div. Inst.* 5. 11. 19).[6] Furthermore, uniquely, a partially preserved Greek inscription from Ephesos (*IK* 11 (Ephesos), no. 217), evidently containing part of the letter of a proconsul to the city, refers to the provisions of ancient laws to be found in Ulpian's *De Officio*, which is clearly also a reference to his *De Officio Proconsulis*. The date might be the Tetrarchic period (see Millar 1986: 279–80).

As a juristic writer who rose to the highest equestrian position, the praetorian prefecture, Ulpian is matched only by Taruttienus Paternus and by Papinian (nos. 4 and 5 above). But even in this role, both an immediate contemporary, Cassius Dio, and the emperor, Severus Alexander, himself, attribute to Ulpian a unique, if perhaps very short-lived, status and influence. In a characteristically suggestive lecture Ronald Syme (1972) saw him as an intellectual who had perhaps been propelled by excessive ambition into a position too dangerous for his talents. As for his contemporary standing as a jurist, it remains puzzling that the role as *a libellis* which Honoré assigns to him for 203–9 lies so separate in time from his prefectures of the annona and the praetorian cohorts (and the very curious inscription from Tyre in his honour mentions only these two posts, while

[5] The question of the date of Ulpian's death, generally assumed to have been in 223, because of the emergence of evidence (*P. Oxy.* no. 2565) that Epagathus, regarded as responsible for his death, was already in Egypt by 224, is reopened by Bauman 1995.

[6] For a recent study of the *Institutiones Divinae* see Digeser 2000.

also once again, describing him as 'iurisconsultus'[7]). But, given the combination of the exceptionally prominent public role to which he finally attained, and the even more exceptional scale and range of his output of learned works, we cannot but see him as the prime example from the Empire of the intellectual in politics. Indeed 'intellectual' is too weak a word. What is at issue is not just a high level of education, very possibly in a second language, or high intellectual ambitions, but a massive output of very detailed technical or professional work, demanding close attention to learned works written by other experts. No one who has read through the 478 columns in Lenel's *Palingenesia* occupied by the remains of the eighty-three books of Ulpian's *Ad Edictum* (Lenel 1889: ii. 421–898) will fail to recognize the spirit of a fellow academic, in which nothing is too mundane to escape definition, along with appropriate reference to earlier authorities. One example will perhaps suffice, from the second book on the *edictum* of the curule aediles:[8]

> Caelius also writes that it is not all animals which, being castrated, thereby become defective, unless the very fact of their castration diminishes their powers; the mule [if castrated] is therefore not defective. The same writer records that Ofilius took the view that a castrated horse is sound, as is also a castrated slave; but if the buyer knew nothing of this but the vendor did, the action on purchase will lie.

Two features of Ulpian's learned output, recently analysed in detail in Tony Honoré (2002), deserve particular attention if what concerns us is the connection, or tension, between public life on the one hand and intellectual, or even philosophical, commitment on the other. The first is the important place occupied in Ulpian's writing by works *De Officio*, on the duties of particular office-holders. The most salient of these, already referred to several times, is the *De Officio Proconsulis* in ten books (Lenel 1889: ii. 966–91); but there was also, for instance, his *De Officio Consulis* in three books; one book *De Officio Curatoris Rei Publicae*, and another *De Officio Praefecti Urbi* (much influenced by the *epistula* of Severus and Caracalla to Fabius Cilo, Praefectus Urbi, referred to above);[9] and another work in one book *De Officio Quaestoris*.

The latter is a striking example of the antiquarian strain found in Roman legal scholarship, and also shown at its fullest in Pomponius' erratic sketch of the history of the Roman constitution in his *Enchiridion* (Lenel 1889: ii. 44–52), and connecting directly to a similar strain in Aulus Gellius, and in

[7] *AE* 1988: no. 1051: 'Domitio Ulpiano, Praefecto/Praetorio, eminentissimo viro,/iurisconsulto, item Praefecto/Annonae Sacrae Urbis . . .'

[8] *Dig*. 21. 1. 38. 7 (= Lenel 1889: para. 1792), tr. in Watson 1985, with emendations.

[9] See p. 80 above. For the *De Officio Praefecti Urbi* see *Dig*. 1. 12. 1 (Lenel 1889: ii. 959–60).

excursuses in the *Annales* of Tacitus, writing a century before Ulpian.[10] Ulpian shows himself fully worthy of this tradition:[11]

The original occasion for electing quaestors was most ancient, and almost earlier than all the other magistracies. Indeed Gracchanus Iunius reports in his seventh book *De Potestatibus* that Romulus himself and Numa Popilius had each two quaestors whom they appointed not on their own say-so, but by popular election . . .

The composition of works *De Officio* was not of course unique to Ulpian. For instance, Ulpius Marcellus (no. 1 above) had written a *De Officio Consulis* in at least five books; Q. Venuleius Saturninus four books *De Officio Proconsulis* (Lenel 1889: ii. 1216); and Iulius Paulus (no. 8 above) wrote works in one book each *De Officio Adsessorum*, *De Officio Praefecti Urbis*, *De Officio Praefecti Vigilum*, and *De Officio Praetoris Tutelaris*, as well as two *De Officio Proconsulis* (Lenel 1889: i. 1143–5). All could be seen as attempts to relate the inherited principles and procedures of Roman law to the changed—and still constantly changing—structure of the offices whose holders now exercised jurisdiction, and the evolving rules under which they did so. We may, however, think that it was not an accident that it was Ulpian's *De Officio Proconsulis* which was to be the one which was most fully preserved and (as it seems, p. 82 above) most often quoted.

Finally, it is very significant that Ulpian, as an academic with the ambition to expose the basic principles of his field, wrote two books of *Institutiones* (Lenel 1889: ii. 926–30). This term of course was not peculiar to juristic writing, as Quintilian's choice of the title *Institutiones Oratoriae* shows, and it was later to be borrowed by Lactantius for his *Institutiones Divinae*. But it was characteristic of legal writing, as in the *Institutiones* of Gaius (the only example surviving *in extenso*), and in the two books of *Institutiones* by Ulpian's contemporary Iulius Paulus (no. 8 above), of which very little survives. More significant are the sixteen books of *Institutiones* by another direct contemporary, Aelius Marcianus (no. 9 above; Lenel 1889: i. 652–75). Marcianus, like Ulpian, begins by trying to define the nature of law, quoting Demosthenes and Chrysippus in Greek (*Dig*. 1. 3. 2); the twenty-three columns of this expository work which survive in Lenel's *Palingenesia* deserve a more prominent place than they have ever received in the canon of classical Latin prose writing.

But it is Ulpian himself who makes the most ambitious claims for the intellectual status of the study of law as the true philosophy. Stimulated by the example of Seneca as the 'philosopher in politics', this paper had origin-

[10] For the overlap between juristic and antiquarian studies see especially Nörr 1976.
[11] *Dig*. 1. 13. 1 (Lenel 1889: ii. 992), tr. Watson 1985, with emendations.

ally aimed to start from these claims, not to end with them. But there has been too much to say by way of preliminaries, and the question remains to be pursued by future students of this vast corpus of writing: does Ulpian's thought in any consistent way step outside the bounds of purely legal reasoning, to apply philosophical principles about the nature of man or of society or of nations or of political authority? And, if so, which principles?[12]

Even if it were to turn out that he does not live up to his own claims, the terms in which he presents them are significant in themselves, and should serve to invite students to ask what Ulpian's place is in the history of Roman thought and of Latin prose writing. Three extracts from the first book of the *Institutiones* will suffice. They are given in the order in which they appear in the first book of the *Digest*, interspersed among extracts from other jurists, but almost certainly in their correct order in the original. Since one of the purposes of this paper is to give a sense of juristic writing as a branch of Latin prose, they will be given in the original, followed in each case by the translation from Alan Watson's edition.

Ulpianus libro primo *Institutionum*. Iuri operam daturum prius nosse oportet, unde nomen iuris descendat. est autem a iustitia appellatum: nam, ut eleganter Celsus definit, (1) ius est ars boni et aequi. Cuius merito quis nos sacerdotes appellet: iustitiam namque colimus et boni et aequi notitiam profitemur, aequum ab iniquo separantes, licitum ab illicito discernentes, bonos non solum metu poenarum, verum etiam praemiorum quoque exhortatione efficere cupientes, veram nisi fallor philosophiam, non simulatam affectantes. (2) Huius studii duae sunt positiones, publicum et privatum. publicum ius est quod ad statum rei Romanae spectat, privatum quod ad singulorum utilitatem; sunt enim quaedam publice utilia, quaedam privatim. publicum ius in sacris, in sacerdotibus, in magistratibus consistit. priuatum ius tripertitum est: collectum etenim est ex naturalibus praeceptis aut gentium aut civilibus. (3) Ius naturale est, quod natura omnia animalia docuit: nam ius istud non humani generis proprium, sed omnium animalium, quae in terra, quae in mari nascuntur, avium quoque commune est. hinc descendit maris atque feminae coniunctio, quam nos matrimonium appellamus, hinc liberorum procreatio, hinc educatio: videmus etenim cetera quoque animalia, feras etiam istius iuris peritia censeri. (4) Ius gentium est, quo gentes humanae utuntur. quod a naturali recedere facile intellegere licet, quia illud omnibus, hoc solis hominibus inter se commune sit. (*Dig*. 1. 1. 1. pr. 4)

Ulpian, *Institutes*, Book I: A law student at the outset of his studies ought first to know the derivation of the word *ius*. Its derivation is from *iustitia*. For, in terms of Celsus's elegant definition, the law is the art of goodness and fairness. (1) Of that art we [jurists] are deservedly called the priests. For we cultivate the virtue of justice

[12] For studies of Ulpian's thought, which in the end cannot be pursued here, see esp. Nörr 1973; Crifó 1976; Schermaier 1993; but see now Honoré 2002, esp. Ch. 3.

and claim awareness of what is good and fair, discriminating between fair and unfair, distinguishing lawful from unlawful, aiming to make men good not only through fear of penalties but also indeed under allurement of rewards, and affecting a philosophy which, if I am not deceived, is genuine, not a sham. (2) There are two branches of legal study: public and private law. Public law is that which respects the establishment of the Roman commonwealth, private that which respects individuals' interests, some matters being of public and others of private interest. Public law covers religious affairs, the priesthood, and offices of state. Private law is tripartite, being derived from principles of *ius naturale*, *ius gentium*, or *ius civile*. (3) *Ius naturale* is that which nature has taught to all animals; for it is not a law specific to mankind but is common to all animals—land animals, sea animals, and the birds as well. Out of this comes the union of man and woman which we call marriage, and the procreation of children and their rearing. So we can see that the other animals, wild beasts included, are rightly understood to be acquainted with this law. (4) *Ius gentium*, the law of nations, is that which all human peoples observe. That it is not co-extensive with natural law can be grasped easily, since this latter is common to all animals whereas *ius gentium* is common only to human beings among themselves.

The next passage does indeed concern itself with *ius gentium*, but it seems clear that some other aspects of this topic had been treated in a section which was not included in the *Digest*. It too is characterized by careful, not to say laboured, definition.

Ulpianus libro primo *Institutionum*. Manumissiones quoque iuris gentium sunt. est autem manumissio de manu missio, id est datio libertatis: nam quamdiu quis in seruitute est, manui et potestati suppositus est, manumissus liberatur potestate. quae res a iure gentium originem sumpsit, utpote cum iure naturali omnes liberi nascerentur nec esset nota manumissio, cum servitus esset incognita: sed posteaquam iure gentium servitus invasit, secutum est beneficium manumissionis. et cum uno naturali nomine homines appellaremur, iure gentium tria genera esse coeperunt: liberi et his contrarium servi et tertium genus liberti, id est hi qui desierant esse servi. (*Dig*. 1.1.4)

Ulpian, *Institutes*, Book I: Manumissions also belong to the *ius gentium*. Manumission means sending out of one's hand, that is, granting of freedom. For whereas one who is in slavery is subjected to the hand (*manus*) and power of another, on being sent out of hand he is freed of that power. All of which originated from the *ius gentium*, since, of course, everyone would be born free by the natural law, and manumission would not be known when slavery was unknown. But after slavery came in by the *ius gentium*, there followed the boon (*beneficium*) of manumission. And thenceforth, we all being called by the one natural name 'men', in the *ius gentium* there came to be three classes: free men, and set against those slaves and the third class, freedmen, that is, those who had stopped being slaves.

Ulpian does not comment here, as he might have done (and perhaps should have), that although slavery and liberation from slavery were no doubt to be found in all the societies with which the Roman Empire had contact (and indeed in the private law of those within the Empire who—until this very moment—had not been citizens), it was within Roman law alone, so far as we know, that, given certain conditions, those who 'ceased to be slaves' gained not merely freedom but citizenship.

Finally, among these preliminary reflections at the beginning of his *Institutes*, Ulpian attempts to distinguish between *ius naturale*, *ius gentium*, and *ius civile*:

Ulpianus libro primo *Institutionum*. Ius civile est, quod neque in totum a naturali vel gentium recedit nec per omnia ei servit: itaque cum aliquid addimus uel detrahimus iuri communi, ius proprium, id est civile, efficimus. (1) Hoc igitur ius nostrum constat aut ex scripto aut sine scripto, ut apud Graecos: τῶν νόμων οἱ μὲν ἔγγραφοι, οἱ δὲ ἄγραφοι. (*Dig*. 1. 1. 6)

Ulpian, *Institutiones*, Book I: The *ius civile* is that which neither wholly diverges from the *ius naturale* and *ius gentium* nor follows the same in every particular. And so whenever to the common law we add anything or take anything away from it, we make a law special to ourselves, that is, *ius civile*, civil law. (1) This law of ours, therefore, exists either in written or unwritten form; as the Greeks put it, 'of laws some are written, others unwritten'.

The reasoning seems loose, for from the fact that the Roman *ius civile* had some characteristics which it shared with the universal *ius naturale* (common to all living things, or at least all which reproduced themselves by relations between two sexes) and with the *ius gentium* (notionally common to all peoples) it does not seem to follow (*igitur*) that some of its provisions should be written and some unwritten.

These passages certainly embody a serious claim by Ulpian with regard to the status of his chosen branch of study. But they may at the same time leave us unconvinced by the idea that his vast contribution to the literature of Roman law was really informed by a profound capacity for philosophical analysis. Further study of this question, pursued through the mass of Ulpian's writing as reassembled in Lenel's *Palingenesia*, could only be conducted successfully by an expert in the philosophy of the Imperial period (another Miriam Griffin, one might say), who came from that background to confront the extensive corpus of juristic writing in Latin.

None the less, Ulpian, both as a 'provincial at Rome' and as an 'intellectual in politics', whose scholarly writing and public career were pursued in difficult and dangerous times, deserves to take his place along with Seneca, and in some senses even with Cicero and Tacitus.

PART II

The Power of Philosophy

Academic Therapy: Philo of Larissa and Cicero's Project in the *Tusculans*

MALCOLM SCHOFIELD

INTRODUCTION

'Empty', said Epicurus (Porph. *Ad Marcellam* 31), 'is that philosopher's discourse which offers therapy for no human passion. Just as there is no use in medical expertise if it does not expel the sickness of bodies, so there is no use in philosophy if it does not expel the passion of the soul.' In a different but related vein we find Sextus Empiricus concluding the *Outlines of Pyrrhonism* with a chapter on sceptical arguments as cures for the pathological conceit and precipitancy of the dogmatists: on what might be called philosophy as a remedy for philosophy itself (*PH* 3. 280–1). The ideas implicit in these formulations, and their antecedents in earlier Greek philosophy, have attracted a good deal of attention in recent years, particularly from writers on the Hellenistic schools. Martha Nussbaum's big book *The Therapy of Desire* (1994) examined at length Epicurean, Stoic, and Pyrrhonist treatments of the conceptual matrix indicated by her title. More recently another big book, by Richard Sorabji, entitled *Emotion and Peace of Mind* (2000), has explored the Stoic material and its appropriation by early Christian writers.

The contribution of the Hellenistic Academy to this way of thinking about philosophy has not much figured—so far as I am aware—in the recent scholarship. The prime exhibit is a report in Stobaeus of an extended analogy between philosophy and medicine elaborated by Philo of Larissa, the last of the Academic Sceptics. During the last decade this text has received brief but glancing attention in studies as diverse as Julia Annas's *The Morality of Happiness* (1993), Harold Tarrant's *Thrasyllan Platonism* (1993), and Simon Slings's Festschrift piece on 'Protreptic in ancient theories of philosophical literature' (1995). The only extended analysis I have seen is that worked out in the ethics chapter in Charles Brittain's new monograph on Philo (2001). I shall begin this paper with a translation and re-examination of the Stobaeus text (consigning some of the more detailed detective work this has involved to an appendix). Is there anything distinctively Academic in Philo's presentation of the analogy as mediated by Stobaeus? I shall argue that, if there is, what it consists in is not a Sceptical stance of any kind, but a return to a Socratic outlook on the scope and function of philosophy itself. As Slings puts the point, rather too sweepingly, 'the whole point of the analogy between doctor and philosopher is precisely [the] reduction of philosophy to ethics; Philo ignores physics and logic altogether' (1995: 180).[1]

Exhibit 2 is Cicero's *Tusculan Disputations*. As a young man Cicero sat at Philo's feet; and the moderate form of Academic Scepticism he himself avowed and practised probably has some sort of Philonian pedigree. How far the conception of philosophy implicit in Philo's version of the medical analogy, or the organization of philosophical discourse he used it to articulate, left their mark on Cicero's philosophical writings is a matter for debate. In a short article published in 1971 Alberto Grilli suggested that it was Philo's scheme which prompted Cicero to compose *Hortensius—Academica—De Finibus—Tusculan Disputations* in that order (recapitulated in the catalogue at the beginning of book 2 of *De Divinatione*); and the *Tusculans* certainly make explicit mention and use of the analogy of medicine and philosophy, not just in books 3 and 4, which are usually read as simply reproducing the Stoic theory of Chrysippus. I shall be looking afresh at the catalogue of *De Divinatione* 2 and proposing that Cicero's account there of his writings on philosophy betrays a view of its function that bears a significant resemblance to Philo's 'Socratism'. For their part the *Tusculans*, which seem to figure as the *chef d'œuvre* of the entire catalogue, present themselves in a similarly Socratic light. I shall end, however, with some reflections on their specifically Ciceronian features, and particularly on what one might call their Academicism.

Philo's Programme

Before presenting his substantive accounts of ethical systems, Stobaeus decides that it is appropriate to say something about the way the subject of ethics is best organized. He discharges the obligation by giving summary

David Sedley kindly read a draft of this paper and gave me some comments and bibliographical advice: my thanks to him. The paper as a whole has grown out of part of a talk Miriam Griffin once heard me give on genres in practical ethics, and which she has subsequently with characteristic generosity and enthusiasm more than once urged me to publish. It has turned into something a bit different: another contribution to one of our mutual pleasures, the study of Cicero's *philosophica*.

[1] I would rather say that philosophy becomes an ethical project—in which logic and physics might have a role, but one that would have to be subordinate to ethics.

accounts of schemes articulated by two Academics of the first century BC, Philo of Larissa and Eudorus of Alexandria. He clearly prefers Eudorus' version (Stob. *Ecl.* 2. 42. 7–45. 6), and appears to have made some use of it in his presentation of Stoic ethics (see Long 1983). One may suspect that the reason why he included an account of Philo's scheme was that it was in fact a popular one. If I were lazy, he says, I would make do with Philo and string together my doxographies following his six-part division of ethics (Stob. *Ecl.* 2. 41. 26–42. 1). The implication is presumably that this is what other authors *have* done.[2] Eudorus' approach, however, is more challenging. It puts theoretical consideration of the essence of the subject-matter first in order of presentation, before turning to concerns such as quality or relation (Stob. *Ecl.* 2. 42. 2–6). The implication here is that Stobaeus' doxographies will accordingly exhibit a rare and distinctive rigour and coherence—though, if so, then sadly promise was not matched by performance.

Here anyway is what he tells us about Philo's scheme (Stob. *Ecl.* 2. 39. 20–41. 25):

Philo of Larissa, an Academic philosopher, a pupil of Clitomachus, was one of those who introduced a significant advance in the other areas [sc. *other than definitions, just dealt with*]. This Philo has done a skilful job in other respects, and particularly as regards his division of philosophical discourse, which I am going to make available.[3]

So: he says the philosopher is like a doctor.

Just as it is a doctor's job first to persuade the sick person to receive the treatment and second to demolish the arguments of those who give contrary advice, so also with the philosopher. So each of these finds its place in the so-called protreptic *logos*, for protreptic is what stimulates us to virtue. One part of it displays its great benefit,[4] the other refutes those who argue against philosophy or make accusations against it or otherwise malign it.

In second place after this is the logos which by the analogy with medicine has to be ordered second. Just as it is a doctor's job to apply the treatment[5] after he has persuaded the patient to receive it, by first removing those causes which produce disease, and then by introducing those which produce health, so also it is in the case of knowledge. For after protreptic devices he [sc. *the philosopher*] tries to apply therapeutic ones, and for this purpose he uses two sorts of stimulant: he applies a *logos*

[2] Or perhaps only what Eudorus says they have done, if we make the Ockhamist assumption that Eudorus was Stobaeus' source for Philo.

[3] With Heeren I delete the words περὶ ἧς ὁ λόγος (as a doublet). Mette (1986–7: 14) has them as the first words of the next sentence—or what would have been the next sentence, since he proposes a lacuna after λόγος.

[4] The greatest benefit of virtue as perceived by any Hellenistic philosopher working in a broadly Socratic tradition is of course happiness.

[5] With Heeren, Wachsmuth, and Mette I delete the words τοῦ μὲν θεραπευτικοῦ.

which removes beliefs which have arisen falsely, and which cause disease in the critical faculties (κριτήρια) of the soul; and also one which introduces beliefs in a healthy condition. *So second comes the topic of good and evil things—that is, the topic to which protreptic points and on account of which it is employed.*

The third logos will correspond again to the third element in medical treatment. For as in medicine all efforts relate to the goal, which is health, so in philosophy they relate to happiness.

But conjoined to the logos on goals is the logos on ways of life. In the case of medicine it is not enough to implant health. There is also a need to provide instructions on health, so that if people pay attention to them they will preserve a good physical condition. In the case of life too there is need for some theorems, by which the end will be preserved. And the *logos* on ways of life is also double, with a particular and a general part. The particular part has to consider questions relating to the individual, for example, whether the person of sense will engage in political activity or live with members of the ruling class, or whether the wise person will marry. The general part has to do with questions which concern everyone, such as what is the best constitution? Must offices be open or subject to a property qualification?

This general logos should be called 'political', and on account of its importance and generality should be treated as a topic on its own, even though it is a part of the logos on ways of life.

If it were possible for all to be wise, there would be no need of still more topics. For finer divisions are only branches of those we have proposed. But since we must also make provision for people in an intermediate condition, who in some cases derive benefit from advisory logoi, *since they are unable to make time for extensive and exhaustive reflection (through limitations of time or necessary business), we must additionally introduce the hypothetic* logos. *This will give them in abbreviated form suggestions which will promote safety and correct practice in individual cases.*

In his monograph on Philo Brittain argues that this text actually articulates not one but two six-part divisions, the one superimposed on the other. I agree with Brittain's diagnosis; and in the quotation above I have italicized the sentences in the text I take to belong to the later structure. If we distinguish the two as Original and Revision, then with Brittain we get the following schemes:

Original

A. Protreptic	(i)	positive, showing 'the great benefit of virtue'
	(ii)	negative, refuting the opponents of philosophy
B. Therapeutic	(i)	negative, 'removing beliefs which have arisen falsely'
	(ii)	positive, 'introducing beliefs in a healthy condition'

C. Preservative (i) prescriptions for the individual
(ii) prescriptions for the government of the community

Revision

(1) Protreptic
(2) On good and evil things—focus of therapeutic
(3) On goals
(4) On ways of life—individual life-choices
(5) Politics
(6) Precepts—'hypothetic' or suggestion[6]

In what follows I shall simply assume the correctness of this stratigraphical analysis: as noted above, a defence of it is relegated to the Appendix. But it is interesting to note that the basically tripartite structure of Original finds echoes or at any rate analogues in later writers: Epictetus' protreptic, refutative, and didactic *logoi* (*Diss.* 3. 23. 33–4), for example, or Clement of Alexandria's protreptic, therapeutic, and advisory *logoi* (*Paed.* 1. 1) (see Slings 1995).[7]

There is one salient tension in the text as it has reached us that underlies everything else: between a scheme of ethical divisions (Revision) and an account of philosophy as a craft analogous to medicine (Original). At various particular points the tension is reflected in a contrast between topics and functions (see the Appendix). But it is perhaps more significant in the

[6] The author of Revision clearly distinguishes between strict precepts (παραγγέλματα) we are required to follow if we are to act as the perfectly rational person would, and advice (παραίνεσις, ὑπόθηκαι) helpful to the average person. This may reflect Posidonius' treatment of practical ethics, and the distinction Seneca ascribes to him (*Ep.* 95. 65) between *praeceptio* and *suasio*, on which see Kidd 1988: 647–51. Following Bernays, Slings (1999: 84 n. 187) rightly points out that ὑποθετικός in this kind of context is 'normal philosophical terminology for "advisory"' (cf. the genre of advice poetry: Kurke 1990), but in my translation 'advisory' renders παραινετικός, and 'suggestion' has the advantage of capturing the ὑπο- element in ὑποθετικός and ὑπόθηκαι, so hinting at a *non*-prescriptive form of advice. The examples in the discussion of Philo's third 'preservative' element in therapy are couched in the question form characteristic of a rhetorical θέσις or *quaestio infinita* (see e.g. Aphthonius *Progymn.* 13, in Spengel 1854: 49. 14–30; Cic. *De Oratore* 3. 109–18, *de Part. Or.* 4, 61–7). One might be tempted to suppose that Revision's ὑποθετικὸς λόγος would therefore correspond to the rhetorical ὑπόθεσις or *quaestio finita*—e.g. whether the Lacedaimonians should fortify Sparta under attack from the Persians. In favour of this conjecture is that ὑπόθηκαι are for the benefit of people who do not have the time to work out from general principles what they should do in particular circumstances. Against is that nothing in the text specifically suggests this further characterization of ὑπόθηκαι. For further discussion of the possible relationship between the treatment of the ὑποθετικὸς λόγος in this text and Philo's work on rhetoric see now Reinhardt 2000.

[7] See the discussion in Slings 1995 (but not perceiving the tripartite structure of Original Slings thinks there are more differences than similarities between Philo and Epictetus).

end that in the one perspective Philo is telling a story about just one part of the subject-matter of philosophy, ethics, whereas in the other he is articulating an account of philosophy as such, conceived as an ordered argumentative craft. Modern writers habitually refer to our text as a presentation of Philo's ethics. If the distinction drawn above between Revision and Original is correct, this must in some degree misdescribe Philo's intentions. What he was meaning to offer was an account of the mission of philosophy itself, conceived of course as a methodical ethical programme.

I do not think there is much mystery about the programme's ultimate pedigree: I have used the word 'mission' advisedly, to recall Socrates' account in the *Apology* of his conviction that his philosophical activity represents his fulfilment of a divinely imposed obligation to sting the Athenians into examining their lives and caring for their true selves or souls.[8] In support of this diagnosis, Slings (1995: 182–3) adduces a statement made in connection with the explicitly aporetic and elenctic picture of Socrates painted in book 1 of Cicero's *Academica* (1. 16): 'All Socrates' talk was taken up in praising virtue and exhorting people to the pursuit of virtue, as can be understood from the writings of the Socratics, especially Plato.' That comes from Varro's speech, which presents the views of Antiochus of Ascalon. But Varro says that everyone agrees on this assessment of Socrates, and there seems to be no reason to think his account would have been controversial. One might say that all Philo has done (not without Platonic authority) is rewrite and articulate the Socratic conception of philosophy in the language of the favoured Hellenistic metaphor of therapy.

Of course, we do not encounter Plato's or Xenophon's Socrates making a tripartite division of philosophy so understood into protreptic, therapy, and 'preservative'. However, there is plenty of evidence of a preoccupation with philosophy as protreptic and as therapy in Plato's Socratic dialogues.[9] We need think only of the teasing exploration of protreptic in the *Euthydemus* or the idea of therapy of the soul ascribed to Zalmoxis in the *Charmides*. And the *Cleitophon*, which is entirely devoted to questions about protreptic, ends with Cleitophon pointing out to Socrates (410c–e) that he would follow up a protreptic *logos* on physical training with an

8 Slings (1995: 183) thinks it remarkable that, despite its Socratic inspiration, Philo's text makes no reference to the central idea of care of the soul. I would guess that this is because the *Apology* was not the most immediate source he was turning to for his articulation of the idea of philosophical therapy.

9 In speaking of 'Socratic' dialogues I imply nothing about relative date within the Platonic corpus (I actually think the *Euthydemus* relatively late). I mean simply those dialogues which are largely free of metaphysical concerns, and present a Socrates engaged mostly in elenctic conversations on mostly ethical matters.

account (supplied by gymnastics or medicine) of the body and the treatment it needs. So he should do the same with the soul, and use the appropriate analogue art to articulate what the care of the soul requires—once protreptic has served its purpose of making us want to acquire virtue.

The Socrates of the *Cleitophon* exhorts people to *virtue* (e.g. 408d), as did most ancient philosophical protreptic in one way or another, and just as Philo does (A(i)). Grilli (1971: 303 n. 5) argued that in the Stobaeus text the words 'for protreptic is what stimulates us to virtue' are a gloss, and that the proper reference of 'its' is 'philosophy', not 'virtue'. Now it is true that there developed over time a discrete genre of protreptic which made its object in the first instance conversion to the study of *philosophy*, not to virtue (e.g. Slings 1999: 59–63, 90–3). The most celebrated ancient examples of protreptic in this more specific sense were Aristotle's lost work of that name and Cicero's lost *Hortensius*. It is also true that A(ii) in Philo's account of protreptic—refuting the opponents of philosophy—presupposes the more specific sense, and was a prominent feature of the *Hortensius*, which Cicero describes for example at *TD* 5. 4 as a reply to those who revile the whole project of philosophy. But Grilli's proposal must be wrong: Philo needs the goal of protreptic to be analogous to health. We should simply conclude that the situation is what one might expect with a thinker determined to interpret philosophy as essentially an ethical project. Protreptic as a discrete division of philosophical discourse has then to function *both* as the prelude to philosophizing as such (cf. A(ii)), *and* as a call to virtue (cf. A(i)). Hence the nature of Philo's account of it; hence too the main ethical thrust of the *Hortensius*, as it appears from the surviving fragments and testimonia (MacKendrick 1989: 109–13).

The most distinctively Socratic ingredient in Philo's scheme is the second element in his programme: therapeutic. The whole idea of philosophical therapy implicit in the account given in the text presupposes the fundamental and fundamentally Socratic idea that virtue and happiness are functions above all of knowledge (Stob. *Ecl.* 2. 40. 15: Wachsmuth 1871) and the state of one's beliefs (40. 18–20). And its negative component—'removing beliefs which have arisen falsely' (40. 18)—is obviously nothing other than the Socratic *elenchus*. Plato himself had already theorized the *elenchus* in medical terms in the famous *Sophist* passage (226b–231b) on the sophistry 'of noble lineage'. Those afflicted with the worst form of ignorance—thinking you know something when you do not (229b–c)—need to be purged of their opinions by the *elenchus*. Physicians of the body take the view that it cannot take in food until the patient has expelled internal blockages. Similarly those undertaking purges of the soul proceed on the assumption that, before anyone in that condition of ignorance can get the benefit of any knowledge they take in, they need to be shamed by the *elenchus* and have it remove from them the opinions which are blocking knowledge (230b–d). The *elenchus* is the greatest and most decisive of purges; and nobody who remains unpurged with regard to the most important truths will be really happy (230d–e).

It is hard to resist the conjecture that Philo relied heavily on this passage in working out his description of philosophical therapeutic. Our first reaction might be to see the positive component in the treatment as distinctly un-Socratic: surely the Socrates who denied that anyone could transmit knowledge to another person would not have seen the acquisition of true beliefs as a matter of 'introducing beliefs in a healthy condition' (40. 20) or as implanting causes of knowledge? The *Sophist* passage shows us that this verdict would be mistaken. There Plato has the Eleatic Stranger envisage the sequel to *elenchus* as something analogous to the ingestion of nourishment: the absorption of knowledge.[10] Not a very Sceptical way of talking about education or intellectual progress, to be sure. But Philo's epistemological views developed over time through a number of stages, as Brittain's monograph brilliantly demonstrates. Contrary to what Brittain argues, however, the conception of medicine implicit in the analogy is one elsewhere associated with medical dogmatists rather than medical empiricists, for the account of therapeutic involves commitment to the typically dogmatist theses that (i) there are some causes which produce health and others which produce disease, and (ii) the practitioner of the art of medicine has the ability to identify them and to implant the one and remove the other.[11] If Stobaeus is right in having Philo refer to what is produced by philosophical therapeutic as knowledge (ἐπιστήμη: *Ecl.* 2. 40. 15), it looks as though he will have taken an optimistic view of the prospects for similar cognitive and practical success in this sphere also.

I cannot identify any specific Socratic antecedent for Philo's idea of a 'preservative' function for philosophy alongside protreptic and therapeutic. Perhaps this was his own contribution to the analogy between philosophy and medicine. The closest parallel I have come across is a line of argument attributed by Plutarch (*De Cohibenda Ira* 453d–e) to the Roman Stoic Musonius Rufus, who may of course have borrowed it from Philo. Musonius insists that care (θεραπεία) needs to continue throughout life.

[10] Nor is the *Sophist* treatment of education an isolated one: see e.g. *Rep.* 3 (401d–402a) on the nourishment someone gets by receiving into the soul fine rhythms and modes, which are 'like a breeze bringing health from good places' (401c–d).

[11] It is true that empiricist theory did sometimes allow for talk of antecedent causes, but as signs rather than as what we might call causes proper: see Hankinson 1987.

Reason is not *just* a purgative like hellebore, to be flushed out along with the illness it cures. It should stay put in the soul and sustain and guard its judgements.

Another reason for suspecting innovation from Philo at this point is the very different kind of rationale offered for subdividing 'preservative' from what we get in the case of the other two functions. In those two cases the functions were divided into subfunctions. Here there is no differentiation in function, merely in the domain over which the function is exercised. It is as if Philo was more concerned to ensure that his scheme could accommodate two of the major genres of the literature of practical philosophy: 'on ways of life' and 'politics'.[12] Selection of those two genres in particular suggests that there is something else here not altogether integrated into the medical analogy: a concern not with ethical prescription as the means of ensuring preservation, which ought to have been the focus, but with the articulation of a social and political framework within which virtue and happiness can be sustained. In developing his account of preservative to give so much weight to this theme, Philo is perhaps asserting a distinctively Academic and Peripatetic view of the philosopher's intellectual responsibilities—and naturally one which would have commanded Cicero's allegiance and respect.

Philo's Programme and the *Tusculans*

At the beginning of book 2 of *De Divinatione* Cicero offers the reader a retrospective catalogue of his philosophical writings. The passage is usually read just for the information it contains—which to be sure is of extraordinary interest and value. We shall be more concerned with *how* Cicero tells the story he tells, and with what sort of story it is.

His account begins as follows:

> I ransacked my brain and pondered a great deal and for a long time how I could be helpful to as many people as possible, and not interrupt at any point the service I perform for the commonwealth. No more important project occurred to me than the idea of transmitting to my fellow citizens the methods of the best of the arts. And I think that through numerous books I have by now achieved this aim.
>
> In my book entitled *Hortensius* I encouraged readers as best I could to take up the study of philosophy. In the four books of my *Academica* I set out the brand of philosophizing I thought least arrogant and most consistent and discriminating. Since the foundations of philosophy are set at the limits of good and evil I gave a thorough

[12] In elaborating Revision as he did, its author was not wholly mistaken in his reading of Original as an articulation of the main topics of practical ethics.

treatment of that subject in a work of five books [sc. *De Finibus*], so that readers could appreciate what different philosophers say and what can be said against each of them. My five subsequent books of *Tusculan Disputations* explained the key prerequisites of a happy life. The first is about making light of death, the second is on putting up with pain, the third deals with the alleviation of distress, and the fourth with other mental disturbances. The fifth covers the subject which sheds more light than any other on the whole of philosophy. It teaches that virtue is sufficient on its own for a happy life.

We should note at once how Socratic all this is: the focus on virtue and happiness as the core preoccupation of philosophy; the Socratic virtues of the style of philosophizing characteristic of the Sceptical Academy, whose distinctive encyclopedic method of inquiry (Algra 1997) is intimated in the brief description of *De Finibus*; above all the emphasis on philosophy's practical responsibilities.

Cicero goes on (*Div.* 2. 3) to mention as next in his sequence of publications the trilogy dealing with a particular *quaestio*: *De Natura Deorum* (completed), *De Divinatione* (in progress), *De Fato* (projected):

After publishing these ideas I finished three books *On the Nature of the Gods*, which contain an investigation of that whole topic. To ensure that the investigation was brought visibly and more than amply to conclusion, I started to write these books *On Divination*. And if I add to them one *On Fate* (as I have it in mind to do), I shall have done full justice to this entire field of investigation.

In context this section of the catalogue reads like a digression into theory, not integrated into the general conception of philosophy Cicero has so far been unfolding—and to which he now at once returns. He tracks back in time (*Div.* 2. 3–4):

To these books I must add the six of *On the Commonwealth*, which I wrote when I was steering the fortunes of the commonwealth: an important subject and one appropriate for philosophy, which had been treated copiously by Plato, Aristotle, Theophrastus, and the entire Peripatetic school. I don't need to say anything about my *Consolation*. It certainly does a bit to heal my own hurt, and I reckon it will also be very helpful to others. I have also intervened recently with the book *On Old Age* that I sent my friend Atticus.[13] And since it is by philosophy that a good and brave man is produced, I must make a particular point of including my *Cato* [sc. the lost Laus Catonis] in this list of books. Again, since Aristotle and also Theophrastus—men who stand out for their combination of acuteness and productivity—have connected their rules for public speaking with philosophy, it seems appropriate to associate my own books on rhetoric with this same list of books. So *De Oratore* will make three, with *Brutus* as a fourth and *Orator* as a fifth.

[13] *On Old Age* is the one work mentioned in this part of the dialogue which post-dates the *Tusculans* and the theological trilogy. It was probably written in the first months of 44 BC.

There is much in this bibliographical story which seems to breathe the same air as Philo's Original. What Cicero like Philo is presenting is *philosophy* (the word itself recurs again and again), and philosophy as in essence an ethical project, with a variety of component subprojects and—in the back-tracking section—associated enterprises (these distinctly a rag-bag). Philo thinks of philosophy as a craft like medicine; in Cicero this same emphasis is expressed in a concern with methodology. He announces at the outset his desire to communicate 'the methods (*vias*) of the best of the arts'; the accounts of *Academica* and *De Finibus* are plainly focused on philosophical method, and at the end of his list the treatment of the oratorical writings suggests a similar focus. Had Cicero wished, he could no doubt have organized the material differently to fit into what he describes elsewhere (*Acad.* 1. 19; cf. e.g. *TD* 5. 68) as the *philosophandi ratio triplex*—physics, ethics, logic. But it is notable that he introduces *Academica* not as a treatment of epistemology, as it is often thought of nowadays, but as dealing generally with the right way to do philosophy (Griffin 1997: 2–8).[14] As for his 'theological' trilogy, we might be tempted to see it as Cicero's contribution to physics and so to one of the three major divisions of philosophy. But in this context these dialogues figure rather as a discussion of a particular and in truth more limited topic or *quaestio*—albeit an extremely full discussion, as Cicero emphasizes. As I suggested above, they are made to seem almost like an interruption in the account of his publications in philosophy ethically and methodologically conceived. For he subsequently turns to describe a medley of earlier writings which are all now construed as illustrating philosophy at work in one way or another as a practical enterprise.

Cicero presents the opening sequence, by contrast, very much as a connected plan of campaign. It is likely enough that this is just what it was or at any rate quickly became (cf. *ND* 1. 9), given that all of them were composed (and in the case of *Academica* also revised) within the space of a few months in spring and summer 45 BC. The protreptic *Hortensius*, celebrated for its impact on the young Augustine (*Conf.* 3. 4. 7), has not survived intact. But from both the numerous fragments and Cicero's own references to it in other writings (e.g. *Acad.* 2. 61, *Fin.* 1. 2, *TD* 2. 4) it is plain that it was conceived in the first instance as a refutation of arguments attacking philosophy (cf. Original A(ii)), although positive discussion of virtue and happiness figured prominently too (cf. Original A(i); MacKendrick 1989: 109–13). While there is no trace in the evidence of Cicero's deploying or exploiting Philo's medical analogy, it seems not improbable that it was acceptance

[14] Much of the material in this and the next two paragraphs is indebted to the fuller and more thorough treatment in Griffin 1997, which also gives references to earlier scholarship.

of Philo's Socratic conception of the philosopher's strategy which led him to launch his re-entry into philosophical writing with a protreptic of just this type.

The preface to *De Divinatione* 2 suggests that Cicero thought that, before he could then go on to argue on his own account for some substantive philosophical theses in the *Tusculans*, he needed to tackle at length two crucial preliminary questions which might naturally arise from the argument in the *Hortensius* that we need to do philosophy: (i) what is the best way to do philosophy? (ii) what are the options open to us in trying to determine the foundations on which philosophy will have to build—specifically as regards the nature of the good which philosophy urges and helps us to pursue?[15] On (i) we should note that at *TD* 2. 4 he makes an interesting contrasted pairing of *Hortensius* and *Academica*, confirming the role of *Academica* in Cicero's writing programme already indicated by the formulation in (i), and very likely reflecting his original conception of the work: *Hortensius* replies to critics of philosophy in general; *Academica* speaks in favour of the Academy in particular. On (ii) we should note that the preface to book 1 of *De Finibus* stresses the work's encyclopedic scope. Cicero says he has explained the view he himself accepts, although it is not clear that *De Finibus* really does this, and the catalogue in *De Divinatione* 2 does not repeat the claim. But he puts the emphasis on the thorough coverage he has given to the disputes on these matters in the philosophical schools (*Fin.* 1. 11–12), after explaining the ambition he has conceived (alluded to at the very beginning of the catalogue) of providing Roman readers with a guide to Greek philosophical teaching.

What is most striking in the catalogue, however, is the status accorded to the *Tusculans*. To the surprise and perhaps dismay of the modern reader (who may get more intellectual profit from several of the other writings of 45–44), this work is indubitably the centrepiece of the whole account. It figures at the climactic point in the opening section of the book, which then breaks off into the theological digression. Uniquely the topic of each of the five books of the *Tusculans* is separately—albeit succinctly—listed; and book 5 is singled out as addressing the key issue in the whole of philosophy. This is just the sort of emphasis one might expect of an author taking inspiration from Philo's conception of philosophy as articulated in Original. Therapy is for Philo clearly the heart of the matter, and the *Tusculans* fill the place in Cicero's scheme that corresponds to Philo's

[15] But Griffin (1997: 2–8) may be right that when Cicero started on his writing project, he may have had in view only the composition of *Hortensius* and *Academica* (or rather the trilogy *Hortensius*, *Catulus*, *Lucullus*).

therapeutic *logos*.[16] As we have already noted, in the text of the *Tusculans* themselves the medical analogy is put to work; and their whole project is described in retrospect as 'alleviation' (*levatio*: *TD* 5. 121). Accordingly, and in marked contrast to the way he describes *De Finibus* as a scholarly survey, Cicero makes his account of the *Tusculans* in the catalogue focus on the practical results they are designed to achieve. He could scarcely have given a clearer signal that, from the Socratic viewpoint, the project of *De Finibus* is to be regarded as subordinate to the more direct and urgent concerns of the *Tusculans*.

THE *TUSCULANS* AS THERAPY

In the retrospective mode and moment of *De Divinatione* 2, then, Cicero viewed the *Tusculans* as his core contribution to the Philonian conception of philosophy as a disciplined ethical project. The *Tusculans* themselves had indeed represented the search for the identity of the good life as philosophy's main preoccupation (e.g. *TD* 1. 1, 5. 1–2; cf. 5. 19–20), and as something particularly associated with its reorientation by Socrates (*TD* 5. 10—the famous passage which tells how he was the first to 'call down philosophy from the heavens and set her in the cities and bring her even into people's homes and force them to ask questions about life and morals and things good and evil'). But how deeply committed is Cicero to a specifically therapeutic construction of the practical enterprise undertaken by the *Tusculans*?

The conception of philosophy as medicine for the soul is worked out mainly in books 3 and 4, where Cicero evidently relies on Chrysippus' anatomy of the passions and emotions as forms of cognitive and volitional disease requiring therapy. But it would be a mistake to suppose that this is a line Cicero adopted solely for the argumentative purpose in hand. Already in the preface to the un-Stoic book 2 we find philosophy treated in this way (2. 11), as also later in the same book (2. 43). In book 3 itself Cicero makes it clear that he intends to be discriminating in his appropriation of Stoic material. He will not render πάθη by *morbi*, 'diseases', but rather by *perturbationes*, 'disturbances' (3. 7; similarly at 4. 23 he criticizes Chrysippus for making too much fuss over the analogy of diseases of the body and diseases

[16] So broadly speaking Hirzel 1883: 479–90, who also marries *Hortensius* with Philo's protreptic. But he makes book 5 take up section (3) of Revision: the *logos* on goals. Grilli 1971 thought the whole sequence from *Hortensius* to the *Tusculans* (together with *On the Commonwealth*) could be matched with successive elements in Philo's scheme, but this produced some gross implausibilities, such as making a therapeutic *logos* out of *Academica* and turning the *Tusculans* into the particular form of a *logos* on ways of life. The fact is that neither *Academica* nor *De Finibus* correspond to anything at all in Philo's programme.

of the soul). On the other hand he compliments the Romans on choosing a word for distress, *aegritudo*, which by its etymology implies a comparison with physical sickness (3. 23)—something not conveyed, of course, by Greek λύπη.[17] And when the preface to book 3 develops the idea of sickness in the soul and the need for philosophy as its medicine (3. 1–6), there is no particular reason to think that Cicero is drawing on specifically Stoic sources. He certainly manages to make his discussion thoroughly and distinctively Ciceronian, engineering an occasion for introducing one of his own favourite politically charged moral contrasts—between true and false glory (3. 4–5)—and then for deploying a handy quotation from Ennius (3. 6). We may in fact be reminded of Philo by the answer Cicero gives to the question he puts at the very beginning of the preface: why does the idea of a medicine of the soul provoke such suspicion and hostility? He suggests that it is because the soul is making a judgement about itself precisely when the actual instrument of judgment (*id ipsum, quo iudicatur*) is sick (3. 1). This recalls Philo's reference to beliefs which 'cause disease in the critical faculties of the soul' (that is, in its instruments of judgement),[18] and which the philosopher's therapy will accordingly remove.

In book 4 Cicero stages a confrontation between the Peripatetic and Stoic stances on the emotions. The Peripatetics 'say that souls are necessarily subject to disturbances, but they introduce a certain measure beyond which one should not go further' (4. 38). In arguing as they do 'they admit that they [*sc.* various forms of distress] need cutting back, but say that complete extirpation is neither possible nor necessary, and take the view that in almost all matters the mean is best' (4. 46). Cicero is asked by the interlocutor how he would answer this line of argument. He steps back a moment before responding (4. 47):

> Do you see what restraint is maintained by the Academics? They just say right out what is appropriate to the issue. Answering the Peripatetics is something undertaken by the Stoics. These parties have my permission to cross swords and fight it out. For me the only necessity is to look carefully for the whereabouts of what seems closest to the truth. So what is there available that might make it possible to reach something close to the truth in this problem? The human mind cannot advance further than that.

That said, however, Cicero has immediate recourse to Zeno's definitions of 'disturbance', and with it launches a torrent of argument which eventually

[17] On these matters of vocabulary see further White 1995: 226–7, although I have resisted his argument against 'distress' as an equivalent for *aegritudo*.

[18] So Hirzel 1883: 485–6; Dougan and Henry 1934: 1–2 (following the old edn. of Davies) aptly cite also Plut. *Animine an corp. affect.* 500–1.

returns to a critique of the Peripatetic thesis, culminating in the ringing assertion that all so-called 'natural' emotions are growths rooted in errors, and must be torn up and pulled out, not trimmed and cut back (4. 57). So—to change metaphor—an appropriate therapy is needed, not for the wise person but for the likes of Cicero's interlocutor. And philosophy (and the rest of book 4) supplies him with it: for assuredly there is a treatment available (est enim quaedam medicina certe (4. 58)). What sort of therapy is that? Reason at work (4. 84), a sort of Socratic medicine (4. 24).

That is probably the high water mark of the endorsement of philosophy as therapy in the *Tusculans*. Book 5 is no less stoutly Stoic in its defence of the proposition that virtue and virtue alone is sufficient for happiness. But as Douglas points out (1995: 210), Cicero in his preface confesses that he 'sometimes loses confidence in this opinion and feels terrified at the weakness and frailty of the human race' (5. 3)—although he goes on at once to reprimand himself for falling into this state of mind (5. 4). At the end of book 1 he had described the project of the *Tusculans* as a whole as a series of discussions which 'may provide alleviation (*levationem habeant*) from distresses, fears, desires—of all philosophy the fullest fruit' (1. 119). Alleviation, not cure, is what Cicero will settle for, as the last words of the work confirm (5. 121): 'In writing this work I could not easily say how much help I shall be to others. Certainly in the bitter sorrows I feel and the various troubles which wash around me on every side it was impossible to find any other form of alleviation' (*levatio* again: the final word in Cicero's Latin as in my translation).

Epilogue

I suppose that all too many contemporary readers will have to confess that they do *not* find the *Tusculans* much help. It is easy enough to guess the main reason why the bereaved and politically vulnerable Cicero himself found *levatio* there: sorrow and grief are predominantly passive, writing is active—and so has potentially therapeutic properties of a self-reflexive kind. What makes it harder for the reader to feel the same is not just that reading is the more passive activity, but that so much of the *Tusculans* is not actually addressed to the business of practical ethics: of sorting out our ideas about death and pain and distress, and thereby doing something towards shifting our reaction to them. For what the *Tusculans* offer us is writing fascinated with its own performance as a paradigm of philosophy and of the communication of philosophy: in Latin and for Romans (in this regard Cicero never made stronger claims for the potential of his authorial activity than in the *Tusculans*: see especially 1. 1–6, 2. 5–8), showing off in particular the author's capacity to turn Greek verse into Latin analogues and find Latin equivalents for Greek philosophical terminology; employing a range of rhetorical as well as dialectical resources, notably the cumulation of *exempla* both Greek and Roman; pursuing truth or rather approximation to it in a Socratic and Academic mode which Cicero simultaneously makes his personal hallmark.[19]

These self-reflexive themes surface at various points throughout the work. But Cicero writes a preface for each book specifically devoted to characterization of philosophy as he is practising it in the pages that are to follow. And here his general themes get a more extended treatment, culminating in an extraordinary prose hymn to philosophy in 5. 5 which begins:

O vitae philosophia dux, o virtutis indigatrix expultrixque vitiorum! quid non modo nos, sed omnino vita hominum sine te esse potuisset?

O philosophy, guide of life, you who instil virtue and expel vices! What could not only we, but the life of mankind as a whole be without you?

The aura of triumph Cicero causes to hover over book 5 derives from the thought not merely that it is philosophy itself which brings a happiness invulnerable to fortune, but that—as the Academic method is particularly well-equipped to bring out—this is the conclusion virtually every school of philosophy can be represented as reaching, however much they may disagree on other issues.

So in the end the therapy proffered by the *Tusculans* is in danger of being academic in more senses than one. In the preface to book 2 Cicero tells the reader that he likes the Peripatetic and Academic custom of *in contrarias partes disserendi*, of putting both sides of the argument: on account of the exercise in speaking it provides, as well as because it is the only way to determine with respect to any question what solution is 'close to the truth' (*veri simile*, 2. 9). This is his formal reason for writing the *Tusculans* as dialogues (cf. 1. 8). In reality the promise of *in contrarias partes disserendi* is honoured by turning the treatment of all the questions examined in the *Tusculans* into

[19] For an excellent brief analysis of most of these features of the *Tusculans* see MacKendrick (1989: 163–8), who locates the work's originality principally in its 'use of rhetoric for philosophical ends' (in line with his general view of Cicero's philosophical works: see 1989: 13–16), and in 'the ingenuity with which Cicero has contrived to find Latin equivalents for Greek technical terms'. He has little to say, however, about the encyclopedic method, although I suspect Cicero was particularly proud of his use of it in book 5 (whether original or not) to argue for *universal* agreement among philosophers—including Epicurus—about the key to happiness: which according to the official theme of the book is virtue, but then from around 5. 68 onwards turns into wisdom (see especially the move at 5. 28): this is how even Epicurus is made to end up on the side of the angels at 5. 119.

debates between or arguments with different philosophical schools, or into expositions of their doctrines. These debates and arguments and expositions occupy a considerable part of the entire text. Cicero's assertion (4. 47) that Academics 'just say right out what is appropriate to the issue', leaving other philosophers to scrap with each other, is a travesty of what actually happens in the *Tusculans*.

The consequence is that not nearly so much time and energy as one might have expected are devoted to the ground-level business of showing (for example) that disturbances of the soul are not natural but creations of our own beliefs and decisions. Cicero's predilection for debate reinforces the self-reflexive and rhetorical tendencies of the *Tusculans* and his own encyclopedic ambitions and inclinations: those features of the work, in short, which no doubt explain much of the special pride in it communicated in the *De Divinatione* 2 catalogue, and which attract such readership as it still commands; or at any rate did so until the argumentative matrix of books 3 and 4, in particular, came to new life with the renewed interest in philosophy as therapy.

Appendix: The Two Versions of Philo's Philosophical Programme

To defend the Brittain hypothesis of two versions of Philo's programme, we need to begin with what I have prejudicially labelled Revision.

It is easy to make out the identity of the six parts of Revision (i.e. the scheme presupposed in the text as we have it now). The protreptic *logos* is simply the first discussed: so (1). (2) and (3) are explicitly picked out as second and third, and (2) is at the same time categorized as 'the topic of good and evil things'. (3) is initially more informally described, but given that description and its placing after (2), reference to 'the *logos* on goals' can hardly not relate to (3). Some scholars (e.g. Grilli 1971) have taken the statement that the *logos* on ways of life is 'conjoined' to the *logos* on goals to mean that it is a subdivision of (3). But the point is rather that, since its focus, like that of (3), is happiness—but preserving rather than implanting the end—it has to be the next or adjoining topic to (3): (4). Politics is given the status of a separate *logos*, and so must count as (5), even though it is initially treated as a subdivision of the *logos* on ways of life. Finally, the hypothetic *logos* is likewise introduced as a separate *logos*: therefore (6).

There can be little doubt that Revision represents a reworking and expansion of a scheme that was originally rather differently organized. The most palpable sign of this can be detected in the handling of (2). The long description of (2) makes it plain that, in line with his medical analogy, what Philo has in mind here is the treatment a philosopher can apply once he has persuaded someone they are in need of it—philosophical arguments which have the therapeutic purpose of removing false and toxic beliefs and introducing true and healthy ones. The subsequent definition of 2) as 'the topic of good and evil things, i.e. the topic to which protreptic points and on account of which it is employed', constitutes a considerable distortion of that description—which had concentrated on the function of therapeutic arguments, not their purported subject-matter or focus.

Moreover, the specification of that focus offered by (2) is problematic. According to Philo's account of protreptic earlier, its focus is virtue (not good and evil); alternatively one might think it looked to happiness, the focus of all efforts in ethics, according to (3). Of course, within a systematic ethics virtue is a subject which might well be treated under the general heading 'on good and evil' (as in Stobaeus' account of Stoic ethics: *Ecl.* 2. 57. 18–58. 4); or again, discussion of the passions (presumably a prime candidate for therapy) will need to consider whether the evils which make us angry really are evils. But these observations merely reinforce the obvious point that 'on good and evil' is a much broader topic than anything in the description preceding the definition of (2) would have led one to expect.

Other features of Revision also betray their probably revisionary status. As Brittain points out, (6) is explicitly characterized as an addition, and as presented falls outside the medical analogy.[20] Revision says only as much about (3) as is needed to indicate what its subject is, namely, the goal, happiness. It is quite difficult to see how any analogue of medical activity might be non-redundantly associated with it. If we were tempted to take 'implanting health' as our cue, we run into the immediate problem that one element in the therapy in (2) was to be the analogue of 'introducing those causes which produce health': so it sounds as though (2) already covers the philosophical equivalent of 'implanting health'.[21] Alternatively one might interpret the claim 'conjoined to the *logos* on goals is the *logos* on ways of life' as licensing us to take the material under (4) and (5) on individual life-choices and on politics as in effect the main content of (3). Brittain suggests that this was in fact Philo's original idea. The more obvious conclusion to draw is that (3) simply did not exist in Original. The author of Revision, however, will have supposed that the original scheme was intended as a fairly comprehensive division of the subject-matter of ethics like that of Eudorus (I do not debate the question whether Revision ante-dates or post-dates Eudorus' scheme).[22] He was doubtless convinced accordingly that Philo must have meant to include a section on goals (also one on good and evil), and at these points—(2) and (3)—in the sequence of topics.

[20] The author of Revision perhaps included it because of Philo's apparently celebrated interest in hypothesis, assuming that on second thoughts he would have added it into his scheme (Cic. *De Oratore* 3. 110). But in Original such cases might have been fitted into the particular division of the *logos* on ways of life.

[21] What (2) had in view as the equivalent of health was virtue. There is a problem anyway with Revision's notion that the equivalent of health will be happiness: it is one thing for the philosopher to try to introduce beliefs which will make someone virtuous, from which happiness will result; it is another and odder thing to try simply to 'implant' happiness—unless that reduces to the first option.

[22] But in the Ockhamist spirit of n. 3 above we might guess that it was in fact Eudorus who was the reviser.

Beyond Comparison: M. Sergius, *Fortunae Victor*

MARY BEAGON

POWER, DISABILITY, AND MORAL VICTORY

In these cases it is clear that courage played a great part but fortune played one greater still. In my opinion at least, no one could justly rate any man higher than Marcus Sergius, even though his great-grandson Catiline detracts from the honour of his name. In his second campaign, he lost his right hand; in the course of two campaigns he was wounded twenty-three times with the result that he was partially crippled in both hands and both feet, his spirit alone remaining undiminished. Though a disabled soldier, he fought on through many subsequent campaigns. Twice he was captured by Hannibal (for it was with no ordinary enemy that he was engaged), twice he escaped from captivity, although he was kept shackled hand and foot every day for twelve months. He fought four times with his left hand alone, and two horses he was riding were killed under him. (105) He had a right hand made for himself out of iron and, fighting with it tied on, he raised the siege of Cremona, defended Placentia, and captured twenty enemy camps in Gaul. All these incidents appear in the speech he made during his praetorship when his colleagues were trying to debar him from the sacrifices because of his infirmity. What piles of decorations would he have accumulated with a different enemy; (106) for it makes the greatest of differences in what historical circumstances each man's heroism occurs. What crowns did Trebia, Ticinus, or Trasimenus bestow? What crown was won at Cannae where flight was the summit of courage? Others certainly have conquered men but Sergius conquered fortune also. (Pliny, *HN* 7. 104–6)

This, the only extant written account of the remarkable exploits of M. Sergius Silus, is to be found halfway through book 7 of Pliny's *Natural History*. If we think of book 7 as falling into three main sections, Sergius appears in the middle one, among the statistics and achievements of human maturity. More precisely, he tops the list of *exempla virtutis* in a military context, paradigm of the quality which, in its wider sense, is exemplified by the Roman people as a whole, as Pliny remarks at the close of this list of records (*HN* 7. 130). Outside Pliny, his praetorship, in 197 BC, is attested

I am delighted to be asked to contribute to a Festschrift for Miriam Griffin. Her teaching has inspired my enduring interest in the historical period and many of the themes incorporated into this chapter.

by Livy.[1] He has also been identified beyond all reasonable doubt as the horseman featured on a coin issued by a namesake quaestor, M. Sergius Silus, *c.*116/115.[2] The portrayal is unusual: the rider holds both sword and a barbarian head in his left hand, thus fitting one of the more memorable details of Pliny's story, the loss, in an early campaign, of his right hand. This catastrophe, which would have ended the military careers of lesser men, was in Sergius' case ingeniously overcome. The succession of military distinctions which follows this early mishap is impressive;[3] all the more so in a family whose profile was for the most part obscure, despite patrician status and a mythical Trojan ancestor[4] to go with it. The break in obscurity for which the family was best known was not one they would have welcomed and is mentioned by Pliny in the same breath as Sergius' name and fame; his great-grandson was none other than the notorious L. Sergius Catilina, the conspirator of 63 BC. Perhaps surprisingly, the shameful contrast between great-grandfather and great-grandson was never thrown in the latter's face when he was attacked in the most scathing terms by the man who sought to destroy him, Cicero.

The situation in which Cicero found himself attacking Catiline and the line of argument he chose to take offer some plausible reasons for ignoring the possibilities inherent in such a comparison, as we shall see. However, it is possible that the emphasis placed on Sergius by Pliny in the first century AD is more significant than Cicero's apparent oversight in the first century BC. I will argue that the elevation of Sergius to the status of pre-eminent *exemplum virtutis* in the *Natural History* owes a great deal to the cultural and philosophical atmosphere in which Pliny was writing; more, perhaps, than it does to the actual historical significance of the hero himself. The key lies in Pliny's final words: 'Others certainly have conquered men but Sergius conquered fortune also'; a statement which reflects a popular philosophical paradox by which virtue in effect turns failure into success. Its significance is, however, enhanced by consideration of the final chapter of Sergius' story in Pliny. An attempt was made to debar the maimed praetor from public sacrifice; the outcome is not recorded. The nature and context of this anecdote are of interest; so, too, is the dichotomy between disability and power

[1] Livy 32. 27. 7, 32. 31. 6, 33. 21. 9, 33. 24. 4. Broughton 1951: 333.

[2] Coin of M. Sergius Silus, quaestor, probably a great-grandson: Crawford 1974: no. 286, p. 301 (pl. 39, no. 24).

[3] A plausible chronology can be constructed for Sergius' career, provided that we identify the campaigns which post-dated the loss of his hand, i.e. those around the Po area and the 'enemy camps in Gaul', with those against Mago in 205–203 BC: see Beagon forthcoming: (104–5).

[4] Trojan Sergestus, ancestor of Sergii: Virgil, *Aen.* 5. 117, cf. Wiseman 1974: 154.

at Rome which lies at its heart and which in turn informs the philosophical contrast between worldly and moral success.

. . . *CUM SACRIS ARCERETUR UT DEBILIS*

'All these incidents [namely, Sergius' military achievements] appear in the speech he made during his praetorship when his colleagues were trying to debar him from the sacrifices because of his infirmity'. From the content of Sergius' speech as reported by Pliny, it was clear that he had, to all intents and purposes, risen above the disabling nature of his mutilations (in addition to the loss of his right hand, he also had lesser injuries to his feet and left hand). So why the opposition, and is it likely to have prevailed? It has often been stated that Greek and Roman civilization set great store by physical beauty, an attitude which would obviously put all those with any kind of deformity at a basic disadvantage, the objects of popular prejudice. A general scarcity of evidence, however, makes it difficult to judge whether such individuals were officially and legally disadvantaged in any way. For Greece, the recent study of disability by Robert Garland notes determined and exceptional individuals with disabilities making it to the top, but also a general air of prejudice towards the misshapen which may have exercised a '*de facto* if not *de iure*' restriction on their political participation (Garland 1995: 31–2—examples include Medon, the Athenian herald, and Agesilaus, the Spartan king, both lame).

For Rome, the evidence does not seem hard and fast. From the little available, Mommsen (1871: i. 494) had suggested that restrictions on holding public office by reason of disability were of a strictly practical nature: was the candidate able to fulfil his duties, especially with regard to warfare? Hence particular care would be taken over higher offices (Dion. Hal. 5. 25: Horatius Cocles; see the following section). Later, candidates may have been assessed according to the nature of their duties. Thus, Sergius himself has, of course, risen to the praetorship, an office entailing military duties, after his accident, having clearly demonstrated his ability to overcome his disabilities in warfare. A lame tribune, as mentioned by Cicero in a letter of 61 BC, being the holder of a non-military office, was perhaps less controversial (Cic. *Att.* 1. 16). Cicero's only comment is a joking suggestion that his lameness is not a good omen for the success of his legislation. Later apparent evidence sometimes quoted from Dio, that Augustus exempted the disabled from becoming senators, is in context a concession to the disabled rather than a penalty (Dio 54. 26. 9).

Legal sources offer a few more hints. The rule recorded by Ulpian (*Dig.*

3. 1. 1. 5) that those who became blind while in office kept that office but were unable to proceed to a higher one, 'for which there are many examples', testifies to the fact that blindness might have restricted a magistrate in more than just military duties. While the case of the blind Appius Claudius makes the jurist pause, his comment on his participation while blind in senatorial debate does not specifically mention tenure of official positions in that state. The disability seems to have struck after his official career was over. The blind, Ulpian notes, were able to retain their status as senators and act as judges. At law, certain restrictions applied to various types of disability. The same extract from Ulpian suggests that the blind were unable to make application to a magistrate on behalf of others. The deaf are not permitted to make application even on their own behalf (*Dig.* 3. 1. 3. 3–4 (Ulpian)), because they might be in danger of disobeying a decree that they had not heard. These latter, like the dumb (ibid), the mentally impaired (*Dig.* 3. 1. 2. 1, Gaius) and the chronically ill to an incapacitating degree (*Dig.* 3. 1. 5. 1, Ulpian) normally had curators acting for them legally.

Such snippets of legal information do tend to support the notion that decisions on official/legal roles of the disabled might be taken on pragmatic and individual grounds, depending upon circumstances matched against the nature of the disability. There was no blanket ban on all the impaired.

For religious roles, however, the ban may have been more rigid. Certainly, sacrifices and priests were supposed to be without blemish, a theory in keeping with the general emphasis on purification and perfection in the Graeco-Roman religious ambience (Garland 1995: 63–5). Evidence for an actual ban at Rome on priests with physical impairments has been assumed from Dionysius of Halicarnassus' statement that Romulus enacted that priests should be without any bodily defect (Dion. Hal. 2. 21. 3); and from Aulus Gellius' account of the appointment of Vestals, where he says they should not have any bodily defect, specifying in particular that they should possess intact speech and hearing (*NA* 1. 12. 3). Then there is the rhetorical exercise included in the Elder Seneca's collection, to which we shall return later, which is based on the premiss that 'a priest should be without defect' and in the course of which it is stated that 'a priest of unsound body should be avoided, as being of evil omen' (*Contr.* 4. 2; see further below, p. 117). Plutarch says that priests with sores were forbidden to watch for omens, from which we could conclude that even temporary infirmities would necessarily lead to a suspension of religious duties. Certainly, the last two examples suggest that no allowance was made for accidents or illnesses, as opposed to congenital disabilities (Plut. *RQ* 73).[5]

[5] Though note that one of the theoretical arguments in the Elder Seneca, *Contr.* 4.2 (below,

These passages, while broadly supporting the notion of a ban on deformed priests, do not necessarily help us to reach a firm conclusion about Sergius. For one thing, Pliny's wording need not mean that he was participating in the ritual as a priest. In fact, the most natural way to interpret Pliny's words is to assume that Sergius was taking part in the sacrifices in his capacity as praetor, and the 'colleagues' attempting to debar him were his fellow praetors. Unfortunately, we have no clear evidence as to the degree of bodily wholeness required of participants other than priests. Does the Sergius story itself offer evidence, unmatched as far as I know elsewhere, that disabled individuals, who were acceptable in all other respects as magistrates, were able to hold office but had to step aside whenever specifically religious duties were required? The smooth unbroken running of the ritual was important, as the requirement for perfect speech and hearing in a Vestal implies, and Garland has suggested that some disabled individuals at least (presumably those who lack control over their movements or speech) may have been excluded from even a passive observatory role in religious ritual (1995: 64–5).

It would certainly seem unlikely that *all* persons with a disability were excluded from *any* participation in ritual. For one thing, the evidence we possess on the possible effects of disease and injury, including military injuries, suggests that the numbers of the *populus* thus afflicted to a greater or lesser extent would have been considerable. On the illness front, diseases from osteoarthritis to malaria, measles, or meningitis could inflict permanent disabilities, from the crippling of joints to blindness (Garland 1995: 18–22). The nature of ancient warfare may have left many with non-fatal but disabling wounds to limbs and the left side of the face (Grmek 1989: 60–1, 32, 59, cf. Hanson 1989: ch. 18). But perhaps most serious of all were the potential complications of what in modern opinion are comparatively minor injuries. Ignorance about the nature of infection could have devastating effects, as the medical sources attest: the Hippocratic Corpus offers examples of minor leg wounds which ultimately produced a bone infection, leading to retarded growth in the affected limb (Hanson 1989: 126–8; Hipp. *Epidemics*). Other writers, including Celsus, offer evidence that combinations of wounds and fractures could turn gangrenous, resulting in amputations, and that a simple but badly healed break in the thigh bone could leave the leg shorter (Celsus 8. 10. 5, with Garland 1995: 21; also 7. 33, 5. 26, 34 D).

The fact that Sergius appears to have been able to argue his case at all suggests that the slight flexibility seen with regard to public office and legal

p. 117) was that the law concerning priestly lack of blemish was intended for assessing prospective priests, not those already in office. See below, n. 8.

business may in certain circumstances have pertained to public religious function as well. But more specific consideration of the problem seems to raise questions rather than provide answers. Certainly, his particular disabilities should not have made him a practical liability as far as disruption was concerned. We have seen that his account of his post-disability war exploits would have implicitly shown that he was perfectly capable of controlled and complex manœuvre and therefore, presumably, of ensuring the smooth operation of the practicalities of ritual, with his left hand. But there is still a problem. Would using his left hand have been acceptable, especially in a religious context, given the traditional beliefs which connected the left with the bad, the unlucky, the inferior, and the female and which remained long ingrained in many areas of ancient thought from ritual and magic to embryology and obstetrics? (Lloyd 1962: 55–66; Beagon forthcoming, (37)).

Again, it was probably not just the nature and extent of the disability, but also the degree to which an individual was involved in the ritual which had to be taken into account. Sergius might, as a magistrate, be expected to take a leading role, as did others, besides priests, in different sacrificial contexts; for example, the *paterfamilias* in the religious ceremonies of his household. Were disabled heads of households in any sense restricted in their domestic religious activities? Surely it would be statistically likely that some such always existed. Or was it the public nature rather than just the centrality as such of Sergius' projected role which caused, or at any rate, added to, his problems?

Finally, the relative scarcity of comparative evidence concerning the religious role of magistrates makes it difficult to assess whether the reaction to Sergius was typical or unusual. Certainly, Sergius' praetorship fell within a period in which the anxieties of the recent wars were reflected in increased reportage of portentous occurrences, including monstrous births,[6] for the most alarming of which, intersexuals, special expiatory rites had been introduced only ten years earlier (Livy 27. 11; see also below, pp. 118–19). It would come as no surprise if there was heightened sensitivity about the participation of the maimed praetor in the state sacrifices. Nor, of course, can we rule out a political subtext: a feud motivated by political enmities, the details of which are now lost to us, but illustrating once again the close and often complex interrelation of politics and religion in the late Republic.

It is easier, however, to rule out a rather different solution to the Sergius problem; namely, that there was no problem, due to the story's being wholly or partly a fiction of later rhetorical debate. This, for example, has been the verdict on the famous incident involving the Pontifex Maximus L.

[6] Bloch 1963: 115–18; Rawson 1971: 158–69; Briscoe 1973: 88–91; MacBain 1982: 126–35.

Caecilius Metellus. A number of sources recount his rescue, in 241 BC, of the Palladium from the burning temple of Vesta.[7] That he was blinded as a consequence and subsequently denied his rights as a priest is a detail first found in the rhetorical exercises of the Elder Seneca (*Contr.* 4. 2, cf. Pliny *HN* 7. 141).[8] There is no other evidence that he was so deprived and we also know that he went on to hold further secular office after the incident, which would apparently infringe the rule in Ulpian debarring the blind from further office (Ooteghem 1967: 20; Dumézil 1966: 320–1). We need not assume that the blinding story was wholly fictitious; Metellus may have suffered temporary blindness as a result of psychosomatic reaction or shock[9] which did not terminate his religious or political career. However, some sort of elaboration of the story for the rhetorical context seems likely; rather contrived exercises of a similar nature which hinge on a disability occur on several occasions in Seneca's collection (*Contr.* 1. 3, 3. 1). In the case of Sergius, it is possible that the religious controversy was a later invention. Yet the details of his career seem reasonably firm: we know he held the praetorship and can, with the corroborative evidence of the coin, assume that during the course of his military career he was mutilated. Therefore, it seems at least as likely that the question of his eligibility to undertake such religious duties as the praetorship entailed really did come up. However, this does not preclude Pliny from having an ulterior motive for the emphasis

[7] Cicero, *Pro Scauro* 48, Dion. Hal. 2. 66, Ovid, *Fasti* 6. 440–540, Livy, *Per.* 19.

[8] See Leuze 1905: 95–115; Wiseman 1979: 33, 36; Winterbottom 1974: 438. Metellus' case is different from those in Dion. Hal. (2. 21. 3) and Gellius (*NA* 1. 12. 3), which refer to screening of potential priestly candidates, and that in Plutarch (*RQ* 73), which refers to a temporary suspension of an incumbent priest.

[9] Augustine, *Civ. Dei* 3. 18, from Varro, is the source which most clearly implies that Metellus' injuries were extensive enough to cause permanent disability. However, he does not specify blindness, the choice of which in Seneca and the later sources seems more than fortuitous: the sudden onset of blindness was traditionally believed to be the result of seeing that which ought not to be seen (Forbes-Irving 1990: 166–7; more refs. in Garland 1995: 194–5 nn.), in this case the Palladium. Moreover, such 'religious' blinding was apparently reversible by appropriate propitiation according to Plut. *Mor.* 309f, whose two examples involve individuals who touched the Palladium, the second of whom, with a slight textual emendation, may in fact be Metellus (cf. Val. Max. 1. 4. 5; also the popular story of the poet Stesichorus' blinding, *PMG*, fr. 192–3, with nn.). As with sacrilege generally, the intentions of the offender appear to have made no difference: thus Cicero ironically contrasts the deliberate intrusion of P. Clodius on forbidden rites with the case of his ancestor. The latter was stricken with blindness, although he had never knowingly seen the forbidden, whereas the former, who had, was not stricken with physical blindness, though Cicero attributes to him a subsequent mental blindness (*De Domo Sua* 105). It should be mentioned that this unnamed ancestor of Clodius has on occasion been identified with our Metellus. If this were correct, it would give a pre-Senecan reference to the story of his blinding, but the identification seems highly unlikely in view of the existence of an obvious candidate in Appius Claudius Caecus; see Nisbet 1939: 158. Cf. also blindness as punishment for sexual crimes, Devereux 1973: 36–49; Forbes-Irving 1990: 166–7; Garland 1995: 194–5 nn.

which he gives to the controversy and the moral to be drawn from it. The purpose for Pliny of the Sergius story will be the subject of the next section.

Leaving aside the rhetorical exercises, but staying with the early imperial period, it is also worth considering whether the most famous example of disability from Pliny's own era can add anything to our understanding of the religious role of the disabled. Rhetorical treatments of the merits of the case for and against the role of the disabled in religious ceremony may even have been given an added topicality in the early/mid-first century AD by the acquisition of a cluster of minor priesthoods and an augurate by the disabled future Emperor Claudius,[10] despite being left out of the running for all political office by Augustus and Tiberius. The severity and nature of Claudius' disability have been debated (e.g. Levick 1990: 15; Garland 1995: 189 n.) and while there is no evidence he was actually deformed, the ancient evidence suggests, at the very least, physical ungainliness and a speech impediment, neither of which, on the evidence we have so far seen, look very promising attributes for a potential priest. His case was of course unusual, decisions about him hinging, to judge from Suetonius, on whether positions, secular or religious, which placed him under the public gaze, would erode the dignity of the highest family of all. Thus it was secular office which was ruled out, religious positions apparently being regarded as of less public significance. Any physical problems in his execution of his priestly duties were no doubt to be forestalled by careful supervision from a colleague acting as minder, as Augustus suggests in the letter to Livia quoted by Suetonius, another of which suggests that his speech in formal circumstances might actually be better than in informal conversation (Suet. *Claud.* 9. 2, cf. *Aug.* 38).

It is hardly legitimate to allow this imperial problem case of the first century AD to reinforce arguments for possible earlier precedents of religious flexibility in the very different circumstances of two to two and a half centuries earlier. Taken in its own historical context, even allowing for the exceptional nature of his case, it is certainly interesting that there are no hints of religious reservation being voiced about Claudius' priesthoods, minor as some of them may have been. But again, rather than looking to the later case of Claudius for help in unravelling those of an earlier era, it may be more appropriate to link it to a change of public attitude mentioned by Pliny himself as being comparatively recent, when he comments on intersexuals that, whereas once they were considered portentous, they now function as *deliciae*, pets, a source of entertainment rather than religious

[10] *Sodales Titiales*, *Salii Palatini*, *Sodales Augustales* and augurate: Suet. *Claud.* 3–7; *CIL* iii, 381; Tac. *Ann.* 1. 54. 2. cf. also *Claud.* 9.2 .

horror and fear. We cannot now examine the wider issues, such as the social and chronological scope of Pliny's reference, not to mention the reason for such a change, raised by this interesting statement (*HN* 7. 34 with Beagon forthcoming: ad loc.). Intersexuals as officially reported portents are not recorded after the early first century BC. If the religious taboos connected even with what were once the 'most accursed' of monstrosities were waning,[11] at least among the pet-keeping classes, possibly strict rules, if they were strict, about priestly imperfections were also relaxing. The capacity of even the grossly abnormal to shock and inspire religious fear had in some sections of society given way to its capacity to entertain; and while lesser deformities had always been liable to ridicule from the public at large, and ridicule was itself one means of dealing with the perceived threat of the abnormal, as Garland reminds us (1995: ch. 5 esp. 83), it was hardly surprising that laughter rather than respect, far less horror at a religious role, was the anticipated reaction to the public exhibition of Claudius. It may not be coincidental that Pliny, writing shortly after, in the second half of the first century AD, apparently shows little interest in the specifically religious aspect of the Sergius controversy, as opposed to the controversy itself, and omits, in his discussion of Metellus (*HN* 7. 141), to mention the religious outcome of the latter's blindness altogether, despite the evident influence of the rhetorical schools upon his work.

The lack of comparative material on the religious role of the disabled means that we cannot be sure what the outcome of Sergius' plea was, nor can we even be certain, given the rhetorical nature of some of the evidence we do have, that the plea was historically authentic. All we can say is that his previous achievements can be given a reasonably plausible historical context and had been exceptional enough to raise him above the confines of a society in which the number of disabled war veterans was possibly quite high and the general attitude towards the disabled distinctly lacking in compassion. Valerius Maximus conveniently preserves the names of one or two other exceptional individuals who, deprived of their right hands, none the less fought on with their left hands, or even with no hands at all (3. 2. 11, 22; cf. Suet. *Jul.* 68. 4, Herod. 6. 114). War wounds generally may have excited a certain respect and sympathy and might of course on occasion be displayed even in court to this end; Cicero in the *De Oratore* (2. 195; *HN* 7. 133–52) has Antonius describe how, in 98 BC, he milked the situation of the war-crippled Manius Aquilius for all it was worth, recalling the emotional

[11] 'Most accursed', special rites, Livy 27. 11, cf. 27. 37, 31. 12; MacBain 1982: 127. 'Not monsters', Diod. Sic. fr. 34. 10. 2, a century or so before Pliny's *Natural History*; and refs. above, n. 6.

reaction of the jury when he summoned his unhappy old client, tore open his tunic, and exposed his scars. The effect, however, may not have been entirely attributable to the scars as such; reaction to Aquilius was heightened by consciousness of his previous glory: according to Antonius, on seeing 'the man I remembered as having been consul, commander-in-chief, honoured by the senate and processing to the Capitol . . . cast down, crippled, sorrowing and brought to risk of all he held dear, I was myself overcome by compassion'. It is part of a wider rhetorical interest in the contrast between past and present, the latter with implications for the future situation of the defendant; an interest to which, in a theoretical context, the use by Pliny in a long section of book 7 (133–52) of the vicissitudes of fortune as a framework for the extremities of the human experience is also related.

In fact, even with war disabilities, familiarity, not to mention fake claims, may have bred contempt; witness Plautus' imposter dishonestly claiming respect for an apparent war wound and the cynical reaction of his listener (*Curculio* 398). And even genuine cases may have met with indifference or ridicule, as Cicero's anecdote, again in *De Oratore* (2. 249; see also below, p. 125), about the young man ashamed to venture out because of the crippling effect of a leg wound, despite his mother's exhortation to remember his bravery with every step he took, suggests. By contrast, toughness of mind as well as body was needed to survive, let alone thrive, in such circumstances. Sergius continued and enhanced a military career that should have been destroyed by his disability, making him for Pliny the outstanding example of *virtus*, one that had, moreover, conquered fortune, rather than been compromised by it. It is to the significance of this assessment of Sergius that we can now turn.

Sergius vicit etiam fortunam

As mentioned at the beginning, the example of Sergius occurs in the central section of book 7 of the *Natural History*, devoted to the statistics and achievements connected with human maturity. Sections 100–30 introduce examples[12] of various kinds of *virtus* (excellence) and 101–6 deal specifically with *virtus* in the military context, the courage and skill of the fighter: Pliny uses *fortitudo* (bravery) and *virtus* synonymously in this passage. Sergius, however, as we can see from the opening of the passage, is the supreme

[12] Pliny may have got Sergius and the preceding *exemplum*, that of Siccius Dentatus, from Varro. Valerius Maximus, who has Siccius but not Sergius, mentions Varro as a source for the former (3. 2. 24). However, he also attributes the Siccius story to 'others' besides Varro, suggesting that such *exempla* were standard.

example. In the previous examples, we are told, 'courage played a part but fortune played one greater still'. Again, at the end of the extract, Sergius' achievement is summed up with another reference to fortune; others have conquered men, but Sergius conquered fortune as well.

Virtus and *fortuna* could be complementary or contrasting qualities. In the opening line, the pairing, together with the fact that the previous examples have been exclusively military, might bring to mind a more specialized meaning of *fortuna*, as a synonym for the *felicitas* or good luck of a Roman general, which he needed to possess in addition to *virtus*. Whether this good luck was originally believed to be innate or the external gift of the gods is disputed (Wistrand 1987: 10; Kajanto 1981: 502–58, esp. 523). Bravery, however, was indisputably part of the individual's personality and Roman writers tend implicitly to attach a greater value to *virtus* than to good luck. The former epitomized the active dynamism of Roman identity itself; a characteristic which Cicero liked to appropriate in particular for the *novus homo*, the man who made his way up the political ladder by virtue of his own ability rather than by the good fortune of high birth.[13]

The final reference to *fortuna* in our passage, however, where it is set in contrast to *virtus*, as something, indeed, which has been conquered or overcome by means of *virtus*, suggests that Pliny's overriding concern here was not with *fortuna* as synonym of *felicitas*, good luck, whether god-given or innate, but with *fortuna* as chance, whether good or bad. Literary references to *fortuna* in the late Republic and early Empire were influenced by the enhancement in Hellenistic philosophies of the dichotomy between moral effort and random chance.[14] In general, these suggested that undeserved good fortune was inferior to, if not actually opposed to, the moral idea of a life spent striving after virtue. The Stoics denied the relevance of fortune's goods to true, *virtus*-based happiness, although the Academics allowed such goods to add to its completeness.[15] The idea developed that virtue

[13] Asconius, *Pro Scauro* 22 (1. 4); cf. Sall. *Jug.* 1. 3; in general, Cic. *Pro. Mur.* 15–17 and below, n.15.

[14] See e.g. Kajanto 1981: 502–58. Hints of such a dichotomy are seen at least as early as Aristotle (*Nic. Eth.* 1099^a–1101^a), as well as in the Greek historians (G. Herzog-Hauser, *RE* vii.A.1, s.v. Tyche 1663–5). For the Roman period, see e.g. *Rhet. ad Her.* (below, n. 15), Sall. *Cat.* 58. 21, Virg. *Aen.* 12. 435 ff.

[15] Cicero, *Fin.* 5. 71, 78, 81 ff. The Stoics emphasized the importance of intention: *virtus*, as the result of the individual's own judgements, is within his control, unlike the external vicissitudes of fortune; cf. Cic. *Parad. Stoic.* 3. 20. See Colish 1985: 42–6. In many ways, this was a philosophical enhancement of the Roman preference for effort over luck, as epitomized by the commonplaces of the *Rhet. ad Her.* which include the maxim that all the rules for life should be based on virtue because virtue alone is within our own control, whereas all else is subject to the sway of fortune (4. 2. 24, 27). A basic *Virtus–Fortuna* antithesis was clearly well established by the 1st cent. BC.

could overcome fortune morally if not physically and can be seen already in Cicero's *Tusculans* (2. 30, 3. 36, 5. 2, 5. 17, etc.). But it is in the Stoic writings of Pliny's older contemporary, the younger Seneca (e.g. *Ep.* 76. 21, 98. 2; *Prov.* 4. 12; *Vit. Beat.* 4. 2, 7. 15. 2), that the contrast between personal moral effort and impersonal chance is most frequently expressed. It is moreover enhanced by another Hellenistic influence on the interpretation of *fortuna*. This was the popular concept of *fortuna-tyche* as divinity, a personification which endowed the impersonal with the characteristic of ambiguity at the very least and sometimes malice and jealousy as well. Seneca's Stoic must overcome a fortune which is in effect misfortune. To the Roman preference for attributing success to personal effort, a tendency echoed in the Greek Polybius' occasional attempts to distinguish between Roman success resulting from random luck and that which results from conscious striving (1. 13, 18. 28, 36 .17), was added philosophy's moral contrast between virtue and fortune, the latter acquiring an extra malign sting from the popular goddess (Kajanto 1981: 532).

Overcoming fortune, therefore, was in effect engaging with a hostile force, an enemy. The notion of a contest appears in earlier references, the portrayal of fortune as enemy being, of course, enhanced by the existence of military as well as moral connotations in the concept of *virtus*. But it was its adaptation and development by Stoic sources which seems to have generated a strong and distinguished tradition for the analogy. Lucan, significantly, puts it in the mouth of the man who, by his day, had become a Stoic icon, Cato of Utica. It was to continue long after, into the Christian era, through the writings of Augustine and Boethius, and thence into the humanistic tradition, culminating in Petrarch's *De Remediis utriusque Fortunae*.[16] It is in Lucan's uncle, Seneca, that the analogy is developed at greatest length. The virtuous man must prepare and arm himself against fortune, so as not to allow her victory. He will not, however, be content to remain on the defensive; he must issue a challenge to fortune, offering himself to her blows in order to be able to prove his *virtus* (Sen. *Ep.* 98. 4, 14; *Prov.* 4. 12). Sometimes the analogy is that of the Olympic competitor, actively challenging fortune to prove his pre-eminence (*Prov.* 4. 2); but at other times it is that of the battle-hungry soldier, or even, as in the famous anecdote in *De Providentia* 4. 4, of the gladiator, bemoaning, in the reign of Tiberius, his lack of opportunity in an age bereft of shows.

Thus, when Pliny talks of the war-hero Sergius overcoming fortune, he

[16] Lucan, *Phars.* 9. 569–71; Aug. *C. Acad.* 11. 1. 1 = *PL* 32. 919; Boethius, *Cons. Phil.* 2. 8. 1–2. Petrarch's work took the theme of 'our ever-present war with Fortune, in which only virtue can make us victorious' (*Rem.* 1, pref., 4): see Rawski 1991: ad loc.

is primarily writing in the manner of a Stoic like Seneca and Sergius' achievement is all the greater for overcoming fortune at its most negative. We have already seen in the previous section that the war-wounded were not necessarily accorded much sympathy in Greek and Roman society generally, due in part to cynicism and, in all likelihood given the conditions of ancient warfare and even everyday life, the contempt bred of familiarity. In addition, deep-seated prejudices against the congenitally deformed may, consciously or not, have coloured attitudes towards post-congenital injury. A tendency to equate beauty and virtue was ingrained in the popular consciousness and found expression in the 'art' of physiognomy (Garland 1995: 88–104). More startling, however, than popular prejudice, was the intellectual respectability such ideas assumed through association with some philosophies. According to one tradition, Pythagoras had admitted followers only after physiognomical examination (Aul. Gell. *NA* 1. 9. 1–2); while comments attributed to some Stoics seem to imply an acceptance of the basic idea that character propensities may manifest themselves physically.[17]

While none of this applies directly to dramatic non-congenitally acquired injury, it none the less serves as a reminder not to take for granted what Seneca feels impelled to argue at length in *Ep.* 66: namely, that the body, even when ugly, deformed, or maimed, is beautified by a virtuous soul. The topic is broached directly in the first four sections of the letter and then developed within the broader context of an argument for the equal value and validity of all displays of virtue, whatever their external circumstances. Virgil is wrong when, at *Aeneid* 5. 344, he writes that *virtus* is more pleasing in a beautiful body (*Ep.* 66. 1); the *virtus* displayed by the maimed is equal to that displayed by the able-bodied. Significantly, Seneca eventually expresses some preference for those who show *virtus* in adversity (*Ep.* 66. 49–53). Moreover, he produces as climax to his argument a famous *exemplum* in many ways parallel to that of Sergius: the legendary Mucius Scaevola showed his contempt of torture after a failed assassination attempt on Lars Porsenna by deliberately burning his right hand. Thus, says Seneca, he finished his war unarmed and maimed but with his stump of a right hand conquered two kings:[18] a moral victory, expressed in military language, over and in spite of adverse physical circumstances. That the wounds of the brave glorified rather than disfigured was a commonplace. It

[17] Mainly in connection with their theory of the corporeality of the emotions, which may therefore leave their marks upon the body. See Beagon 1992: 113–19.

[18] i.e. Porsenna himself and the king he was trying to reinstate at Rome, Tarquinius. See Livy 2. 12 ff., with Ogilvie 1965: 162–3. For Scaevola as *exemplum* (of endurance), see Val. Max. 3. 3. 1.

was worked into a forceful Stoic *sententia* by Lucan, who took the famous example of Caesar's centurion Caesius Scaeva and described him as deified by his wounds into a personification of *virtus* itself.[19]

The crucial point in determining the outstanding nature of Sergius' victory over adverse circumstances is not, however, simply the physical loss of his hand, but the lack of official reward for his valour. Like Scaevola, he was on the losing side. Whilst Roman ideology set a high value on such rewards as a visible enhancement and recognition of an individual's *dignitas*, the Stoic, strictly speaking, should regard the rewards and ornaments of military and political office as, at best, irrelevant to his true moral happiness. Like wealth, a great house, and troops of clients, honours are, according to Seneca, borrowed and dependent on unstable chance (*Ad Marciam* 10. 1). The Stoic takes part in political life, 'not to obtain honours but to be useful to friends, citizens, all mankind' (*Tranq. An.* 1. 10); in other words, to fulfil his wider duty to humanity. Such demotion of military and civil offices and honours to the role of *adiaphora*, mere trappings of life, irrelevant to the true life of virtue and the happiness of the sage, seems to appear in this specific form for the first time in Seneca. It does, of course, reflect not only the growing interest in Stoicism of the first century AD but also the diminishing in that period of the opportunity for traditional political and military careers and their associated trappings, not to mention the friction between emperor and members of the 'Stoic opposition' on the question of political participation or withdrawal from public life, of a compromising endorsement of the regime or a principled stance for moral independence.

The historical setting of Sergius himself was very different but the philosophic background of the first century AD may be of significance in understanding Pliny's giving him pride of place among other possible examples of *virtus*. For, in respect of his lack of official honours, Sergius stands in stark contrast to the other examples of *virtus* in Pliny's catalogue. L. Siccius Dentatus and even the tainted Manlius Capitolinus have their decorations listed in exact detail, a pattern which, as Valerius Maximus's account of Dentatus also suggests, was no doubt the customary one in such accounts (*HN* 7. 101–4; Val. Max. 3. 2. 24).

A question thus suggests itself. Was Sergius a prominent example of military bravery before Pliny took him up? Valerius Maximus, at least, used Dentatus without mention of Sergius, and we have no textual references to Sergius outside Pliny, with the exception of the bare mentions of his name in Livy. Dentatus in both Maximus and Pliny is treated as a straightforward

[19] Lucan, *Phars*. 6. 254; cf. Suet. *Jul.* 68; Caes. *BC* 3. 53; Val. Max. 3. 2. 23.

example of outstanding military bravery appropriately and officially rewarded.

The moral/philosophical dimension of the Sergius *exemplum* is rather different, though the structure is essentially the same; the enumeration of the military decorations has been replaced in Sergius' case with the decorations he did not win, or, rather, the decorations he would have won, had fortune been on his side. But, as it was, fortune, too, was another adversary, over which he gained a more significant, moral victory. The example, even such a treatment of it, may have come from Varro. Certainly, the Stoic resonances of the conquest of fortune by *virtus* are, as we saw, familiar to Cicero and appear on several occasions in the *Tusculans* (45 BC). It is, however, also possible that Pliny, who opens his account of Sergius' career by stressing the contrast between this and the preceding examples and emphasizing the superiority of this example to all others, gives Sergius a prominence he had not had before. Not judging the moral contest by the criteria of worldly success does, of course, go back to Aristotle (*Nic. Eth.* 1099ᵃ–1101ᵃ), but its most forceful summary is, once again, that attributed to the Stoic Cato by Pliny's contemporary, Lucan, for whom 'noble purpose is enough and virtue becomes no more virtuous by success' (*Phars.* 9. 569–71). The final act of the Sergius story, the clash between the disabled praetor and his able-bodied colleagues, is significant here. It is, in a sense, an extension into political life of the *virtus/fortuna* struggle in which Sergius had previously been engaged in a military context. Moreover, it is inextricably linked to it, since the narrative of the military struggle is being re-enacted by Sergius in his speech as his prime weapon against his new adversaries. Even the fact that we are not told the outcome of this second contest serves to enhance the moral/philosophical significance of the *exemplum*. Unfinished, it mirrors the ongoing nature of the virtuous man's lifelong struggle to maintain his spiritual integrity against the blows of fortune.

A possible comparison to Pliny's use of the Sergius controversy is the variant of the Horatius Cocles story found in the fourth-century commentary on the *Aeneid* by Servius (Serv. *Aen.* 8. 646). Dionysius of Halicarnassus' earlier version of the Horatius story, written in the Augustan era, had mentioned the leg wound incurred while defending the bridge and the fact that it 'rendered him useless' for further service to the state as soldier or consul. He implies a straightforward debarment on practical grounds (Dion. Hal. 5. 25; see above, p. 113), with no hint of controversy or strife. In Servius' version, however, the hero actively campaigns for election, only to encounter opposition on account of his limp. He retorts that every step he takes reminds him of his glorious deed. His words echo, probably deliberately, those of the mother of the disabled soldier in the anecdote quoted in the last section from Cicero's *Tusculans* but are now incorporated into the later Stoic elaboration of the *virtus–fortuna* antithesis. The *sententia* on the non-disfiguring nature of the wounds of the brave mentioned earlier (p. 123) is placed within the framework of the figurative battle between *virtus* and *fortuna*. Perhaps significantly, both the Sergius and the Horatius *exempla* featured prominently in Petrarch's great tribute to the Stoic tradition on *virtus* and *fortuna*, the *De Remediis*.

To conclude: Pliny's emphasis on M. Sergius as *victor fortunae*, and so supreme example of *virtus*, may in some ways be the product of first century AD Stoic-influenced thought,[20] stressing the superiority of the moral achievements of *virtus* in the face of a hostile fortune which has made the normal rewards for outstanding valour impossible to achieve. The following words of Seneca in the *De Tranq. An.* offer a hypothetical illustration of the Stoic priorities which underlie the Sergius story in Pliny. Seneca's choice of the praetorship is fortuitous, but serves to emphasize the sentiment's applicability not only to Sergius' lack of official military honours but also to the threatened loss of one of his praetorian duties: 'Does he accomplish more, who, in the office of praetor, delivers the verdict his assistant has formulated, than he who teaches the meaning of justice, piety, endurance, bravery, contempt of death . . .?' (*Tranq. An.* 3. 4).

PRONEPOS CATILINA . . .

The only stain on the glorious example of M. Sergius, is, according to Pliny, the fact that his great-grandson was the notorious conspirator, L. Sergius Catilina. Rather surprisingly, perhaps, Cicero never mentions the illustrious ancestor whose patriotic probity would have made an effective rhetorical weapon with which to berate the adversary whom he portrays as arch-traitor of his country. One reason for this apparent omission, may be that, as suggested in the last section, Sergius may not have been the best-known *exemplum virtutis* in Cicero's day. The contrast might not have had

[20] It has been suggested (Picard 1990) that Sergius was the subject of the monument portraying a soldier dragging a Gaul by the hair, which was seen by Nero as he journeyed back to Rome at the time of the revolt of Vindex (Suet. *Nero* 41. 2). The singling out of such a portrayal is, of course, related to the revolt and unlikely to be more than coincidental with regard to the increased focus on Sergius in the 1st cent. AD which I have posited here; piquant though a confrontation between Sergius, the epitome of *virtus* and its antithesis, Nero (see below, p. 131 and nn. 27–8), would have been. In any case, the attempt made to identify a Gaul being 'dragged' with the Gallic head held aloft in the coin portrayal of Sergius (above, p. 112 and n. 2) is not convincing. Other, closer, artistic parallels have been suggested: see comments by Chamoux and Turcan in Picard 1990.

the same impact if Cicero had had to explain at length who Sergius was. But even if he wasn't as high-profile an *exemplum* as the blind Appius Claudius, whom Cicero was later to use to devastating effect against a delinquent descendant (*Pro Caelio* 33–4), the possibilities for a rhetorical antithesis between great-grandfather and great-grandson still look tempting—and that Sergius had status as his family's role model some fifty years earlier is at least suggested by the coin already mentioned (p. 112).

Possibly the very fact that Sergius was a military hero, veteran of numerous campaigns against Rome's enemies, and bearing not only scars but bodily disablement as a physical reminder of his patriotic sacrifices, might have backfired on Cicero. The consul of 63, hardly experienced in military matters himself, had not so far come across as a champion of Rome's soldiery. He could, by his successful opposition to Rullus' land bill, be argued to have failed the veterans of Pompey's Eastern campaigns amongst others, despite his protestations that he was acting in their best interests. Moreover, numbers of soldiers from a previous era, veterans of Sulla, had joined Catiline; a fact which requires tactful handling by Cicero in the *Second Catilinarian* (2. 20), where he attempts to fillet out the profligate rebellious few from the law-abiding, patriotic majority. Notwithstanding his protestations, here was a group who may very well have had genuine grievances about their treatment by the state. Sergius too, if the attempt at religious debarment is historical, may have ended his official career as in some respects a veteran snubbed by officialdom.

We also know that lineage was one of the weapons wielded by the patrician Catiline against Cicero, whose relatively humble equestrian origins inspired the famous jibe *inquilinus civis* in reply to the *First Catilinarian*. But Sallust also says that, earlier in the same speech, Catiline had defended himself by reference to the patriotic ideals inspired by his old and honourable family. We cannot know whether his great-grandfather Sergius was cited in this context, nor, if he was, how he was deployed; but it is possible that Cicero thought he stood to lose more than he might gain by engaging with Catiline on the subject of ancestry (Sall. *Cat.* 31; cf. Cic. *Sull.* 22).

However, it may well be that the apparent omission to take advantage of Catiline's virtuous ancestor is due primarily to the nature of Cicero's portrayal of Catiline himself in the consular speeches of 63 and those made shortly after. Of particular interest in this respect is the description of Catiline as *monstrum atque prodigium* (*In Cat.* 2. 1) and the way Cicero's imagery develops the idea, especially in the *First Catilinarian*. At Rome, *monstrum* (etymologically related to *monere*, to warn) was a portent of evil, a malfunctioning of nature which might suggest a malfunctioning of the city's relationship with the divine. Prodigies of this type were particularly prone to be noticed at times of national crisis, as had been the case, most recently, less than thirty years earlier, in the Social War period. Rome's ancient law code, the Twelve Tables, required that the father of a dreadfully deformed child should kill it quickly, and in a more violent and unambiguous way than simply exposing it, if a passage in the Elder Seneca's *Controversiae* is anything to go by.[21] Cicero uses the phrase *monstrum et prodigium* on a number of occasions to vilify those whom he regards, or at any rate wishes to depict, as unnaturally wicked and depraved beyond the boundaries of normal human delinquency, anomalies to the point of being barely human. Thus, for example, he describes in a private letter Appius Claudius' depredations in his province (*Att.* 5. 16. 2); and had earlier publicly denounced another errant governor, Verres (*Verr.* 4. 47). Catiline's co-conspirators are described in *Pro Sulla* as 'wild beasts spawned by monstrosities (*portentis*)' (*Sull.* 76).[22]

This idea of anomaly, of difference, was to be found in Aristotle's basic biological definition of *teras*, the Greek equivalent of *monstrum*, which, he said was 'that which is unlike its parents' (*GA* 767^b5–7). A person designated *monstrum* would therefore be regarded as a deformed parody of its parents and indeed of its normal ancestors. And if we return to Catiline and Sergius, we can see that this is indeed the relationship between the two. Leaving aside the straight contrasts between them; Sergius the patriot, Catiline the traitor, Sergius fighting to rid Rome of enemies, Catiline deliberately inciting civil war (delighting in it, according to Sallust, *Cat.* 5), it is even more illuminating to note the apparent similarities: the physical and mental strength and endurance, which powered Sergius' extraordinary career in the face of apparently overwhelming odds, is matched by his descendant, as Cicero and Sallust attest. Besides Catiline's ability to endure hunger, cold, and lack of sleep, the mental toughness of a Sergius is also evident in Sallust's description of a daring and versatile mind, his intense passion and ambition.[23] Both Cicero and Sallust, of course, make it clear

[21] Twelve Tables, cf. Cicero, *Laws* 3. 8. 19. Sen. *Contr.* 10. 4. 16: they are 'thrown out', not exposed, possibly drowned, according to Garland 1995: 17, quoting the younger Seneca, *De Ira* 1. 15. 20. However, the extent to which this was actually done, as indeed the extent to which such things were still taken seriously as portents by the late Republic, is open to debate. Certainly in the case of minor deformities, Seneca's comments (*Ep.* 66. 26) on the extra care and protection lavished on the 'sickly' child by its parents may be relevant.

[22] The imputation of certain crimes, such as human sacrifice (*Vat.* 14), or the incest and familial murder attributed by Cicero to Catiline himself (Asc. *In Tog. Cand.* 91; *In Cat.* 1. 14) could have a similarly dehumanizing effect: see Rives 1995: 72–3.

[23] Cicero, *In Cat.* 1. 26: 'your famous ability to endure hunger, cold and deprivation of every necessity'; and *In Cat.* 2. 9, echoed by Sallust. *Cat.* 5, cf. 14–16. It is surely right to see

that these potentially positive character traits have been comprehensively perverted towards the perpetration of a range of criminal and ultimately treasonable ends; although, in Sallust's account of the final battle, these perverted ends could almost be forgotten as he chooses to stress the military leadership and personal bravery which led Catiline to fight to the death against his own set of overwhelming odds.

Cicero could, then, have made an effective contrast between the patriotic ideal, Sergius, and his monstrous great-grandson. So why not construct, for example, an effective piece of *prosopopoia*, as he was later to do to point the contrast between Clodia and her ancestor Appius Claudius? There is, however, a huge difference in circumstances and thus in tone between the attack on Catiline and that on Clodia. The latter is essentially light-hearted. The overwhelming figure of Appius is set against the sorry specimen of the present generation, trivialized by her own immorality to comic effect. The contrast is grotesque in its lack of balance. With Catiline, however, Cicero chooses to set up a villain of an altogether different type. His crimes represent a deadly serious threat to the whole country. To represent him as a sad disappointment to and departure from the ideals of a patriotic great-grandfather may well have seemed an inadequate comment on the stature of this criminal. Cicero does of course use the same rhetorical device—*prosopopoia*—twice in the *Catilinarians*, but with Catiline the monster rejected not by a horrified parent or ancestor but by the 'mother of us all', his country, who also reproaches Cicero with his slowness to remove and destroy the traitor (*In Cat.* 1. 18; 1. 27–9).

Cicero's Catiline is *monstrum* on a grand scale, the deformed offspring and misbegotten son not merely of a single set of parents, or even a single family, but of Rome itself. 'If your own parents feared and hated you . . . you would retire somewhere out of their sight. As it is, your native land, which is the mother of us all, hates you and dreads you' (*In Cat.* 1. 18). Later, in reply to her complaints, Cicero says that the removal of Catiline himself will not on its own solve the problem, given that he has recruited

these as genuine virtues counterbalanced by appalling defects, rather than as intrinsically dubious qualities ('animal-like' according to May 1988: 53, though cf. 109–10). Later, in the *Pro Caelio* (14), Cicero described the 'monstrous vices' of Catiline as perversions of genuine qualities of ability and endurance, a paradoxical and misleading combination. Counterbalance of extremes was the thrust of Livy's later imitation of the Sallustian portrait of Catiline, when describing (21. 4. 5) Hannibal's ability and endurance as great *virtutes* balanced by equally great *vitia*, of which *inhumana crudelitas* is clearly related to the earlier portrayal of Catiline as monster. They are, in fact, the *virtutes* which despise and counteract luxury (cf. Vretska 1976: 243) and offer a physical counterpart to the non-pampering of the soul which is an essential prerequisite for the Stoic (cf. Sen. *Ep.* 51) in the fight against *Fortuna* discussed in the previous section.

co-conspirators, infected by the wickedness of their leader. Rather than advocating the straightforward ejection of the monstrosity, Cicero instead uses the language of disease. The use of disease or pestilence as a term of abuse was not of itself uncommon in Cicero's range of insults or in invective generally. Antony and his henchmen suffer (*Fam.* 12. 25. 4; *Phil.* 8. 9), as, more elaborately, does Clodius, *nefanda et perniciosa labes civitatis* (*De Domo Sua* 133). As this example illustrates, the language of disease was the natural choice when describing the undermining and disruption of the metaphorical 'body politic'. But with Catiline, the metaphor is developed: if Catiline takes his followers as well as himself out of Rome, 'then there will be wiped out and destroyed not only this *pestis* now grown so large in the state but with it the root and seed of all our ills' (*In Cat.* 1. 30).[24] But 'if he alone is removed out of all this band of brigands, we shall appear perhaps to have gained a short respite from anxiety and fear, but the danger will remain and be set deep in the veins and vitals (*viscera*) of the republic' (1. 31).[25] The analogy Cicero goes on to develop is that of the recurrent illness whose feverish symptoms can be only temporarily relieved, but the nature of Catiline's infection and the problems associated with its eradication suggests not so much infectious disease as a malignant growth, whose physical remnants may remain deep in the *viscera* of the mother state, even when the main tumour is expelled. The *pestis* which has grown so large (*adulta*) is, then, not so much a monstrous offspring that has grown inside the mother state, as something even less recognizably human—a cancerous mole, the monstrous product of a misbegotten conception which was a recognized medical phenomenon in antiquity.[26] Rather than seeing in Catiline the distorted image of his heroic ancestor, Cicero portrays him as a malignant growth, a *monstrum* deformed beyond recognition as, and therefore clearly beyond comparison with, any human creature.

[24] *In Cat.* 1. 30: Hoc autem uno interfecto intellego hanc rei publicae pestem paulisper reprimi, non in perpetuum comprimi posse. Quod si sese eiecerit secumque suos eduxerit et eodem ceteros undique conlectos naufragos adgregarit, exstinguetur atque delebitur non modo haec tam adulta rei publicae pestis verum etiam stirps ac semen malorum omnium.

[25] *In Cat.* 1.31: . . . si ex tanto latrocinio iste unus tolletur, videbimur fortasse ad breve quoddam tempus cura et metu esse relevati, periculum autem residebit et erit inclusum penitus in venis atque in visceribus rei publicae. Ut saepe homines aegri morbo gravi, cum aestu febrique iactantur, si aquam gelidam biberunt, primo relevari videntur, deinde multo gravius vehementiusque adflictantur . . .

[26] *Myle* (Arist. *GA* 775^b 25) or *mylos* (Soranus 3. 9. 36); = unformed flesh, not *zoon* but not *apsychon* either: Arist. *HA* 638^a 24; pregnancy gone wrong: Arist. *GA* 776^a1 ff., cf. Galen; and *GA* 769^b11 on formation of monstrosities.

Conclusions

In conclusion, then, the emphasis that Pliny gives to M. Sergius is probably the product of his own particular moral/philosophical outlook, reflective of the cultural conditioning of his own day, rather than that of an earlier era. The political constraints of the Roman elite in the first century AD gave the *virtus/fortuna* antithesis an extra topicality in the philosophical atmosphere of the period which left its mark on Pliny. This is particularly noticeable in his treatment of Sergius, which differs significantly from the more conventional *exempla virtutis* which precede it in book 7, the implication being that Sergius was the one that really mattered to him. Here, the lists of worldly decorations and honours and triumphs cease, their place filled solely by instances of personal endurance against a wider backdrop of defeat and disgrace.

That he chose an *exemplum* in which the challenge to fortune in the form of political authority is mounted by the *virtus* of the physically disabled is due in part to the topicality of the latter in rhetorical exercises of the period, as discussed above. This may in turn be influenced by a real-life, high-profile example of disability seeking power, the future Emperor Claudius; although ironically the career of Claudius may have softened the actual dichotomy between disability and power in a period when attitudes to deformity generally were changing. Changing times and attitudes towards religion and deformity may have left Pliny comparatively indifferent to or unaware of the significance of the final chapter in the Sergius story, the attempt to debar him from sacrifice, unless this was a literary fiction. But it may also be that the outcome was less important to him than the moral/philosophical image of the struggle itself.

Finally, it is worth considering briefly the contrasting attitudes of Pliny towards two imperial embodiments of power: the disabled Claudius and his able-bodied successor, Nero.[27] The maimed but scholarly Claudius is in the main a positive exemplar of imperial power in the *Natural History*, even if Pliny does not praise his *virtus* as a ruler in so many words. No hint is given of his disability. His able-bodied successor, however, whose physique was

[27] Claudius and Nero in Pliny: see Beagon 1992: 17–18; Beagon forthcoming: introduction; (45); (46); Baldwin 1995: 56–78; Darwall-Smith 1996: 54. For the Flavian rehabilitation of Claudius, see Levick 1990: 187–93 and Darwall-Smith 1996: 48–55. However, the contrast was not straightforward. Miriam Griffin (1994: 307–15) has stressed the complexity of the responses to Claudius on the part of the Flavians: Pliny and, by implication, Vespasian, recognized negative elements in Claudius' rule. For Neronian tensions with regard to the Claudian past, see Griffin 1994: 307–15; 1976: 96–8. For those who wished to flatter or glorify Nero, the physical disparity between the imposing young man and his crippled, undignified predecessor was an obvious means of emphasizing the contrast between them in the former's favour: witness, of course, Seneca's *Apocolocyntosis*.

on public display athletically and aesthetically, in his roles as charioteer and singer, is condemned for his abuse of power and crimes against humanity. Inherently unnatural—his breech birth is described as *contra naturam*—Nero's lack of *virtus* as ruler is the true and ultimate deformity.[28]

For Cicero, writing 130 years earlier, in a period nearly midway between Sergius and Pliny, it was the misdeeds of a great-grandson, rather than the heroism of the great-grandfather, which dominated perceptions of the Sergian *gens*. Neither the *virtus/fortuna* antithesis nor its expression in the *exemplum* of the disabled war hero had yet acquired the resonances that they were to have in Pliny's day. But, in any case, the statesman and orator had developed his own agenda in engineering the destruction of Catiline, the unnatural monster whose moral deformity rendered him unique and removed him well beyond the scope of even the most unfavourable comparisons.

[28] Pliny derived the Neronian breech-birth anecdote from the memoirs of the emperor's mother, Agrippina. Directly or indirectly, his account probably influenced the recurrence of the motif in a later era, as an attribute of Shakespeare's Richard III: 'For I have often heard my mother say | I came into the world with my legs forward' (Henry VI, Part 3, s. 6. 70–1). See Scarcia 1991: 243–63; Beagon forthcoming: (46). He was, of course, a deformed ruler in the physical as well as the moral sense.

Women, Power, and Philosophy at Rome and Beyond

BARBARA LEVICK

PHILOSOPHY AND HISTORY

Is it more of a compliment to tell a philosopher that s/he might be an historian or vice versa? That depends partly on the source of the compliment. Certainly the second may be said of Miriam Griffin, and it is one of the qualities that for me are most admirable about her—quite apart from those of personality that endear her so much to colleagues and friends.

Historians should not be over-modest. Neither history nor philosophy is a field in which women came to the fore in antiquity. The woman philosopher was a rare bird—only one known in recorded history, it could be said,[1] leaving out the Pythagorean texts ascribed to women;[2] the female historian, as opposed to memoir writer, was virtually unheard of.[3]

AMBIGUITIES

The inquiry as to what part philosophy played in Roman women's education, what difference it made to their lives, if it 'empowered' them at all, involves ambiguities. We are better informed about the Roman Empire than about classical Greece or the Hellenistic world. More material survives from Rome and Italy and from the Empire that Rome governed, colonized, influenced, and educated; and *matronae* are now the subject of

It was while enjoying the generous hospitality of the Maison Suger, Paris, and the help of the director and staff of the library of the École Normale Supérieure, Paris, that I was able to read for this paper. I should like to record my grateful thanks to both institutions, as well as to the editors of this volume, first for the opportunity to contribute to it and then for their comments on the original draft.

[1] Lact. *Div. Inst.* 3. 25. 5. Ménage in 1690 found sixty-five, fifteen from the period 200 BC–AD 300; his translator admits definition problems (Zedler in Ménage 1984: pp. xvii–xix).

[2] Pohlenz 1964: 133; Thesleff 1965: 193–201 (Theano); Lefkowitz and Fant 1992: 163, no. 208 (abbrev. LF).

[3] But note Pamphile of Epidaurus (1st cent. AD): *Suda* iv. 15; *FHG* 3. 520–2, tr. LF 168, no. 219.

Hemelrijk's monograph (1999). But the boundaries of 'Greek' and 'Roman' are not clear, especially after the beginning of the Principate; nor is what counts as philosophy, as a philosopher, as power, even as education. The wide range of activities that counted as philosophy needs particular note: in antiquity rhetorical theory as well as logic, physics, and ethics;[4] by the fourth century, as the 'philosopher' Sosipatra shows, clairvoyance (Eun. *Vit. Phil.* 466–70). Further, it is hard to exclude the pub debater from being a *philosophus*, a lover of wisdom, even if s/he will never be *sapiens*.[5] Euphrosyne of Rome was 'pia, docta novem Musis, philosopha', dying at 20 (*ILS* 7783 (LF 169 no. 222)): the first two are achievements; so surely the third, if not of *sapientia*; Aurelia Leite of Paros 'loved wisdom, her husband, her children, her native city' (Pleket 1969: no. 31 at Lefkowitz 1983: 57).

The inquiry also and primarily deals with conflict in society and with attempts to resolve it. A brilliant essay by Blok (1987) attributes specific and normative ideas of sexual asymmetry, and consequent difficulties in writing about women in history, to nineteenth-century thinking. Another contributor to her volume, Versnel (1987: 73), observes that in stressing recent thinking, Blok has not drawn attention to the fact that men in the ancient world had similar ideas (which may have influenced modern ones).[6] Her work is also important for ancient historians concerned with gender issues and the ways they were managed, intellectually and practically, in ancient societies.

The Dangers of Philosophy

Philosophy, asking, as it does, fundamental questions, should be dangerous, and so it has been seen, especially in insecure polities: Athens after the Peloponnesian War, Eastern Europe under Soviet domination, the Roman Republic. For elite men in the mid-second century BC the arrival of philosophers enlivened intellectual and political life. Philosophy gave weight to

[4] e.g. Cic. *De Orat.* 3. 142, with Gwynne 1926: 112–18; Quint. 1. 1 pr. 15 (cf. Cic. *Brut.* 309); cf. Marrou 1956: 289. Triad: J. Barnes 1997: 1.

[5] It is not clear what *φιλόσοφος* means in relation to non-professionals. The verbal *γυνὴ φιλοσοφοῦσα* in Mus. 3. 11. 1. 1H is plain, and the following *ἡ φιλόσοφος* is surely also the woman in pursuit of *σοφία*, *sapientia*; cf. 'sapientiae studium' in Pliny *Ep.* 1. 22. 6, and Lact. *Inst. Div.* 3. 25. 6; a *sapiens* after years of study: Pliny *Ep.* 5. 16. 8. Hence Harmon's caution with the word in Luc. *Merc. Cond.* 36 (Loeb 3, 473). Cf. Barnes in this volume: 293–306.

[6] Elm 1994: 15–17, cautions against accepting such ancient polarities as public/private and male/female: in the first the categories are not distinct, the second 'denies . . . women imagination, creativity, and thus the potential . . . to appropriate dominant symbols and ideas in ways that revise and undercut them'. We need to operate with these polarities to understand the dominant ideology and what had to be undercut.

forensic and political argument; it became worth demolishing a politician's philosophical pretensions (Cic. *In Pis.* with Nisbet 1961 ad loc.; Vell. Pat. 2. 100. 5). But philosophy, by laying down principles that govern politics, might seem to threaten a dominant regime. Even acquiescence in a framework assumes the right to change it. Reservations at Rome led to bans on rhetoricians and philosophers, although, as Miriam Griffin has noted, they simply inhibited teaching in public: the philosopher in the street was not to be encouraged (1989: 3).

Philosophy's pedigree and high claims made it a natural question whether any but males in full possession of citizen rights were fit for it. Philosophers' discussions focus on whether women and slaves should study it or not; it was a convenient belief that it was 'suspect and hateful' to the 'multitudo' (Lact. *Inst. Div.* 3. 25).[7] But its very standing as the ultimate occupation for good men (although cf. Marrou 1956: 125 on Isocrates) gave rise to a cloud; there could be objections to men doing it, deriving from their station (Griffin 1988: 143–5).[8]

One-man rule, even after 27 BC, presented sharp decisions—to collaborate or not with a regime that approached the tyranny excoriated by Plato and Polybius. An indicator in this change was the life and suicide of Cato the Younger. As Flavius Aper comments to Curiatius Maternus in Tacitus' *Dialogus*, to offend for a friend was one thing, another to offend on Cato's behalf (10. 6).[9] His example headed the enforced suicides of politicians in the following century and a half. Less dramatically, the philosophy that taught adherents to despise external 'goods', in which the benefits of *principes* would figure, could seem subversive. 'Are you philosophers teaching us to despise our emperors, then?' (Epict. 1. 20. 9, at Millar 1965: 148).

Miriam Griffin has observed that Stoicism won when oratory lost

[7] Cicero reserves philosophy for the special; Epicurus allows it to all, including women and slaves: Quae universa perdiscere neque feminae possunt, quibus intra puberes annos officia mox usibus domesticis profutura discenda sunt, neque servi . . . neque pauperes aut opifices aut rustici; ob eam causam Tullius ait abhorrere a multitudine philosophia . . . Denique nullas umquam mulieres philosophari docuerunt praeter unam ex omni memoria Themisten neque servos praeter unum Phaedonem quem male servientem redemisse ac docuisse traduntur (12, 15). (These universal things women cannot learn, who in their youth must be taught those duties which will soon be of use in domestic tasks, nor can slaves . . . nor poor men, nor artisans, nor agricultural labourers. For this reason, Cicero says philosophy recoils from the crowd. Finally they taught no women to philosophize except one, from all recorded history, Themiste, nor any slaves except one, Phaedo, who, they say, as he was ill-suited to being a slave, was released and taught.) The multitude: 'et suspecta et invisa': Cic. *Tusc.* 2. 1. 4.

[8] Griffin 1989: 12: the attitude depending on attitudes to things Greek; Roman exemplary conduct was superior. Possible subversion of religion: Brunt 1989.

[9] Cato 'the philosopher': already in 63 (*Pro Mur.*); Sen. *De Clem.* 2. 5. 2. Augustus: Malitz 1988: 161 (favourable).

importance in politics (Griffin 1989: 10; see Tac. *Dial.*). The consolations of philosophy were attractive when political frustration was added to natural disaster and the grief of bereavement. 'Liberalia studia', Cicero's resource (*De Off.* 2. 2), the remedy that the exiled Seneca recommended to his mother (*Ad Helv.* 17. 3), were the refuge for everyone in flight from Fortune. But even philosophy as a time-consuming refuge might seem to defy established authority when the dull Gazette was read everywhere with greater attention to discover what public events Thrasea Paetus had boycotted (Tac. *Ann.* 16. 22).

Hence in part a misleading notion, the 'Stoic Opposition', compressing varied political cases into an undifferentiated mass and eliding issues that differed between generations over a period of about seventy years.[10] Contemporaries and careful historians differentiated between their conduct. The actual effect of philosophy in politics was patchy, beyond giving moral backing to political resolve. It is described by Brunt in connection with Epictetus:

> It would be wrong to infer that he sought to change society except by effecting a spiritual change in the minds of men, or that men whose minds had been so changed would have taken actions different in objective content from those ordinary, decent persons who had never heard a word of Stoic philosophy thought it proper to take. (Brunt 1977*a*: 30)[11]

The reinforcing function of Stoicism,[12] as Brunt points out (1977*a*: 34), lay in uncompromising rigour, buttressed by a claim that Cicero makes in a Posidonian section of the *De Officiis*: what it is right to do cannot conflict with what is in the agent's own true interest (3. 21–32). Power and mastery in living rests in knowledge of how to live, about which an emperor can do nothing (Epict. 4. 1. 63). Miriam Griffin concludes that ethical doctrines were too general to provide unambiguous directives (1989: 32). Helvidius Priscus' purpose was to engage in politics in the face of what chance might bring.[13] Under the conciliatory regimes that followed the death of Domitian, and with the protagonists gone, it was safe for philosophical interest to become what Malitz calls a kind of upper-class state religion (1988: 179, citing C. P. Jones 1971: 53); relations between the élite and pro-

[10] O. Murray 1967: 251: 'The very existence of a Stoic ideology is obscure'. Other sceptics: Griffin 1989: 11 n. 20; cf. ibid. 21 (seventy years, with Sen. *Ep.* 73, rebutting an established reputation for trouble-making).

[11] Swain 1990: 199: Cato's qualities 'owing more to nature'. Note Hor. *Sat.* 1. 4. 115–17.

[12] Annas 1989: 167, cf. 170, notes Chrysippus defending some institutions; Stoics might be too ready to accommodate existing institutions.

[13] Brunt 1975: 9; Griffin 1988: 149, 1989: 33; Tac. *Hist.* 4. 5: 'quo firmior . . . rem publicam capesseret' (so he might engage in politics in a more constant fashion).

fessional philosophers also bloomed—with some feeling that the Academy was to be preferred to the Stoa (Swain 1997: 186). The integration of philosophy into Roman life, already noticed for the period between Cicero and Seneca, was helped, perhaps, by the growing presence of Greeks in the Senate (Griffin 1988: 138).

In all the well-known cases of youths, Nero (Suet. *Nero* 52), Agricola (Tac. *Agr.* 4. 5), and Alexander Severus (HA *Sev. Alex.* 14. 5), being warned off philosophy, it is the mother who advises. The widows Agrippina and Procilla were taking over the father's function, and Julia Mamaea, not her equestrian husband, made her son a claimant for power.[14] But women were in charge of a child's first instruction, and would have recommendations for his second stage. For satisfactory education, Quintilian believed, both parents should be as well educated as possible (1. 1. 6, in Pomeroy 1975: 171).

Philosophy did not fit these boys' station in life, 'imperator' and 'Roman and senator'. In the last instance Mamaea brings on Virgil's injunction to leave art, forensic oratory, and astronomy to others and concentrate on government (*Aen.* 6. 848–54).[15] A weak form of the objection was that philosophy was a mere accomplishment, to which practitioners gave excessive importance,[16] to be left to others, some tainted by inferior status (Malitz 1988: 174 n. 145).[17] A stronger, unexpressed, was that philosophy set up values that could negate those of the statesman. A man who took Epicureanism seriously might abstain from politics altogether,[18] an unwelcome outcome for mothers dependent on vicarious political satisfaction (e.g. Sen. *Ad Helv.* 14. 2).

Epicureans were not absent from politics, though doubts might be felt about their seriousness as philosophers.[19] For Stoics the choice of a senatorial career was 'appropriate for a man of a certain station' (Brunt 1977*a*: 31). But, as Brunt points out, 'it was no less in accord with Stoic teaching that he (in this case Arrian) retired from official life with . . . many years of activity before him. . . . Seneca continually recommended this course to officials like Lucilius'. Even without direct challenge, alternative standards might blunt the claims of practicality, ambition, and self-interest, and, in a

[14] Malitz 1988: 152, noting Seneca's father (*Ad Helv.* 17. 4; *Ep.* 108. 22); Alexander Severus' father: *PIR*[2] G171 (procurator).

[15] Mus. 8. 32–40H: studying philosophy is a ruler's duty.

[16] Plut. *De Lib. Educ.* 10: they should have a taste (γεῦμα) of the rest, but philosophy should take precedence (τὴν δὲ φιλοσοφίαν πρεσβεύειν).

[17] Tac. *Hist.* 3. 81. 1, is unmerciful to Musonius.

[18] Temporini 1978: 164; Fowler 1989. Conditions for participation: Griffin 1988 esp. 145; general effect of philosophy: Marrou 1956: 282; Griffin 1989: 20.

[19] Notably Cicero's victim of *In Pis.*; scepticism: Griffin 1975: 12; criteria for participation, Griffin 1989: 33.

princeps, weaken his grasp on power (not that Marcus Aurelius failed the test—cf. Brunt 1975: 23 for his conventional view of Pius).

Special factors may have been operating in the first two mothers. From 54 onwards Agrippina had to fear the influence of Nero's Stoic adviser Seneca, while Julia Procilla had lost her husband under Gaius when he refused to bring a political prosecution; such principles, strengthened by philosophical tenets, could endanger her son. But Tacitus' phrasing does not imply this, and under Nerva and Trajan there was good reason to stress ties to link Agricola and his father with the earlier martyrs. In this perspective, the success of his mother's efforts to deter him did Agricola little credit. Rather, Tacitus presents her action as a function of normal aristocratic thinking about priorities.

A Girl's Education

The dangers of philosophy might seem worse for girls. Without irony, apparently, Virginia Woolf included herself in the category of 'uneducated Englishwomen' (1929: 103). She never went to school or university, so did not receive her brothers' formal education. Roman education, less institutionalized, was more accessible for girls in well-off families. Up to a certain level, that is, and according to parental expectations and resources; but formal education ended when they married at 13 upwards.[20]

As a model, Hemelrijk takes Pliny the Younger's letter (*Ep.* 5. 15) on the death of Minicia Marcella, with its emphasis on the moral qualities of the girl whose wedding day had been fixed, rather than intellectual attainment or promise (1999: 60; see also *ILS* 1030). This emphasis was natural, apart from the fact that Minicius Fundanus was a friend of Plutarch and a student of philosophy:[21] Minicia's qualities of character were achieved, and unimpaired on her deathbed; her intellectual promise could not have been fulfilled. Elsewhere, Pliny praises a Quintilianus for bringing up his child 'as befits a daughter of yours and a grandchild of Tutilius' (*Ep.* 6. 32). The praise given to the 'continentissimus' Quintilianus suggests the philosopher; Tutilius is probably the C. Tutilius Hostilianus of Cortona in Etruria, 'philosophus Stoicus' praised as such and for his excellence as a father by his children, who was exiled under Vespasian, perhaps with Musonius, another Etruscan, with whom he evidently returned (*ILS* 7779; Dio 66. 13. 2, with Buecheler 1908: 196).

[20] Sources for this section are in Friedlaender (1920: i. 270–3).

[21] Plut. *De Ira Cohib.* 1 and *passim*; Pliny *Ep.* 5. 16. 8. This point is stressed by Clark 1981: 207.

Exceptional though these parents were, and so perhaps their views on education, Pliny approves and disseminates these views; the stress on other-regarding virtues braced by courage would have been endorsed by every right-thinking Roman as the centre of Roman education for girls, just as the civic and military virtues (naturally including courage) were to be inculcated in boys. Although there was a linguistic difficulty, in that essentially it meant manliness *par excellence*, women too could possess *virtus*, which conventionally corresponds to ἀρετή. Musonius Rufus specifically denies that even the narrower ἀνδρεία is a virtue peculiar to men (4. 15. 1. 3H).[22] The linguistic discord could be played on, as Seneca did when he talked of women (such as Cornelia mother of the Gracchi) 'quas conspecta *virtus* inter magnos *viros* posuit' (whom noted virtue placed among mighty men: *Ad Helv.* 16. 5). Awkward suggestions of equality in ἀρετή could be got round by dividing it into two, men's (commanding) and women's (obeying) as in Aristotle's *Politics* (1260ª8).

Here is scope for an education in philosophy, but we do not know if her *praeceptores* had begun to instruct Minicia.[23] The qualities of character that her father and her friend Pliny were so keen to see inculcated could be taught by precept and example, without theoretical founding (Griffin 1989: 8). Some of the earliest and least well-educated Romans were among the most virtuous (e.g. Livy 9. 16. 9). None the less, the beliefs that underlay their conduct could be brought to the surface, elaborated, and defended.

It is philosophers (not entirely disinterested, perhaps) who argue the question and recommend the inclusion of philosophy in women's education. Plato's *Republic,* no doubt in the face of ridicule, advocated equal education for men and women (452a–b, 456b), women were reported in his audiences, as in those of Pythagoras and Epicurus, and active in the Pythagorean school. The Stoa was especially noted for espousing their cause in philosophy; and Seneca, while not explicitly stating their aptitude, insists on their ability to possess the qualities it encourages.[24] The influential Musonius devoted one discourse to the question (Pohlenz 1964: 303).

[22] He tacitly acknowledges the link ἀνδρείαν/ἀνδράσιν (courage/manliness); women too must have courage (ἀνδρίζεσθαι) and keep themselves clean of cowardice (καθαρεύειν δειλίας). The need was famous: Eur. *Med.* 250; cf. Plut. *Γυναικῶν ἀρεταί* (*Mor.* 242e–263c), following tradition (Ziegler 1949: 221). Later discussions of female virtue and rationality: Clark 1993: 121–6.

[23] Hemelrijk 1999: 61 and n. 7 is properly cautious: 'possibly also philosophy and the mathematical subjects'; in her summary, 63, she writes that 'a thorough education . . . was recommended, . . . literature, philosophy and, possibly, some mathematics'.

[24] Pohlenz 1964: 140, notes failure to draw practical conclusions. Hense 1905 on Mus. 3 cites Lact. *Inst. Div.* 3. 25, on the Stoic view and compares Clem. Alex. *Strom.* 4. 8. (P: 590), and Sen. *Ad Marc.* 16. 1.

Talking on education for girls he insisted that without philosophy neither men nor women could be regarded as properly educated (Mus. 4. 19. 1. 6–8H). He argues from the fact that both sexes derive their reasoning power (λόγος) from the gods and use it in their mutual dealings (3. 9. 1. 1H),[25] and asks why it is right for men but not women to seek the way to the good life, which is what doing philosophy is (3. 9. 1. 14H).

Plutarch, assigning philosophy a more negative, prophylactic aim, wants a wife to receive training in it along with mathematics and astronomy. She will not swallow beliefs in magic charms while she is under the charm of Plato's or Xenophon's words (*Praec. Conj.* 48). The scene is Greece, but Plutarch was a Roman citizen, a cosmopolitan figure writing when the cultural worlds of the Greek and Roman elite were coming ever closer together.

Plutarch's advice to husband and wife envisages not her formal education but its continuation under her husband's guidance; he is to choose suitable doctrines and discuss them with her, while she is to regard him as a guide, philosopher, and teacher of the finest and most inspired type (*Praec. Conj.* 14, 48).[26] No doubt Plutarch's treatise advocating the education of women included philosophy in the curriculum as early as he considered it practicable (fr. 15. 242–9 (Loeb): *Ὅτι καὶ γυναῖκα παιδευτέον*—since even a woman should be educated).

But the culminating nature of the subject and the fact that Greek was required to understand it carried it beyond what a Roman girl could normally reach (Hemelrijk 1999: 40).[27] Plutarch describes Cornelia, daughter of Metellus Scipio and wife of Pompey, as being 'well versed in Greek and Latin literature, in playing the lyre, and in geometry; she had been accustomed to listen to philosophical discourse with profit' (*Pomp.* 55. 1).[28] Philosophy, the last item on this list, might have five other disciplines as necessary preliminaries.[29] If a young woman had any education in philoso-

[25] Lysistrata (quoting Euripides) claims intelligence 'although I am a woman' (Arist. *Lys.* 1125–7, cited by Lefkowitz 1993: 54, with n. 19).

[26] Xenophon had provided an example of what might be achieved in *Oec.* 7. 1–3, where Ischomachus' teaching had made a wife capable of managing his estate. (Ménage 1984: 23, takes philosophical teaching by the husband up to the time of Héloise, cf. Migne 1885: 178. 74.)

[27] Hemelrijk 1999: 252 n. 147 notes that Greek was the language of love at Rome, as well as of intellectual enquiry, and an old woman speaking Greek was open to mockery (Mart. *Ep.* 10. 68; Juv. 6. 184–99).

[28] Clark 1981: 199, suggests that the subjects were physics or ethics (thus not simply moral improvement); cf. Luc. *Merc. Cond.* 36: the woman listens to lectures. Women composers have experienced particular difficulties. Woolf 1929: 53 n. 1 cites a contemporary music critic using Dr Johnson's 'woman preacher' dictum against Tailleferre.

[29] Lact. *Div. Inst.* 3. 25. 11 (grammar, rhetoric, geometry, music, astronomy).

phy before marriage it would be gleaned from father and brothers, or from sitting in on their discussions with their tutors, especially residents (Hemelrijk 1999: 25, 41).[30]

Atticus continued to have his daughter taught after marriage (Suet. *Gram.* 16), and a mistress of a household had a better chance of educating herself by attending the lectures that carried philosophical inquiry forward, though not all the practitioners lived up to their high claims.[31] Young women who did not live in a household with a resident philosopher would have to attend lectures supplemented (or replaced) by discussion and dinner-table conversation. Women who could not attend might, if lucky, have access to libraries, their father's or husband's, much as Victorian girls used collections in their own homes.[32] The Elder Seneca's wife Helvia presumably got her learning from books (*Ad Helv.* 17. 4, with Hemelrijk 1999: 41). A woman could not travel to continue it, unless, as seems to be the case with the pupil of Nicomachus of Gerasa (Hemelrijk 1999: 38 with n. 76), a father or husband posted abroad chose to take his family with him; not many postings would take them to the free city of Athens or to Massilia; Asia Minor, Egypt, and Syria were better prospects.

Important as Minicia's moral qualities were in a Roman woman, they were not necessarily enough to secure her a husband. Beside looks and health, a large dowry was crucial; if it included jewellery it would also enhance her looks (cf. Pliny *Ep.* 6. 32. 1).[33] But skills would add to the girl's value and help to secure a better off, better born, and more influential husband as an ally for the family in its political or material advancement. Moral and worldly considerations could reinforce each other. Notoriously, from the second century BC, when Greek culture became more available, all forms of display were beginning to preoccupy competitive Roman society;

[30] Lysistrata has good judgement because she has listened to many speeches by her father and older men and is not badly educated (Arist. *Lys.* 1127, cited by Lefkowitz 1993: 54; Victorian analogy: Woolf 1976: 103).

[31] Teaching of philosophy: Marrou 1956: 284–6. First lectures at Rome: Plut. *Cato maior* 22; Gell. 6 (7). 14. 8; typical activity: Petr. *Sat.* 71. 12. Women attending (*προσιούσας*) lectures or discussions: Mus. 3. 12. 1. 7H. Professionals despised: Juv. 2. 50, 60, 3. 114. Philosophy as a mask for depravity: e.g. Quint. 1 pr. 15.

[32] Virginia Woolf is an example, lucky in that her father was a man of letters: Woolf 1929: 46, on 'Judith Shakespeare': 'She was not sent to school. She had no chance of learning grammar and logic, let alone of reading Horace and Virgil. She picked up a book now and then, one of her brother's perhaps and read a few pages.' Victorian education: Woolf 1938: 9 and 263 n. 1.

[33] Wiseman 2000: 267, cites Menichetti 1995: 57, for the motif of women washing: 'queste raffigurazioni . . . alludono . . . alla *paideia* femminile della cura del corpo tramite cui si acquisisce quel potere di seduzione dell'uomo mediante il quale si accede alla sfera di matrimonio'. (This motif . . . alludes . . . to the feminine *paideia* concerning the care of the body: a medium by which one may acquire a power of seduction over a man—and through which one approaches the sphere of marriage.)

and fashion will have played its part, as in other social developments (Wolfram 1985: 85), carrying women beyond the minimum required for them to give their children primary instruction.[34]

Up to a certain proficiency and notably in literature and music, women's accomplishments won approval.[35] Pliny boasted of the musicianship of his young wife, who was able to set his verses to music, a double achievement: displaying her attainments Calpurnia was also displaying Pliny's (*Ep.* 4. 119. 2–4; so Stat. *Silv.* 3. 5. 64–6). Dancing was permissible, but not to a professional standard: when Sallust reported Sempronia as a budding geisha, dancing more skilfully than a respectable women needed capped being well read and able to play the lyre; so did 'many other accomplishments which minister to voluptuousness' (*Bell. Cat.* 25. 2; see Clark 1981: 200 with n. 25). Acting and other performance arts leading to public or semi-public appearances were disreputable for both sexes because of the class and moral taint that clung to professionals (Wiseman 2000: 266 n. 12), still more duelling in the arena, the province of slave, often criminal, gladiators (Levick 1983: 101). It was a matter of class, ultimately of the stability of society. Privileges and exclusivity carried a price: the élite had to be seen in possession of the *virtus* that was their justification, deploying it in the service of the state (Sall. *Bell. Jug.* 85, esp. 17). Exclusivity meant keeping apart and accepting restrictions on manners and behaviour, unknown to lower ranks, that defined the aristocracy and protected it from class envy; they seemed essential to its survival.[36] No such objections applied to philosophy.

Problems for Women

Considered so far, problems for girls who pursued philosophy have been mostly practical. There were also positive objections, some raised at the opening stage, others complaints made against those who had already embarked on it, and probably displacements for the first type.

A woman doing philosophy was on a level floor with a man. Like her male coevals, she was at liberty to question the foundations of society, both the

[34] Mothers educating their children are paradigmatic: Cic. *Brut.* 211; Tac. *Dial.* 28; *Agr.* 4. 2; Plut. *Gracchi* 1. 3, cf. Val. Max. 4. 4 pr.

[35] See Clark 1981: 199 for *lanificium* as taking the place of 19-cent. 'accomplishments'; 200 for some reasonably well-educated women, seen through poets' eyes (Catullus 35; Prop. 2. 13. 11).

[36] So Augustus' 'moral' legislation and the Larinum *SC* may be interpreted. British officers might not carry parcels; when in the 19 cent. the actor became a gentleman, he was banned from entering a theatre carrying a parcel (Alec Guinness, BBC Radio 3, 7 Aug. 2000).

way of life on which her own status was based and the political activities that were an expression of it, the more clearly because, like Miss Lucilla Marjoribanks (Oliphant 1865–6: iii, ch. 27), the Romans eschewed political programmes and theoretically at least supported a politician on the basis of personal merit (*virtus*) making him 'the right man'. Yet, while it was salutary for a young Minicia to reflect on her own conduct, she was not quite a free agent: 'With a few exceptions, all Roman women were for their entire lives subject to some degree of limitation on their capacity for independent legal action' (Gardner 1986: 5):[37] there was a difficulty in such a person directing her critical attention to politics.

Two features of an activity might make it objectionable for women: that it was unsuitable for persons of their class or that it took them beyond what was permissible for their gender. (The same objections were distinguished by Virginia Woolf 1938: 241.) The first did not apply to philosophy, unless a woman was associating with radical Cynics. Nor were disturbances of political functions the danger for women, as they had none, but an even more fundamental threat: the perturbation of traditional gender roles, which could finally mean the disturbance of traditional marriage settlements and alliances, uncertainties as to paternity, and an interruption of the supply of manpower at all levels (vital to Rome, and a source of anxiety from the second century BC onwards: Brunt 1971: 345–75).[38]

The nineteenth-century justification for such social objections, beyond the knockdown religious argument that 'the desire for learning in women was against the will of God' (Woolf 1938: 46, from Butts 1937: 138), was twofold and had an ancient pedigree: that the female brain was incapable of going into difficult subjects (so that the effort was pointless)[39] or that it could not do so without endangering its and its owner's proper functions (so that she would become incapable of her duties or unwilling to perform them, becoming unsatisfactory or even unacceptable as a wife). In the earlier part of the twentieth century it could take the form of imputing lack of 'femininity' (a word of approval applied to women) to academic pursuits (Hemelrijk 1999: 89, 282 n. 138).

Attitudes must not be foisted on antiquity, but Hemelrijk rightly points out the defensive character of Musonius' and Plutarch's comments (1999: 70). There might be uncertainty as to how far Helvia's 'smattering' might

[37] Discussion of tutorship: Gardner 1986: 14–22; Clark 1981: 207 with n. 51, and 1993: 15.

[38] Concern was demonstrated in the years before Ti. Gracchus' tribunate of 133 (App. *Bell. Civ.* 1. 7–11); in Augustus' marriage legislation, offering privileges to fecund mothers and penalizing the unmarried and childless; and in *alimenta* schemes under the Empire.

[39] Clark 1981: 208, has a good assortment of weaknesses. Simplification is possible: Hemelrijk 1999: 40, on Nicomachus' *Enchiridion*.

go without danger. When favourable judgement was passed it was worth adding, as Plutarch did about Cornelia wife of Pompey, who listened to philosophical discourses with profit, that 'she had a nature that was free from the unpleasant meddlesomeness (περιεργασία) which such accomplishments are apt to impart to young women', as Pliny the Younger thought it worth calling a political friend of the people '*innoxie* popularis' (*Ep.* 10. 31. 3).[40]

Logic and Morals

We have to distinguish two aspects of philosophy: logical and moral. Barnes has argued that Stoic logic was not in decline in the first century AD, but rather exercised a strong attraction on students, which some philosophers deplored (J. Barnes 1997: 1–11). It was to the ethical wing, one of whose merits was that it helped victims of misfortune to bear their fate, that women might most easily gain approved access; in Lucian a lady is supposed to be listening to a lecture on chastity (*Merc. Cond.* 36). Musonius expressly claims that he is not attempting to lead women to anything more, but they could not have been shut out altogether: Juvenal, the most virulent purveyor of women in philosophy, introduces his victim by saying that 'she sets down definitions on moral behaviour'; syllogisms were whizzing past like slingshot (6. 444, 449).[41] Proper conduct must be based on correct doctrines and theory: making this point, Brunt remarks that: 'though men's primary aim should be to purify their minds and ascertain their duties, they cannot, for this very purpose, dispense with logic, by whose aid alone truth can be distinguished from falsehood in ethical, as in all other, propositions' (1977*a*: 25). And later:

> Epictetus implies that both he and his pupils are familiar with these puzzles (e.g. 2. 19). Moreover, his view of the life according to nature depends on the metaphysical Stoic conception of nature as a rational and moral being. . . . The discourses never present an account or justification of Stoic metaphysics, but they presuppose that its

[40] Hemelrijk 1999: 17, juxtaposes Plut. *Pomp.* 55. 1 (cf. *Zon.* 10. 9), and Sall. *Cat.* 25. 2; Sallust uses his material to justify finding Sempronia guilty of transgressions.

[41] In Mus. 3. 11. 1. 5–10H objectors complain that women in philosophy classes might get above themselves, mixing with men and doing verbal exercises, practising sophistry, and solving syllogisms, when they ought to be sitting at home spinning wool. Nor should men give up their proper duties to spend time on words. The aim of philosophy is action. Musonius deplores verbal felicity and excessive cleverness, if women are to do philosophy as women (4. 19. 1. 9: γρανότητα περὶ λόγους καὶ δεινότητά τινα περιττὴν . . . εἴπερ φιλοσοφήσουσιν ὡς γυναῖκες). They belong elsewhere: Mus. *Disc. ap.* Stob. 2. 31. 126 (Wachsmuth 1871: ii. 239), with Friedlaender 1920: i. 298.

doctrines are known to and accepted by Epictetus' pupils. One must learn Stoic theology as a means of attaining blessedness (2. 14, 7–13) . . . presumably by the reading and exposition of Chrysippus' works. (Brunt 1977*a*: 25)

In its most immediate version the objection was again derived from the questioning nature of philosophy, whatever the questions. Philosophy is not something entirely for a room of one's own. It proceeds through group reading, discussion, and interaction, perhaps after a lecture. Expressions of opinion given on level terms were not expected from women, but, engaged in debate, they might challenge views held by husband or male kin, possibly displaying unacceptable intellectual superiority, and again undermining the 'rational' basis of Roman society and gender relationships (cf. Woolf 1929: 30 n. 2 on Johnson's dictum 'Men fear that women are an overmatch for them'). Juvenal in *Satire* 6 shows the world upside-down by pleading for a husband to be allowed his little errors (6. 456).

Other criticisms come, more seriously, from Epictetus—though as an ex-slave he had no reason to respect the upper echelons of society. Lax women of Rome kept copies of Plato's *Republic* because it advocated sharing wives (fr. 15).[42] Community of women and children was a part of the Stoic programme too, under the influence of Cynic doctrine that life required as little organization as possible (J. von Arnim 1903–5: i. 62, no. 269; iii. 183, no. 278); but the *Republic* was the classic text. If Romans misunderstood the *Republic*, they were not alone: it took Annas (1976) to show that it had little that was 'feminist' about it either. As Lefkowitz went on to note, 'the purpose of educating women . . . was to make women think as much like men as possible, since once women thought like men, they would be able to act in the men's (and their own) best interests' (1990: 800, 806).

Naturally, what struck fathers about the enhancement of a girl's attractions through education was obvious to daughters and wives. There could be affectation—and for opponents it was necessary to invent it. Lucian's woman mistreats her household philosopher: she listens to a discourse at her toilet, interrupting it when she has to reply to a letter from her lover; she puts her tutor in a carriage with her toy-boy; her dog pups in his cloak (*Merc. Cond.* 33, 36). The juxtaposition of 'philosophy' and sexual misconduct, with the instructor in his appropriate position in the woman's social scale, is a piquant literary theme more effective than a bald accusation of treating philosophy as a way of showing off[43] and is already found in

[42] Male philosophers in error too: Luc. *Fug.* 18.

[43] Sen. *Ad Helv.* 17. 4: they do not use it for wisdom, but prepare for indulgence (non ad sapientiam utuntur sed ad luxuriam instruuntur); Juv. 6. 445: she desires too much to seem

Horace, where the old woman in pursuit of the poet has philosophical tracts amongst her silken pillows (*Ep.* 8. 15).[44] Here it takes advantage of the fact that philosophy was considered a 'dignified refuge' for the elderly, especially widows, while continued interest in sex was derided (Hemelrijk 1999: 51, with nn. 147–8, 95).

No doubt there was change over time, and women studying philosophy, even its technical aspects, became more familiar. The tensions that are observable, and defensive tone of advocates and the offensive attacks of detractors show that debate was going on; one was afoot at the same time about slaves, their status, and treatment (Sen. *Ep.* 47, cf. e.g. Tac. *Ann.* 14. 42–5). The impression of change is supported by Seneca's acknowledgement of his father's commitment to ancestral practice and old-fashioned strictness (*Ad Helv.* 17. 3). The progress of divorce over two and a half centuries and the rapid demise of 'illegitimacy', an accepted means of denigration until fifty years ago, show that wagging heads grow tired. But there was no change on the nineteenth- and twentieth-century scale, as pressure from industrial and technological developments and the demand for skilled labour, sharpened by war, opened new jobs and professions to women. Small adjustments were made in women's social and legal status, in part connected with the need to sustain families and fortunes[45] and, at the end of the Republic, with the absence of men on service. Old ideals remained intact.

Women in Philosophy

For all the obstacles to women in philosophy, the list is considerable, though it contains more patrons, listeners, and dedicatees than practitioners (Hemelrijk 1999: 252 n. 148): Cicero's friend Caerellia made a copy of the *De Finibus* before publication (ibid. 55, 257 n. 171; *Ad Att.* 13. 21a. 2(4)); Augustus' sister Octavia, recipient of a discourse by the Stoic Athenagoras (Plut. *Publ.* 17. 8); Livia, accepting consolation from Areus on the death of Nero Drusus (Sen. *Ad Marc.* 4. 2–5. 6); Marcia and Helvia, Seneca's addressees; Nicomachus' patron; Martial's poet Theophila, at home in two schools (7. 69. 1–6); Plotina, patron of the Garden (*IG* 2/3² 1099); Galen's friend Arria, probably the mother of M. Nonius Arrius Mucianus, consul

learned (docta nimis cupit . . . videri). Such charges continued: Clark 1993: 131. Men showed off too: Nep. *Vit. Att.* 17. 3; Tac. *Hist.* 4. 5; Quint. 12. 3. 12; Pliny *Ep.* 1. 22. 6.

[44] Friedlaender 1920: i. 299, collects instances of such opposition.

[45] Women in public life in Asia Minor: MacMullen 1980: 213–16; full and nuanced discussion Bremen 1996.

201 (*PIR*² A1115; Galen, *Ad Pis. de theriaca* 14. 213); the dedicatee of Diogenes Laertius' *Lives and Doctrines of the Philosophers* (3. 47). Julia Domna was ἡ φιλόσοφος Ἰουλία (Dio 76. 15. 7, 78; Phil. *Vit. Soph.* 622); Mamaea, careful for her son, is nevertheless said to have summoned Origen to Antioch (Eus. *Hist. Eccl.* 6. 21. 3). The schools to which we hear of women devoting themselves were largely the Academy and the Porch, increasingly to Platonism; Pythagoreanism was an exotic alternative that seemed to prove particularly attractive (Ménage 1984: 12; Clark 1989: pp. xvi–xviii).

Part of the change was due to the developing role of imperial women, whose social position demanded education to the highest degree consistent with female functions at a court which was the focus of Greek intellectual efforts and aspirations. They could hardly be suspected of subverting the social and political order that their menfolk headed, nor often of planning to replace him. With her husband the Empress Salonina was a patron of Plotinus and, but for the machinations of courtiers, would have promoted his scheme to found a city of philosophers in Campania (Porphyry, *Vit. Plot.* 9. 12–14).[46]

There was another reason for politicians of principle to look kindly on their wives studying philosophy. Women's 'power', from rocking the cradle onwards, consisted in influence over men, for which, in a vocabulary enriched by Roman obsession with dominion, *potentia*, with its undercurrent of disapproval, is often used (Mehl 1974: 67). Informal councils might contain female members of seniority and connections; the most famous met in 44 BC after the death of Caesar (Cic. *Ad Att.* 15. 11). Individuals would consult their wives and necessarily leave them to take decisions in their absence. The wife's value as counsellor was enhanced if her judgement was guided by more than native common sense and authorized by principle, especially one consistent with a philosophy that the husband had shared with his wife.

As participants women appear most often at crises. One of the first to follow Cato's example was his daughter Porcia, wife of the Academic Q. Caepio Brutus, who suffocated herself after her husband's death at Philippi (Val. Max. 4. 6. 5; Plut. *Brut.* 53.4). Sometimes women took the lead, as in the famous case of Arria in AD 42.[47] More commonly they acted alongside male relatives, as with Barea Soranus and Servilia; and as Paulina (Dio 62.

[46] Friedlaender 1920: i. 300, notes that Porphyry married a friend's widow Marcella, mother of seven—and an advanced student of philosophy: Porph. *Ad Marc.* 1–9.

[47] *PIR*² A1113, citing Dio 60. 16. 5–9; Pliny *Ep.* 3. 16; 6. 24. 5; Tac. *Ann.* 16. 34; Mart. 1. 13; *ILS* 6261.

25. 1) and the younger Arria (*PIR*² A1114, with Tac. *Ann.* 16. 34) tried to do when their husbands Seneca and Thrasea died (65–6). They went into exile when their men were killed or forced to suicide, or defiantly sent supplies to exiles (Epict. 2. 7. 8, at Brunt: 1977*a*: 30). For women the formulation of philosophy's role in politics offered by Brunt is particularly significant: their scope for action was limited; all the more important in their mental and moral universe the change that philosophy could bring about in their determination to carry a resolution through.

It remains a question how far such extraordinary actions were the result of conscious adherence to doctrine, how far to Roman tradition about the relationship between fathers and daughters, husbands and wives. Plutarch calls Porcia a philosopher (*Brut.* 13. 6), but as G. Ménage already had to admit, it was not by profession (on Arria, Ménage 1984: 46). A modern scholar could weave them into his account of women's life without mentioning philosophy (Balsdon 1962: 58).

The Meaning of Philosophy for Women

All this, like many discussions of women's education ancient and modern, which are focused on its social significance and what men thought about it, has left out what the subject meant to the woman student (Annas 1976: 312). Not surprisingly: the scanty evidence is not beyond suspicion. Horace, Juvenal, and Lucian were at pains to make sure that we are under no delusions, and Seneca did not deny the received opinion accepted by his father that there were women who did not use their learning to acquire *sapientia* but set themselves up for *luxuria* (*Ad Helv.* 17. 4).

Did women love philosophy for its own sake? Emulation of male philosophers in the family might be relevant, at the start, or attraction to a teacher:[48] but that is not the question. To take instances from mainland Greece, Hipparchia of Maronea in the third century BC 'fell in love with both Crates' discourse and his way of life', and married him. 'She adopted the same dress . . . made love to him in public; she went to dinner parties with him.' But she was able to hold her own against a famous professional, Theodore the Atheist, who, at a loss for answers, could only start to pull off her cloak (Diog. Laert. 6. 96–8).[49] And from an earlier generation, Lefkowitz and Fant cite two women who were Plato's students; one of them, Axiothea of Mantinea, left home in Arcadia after starting Plato's

[48] Note 'Magnilla, philosopher, daughter of Magnus, philosopher, wife of Menius, philosopher' (2nd–3rd cent. AD Apollonia in Mysia): Pleket 1969: 40 no. 30 (LF 169, no. 221).

[49] Cf. *Anth. Pal.* 7. 413 (Antipater), LF 167, no. 217. Her brother was a philosopher too.

Republic and, like a woman in search of a new society, went to Athens to attend his lectures, wearing men's clothes.[50]

At Rome, Caerellia was 'aflame' (*flagrans*) with her passion for philosophy (Cic. *Ad Att.* 13. 21. 2); Plotina's letter to Hadrian of 121, 'How much I am interested in the School of Epicurus, you know very well', and requesting on behalf of the sect that the institution at Athens be permitted to choose its head from among men who were not Roman citizens, instead of being restricted to them, is preserved on stone, with her warm letter to the institution, exulting in her success.[51] Her Greek is said to demonstrate her interest: it bristles with verbal substantives ending in *-ma*, a characteristic of Epicurus' style. The zeal of Arria for Plato and Aristotle was praised by Severus and Caracalla (see above, pp. 146 f.); Plotinus' students included women 'devoted' to philosophy (Porph. *Vit. Plot.* 9. 1: σφόδρα φιλοσοφίᾳ προσκειμένας); Diogenes Laertius naturally stresses his dedicatee's enthusiasm for Plato (3. 47, with Hemelrijk 1999: 241 n. 87). It is the proportion of sincere students or the degree of their sincerity that cannot be determined. The Sceptics' women certainly had something to feign: hope for guidance in leading their life, perhaps preceded by curiosity about the guidance their brothers were receiving; then knowledge beyond what could be acquired from the daily round: cosmology and eschatology, and reassurance about ultimate destiny; lastly the technical side of philosophy, the pleasures of syllogisms, paradoxes, and puzzles that Musonius would deny his female students.

The Failure of Philosophy

The snag about Musonius' recommendation of philosophy for women is that it consists in turning her into a first-rate household manager (3. 10. 12–14H).[52] Epictetus likewise was not interested in the 'rights of women', in the sense of their legal and social standing (Hershbell 1989: 2158). Rather the philosophers (apart, it must be admitted, from Plato) emphasized the importance of the domestic rôle: the view is buttressed by an appeal to Homer's saying that good and evil are wrought at home. Household

[50] Axiothea: *POxy.* 3656; tr. Lefkowitz and Fant 1992: 167, no. 216; Themist. *Or.* 295c, cf. Diog. Laert. 3. 46 (variant details).

[51] Plotina: *IG* 2/3² 1099; *ILS* 7784; *Syll.*³ 834; Smallwood, *Docs. Nerva-Hadrian* 442 = Oliver 1989: 174–80, no. 73; Temporini 1978: 162–7; Oliver 1975; Hemelrijk 1999: 116–18 (language).

[52] αὐτίκα δεῖ οἰκονομικὴν εἶναι τὴν γυναῖκα καὶ ἐκλογιστικὴν τῶν οἴκῳ συμφερόντων (It is to begin with necessary for a woman to be a household manager and to be capable of calculating what is advantageous in the household).

management is indeed part of life, the same principles apply as elsewhere and the saying would have been applauded at many a twentieth-century political platform. And the fact that it does nothing to alter conventional ancient views as to a woman's place is only to be expected, fundamentally because of the Stoic view of what philosophy was: practical.[53] A more immediate reason is the scepticism reinforced by fear that Musonius was evidently already facing: 'some say (*φασί τινες*) that as soon as they are let out of the house and mix with men at philosophy classes they will become self-willed (*αὐθάδες*) and bold (*θρασείας*)' (3. 12. 1.6H). But his limited aim meant offering simplified or stripped down philosophy, designed not for human beings as such, but for human beings with a ready-made role. Musonius immediately continues with the woman's particular need to be *σώφρων*. This is the virtue characteristic of the sex (as opposed to courage), as a Hellenistic Pythagorean treatise, purporting to be a letter from one woman to another, concedes (Thesleff 1965: 151–4, at Lefkowitz 1993: 57).[54] Significantly, it is lauded also on young men's tombstones, although in the next *Discourse* Musonius insists that it is right for (grown) men too, and it is one of the four cardinal virtues (4. 14. 1. 12–14H; 4. 14. 1. 6H, with Laurenti 1989: 2135). The woman must be innocent of illicit sex and the other pleasures that involve lack of self-control (*ἀκρασία*), not be a slave to desires, over-ambitious, extravagant, vain, or unduly done up; she must overcome sloth, and not be a prey to grief: negative injunctions all, and against the female failings that philosophy will mop up, although Musonius rounds off the sentence by returning to his original point, that philosophical discourse enjoins practices that are valuable for an individual of either sex in becoming a supremely well-regulated person (*κοσμιωτάτος*). The woman who does philosophy is presented as righteous (*δικαία*), but that amounts to being a faultless helpmeet, good at working together to create concord, a thoughtful carer for her husband and children (3. 10. 1. 1–4H).[55]

[53] Hense 1905 on Mus. 3. 10. 1. 6: *ἐπιστήμη δὲ περὶ βίον οὐχ ἑτέρα τις ἢ φιλοσοφία ἐστὶ* (knowledge about life is nothing other than philosophy); cf. 4. 19. 1. 9: *φιλοσοφία κάλοκ' ἀγαθίας ἐστὶν ἐπιτήδευσις καὶ οὐδὲν ἕτερον* (philosophy and nothing else is knowledge of what is fine and good); 14. 76. 15: *τὸ ἃ πρέπει καὶ ἃ προσήκει λόγῳ μὲν ἀναζητεῖν, ἔργῳ δὲ πράττειν* (the search for what is fitting and profitable in argument, and the accomplishment of it in deed).

[54] Courage, justice, and intelligence are qualities that men and women have in common, but the first and last are more appropriately male qualities.

[55] Domestic *concordia*: Levick 1978: 227. The partnership of marriage: Pohlenz 1964: 302, referring to Mus. 12–15, esp. 79H. Stress on married love in first and second century writers: Laurenti 1986: 2139; particularly Musonius, 'perchè nessuno aveva visto in esso la base di una rivoluzione tanto grandiosa' (because no one had seen in it the foundation of so glorious a revolution).

And philosophy ought to give the female student the necessary courage as well. Energetic and hardy, she will feed her offspring herself and serve her husband with her own hands, and she will do without shirking what some people consider slave's work; she is a great benefit (ὄφελος) to her husband, an adornment (κόσμος) to her family, and a useful example (παράδειγμα) to her female acquaintance.

The philosophers' views are beautifully in tune with the Victorian writer on 'women's mission' who claims that the transplanting of private values to the wider public arena was:

> the true secret of a woman's political influence, the true object of her political enlightenment. Government will never be perfect till all distinctions between private and public virtue, private and public honour be done away! Who so fit for the operation of this change as enlightened, unselfish woman? ([Lewis] 1839: 66)[56]

So Laurenti claims that the resurgence of the Roman family was the prime condition for a resurgence of the Empire; the (good) philosophizing woman is a *materfamilias* (1989: 2139, citing Mus. 14. 73. 1. 10–13H; Clark 1981: 11).

Ancient philosophy and philosophers failed women. With the exception of Cynicism, it challenged little about ancient society but rather rationalized and justified existing stratifications. In Rome it had to undergo additional scrutiny by an entrenched set of possessors. In the stratification of society by property passed down from one *paterfamilias* to the next, women could be made invisible, and philosophy merely reinforced the status quo. Benevolent philosophers should have found either that the restricted freedom to philosophize that they allowed women imposed illegitimate limits on philosophy or, if philosophy was untrammelled inquiry, women were unfit to undertake it. That potential but unfelt problem exposes the limits of their social criticism.

Christian Women

As Miriam Griffin has remarked: 'Philosophy played an important part in a world where religion had little metaphysics and less ethics' (1989: 37). The energies of philosophers from the third century AD onwards came increasingly to be taken up with the issue of Christianity: Origen, Celsus, Porphyry, especially Plotinus. As Christianity made its way, religion took

[56] Mus. 3. 10. 1. 9H quotes Hom. *Od.* 4.392: ὅττι τοι ἐν μεγάροισι κακόν τἀγαθόν τε τέτυκται (since it is in the home that good and evil are wrought); cf. Cic. *De Off.* 1. 54: *principium urbis et quasi seminarium rei publicae* (the front-line of the city and a nursery, as it were, for the Roman people).

on that role of expounding metaphysics and ethics. By Origen's time, 'Platonism and Christian doctrine have become so similar that one can ask how a Platonist could criticize Christian doctrine' (Frede 1997*b*: 228). Yet the Neoplatonist Hypatia was done to death in 415 by a Christian mob (Soz. *Hist. Eccl.* 7. 15). It symbolizes a change. Christianity turned any quest for spiritual and intellectual fulfilment down a new route. Women became the correspondents and disciples of Fathers of the Church, and in houses of retreat some were able from the fourth century onwards to devote themselves to thought and prayer: Sozomen uses the word 'philosophy' in this context (*Hist. Eccl.* 3. 14. 31) and by the mid-fourth century the 'philosophical' life was the Christian life of virginity (Elm 1994: 44 with n. 49).[57] But now the 'philosophical' life often meant the performance of servile tasks (ibid: 125).

In the women involved in this movement, who sacrificed wealth (not status[58]) as the daughters of aristocratic families to take to asceticism, instruction from learned and holy men, even monastic life, we recognize women who three centuries earlier might have attended Musonius. This was more than a thirst for philosophy, otherwise the part played by women in the Christianization of the Empire would have been less prominent. The 'turning towards individual fulfilment' that Averil Cameron, reviewing a work of Foucault, noticed as a partial explanation used in recent discussions of religious developments (Cameron 1986: 266), makes this a field of particular interest.

Even the language was recapitulated. Bold women who escaped from family functions into a life without those or the sexual roles that in ancient and modern stereotypes characterize and confine women, won the title 'mulier virilis', 'fortis femina' (Drijvers 1987: 266). Some went further and, like Axiothea, dressed as men, creating a category of 'transvestite saints'.[59] Drijvers rehearses the motives that have been suggested. If Christianity turned devotees into functioning persons, it was, as Drijvers's citations show, at the cost of their being women, in the sense that they had to become *quasi*-men (internally, of course: Elm 1994: p. ix), functioning persons proper; 'superior to their sex',[60] thus transgressing gender roles again, but

[57] Consequences of celibacy: Clark 1993: 50–6; philosophic women and their attainments: 130–8.

[58] Clark 1993: 103; Elm 1994: 94; Porph. *Against Christians* 58 (with Harnack 1916) for property.

[59] Anson 1974 thinking of monkish fantasies, is uncertain of their existence. Clark 1993: 117 notes disapproval of unfeminine attire. Ascetics: 129.

[60] Jer. *Comm. in Ep. ad Gal. I* (Migne 1885: 26. 307); *Ad Eph.* 3. 5 (Migne 1885: 533); *Ep.* 71. 3 (Migne 1885: 22. 670).

in a way to win approval in circles that moulded public opinion. They 'even had some influence' (Drijvers 1987: 267), though preaching was banned, on the basis of Paul's prohibition (Jer. *Ep.* 127. 7, cf. Paul, *Ep. to Tim.* 2. 11–14).[61] Clark sees women philosophers listening to discussion and manifesting virtue; teachers, who included Sosipatra and the Christians' victim Hypatia, are non-Christian (1993: 133).

The Christian 'philosophical life', the ascetic life, needed no intellectual content. In Elm's words, the γυνὴ ἀνδρεία such as Macrina displays 'characteristics of the Stoic philosopher' (Elm 1994: 101–2); this was in spirit, without abandoning the clothes, manners, and restrictions of a woman, and still performing woman's work (Elm 1994: 75, 108–10; Basil, *Reg. Brev. Tract.* 210). Philosophy as practical morality was triumphant, and acceptable.[62] The code was ready-made. It took an independent Anatolian prophetess to challenge the durable rules that Elm lists as established for women: refraining from independent interpretation and teaching of dogmatic issues, abstaining from talking, remaining inside the house unseen and unheard (Elm 1994: 133, 165). The germ of such a 'philosophic' life may be recognized in the first centuries of the Empire, with the gradual eclipse of logic by morals, the acceptance of rhetoric into philosophy, and, over the same period, the reconciliation of philosophy and government and rise of 'upper class religion'.

Drijvers notes that virgins and chaste widows had a special place of honour in heaven, borne out by paintings such as Charonton's *The Enthronement of the Virgin* (Villeneuve-lès-Avignon, 1453: Bunt 1947: pl. 15) in which they form a row of peas without distinguishing dress or symbols; while anthropologists point out the vital role of the audience in tribal ceremonies (Overing 1986: 140). No more in fourth-century Christianity than in the early Church did change in the status and power of women in their societies make headway (Cameron 1980).

Conclusion

The society revealed by the role of women in one of its most sophisticated activities was wielding two different schemes of thought. Nineteenth-century philosophies of history responsible for difficulties in handling

[61] Clark 1981: 207, quotes Livy 34. 1 (*ORF* 1. 14) for hostility to women's speech; later came the problem of Eve's bad advice: Clark 1993: 126; Elm 1994: 248 notes some women as *didaskaloi,* and ibid. 147 the participation of *kanonoikai* in doctrinal debate.

[62] Laurenti 1989: 2115, on the expanding concept of philosophy in the 1st cent.; 2146 has Musonius and Epictetus confronting 'l'istaurazione della filosofia nelle cose' (the embedding of philosophy in material things).

women in history had ancient roots. From the eighteenth century, with economic, political, and philosophical change forcing elites to take women more seriously than any ancient intelligentsia had, a pole was found to which women could be relegated, that of the 'natural', opposite the 'civil' pole where even working men now operated, and so be kept from consideration in history and politics. In antiquity, the male with full rights stood at the centre; others were placed in circles of graduated rank and privilege. Lefkowitz has argued that the ancient Greeks had 'distrusted women, not, as is commonly thought, because of their sexual attributes, but because they *thought* like women' (1990: 800). That made women excludable. Beyond the limits of citizenship Romans could see men in animal terms, domestic (provincial subjects) or wild (alien 'barbarians'); even Semonides' bee-woman had been animal (fr. 7. 1. 83–94). Women were not considered, any more than in Marxism (contra de Ste Croix 1981: 98–102). They are adjuncts, seen either as (common) property (*κοιναί*)—Epictetus discussing adultery makes the comparison of a common sucking pig to be divided up at a banquet or theatre-seats allocated to individual patrons (2. 4. 8–11, with Annas 1989: 167 and nn. 19–20)—or as shadows of the males in their appropriate circles, or in a variety of polar opposites including the natural and civil or the related wild versus the civilized; Cato the Elder in Livy argues against the repeal of the Lex Oppia (195 BC) and giving rein to 'unbridled natures' and 'unmastered creatures' (Livy 34. 2. 11–3. 2). Infringement of defensive polarities was disastrous, as rejection of hermaphrodite prodigies shows: they were enclosed in a box and thrown into the sea.[63]

Women in philosophy, as part of the elite and sharing its arrogated merits, notably intellectual power, were an irritant. Those who took the lead in the way that Arria did moved out of the female sphere and shamed men who failed to act as such. Such merits exceptionally outweighed the restrictions and won resounding fame. The outstanding exception proved the rule (and at the same time reinforced the idea of the duty that a wife owed to her husband). And society could claim at once that there was a place for women to shine, while it kept its traditional values.

Martial is satisfied if he has, along with a well-fed household, sleep at night, and the day free of lawsuits, a wife who is not *extremely* learned (*doctissima*) (2. 90. 9). The instructive disagreement as to whether women should do philosophy may be found within one family, perhaps even with an individual in two minds. Such bounds vary and are commonly set just

[63] Hermaphrodites, first noted 228 BC (Dio Fr. 47: Luterbacher 1904: 25; MacBain 1982: 127–35 lists them to the Social War), are 'besonders schlimme Vorzeichen' (especially bad omens): Rosenberger 1988: 110 with n. 113 (refs.).

beyond where the speaker finds himself, another instance of the flexibility (hence durability) of gender boundaries. The doctrine that there had been only a single woman philosopher shows that the thing is in the realm of the possible, but freakish. So there was room for the occasional individualist who put conviction into practice. She helped to define society, even illustrating its durability through deviation from the norm. Steam was let off, society as whole left intact.

One philosopher, no historians? History as a part of literature seemed more accessible at the start, but serious history writing, at its most magisterial in the hands of retired politicians, carried the threat of direct judgement, even less tolerable in a woman.

Philosophy in the Second Sophistic

GLEN W. BOWERSOCK

Miriam Griffin and I have known each other for more than forty years, and it is a particular joy to offer her this paper in celebration of a distinguished career. We met at Harvard University in a class taught by Sir Ronald Syme when he was a visiting professor there in late 1956, and we both left America for Oxford to begin further study in the damp autumn of the following year. Philosophy has always been important in Miriam Griffin's approach to Roman history (I well remember her immersion in Seneca already in 1957), and so her interest in philosophy has prompted me after more than thirty years to revisit some old and familiar territory, the culture of the so-called Second Sophistic.[1]

Dr Griffin published a thoughtful review of my *Greek Sophists in the Roman Empire* (Griffin 1971), and at the end she observed: 'the age of the great sophists is largely the product of the fact that the Roman Emperors had ceased to sneer. It is not only that more and more Greeks were admitted to the imperial administration, but also that Greek values were increasingly accepted. The first of the Julio-Claudians could not have written philosophy seriously in Greek . . .'. If Marcus Aurelius did precisely that, it is undoubtedly right to suggest that Roman culture had changed. The sophists were both symptom and cause, and in subsequent years a lively debate opened up as to their importance and their relation with the Roman government (see Bowie 1970, 1982). But with a few exceptions philosophers did not figure in this debate until recently.

Yet the sophistic movement was, as Marcus's philosophical writing implies, closely allied with the prevalence and practice of Greek philosophy. For about a generation this issue lay undeveloped, as discussion of the Second Sophistic concentrated on the training of *pepaideumenoi* and the

[1] Keith Hopkins had briefly tempted me back to this terrain by inviting me to lecture on the Second Sophistic at Cambridge in March of 1997. Since my lecture consisted largely of personal reflections on the work of others, I chose not to publish it. But it signalled appreciatively the new wave of scholarship in the field, and it provoked a lively discussion to which the present paper is indebted. I am also indebted to Christopher Jones for valuable comments on this paper.

possibility of an implied assertion of Greek superiority over Rome.[2] The discussion became repetitive and sterile.[3] But in the last decade the whole subject has been dramatically reinvigorated, in large part by a powerful group of mostly younger scholars. A series of fresh and exciting studies of the Second Sophistic from the perspectives of anthropology, archaeology, art, and gender studies have located the movement within a subtle system of expectations and prejudices, of values and rewards that were embedded in imperial Greek culture and society. For the older generation the credibility of Philostratus had always been the central issue, which some of us had imagined could be persuasively judged through epigraphy. But the new generation has turned to images, self-representation, public display, and personal conduct (even grooming). This illuminating work has emboldened me to attempt a new look at the relation between sophists and philosophers by way of tribute to Miriam Griffin. Most of the work that has inspired me to do this has appeared between 1994 and 2000. The honorand will, I know, take as much pleasure as I do in saluting the progress that has been made.

If we look back, it is plain that study of the Second Sophistic was gravely impeded by the dismissive opinion that Wilamowitz once expressed of the movement. In reviewing Boulanger's work on Aristides Wilamowitz declared (1925: 421): 'Boulanger has not freed himself from the quite useless invention of Philostratus, the Second Sophistic' (von der schlechthin unbrauchbaren Erfindung des Philostratos, der zweiten Sophistik, hat er sich nicht losgemacht).[4] It was all too easy to fault Philostratus for promoting the likes of himself through his *Lives of the Sophists*, to assert that his heroes were nonentities and that the phenomenon for which he created a name was insignificant and ephemeral. But the burgeoning epigraphical record gradually gave the lie to Wilamowitz's scepticism, and there was no point in fretting over the name. Something of consequence was going on, and it was simpler to take over Philostratus' name for it than to invent another. The role of the sophists in both local and imperial corridors of power proved to be very much as Philostratus had described it.

Curiously an unexpected revival of Wilamowitz's attitude came as late as 1994 in Brunt's provocative paper, 'The Bubble of the Second Sophistic'. Since it appeared just as studies of the topic had indeed become repetitive and unproductive, it was hard at the time not to sympathize with Brunt's

[2] Anderson 1989, 1990, 1993. Schmitz 1997 includes a balanced review of these issues.

[3] Cf. Bowersock 1992: 640, *crambe repetita*, and 1998: 480, 'There is actually little here that is new or different.'

[4] Boulanger must have been appalled to read these words from so great a scholar.

impatience. But much of his argument looks as if it had been assembled long before. It documents Brunt's profound interest in second-century Greek thought, an interest that extends all the way back to his early days as a student of Hugh Last. It is true that thinkers of the age, including philosophers and the great doctor Galen, had no great opinion of the sophists, and Brunt undertook to read their testimony as an accurate account of the historical situation. He opined that the great majority of sophists whose biographies Philostratus chose not to write 'were probably men of little repute resident in small towns' (Brunt 1994: 26).[5] That is simply false. For example, T. Flavius Phylax, called a laughing-stock by Philostratus, was honoured at Olympia and belonged to the Athenian Areopagus. Soteros, roughly treated by Philostratus, turns out to have been an eminent person at Ephesus.[6] Athens and Ephesus were not small towns.

The six categories into which Brunt arranged attestations of the word 'sophist' only serve to illustrate an exceptionally rich semantic field, which cannot be accommodated in pigeonholes. The word could be used pejoratively, as Galen used it, or descriptively to indicate a rhetor. But, more than that, it could be used as a term of abuse even by those to whom it applied. Aelius Aristides is a famous case of this. And, as von Staden (1997) has demonstrated in a brilliant paper on Galen and the Second Sophistic, Galen himself was as much a part of the sophistic phenomenon as any of the professional rhetoricians. His disparaging comments on sophists were part of his own self-representation in a highly competitive environment.

It is precisely the cultural environment and its anthropological coding that the new generation of scholars has been able to expose so persuasively. I think above all of the contributions of Johannes Hahn (1989), Maud Gleason (1995), Thomas Schmitz (1997), Maria Domitilla Campanile (1999), and Stephen Harrison (2000).[7] Their work has been substantially reinforced by that of Paul Zanker (1995) on the image of the intellectual in

[5] Observe his remark (Brunt 1994: 25 n. 1), 'Philostratus' chief value is in comments on style; in exact historical scholarship and judgement it is wanting, and it abounds in anecdotes, never to be trusted.' This reminds me of the statement I once heard from Joshua Whatmough that the chief value of the fragments of Sappho is the Greek forms conserved therein. Such confident positivism is, as Housman put it in his Cambridge inaugural, 'the felicity of the house of bondage'.

[6] On both Phylax and Soteros, see the references in Bowersock 1974: 2. For Phylax see the discussion in C. P. Jones 1972: 265–7 in an account of the family, including Phylax's brother (Phoenix) and his father (Alexander). All three were sophists. For the inscription praising Soteros at Ephesos, see now *IK*, *Inschr. Eph.* no. 1548; cf. Schmitz 1997: 142.

[7] It is worth noting that in the enormous bibliography of Swain 1996 the work of Gleason is conspicuous by its absence. Swain's denigration of Wörrle 1988 ('the now common Stadt und Fest approach to the history of the Greeks under Rome' (Swain 1996: 8)) is equally disquieting, as indicated in Bowersock 1998.

ancient art. Brunt's problem arose from his nearly exclusive emphasis on literary texts and philosophical ideas. Inasmuch as the strength of the sophists did not lie in this area but in public performance and showmanship, it proved easy to dismiss them. Yet their lives proclaimed a disposition and an attitude of mind that linked them with other intellectuals and pseudo-intellectuals, even if they did not contribute much profound thought to those who consorted with them. As Philostratus, the inscriptions, and even the coins (Münsterberg 1915) all make plain, their careers depended upon the commerce in Hellenic traditions—the history of the Greeks, their philosophy, and their language. The sophists were part not only of local aristocracies and the Roman administration but of a vast and complex cultural fabric that is only now becoming clear. Philosophy, like Galen's medicine, was obviously an essential component of that fabric.

Philostratus had seen this perfectly, although in the past his words have given rise to some perplexity. He believed that sophistic rhetoric was in origin philosophic rhetoric.[8] They shared themes in common, but philosophers were in search of knowledge whereas sophists claimed to possess it. Yet it is clear that what really mattered was not knowledge but style. Among those whom Philostratus chose to commemorate in his *Lives of the Sophists* were six whom he recognized to be philosophers rather than sophists in the full sense of the term (*οἱ κύριοι προσρηθέντες σοφισταί*, 492).[9] These are Eudoxus of Cnidos, who was honoured as sophist in view of his brilliant style and improvisatory skill; Leon of Byzantium, a pupil of Plato whose variety of rhetorical styles entitled him to be called a sophist; Dias of Ephesus, an Academic who used his talent effectively for political advocacy; Carneades of Athens, who spoke as splendidly as he practised philosophy; Philostratus the Egyptian, who was alleged to have studied philosophy with Cleopatra and to have adopted a highly perfumed style of oratory; Theomnestus of Naucratis, another philosopher who spoke exceptionally well; and, from the era of the Second Sophistic, Dio of Prusa (Chrysostom) and Favorinus. In introducing this group at the beginning of his work Philostratus explicitly stated that they were not sophists (*οὐκ ὄντες σοφισταί*) but seemed to be (*δοκοῦντες*) and hence acquired the name. When he completed his account of the six figures, he repeated the same point all over again. He tells us that he has written about philosophers who had the reputation of being sophists (*ὑπὲρ τῶν φιλοσοφησάντων ἐν δόξῃ τοῦ σοφιστεῦσαι*).

[8] cf. Brancacci 1985 on *ῥητορικὴ φιλοσοφοῦσα*, concentrating exclusively, however, on Dio of Prusa as if he were unique in his synthesis of philosophy and rhetoric.

[9] All references to the *Vit. Soph.* are given by the Olearius pagination.

It sounds very much as if Philostratus and his readers knew how to tell the difference between a philosopher and a sophist, and yet they acknowledged that rhetorical brilliance might entitle a philosopher to the sophistic label. Since neither in Philostratus nor anywhere else is a sophist said to acquire the reputation of philosopher, it would seem as if the titular mobility did not go in both directions. This may perhaps be the result of a sophist's certainty about what he is saying, but there is an implication here that the rank of sophist is actually higher than that of philosopher. That implication is borne out in Lucian's *Rhet. Pr.* 1. where the name of sophist is presented as the pinnacle of success in public speaking:

ἐρωτᾷς ὦ μειράκιον, ὅπως ἂν ῥήτωρ γένοιο καὶ τὸ σεμνότατον τοῦτο καὶ πάντιμον ὄνομα σοφιστὴς αὐτὸς εἶναι δόξαις.

You ask, my young fellow, how you may become a public speaker and yourself seem to embody this most august and honoured name of 'sophist'.

(Compare *Pseudolog.* 19. 10 ἤδη τιμώμενος πρὸς αὐτῶν, ἀλλὰ νῦν ῥήτωρ καὶ σοφιστής—already honoured by them, but now a rhetor and a sophist.[10]) By contrast, the language that Philostratus used to describe a philosopher who seemed to be a sophist, or enjoyed the reputation of a sophist, is exactly matched by the language of the great second-century sophist Polemo about a philosopher he hated, Favorinus. In his *Physiognomonica* Polemo asserted that Favorinus made use of the Greek language so very well that he was called a sophist (Hoffmann apud Foerster 1893: 163). Although we have Polemo's words only in an Arabic translation, it is clear that he is referring to the dazzling use of Greek in Favorinus' public speaking (*wa kāna qad ta'allama al-lughata-l-yunāniyyata wa-l-kalāma 'layhā wa hadhā min kathrati kalāmihi wa kāna yusammā sūfisṭay*: He had studied the Greek language and its usage, which he mastered so thoroughly that he was called a sophist). He stresses the spoken use (*kalām*) of the language.

But coruscating rhetoric was not the only thing that distinguished the sophists from most philosophers. They looked different, as Philostratus makes embarrassingly plain in his account of the career change of Aristocles of Pergamum. This man had begun as a philosopher of the Peripatetic school but was eventually attracted to the sophists, especially Herodes Atticus. 'As long as he was a student of philosophy,' says Philostratus, 'he was slovenly in appearance, unkempt and squalid in his dress, but now he began to be fastidious, discarded his slovenly ways, and admitted into his house all the pleasures that are afforded by the lyre, the flute, and the

[10] For the σεμνότης of sophists cf. Dio Chrys. *Or.* 6. 21, τοὺς σοφιστὰς τοὺς σεμνούς.

singing voice.' The long unkempt hair and scruffy beard were essential parts of the philosopher's image, as Maud Gleason (1995) has so convincingly shown.[11] That image projected an atmosphere of unmitigated masculinity. Lucian made this all too obvious in his *Demonax*, when the philosopher of the title declares that his ὄρχεις (testicles) constitute his qualifications for doing philosophy. By contrast the sophists were magnificent and fastidious. Polemo travelled in a chariot adorned with silver and accompanied by a grand retinue of animals and slaves (Philost. *Vit. Soph.* 532). Alexander Peloplaton cultivated an elegant appearance that left his audiences gasping. He wore a trim beard, manicured his nails, cleaned his teeth, and always smelt of perfume (*Vit. Soph.* 569–72).

If the categories of philosopher and sophist were traditionally distinct in appearance (and sometimes in odour), the spheres of their activity were distinct as well. In a well-known passage in Artemidorus' *Oneirocritica* philosophers and sophists, as dream objects, are sharply distinguished. The former are associated with priests and prophets, the latter with public figures who come into contact with the masses (ὄχλος) and those who play musical instruments with their mouths (Hahn 1989: 47–8). Philosophers belonged to a closed confraternity, it seems, whereas sophists belonged to the public. Yet it was in the passage into the public arena that these distinctions became confused.

Apuleius confronted the problem directly when he delivered his *Apology* before the proconsul Claudius Maximus at Sabratha. He had a reputation as a philosopher to maintain (*philosophus Platonicus* as he was later to Augustine and was probably styled on an acephalous inscription, Harrison 2000: 5 n. 19, 8 n. 32). The proconsul himself had philosophical interests, to which Apuleius flatteringly alluded. Yet Apuleius was a superb speaker, a Latin sophist, as Harrison rightly calls him, and the very speech he delivered is proof of his prowess. He had, therefore, to look like a philosopher since his accusers had portrayed him as 'good-looking and as effective a speaker in Greek as in Latin' (*formosum et tam Graece quam Latine . . . disertissimum*) (*Apol.* 4). Apuleius presented himself to the court as a man of mediocre looks at best, who had become a human wreck through constant

[11] In an important study of self-representation as indicative of culture and identity, R. R. R. Smith (1998: 80) minimizes the idea of an image of the intellectual as such in the 2nd cent. AD. He notes the scarcity of 'the classic image of the shambling, bedraggled philosopher' and observes: 'It is striking that there are no really philosophical or "sophistic"-looking portrait statues surviving.' He argues that philosophers and sophists would have received statues only in their capacity as local aristocrats, benefactors, or politicians. This may well be true of the statues offered to Dio of Prusa, but one wonders whether the statues of Favorinus would have belonged to that category, or the missing statues on surviving bases—e. g. at Delphi and Ephesus—proclaiming the honorand a sophist. See nn. 6, 12, and 16 of this paper.

study. He was pale and weak, his hair a tangled mess. He must have given particular attention to preparing his hair in a philosophically sordid fashion: ' so, I think, the charge against my hair, which they meant to be so-to-speak a capital charge against me, is sufficiently refuted' (*satis ut puto crinium crimen, quod illi quasi capitale intenderunt, refutatur*).[12]

With Apuleius we have another crossover no less remarkable than Dio of Prusa and Favorinus. The careers of these three, and especially the last, lead us directly to the topic for which the recent work on image and performance in the Second Sophistic has now laid a solid foundation. That is the surprising emergence of certain philosophers as performance artists. Cultural distinctions can often be discerned most sharply when they are violated, as is undoubtedly the case here. The sophist-philosophers ceased to be members of a closed and quasi-sacred confraternity, they ceased to be unkempt, and they performed before the public. The matted hair of Apuleius at Sabratha was, in fact, part of his performance in court. It provided Paul Zanker (1995: 222–9) with the leitmotif of a valuable section of his work on the image of the intellectual: 'Die ungekämmten Haare des Apuleius'. Apuleius' opponents had no doubt observed him on other occasions when he might well have been characterized as *formosus*. The question arises whether these crossover personalities spent their careers switching back and forth between a public sophistic image and a studious philosophical one. This is inherently implausible, and we must assume that Apuleius' quick change was a unique expedient designed for courtroom consumption.

It would appear that the performing sophist-philosopher behaved as extravagantly as any sophist worthy of the name. In a tantalizing brief scrap from the *Florida* Apuleius congratulates his audience in the theatre for coming to hear him, where they might otherwise have been watching a mime, a tight-rope walker, or a comedy:

Bono enim studio in theatrum convenistis, ut qui sciatis non locum auctoritatem orationi derogare, sed cum primis hoc spectandum esse, quid in theatro deprehendas. Nam si mimus est, riseris, si funerepus, timueris, si comoedia est, faveris, si philosophus, didiceris. (Apul. *Flor.* 5, see Harrison 2000: 101).

For you have congregated in the theatre with good intent, you who know that location cannot detract from the authority of a speech, but that which you find in the

[12] Cf. the elaborate defence of his long and unkempt hair that Apollonius of Tyana makes to Domitian in Philostratus' biography (*Vit. Apoll.* 8. 7, 6: Kayser 1870–1: 309–10) or the pride that Dio of Prusa took in his long hair (*Or.* 12. 15, 47. 25). It would be interesting to know how he would have been represented in the portrait busts and statue that Prusa offered him (44. 2). See C. P. Jones 1978: 105.

theatre is something you absolutely must see. For if it is a mime, you will laugh, if a tight-rope walker, you will be frightened and if a comedy, you will applaud; but if it is a philosopher, you will learn.

All good entertainment, but a philosopher provides instruction as well as entertainment. Harrison has properly compared Dio of Prusa's account of the value of his public speeches in his *Olympic*, where he contrasts his mission of imparting wisdom through his oratorical brilliance with that of others who are not philosophically inclined. It is, he asserts, as if he were the owl among birds of varied plumage.

It is fortunate that we have now reached a stage in our understanding of Dio that we have no longer to contend with an unfortunate hypothesis, propagated by Synesius of Cyrene and developed influentially by H. von Arnim (1898), that Dio first had a sophistic phase in his career and then a philosophical one. Four scholars, three of them in the same year, have now independently repudiated this unhelpful notion, as Schmitz (1997: 86 n. 69) correctly observed:

Die von Dion selbst (*Or.* 13. 12) erzählte Geschichte, er habe sich während seines Exils zur Philosophie bekehrt, wurde in der Neuzeit gerne geglaubt, und manche Philologen meinen, alle seine Schriften in eine 'sophistische' und eine 'philosophische' Period unterteilen zu können . . . Die Arbeiten von Desideri, Moles, Jones, und Swain hätten diese Bekehrungshypothese endgültig ein Ende bereiten sollen.[13]

The tale recorded by Dio himself, that he turned to philosophy during his exile (*Or.* 13. 12), has been readily believed in modern times, and many scholars think that all his writings can be divided into a 'sophistic' and a 'philosophic' phase . . . The work of Desideri [1978], Moles [1978], [C. P.] Jones [1978], and Swain [1996] should have finally put an end to this hypothesis of conversion.

Philosophy and sophistic were by no means separate compartments or separate evolutionary phases in the cases of the three major crossover figures. The two activities were inextricably meshed because public performance was integral to both. Furthermore, movement from sophistic practice to philosophy was movement in the wrong direction. Dio himself knew that he ranked as a sophist, and a garrulous one at that, when he amusingly cited a mischievous critic who called him the 'nightingale of the sophists' (*ἀηδὼν τῶν σοφιστῶν*) because he never stopped talking (*Or.* 47. 16).

The cases of both Apuleius and Dio suggest that when a philosopher

[13] It should be noted that in arguing for an early date for Dio's *Alexandrian Oration* C. P. Jones (1973: 308) had already noted the implications for H. von Arnim's conversion hypothesis: 'This indicates once more that von Arnim was wrong to characterise Dio before his exile as a pure sophist, like one of Philostratus' showmen . . . Dio's early development was a more complicated process, in which sophistry and philosophy were closely intertwined.'

accepted the evidently higher calling of sophist he put aside the masculine squalor that was traditionally associated with philosophy. This violation of conventional external signs is nowhere more conspicuous than in the most remarkable of all the crossover philosophers, Favorinus of Arelate. If Polemo hated him and composed in his *Physiognomonica* what Holford-Strevens (1997: 200) has justly called a 'poison-pen portrait', he could not, as we have seen, deny him the appellation of sophist. Favorinus was the embodiment of contradictions, as Philostratus recognized. He came from the Latin West and rose to eminence in the Greek East, he was sexually underdeveloped (with undescended testicles, it seems) but found pleasure with women, he quarrelled with an emperor and survived. But above all he was a philosopher who achieved the reputation of a sophist, and he comported himself entirely in the manner of one. There was no trace of the philosopher's beard, since he had no beard at all, nor, for obvious reasons, could he exude an air of masculinity. As for unkempt hair and a hirsute body, he went to the opposite extreme. According to Polemo, he was greatly concerned with looking after his body, particularly the hair on his head, which he dyed in a manner that would formerly have been thought dissolute and effeminate.[14] He regularly applied allegedly seductive lotions to his otherwise smooth skin, and must have exuded an aura of perfume no less than Alexander Peloplaton. Favorinus calls to mind the great lionized castrati that made their careers in baroque opera. He was much sought after and admired. Both Athens and Corinth at one time had statues of him.[15]

It is all the more astonishing that this singular figure should have been the author of a treatise on the lifestyle of philosophers (περὶ τῆς διαίτης τῶν φιλοσόφων). The work is regrettably lost, but the mere fact that Favorinus wrote it is telling enough. When Miriam Griffin wrote of the acceptance of Greek values, she was not perhaps thinking of the Greek values promulgated by Favorinus in his own person, but Greek values they were none the less. These were the distinctive values generated by the Second Sophistic

[14] The revelation that Favorinus dyed his hair comes from a brilliant reading of the Arabic text of Polemo by the late A. F. L. Beeston, as reported in Holford-Strevens (1988: 73 n. 8). (One would like to know how many other sophists or philosophers dyed their hair.) By the simple placement of a dot over the letter *ṣād*, thereby converting it into a *ḍād*, an ungrammatical expression in the text is eliminated and the word for 'dyeing' emerges from the letters *kh-ṣ-b* as printed by Hoffmann in Foerster 1893. The manuscript contains an unpointed Arabic text, and so this solution is not even an emendation but another reading. A new edition of this fascinating work is badly needed. Hoffmann worked from only one of the five known manuscripts.

[15] We know of the statues from Philost. *Vit. Soph.* 490 (Athens) and Favorinus, fr. 95B (Corinth). The magistrates of both cities brought down these statues when Favorinus' fortunes had momentarily declined in favour of Polemo.

—ostentation, ornament, and performance in both language and presence. These, as Favorinus (and to some extent Apuleius and Dio of Prusa) must have shown, were no longer incompatible with a philosophical mind. Equally the social success and public anatomical displays of Galen had transformed the image of the doctor, so that, as von Staden has shown (1997), if Galen sounded the usual notes of scorn for sophists he nevertheless behaved as if he were one of them. There could hardly be a greater tribute to their cultural impact than this.

The philosophical sophists represented the highest level of a phenomenon that Johannes Hahn has well named *das Phänomen des Konzertphilosophen* (1989: 92). Philosophers who performed in theatres, like Apuleius, and presented philosophy in an accessible way for large audiences were by no means uncommon. Most of these performers did not merit the accolade of 'sophist', but it was the sophistic context that gave them their opportunity. Perhaps the best known of these was Maximus of Tyre, whose forty-one philosophical lectures (διαλέξεις) survive. Maximus clearly failed to work at a level that attracted the attention of Philostratus, but his lectures show that he aimed at beguiling his audiences with learning, not at instructing them as a teacher in the schools would have done. He stated that he left the fundamentals of philosophy, such as terminology and argument, to the διατριβαί since teachers were not hard to find (*Dial.* 1. 8: Trapp 1997: 236–9). Such sophists, as he called them in a purely derisive use of the term, were ubiquitous: πάντα ὑμῖν μεστὰ τοιούτων σοφιστῶν (*Dial.* 1. 8: Trapp 1997: 239). But as a performer, who appeared in θέατρα Ἑλληνικά (*Dial.* 1. 10: Trapp 1997: 315), Maximus was, in fact, following the lead of the professional sophists in abandoning the traditional dress code of philosophers. He felt obliged to excuse himself for being groomed and attractively dressed. One should not judge a philosopher, said Maximus, by his external appearance (*Dial.* 1. 10: Trapp 1997: 290–3). In other words, he is repudiating the traditional coding by asking his listeners to ignore the message conveyed by external signs. He wanted them to assume that he possessed no less wisdom and goodness than those who were properly hirsute and untidy. As Hahn (1989: 96) put it: 'So ist er im Ende, obwohl er sich immer wieder gegen diese Profession verwahrt, doch eigentlich Sophist' (So in the end, although he protests again and again his opposition to this profession, he is after all really a sophist).

The breaking of the visual code is consistent with the blurring of the distinction between philosopher and public speaker. Not surprisingly many philosophers of the time disapproved of what the likes of Maximus were doing. Although a philosopher must naturally be a master of language to convey his thoughts, entertaining the public was not part of the contemplative search for truth. Plutarch expressed himself unambiguously on this matter and by doing so documented the world of the concert philosophers: 'In a philosophic discussion we must set aside the repute (δόξα) of the speaker and examine what he says on its own. For in lectures, as in war, much of what goes on is without substance (πολλὰ τὰ κενά)' (Plut. *Mor.* 41b). Epictetus would have agreed, as Hahn (1989: 86–90) has shown.

The acceptance of sophistic norms of grooming and dress, contrary to traditional coded self-representation, was part of that larger acceptance of Greek values to which Dr Griffin referred in 1971. As in so much, Favorinus is the extreme case. But his naturally smooth skin could be paralleled with a taste for depilation in more naturally hairy sophists. Philostratus tells us that Scopelian was famous for being depilated (*Vit. Soph.* 536). Maud Gleason (1995: 69–70) has admirably examined the traditional prejudice against this practice through the frenetic protests of Clement of Alexandria, who scorned those who renounced the flower of manliness (τὸ ἄνθος τὸ ἀνδρικόν). He declared that the cities of the Empire were full of depilators of every kind (Clem. *Paed.* 3. 3). In this, as in other things, Clement cannot be taken as a spokesman of the world in which he lived, but rather, like Plutarch, he actually illustrates what is going on by protesting so vigorously. Depilation, which Tertullian (*Pall.* 3) described as a Greek habit (Graecatim depilari), had long since passed from a titillating subject of jibes in Martial (3. 74, 6. 93, 10. 65) or Juvenal (8. 114) to a widespread practice in the Eastern Empire. A recent inscription from Apamea (*SEG* 37. 1434) reveals a company depilator (δρωπακιστής) with the Roman troops installed there, and an Easterner may have been responsible for the appearance of the same word on a newly published Greek graffito at Ostia (*SEG* 45. 1451). It is against a background of depilation as commonplace at Antioch that one must read Julian's *Misopogon* two centuries later.

For Clement, as Gleason observed (1995: 68), one can translate grooming and dress into character traits just as a physiognomist can do with physical appearance. The observation is pertinent here because Polemo, a major sophist whose appearance was nothing if not flamboyant, was himself also physiognomist. His treatise on physiognomy, containing the cruel portrait of his enemy Favorinus to which we have already referred, is a lengthy and manifestly professional manual. Maria Domitilla Campanile (1999: 288–9) has noticed that there is no reference in Philostratus' ample biography of Polemo to his activity as a physiognomist, and this, she believes, requires an explanation. She suggests that the construction of the image of a sophist, at least for Philostratus, implied singularity—a great orator, inimitable and like no other. This construction would be weakened, in her view, by revealing: 'uno scienzato che viaggia per feste e mercati, concorrente di medici, astrologi e interpreti di sogni' (a sophist who travels through festivals and markets, competing with doctors, astrologers and interpreters of dreams). It is not inconceivable that Philostratus would have considered Artemidorus unfit company for Polemo, although both were snobs about their audience, but doctors, with Galen as the pre-eminent one, were certainly respectable enough. On the other hand, Favorinus, as an Academic, certainly had no use for astrologers, as we know from his friend Aulus Gellius (*Noct. Att.* 14. 1, see Holford-Strevens 1988: 1978–9). Philostratus may have been reluctant to recognize the somewhat disreputable ambience of astrology, physiognomy, and dream interpretation within which the sophists operated (Barton 1994). With all of Galen's sputtering, both sophistic and science, including what we might call pseudo-science, went well together, and it must have been tempting for hostile auditors to allege the possession of supernatural powers. Apuleius was not the only one to suffer from this. Dionysius of Miletus was thought to have used magic to improve the memory of his pupils (γοητεύων: Philost. *Vit. Soph.* 523).

Not surprisingly, therefore, the philosopher sophists and their lesser brethren, such as Maximus of Tyre, found themselves in a world far removed from the contemplative life. With the assault on the traditional signs of masculinity and wisdom it became difficult to construct a recognizable image of a philosopher in the Second Sophistic. Personal characteristics peculiar to one individual, such as those of Favorinus, no doubt allowed the sculptors who created his statues at Corinth and Athens to produce a reasonable likeness. But it would have been difficult to find a general code, as earlier with the bearded philosophers. That may be why, in seeking images of the intellectual in the middle of the second century, Paul Zanker had to concentrate on the textual evidence for Apuleius' reversion to a conventional type during his trial. Clear examples of portraits of intellectuals in this period are praeternaturally scarce, as R. R. R. Smith (1999: 452) acutely pointed out in reviewing Zanker's book:

> It is most interesting then that while literature is full of references to intellectual self-styling in life, very few second-century portraits have a unitary or primary intellectual expression. Z. ventures no explanation. One obvious explanation is to hand which may be made explicit: intellectuals qua intellectuals no longer or very unusually received public statue monuments under the Roman empire. . . . It might, in this reviewer's opinion, be profitable to look first at the self-representation of Antonine Rome and the Greek East as two separate strands rather than to run them

together. For the different audiences in (say) Ephesus and Ostia, a beard did not necessarily carry in itself precisely the same meaning.

Marcus Aurelius was well acquainted with the sophists. He heard some of them declaim and presided personally over a trial of Herodes Atticus, one of the greatest of them. His teacher Fronto (van den Hout 1999: 141) was enthusiastic about the union of eloquence and philosophy: 'Philosophy will furnish what you say, eloquence how you say it' (dabit philosophia quod dicas, dabit eloquentia quo<modo dicas>). He described *eloquentia* as *comes philosophiae*. But Marcus himself steered clear of all this when he wrote his own philosophy, and yet he wrote philosophy (remarkable enough) and wrote it in Greek. He was not welcoming to the sophistic movement in his book. His aversion he attributed to the Stoic Q. Junius Rusticus, consul suffect in 133 and consul ordinarius in 162, an aristocratic philosopher solidly rooted in the old Roman tradition. (*Med.* 1. 7. 1–2): *Παρὰ Ῥουστίκου τὸ λαβεῖν φαντασίαν τοῦ χρῄζειν διορθώσεως καὶ θεραπείας τοῦ ἤθους καὶ τὸ μὴ ἐκτραπῆναι εἰς ζῆλον σοφιστικόν* (from Rusticus [I learnt] to gain a conception of the need for correction and treatment in one's moral character and not to be diverted into sophistic zeal). Unlike many others of his time, Marcus believed that philosophy should not have any taint of sophistic rhetoric. He was certainly not alone in that opinion. He displayed his old Roman mores no less than his Stoic convictions even as he wrote in Greek.

With the luxuriant proliferation of philosophical sects in this age it would be difficult to categorize those sects in terms of their sympathy for concert rhetoric. An Academic such as Favorinus or Platonists such as Apuleius and Maximus seem to have had no qualms about performance philosophy. But it seems obvious that Stoics, Epicureans, and Cynics were allergic to it. Like Marcus, the Stoic Timocrates, another enemy of Favorinus, strongly opposed this kind of career, as doubtless did his teacher, the long-bearded Euphrates of Tyre (cf. Pliny, *Ep.* 1. 10, demissus capillus, ingens et cana barba). Epicurean suspicion of rhetorical deception is beyond question (Arrighetti 1973: 175–83).[16] Cynics, almost by definition, were never likely to compete with the sophists. Lucian tells a delightful anecdote in his *Demonax* (50) about a Cynic before a proconsul. The Cynic greatly vexed the proconsul by his slanderous charges against a depilated man—one imagines this might have been a sophist—as being a *cinaedus*. When the governor was considering various severe punishments,

[16] The passage is cited, from the 1st edn., by C. P. Jones 1972: 265–7 in arguing against the identification of the Epicurean Alexander in Plutarch's *Quaest. Conviv.* with the sophist T. Flavius Alexander, honoured on a statue base at Delphi.

Demonax intervened in the Cynic's favour on the grounds that he was doing no more than practising the frank-speaking characteristic of his philosophy. The proconsul relented but asked Demonax what the man's fate should be if he committed such an offence again. The answer came back that the Cynic should himself be depilated. This is a powerful example of coded homoeopathy in the Graeco-Roman context.

The acceptance of Greek values in the Roman world was indisputably greater in the time of Marcus than that of Augustus, and Miriam Griffin knows better than anyone that two extravagantly philhellenic emperors, Nero and Hadrian, played a major role in this evolution. But the ambivalent response of Marcus to Hellenism illustrates R. R. R. Smith's point that the extent and manner of that acceptance was by no means the same everywhere. There were, as we can see among the feuding philosophers, internal variations within Greek culture itself as well as changing nuances as one moved from East to West. If Apuleius was, as Harrison (2000) convincingly claims, a Latin sophist, he is still different from Favorinus with his dyed hair and smooth skin or Polemo with his animals and silver-ornamented chariot. If Tertullian was, as T. D. Barnes (1971) suggested, a Christian sophist, he was none the less able to look down upon depilation as a Greek habit. The Second Sophistic had an impact upon the Empire that Wilamowitz never imagined, but that impact cannot have been uniform. In promoting and rewarding a thriving new class of philosopher lecturers, the sophists not only received a few of them into their lofty ranks at the top, where 'sophist' was a term of honour (*σεμνότατον ὄνομα*). It also created opportunities for lesser practitioners in careers where the word 'sophist' was a term of disparagement. But without the sophists themselves such persons would have been forgotten altogether, toiling in obscurity as schoolteachers or diagnosticians.

Galen and Maximus of Tyre belonged to a generation for which philosophy no longer required a beard and filthy hair. Worldly success and an elegant, even flamboyant appearance had become an acceptable way of life for philosophers who were so inclined. And perhaps one day we shall discover whether Favorinus, who led the assault on the old conventions and codes, chose to celebrate the new dispensation when he wrote his work on the lifestyles of philosophers.

Part III

Power

Cicero: A Man of Letters in Politics

ZVI YAVETZ

In 66 BC, the praetor Marcus Tullius Cicero supported without the slightest hesitation the Manilian law: 'I praise both the spirit and the letter of your law and yet more strongly approve it' ('Istam tuam legem et voluntatem et sententiam laudo, vehementiusque comprobo': *De Imperio Cn. Pompeii* 69). In spite of Lucullus' victories, the war in the East was far from over. Mithridates was still alive and could at any moment destroy the business interests of many Romans in Asia. It was therefore essential—so Cicero—immediately to appoint a general who could restore the Roman power in the East. This man should be Pompey, because he was endowed not only with military genius, but also with integrity, self-control, and trustworthiness. Moreover, his stunning success in his war against the pirates should convince anyone that Pompey was precisely the kind of commander needed for the campaign in Asia. He possesses the four qualities indispensable for a first-rate commander: knowledge of warfare (*scientia rei militaris*), *virtus*, *auctoritas*, and *felicitas* (*De Imperio* 28). Therefore Pompey must be given a free hand in Asia and all the fears and misgivings of the distinguished senators, like Hortensius and Catulus, should be brushed aside. Hortensius in particular should be reminded that he had opposed the Gabinian law as well—and Cicero could now play his trump card and ask:

> Well then, by the immortal gods, if your 'authority' and 'valid argument' had prevailed, would we today be in possession of this our glory and this our power over the globe?

> Quid tum per deos immortales, si plus apud populum Romanum auctoritas tua et vera causa valuisset, hodie hanc gloriam atque hoc orbis terrae imperium teneremus?

It was easy for Cicero to destroy an opponent whose opinion concerning the war against the pirates proved wrong in the end. It would have been much more complicated to take up a matter of principle, because Hortensius never doubted Pompey's abilities. On the contrary, he seems to have emphasized that 'if one man is to be put in supreme command, Pompey would have been the best choice'. However, the principle was wrong: 'ad unum tamen omnia deferri non oportere' (*De Imperio* 52).

A modern reader might have expected a theoretical refutation of Hortensius' argument, especially from a man like Cicero, who was proud of his philosophical background and who admitted that from his earliest youth he devoted no small amount of time and energy to philosophy:

For I have not suddenly begun to engage in philosophy and from my earliest youth I have devoted no small part of my energy and attention to that field. When I least appeared to be so, then I was most fully engaged in philosophy.

Nos autem nec subito coepimus philosophari nec mediocrem a primo tempore aetatis in eo studio operam curamque consumpsimus et cum minime videbamur, tum maxime philosophabamur. (*De Natura Deorum* 1. 1. 6)

Cicero, however, preferred not to pick up a theoretical discussion in a Roman popular assembly. It seemed more convenient to challenge Hortensius by asserting that his line of argument was now out of date and had been refuted not so much by words as by facts ('re multo magis quam verbis refutata': *De Imperio* 52), and the fact was that Pompey had beaten the pirates in a brilliant campaign and never made use of his victory to promote his own political standing in Rome. Why then, should one assume that Pompey would behave differently once the war against Mithridates and Tigranes was over?

Indeed, in 66 BC Cicero won the day, but a few years later he changed his mind and wrote to this friend Atticus that he utterly disliked Pompey's military boots ('mihi caligae eius . . . non placebant': *Ad Att.* 2.3.1), and that the man whom he had depicted as a genius had became a boring mediocrity. Moreover, according to Cicero, Pompey's first public speech was a complete disaster, disliked by the rich and the poor alike and convincing neither the Optimates nor the Populares: 'Not pleasing to the wretched, meaningless to the wicked, unwelcome for the well-off, unimportant for the respectable' ('non iucunda miseris, inanis improbis, beatis non grate, bonis non gravis': *Ad Att.* 1. 14. 1).

Instead of praising Pompey's victories in the East, Cicero seemed to have enjoyed the sarcastic nicknames Pompey received from his enemies:—Epicrates, Sampsiceramus, Arabarches, and Hierosolymitamus (*Ad Att.* 2. 3. 1, 16. 2, 9. 1, 17. 3)—and was suspicious even of Pompey's open expressions of affection for him. He considered these manifestations as sheer envy, badly disguised, and summed up his view about his former favourite:

In no way courteous, in no way straightforward, in no way distinguished in political affairs, in no way honourable, in no way brave, and in no way a gentleman.

Nihil come, nihil simplex, nihil ἐν τοῖς πολιτικοῖς illustre, nihil honestum, nihil forte, nihil liberum. (*Ad Att.* 1.13.4).

How could this change of allegiance be explained? Was it due to Cicero's inconsistent character, to his incurable opportunism and shameless careerism? Did he support Pompey in 66 BC only because he understood that, without his patronage, he could hardly win the consulate *anno suo* (in 63 BC)? And after the fulfilment of his supreme desire, did he simply drop him, because he never thought highly of him anyway? Those who believe, like Mommsen, that Cicero was a morbid turncoat and egotist, a man without insight, opinions, or intentions ('ohne Einsicht, Ansicht und Absicht'), one of the 'Half-men, who shrink not from wrongdoing but from its discovery' ('Halbnaturen, die nicht vor dem Unrecht, aber vor dessen Nacktheit zurückschrecken': 1898: 147), could easily ascribe all Cicero's tergiversations to his appalling character. Did he not sicken his interlocutors by his endless boastings to know it all ('omnia comperi') that made Seneca remark that Cicero praised his own consulate 'non sine causa sed sine fine' (*De Brev. Vit.* 5. 1).

As a matter of fact, his meteoric rise to fame and power ended after 63 BC. His inglorious behaviour during his exile, his shameless public surrender to the triumvirs in his speech *De Provinciis Consularibus,* his own acknowledgement that he was ashamed of himself (*Ad Att.* 4.5), and his dramatic cry, 'Goodbye to honesty, straightforwardness and uprightness', may support Mommsen's contempt of Cicero.

In his frustration he wrote to his brother that his lifelong aspiration to excel and be the leader of others has completely vanished (*Ad Qu. Fr.* 3.5.4). He was left with no choice but to accept the advice of Atticus and to make an effort to win the affection of those who had influence:

Since those who have no power do not wish to love me, let me direct my efforts so that those who do have power may care for me. You'll say: 'I wish you'd thought of that before'. I know you've wanted it and that I have been a genuine ass.

Quoniam, qui nihil possunt, ii me nolunt amare, demus operam, ut ab iis, qui possunt, diligamur. Dices: 'vellem iam pridem'. Scio te voluisse et me asinum germanum fuisse. (*Ad Att.* 4. 5. 3)

Nor did his endless waverings between October 50 BC and the battle of Pharsalos in 48 gain him more respect. He understood that a civil war between Pompey and Caesar was no solution and that eventually one tyrant would assume the rule. However, he knew only whom to flee, but not whom follow ('quem fugiam habeo, quem sequar non habeo': *Ad Att.* 8. 7. 2).

Eventually he had to make a decision. He joined Pompey, reluctantly, because he appreciated him neither as a statesman nor as a general, 'A man whom I knew to be a useless statesman of old, but whom I now indeed see even to be a useless general' ('Quem ego hominem ἀπολιτικώτατον omnium iam ante cognoram, nunc vero etiam ἀστρατηγητότατον': *Ad Att.* 8. 16. 1), but he believed that he owed it to him: 'Beneficium sequor—mihi crede—non causam' ('I follow the obligation—believe me—not the cause': *Ad Att.* 9. 7. 3).

Not for long. He was miserable in Pompey's camp in Greece, and since he preferred 'to lose friends rather than a joke' he made many enemies and returned to Italy, but could not find his peace under Caesar's dictatorship either. He was disappointed when Caesar did not take any notice of his recommendations for a new beginning by 'establishing juries, recalling good faith, restraining lusts and promoting the rearing of children' ('constituenda iudicia, revocanda fides, comprimendae passiones, propaganda suboles': *Pro Marcello* 23; cf. ibid. 8–9, 25–9, and *Ad Att.* 13. 27. 1) and thus reanimating all that had been disintegrated and dissipated by the Civil War.

He felt humiliated when he had to wait long hours in Caesar's antechambers before being received by the dictator:

> When at the request of Sestius I was calling on Caesar and was sitting waiting until I should be called, Caesar said: 'I'm sure I must be a most unpopular man, when M. Cicero sits and cannot see me at his own convenience.'

> Cum Sestio rogatu apud eum [i.e. Caesar] fuissem exspectaremque sedens quoad vocarer, dixisse eum: 'ego dubitem quin summo in odio sim, cum M. Cicero sedeat nec suo commodo me convenire possit.' (*Ad Att.* 14. 1. 2–3)

He felt deeply hurt when, at last, the great man accepted the invitation to dine at his villa, arrived with an enormous entourage, enjoyed a lordly meal, and discussed problems of language and literature, but skilfully avoided any political topic. An infuriated Cicero reported to his friend that he would never invite such a guest again: 'Once is enough!' ('semel satis est': *Ad Att.* 13. 52).

In public, however, he never spoke out against Caesar, an attitude which made a French scholar remark: 'Le père de la patrie est devenu le bouffon de la tyrannie' (Duruy 1870: ii. 352). Brutus and Cassius must have known Cicero's state of mind in those days. They refrained from asking him to join the conspiracy. After Caesar's death, Cicero complained that he had not been invited to the 'party' of the Ides of March (he would not have allowed the sparing of Antony's life), but Shakespeare, who never read Cicero's letters, ingeniously reconstructed the reasoning of the conspirators for not inviting him:

Ah, name him not; let us not break with him.
For he will never follow anything
That other men begin.
(*Julius Caesar* 2. i. 150–2)

When dissension grew between the young Octavian and Antony, Cicero enthusiastically supported Octavian in public, but in private he was at least supposed to have been less wholehearted: in a letter to Cicero Brutus reports that:

Caesar himself had, of course, no complaint of you, except for a remark which he said you had made that 'the young man should be praised, honoured and carried off'; he said he would ensure that he could not be 'carried off'.

ipsum Caesarem nihil de te questum nisi dictum quod diceret, te dixisse laudandum adulescentum, ornandum, tollendum; se non esse commissurum ut tolli possit. (*Fam.* 11. 20. 1)

He paid a heavy price for his wittiness. Abandoned by Octavian, he was brutally killed by Antony's henchmen in 43 BC.

He, holding his chin in his left hand, as was his custom, gazed steadfastly at the assassins . . . so that most of them covered their faces as Herennius was killing him . . . he cut off his head and, on the orders of Antony, the hands which wrote the Philippics.

αὐτὸς δ' ὥσπερ εἰώθει τῇ ἀριστερᾷ χειρὶ τῶν γενείων ἁπτόμενος, ἀτενὲς ἐνεώρα τοῖς σφαγεῦσιν . . . ὥστε τοὺς πλείστους ἐγκαλύψασθαι τοῦ Ἑρρενίου σφάγοντος αὐτὸν . . . τὴν δὲ κεφαλὴν ἀπέκοψεν αὐτοῦ καὶ τὰς χεῖρας, Ἀντωνίου κελεύσαντος, αἷς τοὺς Φιλιππικοὺς ἔγραψεν. (Plut. *Cic.* 48. 3–4)

Now, the main question: could Cicero be depicted as a philosopher in politics? I would like to formulate the question differently, because I do not want to enter into a debate with scholars who regard Cicero as an eclectic who never produced anything original in philosophy. I would like to submit that Cicero's literary output was remarkable, and even if his books on rhetoric and politics, philosophy and religion, language and literature, lack originality, his insights were often illuminating and instructive. Nobody can deny that he was a man of letters *par excellence*, and as such he faced the same problems as philosophers in antiquity or intellectuals in politics in our own days.

Just as Paul Johnson (1988) has disclosed the hidden vices in the characters of Rousseau, Marx, Sartre, and Brecht, one could easily point out the striking contradictions between Cicero's thoughts and his actions or between his public speeches and private letters. This might lead us to a further question. Is this kind of behaviour typical for men of letters in politics? The only answer possible would be that it was not typical but not untypical either (a phrase coined by Finley 1973: 36). Keep in mind that one of Cicero's misfortunes was precisely the preservation of so many truthful and sincere letters to Atticus: 'I speak with you as if with myself' ('Ego tecum tamquam mecum loquor') in which he describes the pains and torments he went through, especially when he had to decide which side to join in the turbulent days of the late Republic. He was, after all, not the only senator who changed sides; why then should he take the brunt for all of them?

It is of course true that ancient political groupings do not resemble modern political parties. There were no carefully defined political programmes, and personal ties often meant more than ideologies. But this does not mean that a common belief in a certain political ideal did not play a role at all: 'To want the same things and not want the same things—that ultimately is solid friendship' ('Idem velle atque idem nolle—ea demum firma amicitia est': Sall. *Cat.* 20. 4) are the words Sallust put into Catilina's mouth. Or elsewhere: 'quos omnis eadem cupere eadem odisse, eadem metuere, in unum coegit' ('all those whom the same desires, hatred and fears compel to unite': Sall. *Jug.* 31. 14). In ancient Rome, people understood the difference between giving support to an individual and automatically joining his party. This is how Atticus behaved towards Brutus after the assassination of Caesar. He gave him money, but he not only refused to join his *factio*; he even refrained from meeting Brutus' friends and political associates:

> He, judging that his duties to a friend should be discharged without joining parties and having always distanced himself from such plans, replied that if Brutus wished to use any of his resources he might do so, as far as they extended, but that he would neither discuss nor meet with anyone concerning the affair.

> at ille, qui officia amicis praestanda sine factione existimaret semperque a talibus se consiliis removisset, respondit: si quid Brutus de suis facultatibus uti voluisset, usurum quantum eae paterentur, sed neque cum quoquam de ea re collocuturum neque coiturum. (Nepos, *Att.* 8. 4)

An enmity between people could derive from differences in political opinions (ex rei publicae dissensione: *Pro Sestio* 72), and in the political jargon of the late Republic it was the term *causa* that enabled someone to express his personal allegiance to a leader without supporting his *causa,* or political plans (*Ad Att.* 9. 7. 3). For educated people, belief in a *causa* was essential. And Cicero was an educated man. He, too, adhered to a political ideal.

Concordia ordinum (harmony between the orders) was for him more than just a political catchword. A serious alliance between the *ordo senatorius* and the *equites* would not only serve the best interests of Rome; it could also solve the personal problem of our *novus homo* from Arpinum: he could execute the policies of the senators without neglecting the economic interests of the Roman *equites*. This *concordia* prevailed during the days of the Catilinarian conspiracy in 63 BC, but it collapsed as early as 62 BC, mainly because diehard senators (like Cato the Younger) refused to accommodate some disgraceful economic demands of the *equites* ('turpis postulatio': *Ad Att.* 1. 17. 8–9), and according to Cicero, because he had forgotten that he did not live in Plato's *Politeia*, but in the 'cesspit of Romulus' (in Romuli faece: *Ad Att.* 2.1.8).

It is therefore possible to depict Cicero as a clever pragmatist, a believer in balanced compromises, and not as a shameless opportunist, and this has nothing to do with his being a philosopher or a man of letters. Every compromising moderate faced the danger of being nicknamed *kothornos* like Theramenes in Athens. With an eye to figures such as the former United States Secretary of State Henry Kissinger, some political scientists have differentiated between intellectuals in politics and intellectual politicians. An intellectual politician is a certain type of politician. An intellectual in politics is a special type of intellectual. Does this classification help us to understand Cicero better? To a certain extent, but there is more to it. It is my firm conviction that anyone who goes into politics starts to behave like a politician. He rarely has the time or the patience to think theoretically and thoroughly about the problems he faces in his daily occupation.

Timing is an essential factor in politics, and it was timing that forced even an intellectual like Walter Rathenau to make a quick decision at the Rapallo conference, which eventually led in 1922 to his assassination (see Joll 1960: ch. 2). As chairman of a debating club, which met every Wednesday at his home in Berlin, he had time to reflect and even delay a final, well-considered answer for a week. As minister of foreign affairs of Germany there was no such time at his disposal. And Cicero was not an armchair man of letters. He was an active Roman senator, a consul who carried responsibilities, and was often expected to act under pressure.

A little story concerning a perhaps fictitious conversation between an intellectually bright and curious teenager (Alcibiades) and an elderly, worn-out statesman (Pericles) might be instructive. Pericles comes home after a long and hectic working day, eager to freshen up, take a rest and reflect undisturbed on some complicated issues which had preoccupied him at his office. At that very moment he is asked by young Alcibiades 'to teach him what a law is'. Pericles answers with obvious reluctance, and, indeed, Alcibiades points out the flaws in most of Pericles' definitions. Eventually, the old man—perhaps in order to put an end to a conversation he had resented from the very beginning—admits that when he was Alcibiades' age, he was very clever at this sort of thing:

'For the puzzles we thought about and exercised our wits on were just such as you seem to me to be doing now'.

'Ah, Pericles', cried Alcibiades, 'if only I had known you intimately when you were at your cleverest in these things.'

'τοιαῦτα γὰρ καὶ ἐμελετῶμεν καὶ ἐσοφιζόμεθα, οἷάπερ καὶ σὺ νῦν ἐμοὶ δοκεῖς μελετᾶν.'

Τὸν δὲ Ἀλκιβιάδην φάναι: 'Εἴθε σοί, ὦ Περίκλεις, τότε συνεγενόμην, ὅτε δεινότατος σαυτοῦ ταῦτα ἦσθα.' (Xen. *Mem.* 1. 47)

This story illustrates the disappointment caused by exaggerated expectations, and it is this disappointment that haunted Cicero, not only in his lifetime, but also in his afterlife in scholarship. In *Cicéron et ses amis* (1897) Gaston Boissier tried to understand and forgive. Mommsen did not. One expects a great deal from all people involved in public life, but from philosophers and men of letters, religious leaders, and socialists a little bit more.

Deus or *Divus*: The Genesis of Roman Terminology for Deified Emperors and a Philosopher's Contribution

DAVID WARDLE

To a Roman of the first century AD who chose to reflect on the changes the state had witnessed over the previous century perhaps one of the most striking would be the introduction of imperial cult. By the appropriation and adaptation of Hellenistic ruler cult the early Roman emperors opened up a new way in which their subjects could conceive of and relate to their rulers. While much of this new relationship was expressed in cult actions such as sacrifices and religious ceremonies, language was also crucial. Simon Price has demonstrated (1984*a*) that Roman imperial cult is best understood as a system for negotiating and conceptualizing power, and as concentrated on ritual.[1] Here I shall focus on one word, *divus*, which was to become ubiquitous in Roman imperial cult as the term denoting a deified emperor, and ask how this came to be, relying largely on the evidence in Cicero's philosophical works. I hope I can show that one of Miriam's main interests, Cicero's philosophical works, can also contribute to our understanding of early Roman imperial ruler cult.

Both *deus* and *divus* derive from a common root in **deywos* (Old Latin *deivos*) and have a fundamental connection with the Indo-European terms for 'sky' (Schwering 1914–15: esp. 30; Sihler 1995: 337–9). Schwering, in his detailed study of the uses of both words in Republican Latin, posited an original distinction between *deus* as the generic term (*Gattungsbegriff*) for deity and *divus* as the individual deity (*Gott-Individuum*) and explained its

Miriam taught me as an undergraduate and was the principal supervisor of my D.Phil. thesis. At every stage she has been unstinting in support, encouragement, and sage advice. It is a privilege to be able to contribute to this celebration of Miriam's career.

[1] There has been considerable discussion in recent years on ruler cult in the Roman Empire and on the terminology employed for deified emperors, e.g. Price 1984*b*: 83. The most detailed statement of his views, in a work which has received overwhelmingly favourable reviews, remains Price 1984*a*: esp. 220. Cf. Price 1987: 77; Chirasso Colombi 1993: 796; Clauss 1996: 400–33.

use for deceased emperors on the grounds that, just as during their earthly lives they had manifested a powerful personality, so in their heavenly translation they were perceived as a personal god (*Gott-Individuum*).[2] Thus the choice of *divus* was motivated by theological and philological considerations. Schwering has to admit, however, that much of the force of the distinction was lost over time and that by the first century BC there was a tendency to use *deus* more or less indiscriminately while *divus* was relegated to the literary register (1914–15: 41).[3] Even if, on the basis of the literary and epigraphic evidence which has survived to the twentieth century, Schwering's distinction between the generic *deus* and the specific *divus* is correct, that is no proof that the people of the late first century BC understood the distinction in that way or that such considerations determined its use for the deified Caesar.

Indeed the only extant definition from the Republican period, that of its finest scholar M. Terentius Varro, has no connection with the criteria employed by Schwering. Servius' commentary on Virgil, *Aeneid* 5. 45 'a sanguine divom' and *Aeneid* 12. 139 'diva deam' gives us indirectly Varro's view:

'divum' et 'deorum' indifferenter plerumque ponit poeta, quamquam sit discretio, ut deos perpetuos dicamus, divos ex hominibus factos, quasi qui diem obierint: unde divos etiam imperatores vocamus. sed Varro et Ateius[4] contra sentiunt, dicentes divos perpetuos, deos qui propter sui consecrationem timentur, ut sunt dii manes: quod tangit in duodecimo dicens: 'diva deam stagnis quae fluminibusque sonoris praesidet'.

[2] 1914–15: e.g. 30–1: 'ist sehr charakteristisch und bestätigt die Deutung des Wortes *Divus* als eines Individualitätsbegriffes, wie mir scheint, besonders eindringlich'. (The significance of the word *Divus* is most characteristically and acceptedly that of a conception of individuality, and, it seems to me, particularly forcibly so.) Ibid. 39: 'wie der Kaiser auf Erden als machtvolle Persönlichkeit gelebt hatte, so ging er auch in den Himmel ein als ein persönlicher Gott, ein Gott-Individuum und als solches auch in Jenseits ein in der Vollkraft des Selbstbewubtseins und der geistigen Persönlichkeit lebendes Ich'. (As Caesar on earth lived as a powerful personality, so he entered heaven too as a personal god, as a *Gott-Individuum*, and, as such, in the hereafter, a living 'I' in the full power of self-consciousness and in his spiritual personality.) Sihler (1995: 179) presents arguments from phonological glides—the parallel forms *deus* and *divus* 'result from levelling in opposite directions' from a shared paradigm.

[3] Schwering's comprehensive survey of the uses of *divus* in the *Thesaurus Linguae Latinae* (5. 1. 1649–58) shows that most of the extant examples from the Republic are from verse authors, where constraints of metre may govern the choice of noun. For example, Virgil (*Aen.* 12. 139) uses *diva* of Juno and *dea* of the nymph Juturna, where the distinction owes nothing to differing grades of deity or *Gott-Individuum* as opposed to *Gattungsbegriff*.

[4] Servius probably refers to L. Ateius Praetextatus rather than to C. Ateius Capito (cf. *GRL* 140–1), who is better known as a lawyer (cf. Price 1984*b*: 83 n. 39). The exact identity is unimportant here as Varro's priority is sure in either case.

For the most part the poet uses 'divum' and 'deorum' without distinction, although there is a difference in that we call perpetual divinities *dei* and those who have become gods after a human existence *divi*. But Varro and Ateius hold the opposite view, calling perpetual divinities *divi* and those who are honoured because of their being consecrated *dei*, as are the *di manes*. He touches on this in book 12 saying: 'deity (*diva*) [speaking to] deity (*dea*), she who watches over lakes and sounding rivers'.

deus autem vel dea generale nomen est omnibus; nam quod Graece δέος Latine timor vocatur, inde deus dictus est, quod omnis religio sit timoris. Varro ad Ciceronem tertio: 'ita respondeant cur dicant deos, cum <de> omnibus antiqui dixerint divos'.

deus or *dea* is the generic term for all gods; for what in Greek is called δέος is *timor* in Latin, from which *deus* comes, because all religion involves fear (*timor*). Varro writes in the third book of *De Lingua Latina* (dedicated to Cicero): 'Let them so respond why they say *dei*, since the ancients say *divi* of all divinities'.

Varro's distinction between *divus* as a perpetual divinity and *deus* of a deified human being is the very opposite of the distinction which came to dominate, the distinction which is found in Servius and other later commentators and antiquarians and which official imperial usage seems to have hallowed.[5]

To discover why *divus* was applied to Caesar in the late 40s BC it is more useful to understand what *divus* meant, or what connotations it bore, to an educated Roman of that period, than to pursue a linguistic approach as Schwering did. The second of these Varronian quotations, the sole surviving fragment definitely to be attributed to book 3 of the *De Lingua Latina*, provides a clue how to proceed: *divus* was seen to be archaic. Powerful and detailed contemporary literary evidence for this comes from book 2 of Cicero's *De Legibus*, which is principally concerned with religious law. Cicero in his own *persona* sets out a religious code for his ideal state and provides an extended commentary on its provisions (*Leg.* 2. 19–68). The introduction to the laws themselves, in which Cicero justifies his choice of language, is crucial (see Lebek 1970: 34):

Expromam equidem, ut potero, et, quoniam et locus et sermo familiaris est, legum leges voce proponam . . . sunt certa legum verba, Quinte, neque ita prisca, ut in veteribus duodecim sacratisque legibus, et tamen, quo plus auctoritatis habeant, paulo antiquiora quam hic sermo est. (*Leg.* 2. 18)

[5] Servius' and Varro's exact words appear to be taken up in the later *Differentiae* (ed. Bekker). Isidore (*Diff.* 2. 16) follows more succinctly 'deus semper est, divus fit' (the *deus* is eternal, the *divus* created). For a collection of ancient etymologies, see Maltby 1991: s.v. *deus* and *divus*.

I will present them as best I can, and, since the location and the conversation are between friends, I will set out my laws in the style of laws . . . there are fixed terms for laws, Quintus, not so antiquated as those in our ancient Twelve Tables and sacred laws, and yet, so that they may have more weight, I will use language a little more archaic than current speech.

The text of the laws contains deliberate archaisms which Cicero thought particularly appropriate to legal documents.[6] One of the clearest examples of this is his language to describe the gods. In general they are *divi*, for example in the opening words: 'ad divos adeunto caste, pietatem adhibento, opes amovento' (let them approach the gods in purity, bringing to them piety, leaving wealth behind) whereas in the dialogue section where Marcus is directly paraphrasing the opening sentences of his laws he writes 'caste iubet adire ad deos'.[7] One further use can illustrate this:

divos et eos, qui caelestes semper habiti, colunto et ollos, quos endo caelo merita locaverint, Herculem, Liberum, Aesculapium, Castorem, Pollucem, Quirinum, ast olla, propter quae datur homini ascensus in caelum, Mentem, Virtutem, Pietatem, Fidem, earumque laudum delubra sunto, ne ulla vitiorum sacra sollemnia obeunto. (*Leg*. 2. 19. See Schwering 1914–15: 4–5)

They shall worship as gods both those who have always been considered heavenly and also those whose merits have secured them access to heaven, Hercules, Liber, Aesculapius, Castor, Pollux, Quirinus, and also those qualities through which an ascent to heaven is given to man, Intellect, Courage, Piety, Good Faith. There shall be shrines to their praise, but they shall not undertake annual ceremonies in honour of the vices.

The dialogue passage which comments on this section of the laws, 'fortium bonorumque divinos', uses the adjective *divinus*, which before the fourth

[6] e.g. from *Leg*. 2. 19: 'faxit', 'habessit', 'ollos'. For a contrast with the contemporary practice in laws such as the *lex Coloniae Genetivae*, see below, p. 187. Livy's language particularly in sections dealing with portents reveals more archaic forms than his standard narrative. A comparable feature is the archaism present in Livian prayer formulae (see Hickson 1993: e.g. 24–5, 72); because of the conservatism of Roman religion in this respect these changed little. For the genre of historiography, Lebek (1970: 281–2), on the use of *divi* in a fragment of Sisenna (a correction for *viri*), argues that even as early as the first half of the 2nd cent. BC *deus* was the regular term, whereas *divus* was archaic and probably poeticizing.

[7] For *de Legibus* 2. 19 cf. 2. 24. The other uses of *divus* in Cicero's laws and *deus* in the dialogue commentary: 2. 20: 'quaeque quoique divo decorae grataeque sint hostiae, providento' (let them prescribe whatever victims are fitting and pleasing to each god). Compare too: 'quibus hostiis immolandum quoique deo' (which victims must be sacrificed to each god) and 'divisque aliis alii sacerdotes, omnibus pontifices, singulis flamines sunto' (let various priests be for various gods, the pontifices for all gods, and the flamens for individual gods); and 2. 21: 'divorumque iras providento' (let them foresee the wrath of the gods) and 'quibus divis creverint, procuranto' (let them make offerings to those gods which they decide); also 2. 22: 'eamque cum divum honore iugunto' (let them combine this with honour to the gods) and '†leto datos divos habento' (let them consider those who are dead gods).

century AD serves as the adjectival form of both *deus* and *divus*.[8] Crucially, however, his passage shows beyond doubt that for Cicero there is no theological distinction between 'eternal gods' and those who became gods through deification for their *merita*; both could be called *divi*.[9] At any rate Cicero offers no support to the distinction claimed by Varro, but provides strong grounds for believing that *divus* was, or at the least was believed to be, the term appropriate for a law modelled on an ancient exemplar.

There are, however, two passages in the laws where Cicero uses *deus* which might seem to overthrow the distinction I have posited.

> Quis secus faxit, deus ipse vindex erit. (*Leg*. 2. 19)
>
> Whoever does differently, god himself will punish.

This is the immediate continuation of the opening clause of the laws, 'ad divos adeunto caste' (let them approach the gods in purity), and at first sight presents a problem, but Cicero's use of the singular and the later form both suggest that he is importing a more overtly philosophical notion encompassing all divinity, a notion which approximates to Schwering's *Gattungsbegriff*.[10] The second exception may corroborate this solution:

> impius ne audeto placare donis iram deorum (*Leg*. 2.22)
>
> let no impious man have the audacity to appease the gods' anger by gifts.

In commenting on this injunction Cicero gives the reader Plato's view from his *Laws*,[11] 'qui vetat dubitare, qua sit mente futurus deus, cum vir nemo bonus ab inprobo se donari velit' (which leaves no doubt what the opinion of a god would be, since no good man wishes to accept a gift from a dishonest one). He renders Plato's θεός by *deus* and seems to be thinking of a category wider than the gods acknowledged in Roman state cult.

The third exception requires a slightly different form of argument, as the commentary on it has been lost in the lacuna between chapters 53 and 54:

> deorum manium iura sancta sunto (*Leg*. 2. 22)
>
> the rights of the *Di Manes* are to be sacred.

[8] The dialogue commentary, 'fortium bonorumque divinos' (*Leg*. 2. 28), uses the adjective *divinus* (Schwering 1914–15: 4–5).

[9] Cf. the later position as set out by Price (1984*b*: 77): '*divus* and *deus* were [not] two exclusive categories; rather, *divus* was a subcategory of *deus* and it was thus perfectly possible to refer to a consecrated emperor as *deus*'.

[10] *Leg*. 2. 25: 'quod autem non iudex sed deus ipse vindex constituitur' (for which no judge but a god himself is appointed avenger).

[11] *Leg*. 716e1–3: ἀκάθαρτος γὰρ τὴν ψυχὴν ὅ γε κακός, καθαρὸς δὲ ὁ ἐναντίος, παρὰ δὲ μιαροῦ δῶρα οὔτε ἄνδρ' ἀγαθὸν οὔτε θεὸν ἔστιν ποτὲ τό γε ὀρθὸν δέχεσθαι (He who is bad is impure in his soul, his opposite, pure; neither a good man nor a god can rightly accept a gift from a polluted man).

In extant Latin (outside of poetry) there is only one combination of *divi* and *manes* '[di]bus M[anibus] /infer[is]', and that is a questionable restoration (*CIL* ii. 4424, cf. Lucr. 3. 52). In all probability the phrase *d(i)i Manes* was set by Cicero's time and to present a variant would have seemed odd.

The fourth exception is the most problematic:

separatim nemo habessit deos neve novos neve advenas nisi publice adscitos; privatim colunto, quos rite a patribus <cultos acceperint>. (*Leg*. 2. 19)

No one shall have gods individually, either new or foreign unless they have been recognized by the state. Privately they shall worship those whose worship they have duly received from their ancestors.

In the commentary, 'suosque deos aut novos aut alienigenas coli', *deus* is used. In both law and commentary *dei* may be used to distinguish all kinds of deities from the gods formally recognized by the state, those rightly to be worshipped and because of the legal recognition extended to them properly to be called *divi* (*Leg*. 2. 25, with Schwering 1914–15: 35).[12]

To emphasize the archaic nature of *divus*, beyond the contrast between Cicero's use of *divus* in his proposed laws and his usage of *deus* in his commentary, we need only compare Cicero's other literary output. *Divus* appears only once in Cicero's extant speeches, and then specifically of the deified Caesar, in the Second Philippic, which was composed months after Caesar's death by which time the designation *Divus Iulius* had been legally conferred on him.[13] In his philosophical works *divus* occurs nine times, of which three are quotations from Ennius (*ND* 1.4, 64, 65), four from Cicero's own poetic works (*Div*. 1. 19, 21, 2. 63, 64), one is dictated by etymological considerations (*Div*. 1.1) and the other a translation of the title of a work by Protagoras (*ND* 1. 63). In his letters there are no examples of *divus*, whereas *deus* is found (e.g. *Att*. 1. 16. 6, 6. 3. 3, 8. 16. 1, 11. 2. 2; *Fam*. 10. 8. 6, 11. 18. 3, 14. 7. 1). Cicero, then, believed that *divus* was the appropriate term for a law.

[12] Clauss 1996: 410: 'für ihn sind *divi* die von Staats wegen anerkannten Götter, von denem sichere Vorstellungen verbreitet sind, *dei* dagegen alle göttlichen Wesen, auch fremde, unbekannte und unbestimmte, deren Göttlichkeit aber nicht geleugnet werden kann.' (The *divi* are those deities who are recognized by the state, by whom their cults are spread. *Dei*, on the other hand, have a fully divine nature, and although it may also be foreign, unknown and ill-defined, their godliness can not be denied.)

[13] *Phil*. 2. 110: 'est ergo flamen, ut Iovi, ut Quirino, sic Divo Iulio M. Antonius' (so for Divus Iulius in the same way as for Jupiter and Quirinus, M. Antonius is *flamen*). Cf. North 1975: 175 and Beard *et al*. 1999: ii. 222: 'the *only* explanation for Cicero's apparent knowledge is that he knew of detailed plans for deification drafted in Caesar's lifetime, but only implemented in the years after his death' (my emphasis). In earlier orators there is one passage in Cato the Censor where the manuscripts read 'dium immortalium' (ap. Fest. 268L) and Schwering has posited *divorum*. H. Malcovati 1956: fr. 73 prints *dium*.

This emphasis on the terminology appropriate to a law is directly relevant to the situation in 44 BC, because in Roman imperial cult consecration was achieved first and foremost by the passing of a *senatusconsultum* and then a *lex*. Most discussion has centred on the role of the Senate in debating the late emperor's claim to divinity and in issuing a decree which recognized his ascent to heaven and established divine honours for him—the *consecratio* proper (e.g. Price 1984*b*: 86–93).[14] Crucial, however, for establishing the role of the people, and thus the context of a *lex* proper, is an inscription from Aesernia:

Genio Deivi Iuli parentis patriae quem senatus populusque Romanus in deorum numerum rettulit.

To the spirit of Divus Julius, *pater patriae*, whom the senate and people of Rome placed among the number of the gods. (*CIL* x. 2668)[15]

In arguing, rightly, that *divus* was the correct term for a legally conferred divine status for Caesar, Clauss accepts the philological distinction made by Schwering, but ignores the probability that *divus* had disappeared from Roman legal terminology by the mid-first century BC, even where it would have been the appropriate term. Festus presents two examples of laws he attributes to the regal period which use *divus*: '<nurus> sacra divis parentum estod' and 'puer divis parentum sacer esto' (260L).[16] Even if these laws are not authentic, it may suggest that there was a belief that *divus* was the archaic form. The meagre surviving examples of Roman laws from the Republic preserved via inscriptions use only *deus* (Riccobono 1941), although it is worth mentioning that these all date from the late Republic: the *Lex Bantina* of 133–118 BC (*CIL* i.^{2} 582), the *lex Julia municipalis* of 48 BC (*CIL* i.^{2} 593), and three instances in the *lex Coloniae Genetivae* of 44 BC (*CIL* i.^{2} 594, e.g. LXX). Those laws of which the text survives only through literary sources make no contribution, because by an accident of transmission only those mediated by Greek sources mention gods, and the Greek θεός can represent both *divus* and *deus* (see e.g. Clauss 1996: 410).[17]

[14] Kierdorf 1986 clarifies the official terminology for deification, showing that the Senate's decree should not be called *consecratio*, but rather the introduction of cult—'Kulteinführung' (esp. 48–9).

[15] The vexed question whether this inscription dates from Caesar's lifetime, as the mention of his *genius* and his human titles suggest (on this last aspect, see Chastagnol 1984: 275–87), is unimportant to the question of the role of the people (but see Clauss 1996: 408–9).

[16] But cf. 204L: 'dis piaculum dato' from Numa's *lex spoliorum opimorum*. Cf. other inscriptional evidence from the Republican period showing that the common form was *di Parentes* (e.g. *CIL* v. 3283).

[17] For θεός as the general Greek rendering of both *divus* and *deus*, see Price 1984*b*: esp. 83–5. The earliest extant Greek writer to render *divus* into Greek, Diodorus Siculus, uses various periphrases: 5. 25. 4: ὁ κληθεὶς θεός (the so-called god); 4. 19. 2: τοῦ . . . θεοῦ προσαγορευθέν-

This survey of Roman laws opens up the possibility that the choice of *divus* involved a deliberate archaism by whoever was responsible for deciding on the title to be given the divine Caesar. Weinstock (1971: 391–2) has argued that 'it will have been Caesar, another linguistic expert, who inspired by the Varronian speculations created a real distinction which was to be lasting: "Divus" was from now on a god who had previously been a man' and in particular that Caesar secured this by a clause in his will. However, no evidence exists in Caesar's writings or in the various accounts of his dictatorship to suggest that he expressed any intellectual opinion on terms to express divinity or that his will set out an explanation for the use of *divus*. Moreover it may well be that the divine title had been decided upon during Caesar's lifetime, if the information of the Aesernia inscription does indeed predate Caesar's death and accurately reflects the decision taken by Senate and people.[18]

A passage in Dio Cassius has been used to suggest that Caesar was called *divus* before any *lex* in 44. Dio records a statue erected to Caesar on the Capitol after Thapsus in 46 BC with an inscription calling him ἡμίθεος (43. 14. 6; cf. 43. 21. 2: ὕστερον δὲ τὸ τοῦ ἡμιθέου ὄνομα ἀπ' αὐτοῦ ἀπήλειψεν—later he relinquished the titles of demi-god), the same statue as recorded by Servius (Auctus):

eique in Capitolio statuam, super caput auream stellam habentem, posuit: inscriptum in basi fuit 'Caesari emitheo'. (*ad* Virg. *Ecl.* 9.46)

He put up a statue to him on the Capitol, with a golden star above its head: the inscription on the base was 'the demi-god Caesar'.[19]

τος (the one referred to as a god), which may indicate a perceived difficulty. Cassius Dio, writing when Roman ruler cult had been practised for over 200 years, uses ἥρως of Julius Caesar (51. 20. 6–8, 56. 34. 2) and later deified emperors (e.g. 66. 19. 2, 67. 2. 6, 69. 2. 5).

[18] An inscription found on the island of Cos may corroborate that from Aesernia, but crucially 'divum' has to be restored. (*AE* 1947: no. 5): '[C(ives) R(omani) qui C]oi negotiantur [civitatem] Coam pietatis in [C(aium) Iulium Cae]sarem ponti[ficem maxim]um p[a]trem [patriae divum]que et benevol[entiae erga] se caussa' (Roman citizens who trade with Cos because of the piety of the citizenship of Cos towards Gaius Iulius Caesar, *pontifex maximus*, *pater patriae* and god and their deeds of kindness). See Clauss 1996: 408. A. Alföldi (1973: 99–100) argues plausibly for a senatorial decree passed in early 44 giving Caesar the official title *Divus*. But Suetonius' list of superhuman honours (*Iul.* 76. 1) excludes any such appellation. Cicero's use of *Divus Julius*, on which the argument also rests, may be thought to reflect the popular outpouring after the *ludi victoriae Caesaris* in July 44 and not official senatorial action, but North (1975: 175; followed by Fishwick 1987: 64–6) rightly stresses that, as Cicero presents the three key elements of the divinization—cult title, priesthood, and first *flamen*—this strongly suggests knowledge of the decree, or rather, as I have argued, of the law.

[19] For Weinstock (1971: 41 n. 6), Servius confuses the statue of 46 with that set up by Octavian after Caesar's assassination in the Forum (Pliny, *NH* 2. 94; cf. Suet. *Iul.* 88), but these texts, even when taken together, do not prove an error—more than one statue may have been decorated, although Octavian dedicated only one statue.

Weinstock (1971: 53, 158) grants as a possibility that the inscription 'unquestionably in Latin' read *Divo Iulio*. A. Alföldi suggests an imprecise rendering of 'numini Caesaris' (1975: 165). The most convincing interpretation, however, and one which pays the closest attention to Dio's linguistic usage, has Caesar given the title 'Romulus' (Fishwick 1975: 624–8). It would seem, then, that this passage cannot be brought into the debate.

Before suggesting why *divus* was applied to Caesar, it is worth tracing the rapid attribution of divinity to Caesar after his assassination: soon after the funeral, unofficial worship was paid to him in the Forum (e.g. Suet. *Iul.* 85)[20] and from September 44 BC even Cicero could apply *divus* to him, albeit with no enthusiasm (*Phil.* 2. 110). The intervening period had witnessed the celebration of the *ludi victoriae Caesaris* during which a comet had shone for seven nights and was believed to be Caesar's soul, ascended to heaven.[21] On 1 January 42 BC further honours were paid to Caesar which many have taken to include his formal incorporation 'in deorum numerum', but, as we have seen, that had occurred in 44 BC (see Fishwick 1987: 56).[22] The protagonists of the Triumvirate seem to have been relatively slow in utilizing Caesar's new status: although during the siege of Perusia in 41–40 BC Octavian's troops fired slingshot which bore the inscription 'Divom Iulium' (*CIL* xi. 6721, 21).[23] A. Alföldi and Giard (1984: 152) argue convincingly that the Perusine War, which ended around February 40 BC, was the context for the minting of the first bronze coins for Octavian with the legend 'DIVOS IULIUS' to pay and reward his soldiers for their loyalty to him and the late dictator.[24] *Denarii* were minted in 38 BC in the name of

[20] The Epicurean philosopher Philodemus (*Περὶ Θεῶν* 3: col. 8. 37, col. 10. 2) opposed this popular deification. See Cogrossi 1981: 141. Even Caesar's funeral in the city can be seen as an indication of his divine status (Liou-Gille 1988: 288–93).

[21] The older discussions of Scott 1941: 257–72 and Bömer 1952: 27–40, have in most respects been overtaken by those of Ramsey and Licht 1997 and Gurval 1997: 39–70 (see also Domenicucci 1996: esp. 60–70; Gee 2000: 163–74). Gurval rejects the appearance of a comet in 44, having Augustus himself fashion the myth, but the silence of Cicero is not fatal to the comet's historicity (see Ramsey and Licht 1997: 112–16), and the detailed record of sightings in both Rome and China are not inconsistent with a real comet.

[22] The mysterious *lex Rufrena* (*CIL* i^2. 2972) (from Minturnae): 'Deivo Iulio iussu populi Romani e lege Rufrena' (by order of *divus Iulius*, under the *lex Rufrena*, the Roman people . . .) probably belongs to 44 rather than to 42 or later. It is not certain whether this was the law by which Caesar was deified or one authorizing the setting up of statues to Caesar (cf. Taylor 1931: 268–9).

[23] The attribution of *denarii* with representations of a star to 44 BC is not secure. Crawford (1974: 744) accepts a date in 38 BC; contra A. Alföldi 1975: 157.

[24] A. Alföldi (1975: 178) dates the coin issues of Ti. Sempronius Gracchus and Q. Voconius Vitulus to 43 and thus the earliest numismatic references to that year, but Crawford (1974: 529–30, 742) and Wallmann (1988: 172–4) suggest 40 or later. Gurval (1997: 55–7) argues for 38 and after, seeing the coins as a response to Sex. Pompeius' coins which exalted his divine father.

M. Vipsanius Agrippa with facing busts of Caesar and Octavian with the respective legends 'DIVOS IULIUS' and 'DIVI F' (A. Alföldi and Giard 1984: 151).

The archaic term *divus*, I suggest, was deliberately chosen for the deified Caesar to lend the sanctity of tradition to a novel manœuvre, the only precedent for which was the consecration of Romulus. That itself seems to have been a very late idea introduced under Greek influence (Jocelyn 1988: 39–65; Skutsch 1985: 245–6), and owing considerably to the efforts of Caesar and the Julian *gens* in the first century BC.[25] Certainly during the Republic there was no religious activity relating to Romulus which marked him as other than one of the dead: he was never referred to as *divus* Romulus and in historical times was never the recipient of any cultic action distinguishing him from the undifferentiated group of the ancestors, the *di Manes*. When Cicero was writing *De Legibus* in the late 50s BC[26] he had no idea that Caesar or any other contemporary human being would be formally deified by the Roman state and that the terminology of his 'laws' would be followed in the law by which Caesar was deified. A textual crux, '†nos leto datos divos habento' (*Leg.* 2. 22), prevents us knowing whether Cicero's state made formal provision for the deification of deserving human beings, but the position of this clause between two which deal unambiguously with the continuing worship of ancestors by the family suggests strongly that he is dealing with the dead as an undifferentiated group, and does not conceive of an individual's inclusion in a public cult.[27]

[25] Classen 1962: esp. 191–2 shows that the identification with Quirinus owes much to the influence of the Julii, and particularly to that of Caesar after his election as *pontifex maximus* and that of Sex. Julius Caesar, his cousin and *flamen Quirinalis* in the 50s. La Penna (1988: 284) suggests a Sullan date. Dumézil (1970: 250–1) posits the first visible signs of the identification in 296 BC. By 51 BC in his *De Republica* (e.g. 2. 18, 20) Cicero could present the identification but without a secure attribution of the tradition. Even if the identification of Romulus with Quirinus was inspired or advanced by Caesar in the 50s BC, it is far from clear that Caesar was deliberately preparing the way for his own elevation rather than strengthening the prestige of his *gens* (*pace* Burkert 1962: 374). For the widespread practice of noble families tracing their ancestry to gods and the competitive element in this, see Wiseman 1974: 153–64. Even if Varro was active in tracing or promoting Trojan genealogies at Caesar's command to justify his extension of the patriciate in 45 (Toohey 1984: esp. 6–8), there is no necessary connection between this and Caesar's plans for his own deification.

[26] Even if *De Legibus* received some finishing touches in 44 or 43 BC, Cicero appears to have made no changes to this section of book 2 and the whole work was never published. On the dates see MacKendrick 1989: 330. Grilli (1990: 175–87; 1995: 55–63) has Cicero begin work on *De Legibus* between April and Sept. 46 and finish writing in 44, but Brunt (1989: 185 n. 25) and Fontanella (1995: 5 n. 1) reaffirm that *De Legibus* was not revised after the late 50s and was published posthumously.

[27] The manuscripts read *nos*, which is clearly out of place. Urlichs proposed <*bo*>*nos*, Davies *suos*: De Plinval <*huma*>*nos*; van der Bruwaene *hos*.

Something different was required for Caesar who was to receive the panoply of forms of worship given to any of the Hellenistic monarchs who were the recipients of ruler cult. It was important to underline clearly the change in Caesar's status which deification brought, to provide a form of address for the new divinity, and to distinguish Caesar from the plurality of Julii Caesares in the late Republic. The chosen form Divus Julius required relegating his *cognomen* in favour of the *nomen* and juxtaposing a term specifying 'god': C. Iulius Caesar became *divus Iulius*.[28] Although the juxtaposition of *divus* (or *deus*) with the name of a divinity was rare in non-literary Latin texts, as it was unnecessary for gods whose divinity and function were well known,[29] in 44 BC every assistance was required for the establishment and definition of the cult of Caesar.

Divus, then, was applied first to the deified Julius Caesar because it was perceived as the more archaic of the two nouns for god and the one more appropriate to laws (and thus to a legally conferred status); it was chosen for political rather than philological reasons.

[28] A few examples of *divus Caesar* exist, but the stress is never on his divinity (e.g. Livy 34. 9. 3; Suet. *DA* 96. 1). Rubincam (1992: 88–103) notes in writers of the triumviral period 'an apparent reluctance to make use of the convenient new title *divus*', which she attributes to a 'strong repugnance towards this elevation to divine status of one of their own kind'. Her table of naming practices is incomplete—Valerius Maximus is omitted and some variations in her listed authors are missed (e.g. *divus Caesar* at Suet. *Aug*. 96. 1).

[29] e.g. from inscriptions 'dei(va) Marica', a goddess from Minturnae (*CIL* i². 374), 'deiv(eis) No[v]esede (*CIL* i². 375), the divae Corniscae (*CIL* i². 975); from antiquarian researches: Diva Palatua (Varro, *LL* 7. 45), diva Rumina (Varro, *RR* 2. 11. 5), divus pater Falacer (Varro, *LL* 5. 85). Examples of *deus* from Rome connected with some divinity include Aesculapius (*CIL* vi. 2), Apollo (*CIL* vi. 23), Flora (*CIL* vi. 30867), Liber pater (*CIL* vi. 467), and most frequently Hercules (*CIL* vi. 263, 305, 314, 317, 3686). For the epigraphic uses, see D. Vaglieri in *Dizionario Epigraphico*, ii, s.v. *deus*, 1716–26. I believe that this epigraphic and literary evidence does not support the idea that *divus* was used in 44 BC for linguistic reasons, that the distinction between *deus* and *divus* is syntactical, that *divus* is more frequent in an adjectival function (see Mason 1974: 124). The archaic Latin material in *CIL* i² reveals a roughly equal usage of the two.

Arcanum Imperii: The Powers of Augustus

HANNAH M. COTTON AND
ALEXANDER YAKOBSON

INTRODUCTION

All the emperors after Augustus received the imperial powers in bulk for life at the moment of their accession.[1] Not so Augustus: in January 27 BC, as part of the 'first settlement', he was granted a number of provinces for ten years (Dio 53. 13. 1), and this grant was regularly renewed, for five or ten years, till the end of his reign (Dio 53. 16. 2). Our only source for those prorogations is Dio. His account is remarkable in two ways.

First, Dio understands these prorogations to be no less than the prorogation of the imperial power itself—the Principate.[2] Augustus' control over the provinces allotted him in 27 BC, not least because of the armies concentrated in them, was no doubt of crucial importance, but Dio himself is the source for the generally accepted view that at least since 19 BC Augustus enjoyed *imperium* in Rome and Italy,[3] and many scholars follow him in believing that in that year he was granted this domestic *imperium* for life. Why then should the provincial *imperium* (the so-called proconsular *imperium*) be equated with the imperial power itself? How, for instance, could the renewal of Augustus' *imperium* in the provinces in 18 BC—a year after he allegedly received the domestic *imperium* for life—be said to have added

Dedicated to my dear teacher and friend by her former student as well as by my former student. H.M.C. The translations of Greek and Latin texts usually follow those of the Loeb Classical Library.

[1] Dio 53. 18. 4: καὶ νῦν μὲν πᾶσαι ἅμα αὐτοῖς ὡς τὸ πολὺ . . . δίδονται. True, they may have declined some titles and assumed them later on, but they never declined the essence of power itself.

[2] Cf. Dio 53. 16. 2–3 (27 BC) ἡγεμονία; 54.12.4 (18 BC) προστασία; 55. 6. 1 (8 BC) ἡγεμονία; 55. 12. 2 (AD 3) ἡγεμονία; 56. 28. 1 (AD 13) προστασία τῶν κοινῶν. Especially telling is Dio's observation when Augustus received the supervision of morals for another five years in 12 BC (54. 30. 1): 'this office also, like the monarchy (ὥσπερ που καὶ τὴν μοναρχίαν), he received for limited periods (κατὰ προθεσμίας)'. It is not relevant for our argument here that the testimony on the 'supervision of morals' is suspect.

[3] Which included the command over the praetorian cohorts: cf. Suet. *Tib.* 24, Tac. *Ann.* 1. 7, for the symbolic as well as practical significance of this command as a token of imperial power.

five years to his Principate (*προστασία*)? (Dio 54. 12. 4.) In other words, how and why did the renewals of the provincial *imperium* come to assume such decisive importance? And not merely in Dio's eyes. Dio, after all, might be thought to be merely acknowledging the realities of power and consequently equating the control of the armies and the provinces with the Principate itself. The imperial regime on the other hand had no apparent interest in stressing the importance of the 'military' *imperium* in the provinces at the expense of the 'civil' *imperium* in Rome and Italy. And yet the emperors too treated those prorogations as relating to the imperial power as a whole: Augustus' acts of *recusatio* on these occasions make it clear that he regarded these renewals in this light,[4] as does Tiberius' celebration of his *decennalia* in AD 24 (Dio 57. 24. 1) and 34 (Dio 58. 24. 1). Furthermore,'subsequent emperors', Dio tells us, 'though no longer appointed for a specified period, but for their whole life, once and for all, nevertheless always held a celebration every ten years, as if then renewing their sovereignty once more; and this is done even at the present day' (53. 16. 3).

This brings us to the second remarkable feature in Dio's account. As just pointed out, it was precisely on the occasion of the periodical renewal of his *hegemonia* that Augustus put on an act of *recusatio*.[5] These expressions of reluctance continued until the very end of Augustus' reign, when the imperial system was firmly established and entrenched in people's minds as well as in political reality. In fact they continued, so to speak, after his death, for his successor, Tiberius, in the funeral oration he delivered over the dead Augustus, so Dio tells us, reminded the people that (in 27 BC) they had constrained Augustus 'for a time at least to be your leader', and when that period came to an end, 'you' (the people) 'forced' him, against his will, to agree to having his leadership prolonged time and again (56. 39. 6). Dio's account of the first renewal in 18 BC omits to mention a refusal on Augustus' part (though an echo of reluctance may perhaps be detected in Augustus' remark that a period of five years would be sufficient (Dio 54. 12. 4–5)); but even this is made good by Tiberius claiming that on this occasion, as well as

[4] On the *recusationes* and their significance see below.

[5] 55. 6. 1 (8 BC): *Μετὰ δὲ δὴ ταῦτα τήν τε ἡγεμονίαν, καίπερ ἀφιείς, ὡς ἔλεγεν, ἐπειδὴ τὰ δέκα ἔτη τὰ δεύτερα ἐξεληλύθει, ἄκων δῆθεν αὖθις ὑπέστη* ('After this, now that his second period of ten years had expired, Augustus once more accepted the supreme power—though with a show of reluctance—in spite of his oft-expressed desire to lay it down'). 55. 12. 3 (AD 3): *πληρωθείσης δέ οἱ καὶ τῆς τρίτης δεκαετίας τὴν ἡγεμονίαν καὶ τότε τὸ τέταρτον, ἐκβιασθεὶς δῆθεν, ὑπεδέξατο* ('And now that his third ten-year period was completed, he accepted the leadership for the fourth time, though ostensibly under compulsion'). 56. 28. 1 (AD 13): *τήν τε προστασίαν τῶν κοινῶν τὴν δεκέτιν τήν πέμπτην ἄκων δὴ ὁ Αὔγουστος ἔλαβε* ('Augustus with seeming reluctance accepted a fifth ten-year term as head of state').

on others, Augustus had to be 'forced' to agree to have his leadership of the state renewed (Dio 56. 39. 6).

Although scholars have realized the importance of the grand *recusatio* of 27 BC,[6] the continuing periodic *recusationes* have been all but ignored. What was the political import of these displays of reluctance?

The existence of Augustus' domestic *imperium* triggered off, as we have just seen, the present discussion: its existence makes it difficult to understand the periodic renewals of Augustus' power as applying to the provincial *imperium* alone; and conversely, the periodic renewals of the *hegemonia* make it difficult to accept Dio's claim that the domestic *imperium* of the *princeps* was granted for life. Consequently our discussion will attempt first to disentangle the vexed question of the legal source of Augustus' *imperium* in Rome and Italy. At some stage, as we shall argue, Augustus' *imperium* in the provinces was made to apply to Rome and Italy as well; this domestic *imperium*—contrary to Dio's testimony and the opinion of many modern scholars—was thus granted for limited periods and not for life. The prolongations, related by Dio, could thus be plausibly presented and regarded as renewing the imperial power itself—though, of course, they did not embrace all of the powers of the *princeps*[7]—and became fit occasions for Augustus to display his republican sentiments. In addressing the import and significance of these staged *recusationes* we hope to shed further light on an important ideological aspect of the Augustan Principate: its continuing ambivalent attitude towards the idea of sole rule.

The periodic prolongations of the imperial power and the *recusationes* set the Augustan Principate apart from other monarchical forms in which power was assumed (or even granted) for an unlimited period, that is for life: with every renewal of the imperial power the sovereignty of Senate and People as the bodies granting it was reasserted (compare Bleicken 1998: 371).

THE LEGAL BASIS OF AUGUSTUS' *IMPERIUM* IN ROME AND ITALY

Though this is denied by some,[8] it is obvious that Augustus must have held *imperium* in Rome and Italy;[9] it is, above all, simply inconceivable that he did not. Moreover, Augustus is attested as exercising capital jurisdiction in

[6] 'The Principate was established by an act of denial (*recusatio*), ritually perpetuated from reign to reign', Wallace-Hadrill 1982: 36; cf. Béranger 1953: 137; Yakobson and Cotton 1985: 497.

[7] See above, n. 2.

[8] Mommsen 1887: ii. 872 and n. 2 there; Premerstein 1937: 234–9; note e.g. ibid. 239: 'The successors of Augustus . . . possessed no permanent consular *imperium* either'. See recently Crook 1996: 91–2.

[9] A limited exercise of a proconsul's *imperium* in Italy, outside the *pomerium*, had Republican precedents, see Brunt and Moore 1967: 13.

Rome, commanding troops there, and appointing *praefecti urbi*[10]—none of which could be done without the possession of *imperium*.[11] He also claims in the *Res Gestae* to have conducted a *census* twice *consulari cum imperio*; this happened in 8 BC and in AD 14, when he was not consul (*RG* 8. 3–4). It would have been absurd for the Senate to confer a consular *imperium*, rather than a *censoria potestas*, on him just for the purpose of *census*—although they probably authorized him to exercise his consular power in a 'censorial' way—as apparently happened in 28 BC.[12]

What, then, was the legal source of this *imperium*? The most popular explanation today (found for example in Brunt and Moore 1967: 13–14) is based on Dio's testimony in 54. 10. 5:

τὴν δὲ τῶν ὑπάτων (scil. ἐξουσίαν) διὰ βίου ἔλαβεν, ὥστε καὶ ταῖς δώδεκα ῥάβδοις ἀεὶ καὶ πανταχοῦ χρῆσθαι, καὶ ἐν μέσῳ τῶν ἀεὶ ὑπατευόντων ἐπὶ τοῦ ἀρχικοῦ δίφρου καθίζεσθαι.

He took consular powers for life so that he could use (or: to the extent of having the right to use) the twelve rods always and everywhere and sit always in the curule chair between the two men who were at the time consuls.

This is usually taken to mean that in 19 BC Augustus received a grant of a consular power for life.[13] This seems highly implausible: consular power for life sounds too openly autocratic and 'un-Augustan' (Southern 1998: 133); moreover it is not certain that this is how Dio's text should be understood.[14]

It has also been suggested[15] that the source of his domestic *imperium* was the decision taken in 23 BC, also related by Dio, to allow Augustus' (proconsular) *imperium*, whenever and for as long as he possessed it,

[10] Not only the prerogative of appointing a *praefectus urbi*, but the very nature of the office proves that Augustus possessed domestic *imperium*: traditionally the *praefectus urbi* served as a substitute to city magistrates with *imperium* in the latters' absence. The holder of *imperium* in Rome replaced by the Augustan *praefectus urbi* was none other than Augustus himself!

[11] Cf. Brunt 1977*b*: 96, especially n. 9; A. H. M. Jones 1951: 117–18; Jones mentions there also the 'specifically consular prerogative' of receiving *professiones* for consular and praetorian elections exercised by Augustus in the latter part of his reign when he was no longer consul. Mommsen's (1887: ii. 564) and Premerstein's (1937: 243–4) attempts to explain away the exercise of *imperium* in Rome and Italy are not convincing.

[12] Cf. *ILS* 6123, Venusia: *Imp(erator) Caesar VI M. Agrippa II (cos.) idem censoria potestate lustrum fecer(unt)*.

[13] Ἐξουσία here must be interchangeable with *imperium*, which is often rendered as ἀρχή.

[14] See Premerstein 1937: 237–8, understanding the ὥστε clause following the τὴν δὲ τῶν ὑπάτων (scil. ἐξουσίαν) διὰ βίου ἔλαβε to limit the power to the consular *insignia*; cf. also Crook 1996: 91–2.

[15] Greenidge 1901: 341–2; Pelham 1911: 69–70; Brunt 1962: 71; Brunt 1977*b*: 96; H. S. Jones 1934: 138; see also Badian 1986: 81.

not to lapse—as it normally did—when he crossed the *pomerium* (Dio 53. 32. 5).[16] However, many have felt that a proconsular *imperium* could never have been exercised in Rome; it could only have been exercised in his provinces *from* Rome.[17] This feeling has more to it than the narrowly legalistic view that there was a clear-cut and fundamental difference between a 'consular' and a 'proconsular' *imperium*. Against the latter it has been convincingly shown that, under the Republic, what a proconsul had in his province was a consular *imperium*; that was the original meaning of *pro consule*,[18] and the very expression *proconsulare imperium* was itself an imperial invention, first attested under Tiberius.[19] Yet it is impossible to deny the gut feeling that to allow Augustus to exercise a proconsul's *imperium* within Rome and Italy might have seemed tantamount to subjecting the city to something like 'military rule', or treating Rome and Italy like a province (Premerstein 1937: 242, 244).[20]

However, the arrangement envisioned here need not have resulted in openly assimilating Augustus' position in Rome and Italy to that of a proconsul lording it over his province. On the contrary, we must assume that precisely this was carefully avoided (Pelham 1911: 73, 78).[21] His *imperium* gave him in the city legal powers that were no more than equal to those

[16] *τὴν τὲ ἀρχὴν τὴν ἀνθύπατον ἐσαεὶ καθάπαξ ἔχειν ὥστε μήτε ἐν τῇ ἐσόδῳ τῇ εἴσω τοῦ πωμηρίου κατατίθεσθαι αὐτὴν μήτ' αὖθις ἀνανεοῦσθαι*. The two words *ἐσαεὶ καθάπαξ* are commonly translated 'once for all and for life'—thus contradicting Dio's own specific and repeated testimony on the prorogations. For the translation 'whenever and for as long as' offered in the text: see most recently Crook 1996: 86 (cf. also 92 n. 112); this was observed long ago by Kolbe (1931: 56; cf. Premerstein 1937: 232–3); cf. Bleicken 1990: 96–7 and n. 267. If understood as 'once for all and for life', then Dio may be simply wrong—yet another example of his tendency to exaggerate Augustus' powers (see below, n. 24 and text); alternatively, one may take Dio's claim in the purely technical sense suggested in A. H. M. Jones 1951: 114–15.

[17] Passionately argued by Premerstein 1937: 242; accepted by Syme 1939: 406 n. 2; and recently repeated by Eck in his succinct account of the consequences of the 'second settlement' in the year 23 (1998: 54): 'In Rome itself Augustus could not act by virtue of his proconsular *imperium*'.

[18] Pelham 1911: 65 followed by A. H. M. Jones 1951: 118, and others.

[19] See above all Girardet 2000. We are grateful to Klaus Girardet for putting the manuscript at our disposal in advance of publication; cf. also Brunt 1977*b*: 96, n. 7.

[20] The feeling survived to the 2nd cent. AD and caused Antoninus Pius to rescind Hadrian's policy of sending *legati Augusti pro praetore* of consular rank whose title and competence were identical to those of the provincial governors into regions of Italy: see Eck 1991; cf. Eck 1999: 253; Cotton 2000: 222–3. The *locus classicus* for the contrast between the exercise of *imperium* in Rome and the provinces is of course Cic. *QF* 1. 1. 22.

[21] An echo of this deliberate attempt not to appear to be governing Rome *proconsule* might be preserved in Dio's observation that the emperors were always styled proconsuls [but only] 'when outside the *pomerium*' (53. 17. 4). However, Augustus' absence from Rome in 15 BC may not be the reason for the use of *proconsule* in the new edict from Spain (l. 2), but rather the audience which the edict is addressing; wherever Augustus was, he was *proconsule vis-à-vis* his own provinces; see, however, G. Alföldy 2000: 193–4.

possessed by the two annual consuls;[22] furthermore, only in 19 BC did he receive the consular *insignia*. This *imperium* may have been provincial ('proconsular') in its origin, but it was thoroughly domesticated and made to look relatively inoffensive so as not to provoke the emotional reaction against 'redacting Italy [and Rome] into a province'.[23]

Seen in this light, the idea that Augustus' *imperium* in the provinces was, by a special enactment (either in 23 BC or later, see below), 'applied' to Rome and Italy looks less outrageous than it seems at first sight. Of course, such an arrangement would have been untraditional; but then any arrangement that allowed Augustus to exercise *imperium* in Rome and Italy while he was not consul must inevitably have been untraditional to some extent. At any rate, this explanation has the merit of turning Augustus' *imperium* in the city into a temporary one (as a proper republican *imperium* ought to be): it lasted for ten (or five) years at a time and was prolonged, repeatedly, by Senate and People. On the other hand, the theory of a 'consular *imperium* for life' granted in 19 BC is difficult to accept precisely because it would have been too blatantly untraditional, making a mockery of Augustus' claim in the *Res Gestae* that he never took an office *contra morem maiorum*. Moreover, it would seem preposterous to regard the periodic renewals of Augustus' powers in the provinces as prolonging the imperial power, the Principate (or the 'monarchy', as Dio would have it: 53. 17. 1), if one assumes that Augustus held, independently and separately from his *imperium* in the provinces, a consular *imperium* for life in Rome and Italy. Indeed 'the consular power for life' may well be another instance of Dio's tendency to make sweeping—and inaccurate—statements on Augustus' legal powers and monarchical position.[24] Dio may have misconstrued a source which created a temporal linkage between Augustus' provincial *imperium* in the provinces and the exercise of that *imperium* in the city: whenever and for as long as he possessed the *imperium* in the provinces, he would be able to exercise it in Rome. The phrasing may have been identical to that which, according to our reconstruction (above, n. 16 and text), bestowed on him in 23 BC the

[22] See below for the suggestion that between 23 and 19 BC his *imperium* was less than that of the consuls.

[23] *quasi ... in formam provinciae [Italia] redigeretur,* as C. Albucius Silus put it when L. Piso as proconsul exercised criminal jurisdiction in Cisalpine Gaul (Suet. *Rhet.* 6 with Kaster 1995: 323–4).

[24] Cf. 53. 28. 2 (24 BC) where Augustus is 'freed from all compulsion of the laws' (τῆς τῶν νόμων ἀνάγκης ἀπήλλαξεν); 54. 18. 1 (17 BC) where on Lucius' birth Augustus is said to have appointed him and his brother, Gaius, 'then and there successors to his office'. The so-called *Lex de Imperio Vespasiani*, clause VII, gives the lie to Dio's first statement, cf. Brunt 1977*b*: 108–9; the second statement needs no refuting.

lifelong privilege of not losing his provincial *imperium* when crossing the *pomerium*. If so, Dio may easily have mistaken this formula for a bestowal of a lifelong consular *imperium*.[25]

If Augustus' *imperium* not only did not lapse when he crossed the *pomerium* but could be exercised in Rome itself, a purely formal precedent for such an arrangement might have been offered by the senatorial decrees which allowed proconsuls to keep their *imperium* in Rome on the day of their triumph.[26] Of course, Augustus' case was entirely different: not only was he thus given a real power for a prolonged period, rather than just being allowed to conduct a ceremony, but we must assume that he could henceforward exercise his *imperium* in Rome and Italy even when he was in the provinces (as often happened during that period). The formula devised in 23 BC must have been sufficiently flexible to provide for this. But it would have been entirely in the spirit of his Principate for Augustus to effect a revolutionary change by relying on some ancient precedent or formula, or by devising a formula which sounded sufficiently close to an ancient one.[27]

23 OR 19 BC?

Avoiding the automatic expiry of Augustus' *imperium* on crossing the *pomerium* did not, by itself, make his *imperium* operative within the city and Italy. A proconsul should exercise his *imperium* only within his legally granted province—only by special authorization could he exercise it outside it.[28] The enabling formula must have included some positive indication that Rome and Italy were, for Augustus, a proper sphere of action. Devising such a formula would be a delicate matter. Moreover, since there was no precedent for someone exercising a proconsul's *imperium* in Rome for a prolonged period, it may well have been unclear what exactly it was proper

[25] We are grateful to Werner Eck for this suggestion.

[26] See Livy 26. 21. 5, 45. 35. 4 with Mommsen 1887: i. 128–9. Cf. also Livy 26. 9. 10 (cited in n. 33 below) where in the emergency of the Second Punic War a proconsul was allowed by the Senate to enter the city with his army and keep his *imperium*. Martin Jehne reminds us of Pompey's *cura annonae* in 57, which according to Dio (39. 9. 3) entailed ἀρχὴν ἀνθυπάτου in Italy, perhaps also some powers in Rome, see Cic. *Dom*. 25–6.

[27] e.g. the powerful new office of the *praefectus urbi* created by Augustus had but a formal and superficial connection to the ancient republican office bearing the same name, cf. Tac. *Ann*. 6. 11. Note that Suetonius gives it as an example of the creation of *nova officia* by Augustus, *Div. Aug*. 37. See Mommsen 1887: ii. 1059.

[28] *Proconsul . . . potestatem non exercit nisi in ea provincia sola, quae ei decreta est*, *Dig*. 1. 16. 1. The prohibition had to be re-enacted time and again; evidently, it was much harder to enforce than the automatic lapsing of the *imperium* on crossing the *pomerium* reflected in the *Lex Cornelia*: *lege Cornelia imperium habiturum quoad in urbem introisset*, Cic. *Fam*. 1. 9. 25; cf. Cic. *Pis*. 50.

for Augustus to do.[29] It has even been suggested that the enabling formula was left deliberately vague, so as 'not to declare explicitly what was implied' (Greenidge 1901: 341). It seems likely that at the very least, Augustus' right to command troops in Rome and Italy was firmly secured.

When was the 'enabling' formula devised: in 23 or 19 BC? Opting for 23 BC has the advantage of explaining how Augustus could command the praetorian cohorts before 19 BC (though this could have been arranged by a special enactment), and, generally, it would mean that there was no interruption in his *imperium* in Rome and Italy.

However, this seems to play down the significance of the year 19 BC. But the year 19, it must be conceded, does appear to have been politically significant. This emerges not only from Dio's account of events from 23 to 19 BC—the people, who had repeatedly clamoured for Augustus to accept the consulship since 23 BC, calmed down in 19 BC and remained calm thereafter—but also from Augustus' own remarks in the *Res Gestae* (11–12. 1).

It may be that between 23 and 19 BC Augustus lacked only the trappings of *imperium*, and this was made good in 19 BC to the satisfaction of the common people unduly impressed by the ceremonial side of things.[30] Dio's passage (54. 10. 5) can indeed be read in this light: he lays great stress on the *fasces* and the seat between the consuls. 'On this view, in 23 Augustus lost no real power, but only the outward appearance of it; it was only the *insignia* which he lacked until 19, and he then received them' (Brunt and Moore 1967: 14).

This theory which opts for 23 BC is open to the objection that it turns the 'second settlement' into too transparent a sham:[31] having resigned the consulship in that year Augustus not merely failed to lose any power, but actually increased his power by receiving, instead of the annual consulship, the full consular power for a much longer period. It is thus better to assume that he did lose real power in 23 BC—not only the trappings of it—by resigning the consulship.

One may therefore go back to accepting 19 BC as the year in which Augustus was granted *imperium* in Rome and Italy, but this was not a

[29] Until his *imperium* was formally equated with that of the consuls, see below.

[30] Those who do not believe in the grant of consular *imperium* in 19 take Dio's statement to refer to a grant of the consular *insignia* in that year, cf. above n. 14. However, 'the *insignia* could hardly have been bestowed on a man who did not enjoy the power they symbolised' (Brunt and Moore 1967: 13; Brunt 1977*b*: 96 n. 8). Moreover, Augustus would hardly have taken the *insignia* without the reality of power; on the contrary, if anything, he would opt for the reality of power without the *insignia*.

[31] cf. Velleius Paterculus 89. 5 on the 'republican' nature of Augustus' decision to surrender the consulship in 23 BC.

separate consular *imperium* given for life but the 'widening' of his provincial *imperium*. In other words, the application of the proconsular *imperium* to Rome and Italy was not immediate, it did not happen in 23 BC; only in 19 was Augustus allowed to exercise his *imperium*, hitherto confined to the provinces, in Rome and Italy. A. H. M. Jones, who espouses this theory, suggests that this was done by the Senate declaring 'Augustus' *imperium* to be equal to that of the consuls, thus releasing it from its territorial limitations' (Jones, 1951: 118).[32]

However, equality with the consuls' *imperium* and the release from territorial limitations, that is allowing a proconsular *imperium* to be exercised in Rome, do not have to stand in a cause and effect relationship to each other. Indeed, 'the release from territorial limitations' is more likely to have preceded the equation.[33] Therefore we propose that there was a two-stage process. Augustus' 'domestic' *imperium* was indeed first created in 23 BC, but he *did* lose power in resigning the consulate: any arrangement which allowed him to exercise his so-called proconsular *imperium* in Rome and Italy must have meant that formally the consuls, as the highest magistrates of the state, enjoyed—*horribile dictu*—an *imperium* greater than that of the *princeps*.[34] In 19 BC, under insistent and prolonged popular pressure, further enactment placed him, both in respect of his actual powers and symbolically, on an equal footing with the consuls.[35] Dio's *fasces* and the seat between the consuls are not merely the appurtenances of power but the expression of the acquisition of a greater *imperium* than the one he had had hitherto. If so, it is easy to understand how Dio could have described this as conferring the consular *imperium* on Augustus. Likewise, it makes sense of the behaviour of 'the people'—the urban *plebs*—between 23 and 19: they did not clamour repeatedly for Augustus to assume the consulship merely because they could not bear to see him without the *fasces*; they were satisfied

[32] A similar conclusion is reached by Girardet 1990: 118. In contrast to what he said in 1951, in 1970: 60 A. H. M. Jones appears to accept fully that Augustus took consular *imperium* for life in 19 BC—which may account for Crook's comment: 'Most scholars, nowadays, are only too happy to believe that Augustus accepted [the consular power] for life in 19 [following A. H. M. Jones 1951]' (1996: 91 with n. 111).

[33] Cf. Livy 26. 9. 10 (211 BC): *cui* (the proconsul, Q. Fulvius) *ne minueretur imperium si in urbem venisset, decernit senatus par cum consulibus imperium esset* with Mommsen's comment (1887: i. 638 n.2): 'certainly not merely, as Livy says, to prevent his losing his *imperium* on entering the city . . . but also in order to make it equal to that of the consuls'.

[34] Even in Augustus' own provinces, if we accept Cicero's *omnes enim in consulis iure et imperio debent esse provinciae* ('for all provinces should be subject to the consul's jurisdiction and *imperium*', *Phil.* 4. 9). For although his *imperium* in 23 BC was made superior to that of the other proconsuls, in theory, at least, it was still formally inferior to that of the consuls. This anomaly, we suggest, was corrected in 19 BC.

[35] Cf. the *tribunicia potestas* which Augustus seems to have accepted gradually until 23 BC.

by the arrangement of 19 because it gave Augustus legal powers equal to those of the consuls as well as the consular *insignia*.[36]

Suetonius relates that Augustus toyed with the idea of serving as a third consul (*Aug.* 37); this has reasonably been interpreted as expressing his desire to find some way of keeping his 'domestic' *imperium* without monopolizing one of the two annual consulships. It is clear that he did find a solution—either in 23 or in 19 BC—or perhaps, as we suggest, in two stages over those two years: nothing so outrageous as assuming 'consular power for life' in addition to a provincial *imperium*, but the more elegant extension of an already existing (provincial) *imperium* into Rome and Italy, and later on equating it with that of the consuls. This *imperium* was not for life, but in need of renewal every ten or five years.

That the legal source of the Roman emperors' 'domestic' *imperium* was indeed their 'provincial' *imperium* applied to Rome and Italy—and not a separate *consulare imperium*—is suggested by the terminology Tacitus uses for Nero's *imperium* in AD 51. Nero is said to have received from Claudius a *proconsulare imperium extra urbem*,[37] which, as A. H. M. Jones rightly observes, implies 'that Claudius' *imperium* (which presumably would have been valid *intra urbem* also) was deemed to be proconsular' (1951: 118).[38] *Extra urbem* can hardly mean only 'in the provinces', but must mean that Nero was able to exercise his *imperium* in Italy, though not in Rome. The heir apparent was thus placed just one step behind the *princeps* in this respect; furthermore, his *imperium* was greater than those conferred on Agrippa or Tiberius under Augustus, and on Germanicus under Tiberius —which apparently applied only to the provinces.[39] It may well be that the term *proconsulare imperium* was invented then for the benefit of Augustus'

[36] Premerstein (1937: 236) argues that the special quasi-consular powers as regards his dealings with the Senate (Dio 53. 32. 5, the so-called *ius primae relationis* and the right to convene the Senate whenever he pleased) that were conferred on Augustus in 23 and 22 BC respectively, would have been redundant if he had already enjoyed a consular *imperium* in the city. But this objection does not apply if one assumes, as we do, that an *imperium* equal to that of the consuls was only granted in 19 BC.

[37] Tac. *Ann.* 12. 41. 1. Cf. *HA M. Ant.* 6. 6: Marcus Aurelius received *imperium extra urbem proconsulare* from Pius. Hammond, who denies that Augustus could exercise *imperium* within the *pomerium*, regards this as evidence that 'undoubtedly' by the 2nd cent. and 'possibly' by the reign of Claudius the emperor could exercise his (originally 'proconsular') *imperium* within the walls of the city (1933: 31–2).

[38] The *HA* always describes the emperors as receiving *proconsulare imperium* and *tribunicia potestas*: *Antoninus Pius*, 4. 7; *Marcus Antoninus*, 6. 6; *Pertinax*, 5. 6; *Severus*, 4. 2; *Alexander Severus*, 8. 1; *Gallieni Duo*, 2. 2; *Tyranni Triginta*, 22. 10; *Probus*, 12. 8.

[39] Presumably they too did not lose their *imperium* on crossing the *pomerium*, nor did they have to get it again on setting out; however, they could not exercise the *imperium* in the city.

lieutenants who received *imperium* in the provinces. At first it was probably used informally; only later on did it enter legal usage.[40]

Tiberius, according to Velleius Paterculus (2. 121. 1) and Suetonius (*Tib.* 21), had his *imperium* made equal to that of Augustus *in the provinces and the armies*—but apparently not in Rome and in Italy. This is why a special law needed to be passed to allow him to take the census jointly with Augustus,[41] whereas Augustus could take the census by virtue of his (originally 'provincial') *imperium* applied to Rome and Italy, which he describes in the *Res Gestae*, in the spirit of republican usage, as *consulari cum imperio*.[42] It is thus wrong to claim that Tiberius had equal powers to those of Augustus during the latter's lifetime, or that he had already possessed the totality of imperial power before AD 14. The *relatio consulum* mentioned by Tacitus in describing his accession debate had a significant legal content (contra Griffin 1995*a*: 37–8).

AUGUSTUS' *RECUSATIONES*

Why did Augustus need to be persuaded or, according to what Dio attributes to the funeral oration delivered by Tiberius, 'forced' (ἐξεβιάσασθε) to accept the periodic renewals of his powers? What is the significance of this posture of reluctance, repeatedly adopted by the *princeps*?

It is clear from what Augustus says in *Res Gestae* 5–6 which powers, in his opinion, were to be declined: the dictatorship, the perpetual consulate, and the quasi-dictatorial power of *curator legum ac morum summa potestate solus*—all of which would have clearly marked him as sole ruler of the state, contrary to the republican tradition to which sole rule was an anathema. In Augustus' own words, he would not accept any office *contra morem*

[40] Even as late as AD 20 it may not have yet become a legal term, as implied by its absence from the *SC de Cn. Pisone patre* (ll. 34–6): *ut in quamcumq(ue) provinciam venisset, maius ei imperium quam ei, qui eam provinciam proco(n)s(ule) optineret, esset, dum in omni re maius imperium Ti. Caesari Aug(usto) quam Germanico Caesari esset* ('That in whatever province he entered he would have greater *imperium* than the person who was governing that province as proconsul, with the proviso that in every respect Ti. Caesar Aug. was to have greater *imperium* than Germanicus Caesar'. The English translation is Miriam Griffin's in Griffin 1997*b*: 251).

[41] Suet. *Tib.* 21. 1: *Lex per consules lata est ut provincias cum Augusto communiter administraret simulque censum ageret* ('The consuls had a law passed that he should govern the provinces jointly with Augustus and hold the census with him'). Cf. A. H. M. Jones 1951: 119.

[42] After 19 BC, when the *insignia* as well as the full legal content of consular *imperium* were at his disposal, it would only be natural for Augustus to use this expression. On the strength of *consulari cum imperio* in the *Res Gestae*, Girardet (2000: 201, n. 105) rejects Dio's use of ἀνθύπατος ἐξουσία (55. 13. 5) to describe the power by which Augustus took the census. But Dio's language, even if imprecise, may still reflect the original source of Augustus' *imperium* in Rome, i.e. his provincial *imperium*.

maiorum. *Res Gestae* 5–6, if read together with paragraph 34, present a clear and consistent 'official version': prior to 'the first settlement' of 27 BC Augustus had indeed dominated the state (a situation which was justified by the 'emergency' of the civil wars (*RG* 34. 1)); however, after 'restoring the Republic to the Senate and the People of Rome'—*rem publicam ex mea potestate in senat[us populique Rom]ani [a]rbitrium transtuli*—he became a magistrate enjoying a unique position of *auctoritas*, but fully subject to the republican tradition which rejected any form of autocracy. Whenever any office or power which went beyond the limits of republican propriety was offered him, he rejected it. Augustus' 'resignation speech' in the Senate on 13 January 27, as related by Dio (53. 3–10), is full of similar republican sentiments. Moreover, according to this account, Augustus' position in the state as defined at the conclusion of this session of the Senate had to be forced on him: 'they [the senators] kept shouting out . . . begging for monarchical government . . . until they forced him, as it was made to appear, to assume autocratic power' (Dio 53. 11. 4). It is not surprising that in the *Res Gestae* Augustus, though he seems to take no less pride in the powers that he rejected than in those he was granted by Senate and People, mentions neither the fact that his position under the 'first settlement' had to be 'imposed' on him, nor the fact that his imperial powers were renewed over his repeated objections. Augustus' posture in the *Res Gestae* is that of a proud and ambitious republican noble who does not shy away from power unless this power amounts to autocracy and is contrary to *mos maiorum*. Since Augustus claimed that after returning the Republic to the Senate and People in 27 BC he was no longer an autocrat, he could not admit that the powers he held thereafter justified a gesture of refusal.[43]

Thus there is a contradiction between Augustus' own description of his position after 27 BC in the *Res Gestae* and Dio's account according to which Augustus not only was in fact and for all practical purposes the sole master of the state, but also made this fact clear by public displays of uneasiness with his official position: his powers were so unrepublican that they had to be repeatedly imposed on a reluctant *princeps* against his will. Does this contradiction not cast some doubt on Dio's entire account? Is it possible

[43] cf. Velleius Paterculus 2. 89. 5: Augustus' repeated consulships are said to have been imposed on him against his will (*cum saepe obnitens repugnasset*); his reluctance, in this context, is clearly presented as resulting from republican scruples. The continuous hold on the consulship after 27 BC was indeed a deviation from republican norms, inconsistent with the restoration of *illa prisca et antiqua forma reipublicae*. But this deviation, as well as being involuntary, was merely temporary and of relatively short duration: in 23 BC Augustus had his way and laid down the consulship. Relating his scruples and uneasiness in this respect could only reflect glory on the *princeps*.

that Augustus adopted such a posture after the pretended restoration of the Republic? And conversely, is it likely that he repeatedly pretended to wish to lay down his imperial powers[44] even as he was conducting an openly dynastic policy which, of course, presupposed the continuation of the imperial regime during Augustus' lifetime and beyond it?[45]

The conflicting evidence of the sources seems to make it difficult to reconstruct a consistent 'official version' of the Augustan Principate. What was the image that it wished to project to the public? Did it present itself as a restored Republic, an unabashed hereditary autocracy, or perhaps an 'involuntary autocracy' repeatedly imposed on a reluctant *princeps*, who was hoping that one day he would be allowed to lay it down? Indeed, Fergus Millar noted that Augustus was publicly addressed as an all-powerful and (sometimes) quasi-divine ruler; the unrestrained and wholly unrepublican nature of this adulation, which seems inconsistent with any pretence that the Republic had been restored, led Millar to the conclusion that, contrary to the conventional reading of *Res Gestae* 34, Augustus never claimed that in 27 BC he had restored the republican form of government.[46] Against this it could be argued that Augustus' repeated *recusationes* are inconsistent with an openly avowed hereditary monarchy. But was Augustus obliged to be consistent?

Indeed, the testimony of Tacitus relating to the reign of Tiberius shows that the imperial regime dispensed the ruler, among other things, from the obligation to adopt a consistent posture. It was perfectly possible for the emperor (in this case, Tiberius) to pretend, when it suited him, that he was ruling against his wish and hoping that one day he would be allowed to lay down the imperial power and have the Republic restored; what is more, this could be done in a setting that was blatantly monarchical and dynastic.

44 As implied by Dio's καίπερ ἀφιείς, ὡς ἔλεγεν (55. 6. 1); note the imperfect tense.

45 The fact that Augustus feels not the slightest compunction in revealing his dynastic plans in his letter to his grandchildren quoted in Aulus Gellius' *NA* 15. 7. 3 (= Malcovati 1969: *Ep*. 22) is quoted by Millar 1973: 67, as evidence that Augustus could not have written such a letter had he claimed that he had restored the Republic.

46 See Millar's comment on Vitruvius 5. 1. 7: 'Moreover, and this is the essential point, its obsequious flatteries could certainly be disregarded and considered as of no historical significance *if* they had been written under any conditions *except* those supposed by modern scholars, namely a recently-proclaimed "restoration of the Republic". Had such a thing been proclaimed, Vitruvius' words would have been grossly undiplomatic—and would not have been written' (1973: 66). See his concluding remark (p. 67): 'The victory of Actium, the death of Antonius and the stabilization of affairs in Rome all marked steps towards, not away from, the establishment of a monarchy; and no good evidence suggests that anybody at the time claimed, or supposed, otherwise.' Recently Rich and Williams 1999: 213 concur: 'this—i.e. the restoration of *rem publicam p. R. rest[it]u[it]* for 13 January in the Fasti of Praeneste—does not entitle us to assert that Augustus restored, or claimed to have restored the Republic'.

The passage (*Ann.* 4. 8–9) deals with the 'national mourning' after the death of Tiberius' son Drusus. In the Senate, amid extraordinary displays of grief for the Emperor's son—who was voted posthumous honours exceeding those of Germanicus—Tiberius had Nero and Drusus, Germanicus' sons and his own grandsons through adoption, brought before the senators. Deploring his old age, he committed them, who had lost their father and now their uncle, to the care of the Senate: 'I adjure you to receive into your care and guidance the great-grandsons of Augustus, descendants of a noble ancestry. So fulfil your duty and mine. To you, Nero and Drusus, these senators are as fathers. Such is your birth that your prosperity and adversity must alike affect the state' (Tac. *Ann.* 4. 8. 5). At the height of this dynastic melodrama, Tiberius saw fit to dwell on the question of the restoration of the Republic: 'He now fell back on those idle and often ridiculed professions, about restoring the Republic (*de reddenda republica*), and the wish that the consuls or someone else might undertake the government' (Tac. *Ann.* 4. 9).[47]

If the consuls were to undertake the government this would indeed have meant a 'restoration of the Republic'; for someone else to do it would have meant setting up another *princeps* —presumably, from another family, since no adult Julian was available. The essential point for Tiberius is to stress that he is weary of power and would gladly lay it down. Needless to say, both those scenarios were wildly implausible, and contradicted not merely the true nature of Tiberius' reign and the way he was publicly addressed by others, but also his own clearly dynastic message to the senators on that same occasion.[48] It would be preposterous to claim that the regime of Tiberius consistently projected to the public the image of a 'provisional government' waiting for an opportunity to restore the Republic or transfer the power to someone else.[49] Nevertheless, Tacitus explicitly

[47] *ad vana et totiens inrisa revolutus, de reddenda re publica utque consules seu quis alius regimen susciperet*. Millar insists in fact that *reddere rem publicam* has the specifically 'republican' meaning which he denies the expression *restituere rem publicam* (1973: 67); cf. Millar 2000: 4–7.

[48] The issue of hereditary succession could still give rise to double-thought in the 2nd cent. AD. Pliny expresses outrage at the principle of hereditary succession (*Panegyricus* 7.5): 'For when it is the case of transferring the Senate and People of Rome, armies, provinces and allies to a single successor, would you look to a wife to provide him, or seek no further than the four wall of your home?' This reaches its climax in *imperaturus omnibus eligi debet ex omnibus* ('he who is destined to rule the people, one and all, should be chosen from among them all'). Later it turns into a wish for a son to inherit Trajan's position, while *adoptio* becomes a second choice, a fallback in the absence of a natural son (94.5): *ut quandoque successorem ei tribuas* [i.e. Juppiter], *quem genuerit, quem formaverit similemque fecerit adoptato, aut si hoc fato negatur, in consilio sis eligenti monstresque, quem adoptari in Capitolio decet.*

[49] On the monarchic atmosphere of the first years of Tiberius' principate see the *SC de Cn. Pisone Patre*—published merely six years after the 'republican' *Res Gestae*.

testifies to the fact that the intention to restore the Republic was a theme on which Tiberius dwelt repeatedly (*totiens inrisa*) and not just on that occasion. Thus the imperial regime could afford to send contradictory messages; what made it easier was the fact that nobody would dare point out the contradiction.[50] This freedom to formulate its official ideology unconstrained by the demands of logical consistency is perhaps one of the most important privileges of true autocracy. The Roman *princeps* could simultaneously enjoy kingly power and adulation and claim credit for republican (or quasi-republican) virtues. For an autocratic regime with a republican—and, indeed, a 'popular'—origin, this posture (or combination of postures) was perhaps natural. The twentieth century offers us striking examples of this: 'Stalin is worshipped in terms that would have made Nero blush', wrote George Orwell in 1938 (1970: 370). Stalin was praised among other things for his *civilitas*, for being a simple man of the people and an exemplary democrat.[51] The comparison should not be pushed too far of course, but it does show how a ruler's 'cult of personality' can happily coexist with a republican and popular posture. All this does not mean that such a regime can hold public opinion in open contempt. On the contrary: the inner contradictions of the official propaganda reflect an attempt to take account of the public's sensitivities and manipulate them to the regime's advantage.

If it was still possible for Tiberius to pretend, occasionally, that he intended to lay down his power and restore the Republic, we should not be surprised that it was possible for Augustus. Indeed, it is highly likely that in adopting this posture, as in so much else, Tiberius was following *exempla Divi Augusti*. Had we only the testimony of Tacitus on Tiberius' repeated assertions of a desire to lay down his power, we should have guessed, even without Dio's testimony, that something very similar had from time to time been said by Augustus. It has been pointed out that in staging his famous *recusatio imperii* in the Senate at the start of his reign Tiberius was

[50] Any attempt to call the emperor's bluff or take him at his word was made at one's peril, as Asinius Pollio and Mamercus Scaurus discovered at the debate in the Senate on Tiberius' accession, see Tac. *Ann.* 1. 12. 1 (we owe this observation to Werner Eck).

[51] See *Bolshaya Sovietskaya Encyclopedia*, lii (Moscow, 1947), s.v. *Stalin*: 'While performing, in a masterly fashion, his functions as Leader of the party and the people, and enjoying the full support of the entire Soviet people, Stalin, at the same time, did not display even a trace of pride, arrogance or self-admiration' (570). '. . . All know the crushing, overpowering might of Stalin's logic, the crystal clarity of his thought, his iron will, his devotion to the party, his ardent faith in the people and his love for the people. All are familiar with his modesty, his simplicity, his sensitivity towards human beings and ruthlessness towards the enemies of the people' (618). '. . . In many languages the peoples of the Soviet Union compose songs about Stalin. These express the deepest love and the boundless devotion of the peoples of the Soviet Union to their great Leader, teacher, friend and commander-in-chief' (619).

following in the footsteps of Augustus who resigned his autocratic powers in January 27 BC and then had to be 'forced' by the senators to assume the leadership of the state (Syme 1958: ii. 690 n. 2). Suetonius says that in accepting the imperial power Tiberius held out the prospect that he would lay it down in the future and quotes his exact words: 'Until I come to an age when you will be good enough to grant me a respite' (*Tib.* 24). This declaration of intent may well have been intended as a substitute to setting a time limit on the powers granted to the emperor. It may seem strange that Tiberius accepted for life the powers which had been granted to Augustus only for limited periods; the most probable explanation is that he pretended that the period of ten years, following Augustus' example, would be too long for an old man like him and hinted at the prospect of an earlier resignation.[52] To this theme he returned, from time to time, according to Tacitus, during the early years of his reign. We do not hear of such a posture being adopted by any later emperor, but the gesture of refusal would be repeated time and again by Roman emperors at the moment of their accession to power.[53]

How, then, did the imperial regime present itself to public opinion during the reign of Augustus? What was 'the official version'? It seems that there were three of them. When it suited the *princeps*, he could claim, as he does in the *Res Gestae*, that he had indeed and truly restored the Republic in 27 BC; his extraordinary position in the state could then be explained purely in terms of *auctoritas*, as opposed to actual power. The most natural exponent of this republican theory was of course Augustus himself, the greatest republican of them all; but Velleius Paterculus could claim that Augustus had restored *illa prisca et antiqua forma reipublicae* in a particularly sycophantic passage of his thoroughly monarchist book (Vell. Pat. 2. 89. 3). If so, the powers held by the *princeps* were fully 'republican' and did not need to be legitimized by the ritual of refusal and forced acceptance. Nevertheless, this ritual was performed whenever Augustus' *imperium* was renewed. This was an expression of what may be termed the second, or middling, version: being the supreme leader of the state (which was not, however, quite the same thing as a *regnum* or a *dominatio*[54]) was a heavy burden which Augustus had agreed to bear with great reluctance—only for a

[52] Since Dio dates Tiberius' *decennalia* celebrations to AD 24 and 34 (57. 24. 1; 58. 24. 1), it seems that, whatever *imperium* he possessed before his accession, his *imperium* as *princeps* was counted from AD 14.

[53] See Wallace-Hadrill 1982: 36–7; Béranger 1953: 137; Yakobson and Cotton 1985: 497.

[54] Cf. Tiberius' funeral oration on Augustus as reported by Dio: Augustus could have been *sole master* of the state (μόνος . . . κύριος ἁπάντων 56. 39. 2); when he tried to resign, he was 'forced' by the people, 'for a time at least', to be its *leader* (ὑμῶν προστῆναι 56. 39. 6).

limited period of time, fully intending the whole while to lay it down in the future. Alongside the republican version and the quasi-republican one there existed and flourished a version which was in fact openly monarchist: it was reflected in the unrestrained adulation addressed to the ruler, in the quasi-divine homage paid to him, in the strenuous cultivation of loyalty to the imperial family, and in the open expectation of hereditary succession.[55]

The republican version of the Principate disappears after the death of its founder; the monarchist one was clearly destined to become dominant, and had doubtless become dominant already under Augustus—at least during the later part of his reign. But the quasi-republican version did not wholly vanish. It was echoed in the gesture of refusal at the accession of many a new emperor and, more significantly, it goes a long way to explain the peculiarly Roman ideal of *civilis princeps* and the various patterns of behaviour associated with it (Wallace-Hadrill 1982).

Postscript

Jean-Louis Ferrary kindly sent us in advance of publication his 'A propos des pouvoirs d'Auguste', forthcoming in *Cahiers du Centre Gustave-Glotz,* 12 (2001)—unfortunately too late for his arguments to be integrated into our discussion. In his own words: 'nous sommes parvenus, indépendamment les uns des autres, à des opinions semblables sur plusieurs points importants'. Unlike us, however, he does not believe that the extension of Augustus' provincial *imperium* to Rome (which he puts in 19 BC) made that *imperium* fully equal to that of the consuls. But the twelve lictors and the right to sit between the consuls reported by Dio do imply a formal equality with the consuls, and Augustus would hardly have taken the *insignia* of a greater power than he actually possessed (cf. n. 30). True, Augustus is not attested as taking over the consuls' routine functions, but that was not the purpose of equating his *imperium* with theirs; and he legislated *per tribuniciam potestatem*, rather than by virtue of the consular *imperium*, not—we believe—because he lacked the latter, but because of the symbolic significance of the former.

[55] Cf. the inscription from Pisa after Gaius' death, *ILS* 139: *iam designatus . . . princeps.*

An Emperor is Made: Senatorial Politics and Trajan's Adoption by Nerva in 97

WERNER ECK

Why was Trajan adopted by Nerva in October 97 and made his successor? The few ancient sources all point in the same direction: it was the consequence of the extreme pressure under which Nerva stood. The praetorian troops in Rome compelled him to hand over to them the men who had been responsible for Domitian's murder[1]—Petronius Secundus, one of the serving praetorian prefects, and the *cubicularius* Parthenius are mentioned in particular.[2] The soldiers acted summarily and killed them both. They were incited to their action by the other prefect, Casperius Aelianus, who after his dismissal by Domitian had been reinstated in this position by Nerva himself.[3]

At any rate, according to the ancient account, this shameful humiliation which he had suffered at the hands of the praetorians and one of their prefects, prompted Nerva, in October 97, during a sacrifice on the Capitol to Jupiter Optimus Maximus just after the report of a victory over the Germans from the Danube region, and under divine inspiration to adopt Marcus Ulpius Traianus, then *legatus Augusti pro praetore* in the province of Germania Superior,[4] as his son, and immediately afterwards to appoint him as his partner in government. For his part, Trajan is said, above all by Pliny in his *Panegyricus*, to have accepted this adoption only reluctantly; nothing

Dedicated to Miriam Griffin in friendship and devotion. For critical remarks I am grateful to Hannah Cotton (Jerusalem), Oliver Verlage (Cologne), and especially to Anthony R. Birley (Düsseldorf). I am also grateful to Hannah Cotton for helping with the final version of the English text. This contribution takes some steps further ideas already partly developed by Syme 1958: *passim*, and Schwarte 1979.

[1] Cassius Dio 68. 3. 3; *Epit. de Caes.* 12. 8; Plin. *Pan.* 6. 1–2.

[2] *PIR*² P 308; C 951a.

[3] See Griffin 2000: 84–96 for a general account.

[4] Unambiguously stated only in the *HA Hadr.* 2. 5; but cf. Plin. *Pan.* 9. 2; Cassius Dio 68. 3. 4. However, there is no reason to suppose, on the basis of certain Byzantine authors, that Trajan himself might have won the victory in Pannonia to which Bennett 1997: 46 refers and from which he infers that Trajan had governed that province before he went to Germany. This supposition has nothing to support it.

but the dire plight of the *res publica* could make him bow to Nerva's decision. Thereupon the praetorians' mutiny in Rome collapsed (Pliny, *Pan*. 9–10).

This is essentially the picture painted by the sources, which even today is accepted by some scholars as more or less accurate. To be sure, it has also long been recognized, notably by Ronald Syme (1958) and Karl-Heinz Schwarte (1979), that events cannot have followed such a simple course; rather, the ancient reports reveal only the surface of a process that was in reality far more complex and many-layered (see also Birley 1997: 37, 38–9). In fact, it is claimed, Trajan prevailed in an internal power struggle, in which he personally led one party while the other party gathered behind M. Cornelius Nigrinus Curiatius Maternus. The discovery of the latter's *cursus honorum* in an inscription from Liria Edetanorum in Hispania Tarraconensis[5] made it possible to flesh out the remark recorded by the younger Pliny in 97 that a governor in an eastern province had aspirations to the throne (*Ep*. 9. 13. 10–11).[6] Sound speculation on Schwarte's part made it appear probable that Cornelius Nigrinus was associated with the praetorians' mutiny.[7] It had always seemed surprising that Casperius Aelianus, the *praefectus praetorio*, should have turned against his patron Nerva, who had reinstated him in command of the praetorians after he had been dismissed by Domitian. Normally this post was not subject to a time limit; a prefect remained in office so long as he appeared loyal and useful to the emperor; conversely, if Domitian had dismissed Casperius, there must have been a breakdown in trust between them. It is all the harder to understand why Casperius, on this hypothesis, should turn against Domitian's murderers. Schwarte, however, was able to account for Casperius Aelianus' seemingly inexplicable conduct with the highly plausible explanation that, as hinted in the *Epitome de Caesaribus*, he had taken a bribe from Cornelius Nigrinus (12. 8) to lead the praetorians' mutiny against Nerva. The purpose of the uprising was the rehabilitation of Domitian through the punishment of his murderers, thereby making Cornelius Nigrinus, as his most highly decorated general, the natural successor to Nerva; none of the senators who had obtained military honours under Domitian could compete with Nigrinus' prestige. In this way Casperius could look forward to a longer and more promising future than under the already aged Nerva. However, once Nerva adopted Trajan, whose army stood ready just across the Alps, Cornelius Nigrinus' attempt to put pressure on the emperor was thwarted. He was relieved of his duties in Syria, but his confederate Casperius Aelianus was dispatched to Trajan in Germany and there executed.

5 On this see G. Alföldy and Halfmann 1973: 331–73. *AE* 1973: 283.

6 See also Syme 1958: i. 15–16.

7 Schwarte 1979; cf. also Franke 1991: 170–5.

In principle this reconstruction, especially as regards the actual events, must be right. However, it does not deal with the crucial question how Trajan found himself in Germania Superior in the first place, thereby having at hand the decisive force to make his adoption by Nerva effective. In general, this governorship of Trajan's seems to be regarded as an appointment with nothing remarkable about it. Trajan passes for one of the outstanding military men of the time, a *vir militaris*, to whom a province like Germania Superior with three legions and numerous *auxilia* would naturally be entrusted. Some have even supposed that before Germania Superior Trajan had already governed Moesia or Pannonia, having been appointed governor there by Domitian between AD 92 and 96.[8]

This reasoning, however, leaves out of account certain significant facts that we know about the careers of senators in general and of Trajan in particular. In the Flavian period it had become normal for the legates of the great consular provinces in which legions were stationed to have accumulated experience in various posts, in some of which they acquired also military experience, before their appointment as consular governors. First came a legionary tribunate at the age of about 20, next the command of a legion as a young *praetorius*, and after that some further responsible service, such as rule of a praetorian province like Lugdunensis or Belgica, or Lycia-Pamphylia or Judaea in the East, the command of Legio III Augusta in Africa, a proconsulate in a praetorian public province, or an important office in Rome such as the prefecture of the *aerarium Saturni*.[9] With the consulate to follow, a man had accumulated sufficient experience and was prepared, by Roman standards, to undertake the most important duties in the Empire, namely the great commands in provinces with a legionary garrison.

However, Trajan's career, to the extent that we know anything about it prior to Domitian's death, does not fit this model: in fact we know nothing, beyond what the younger Pliny tells us on the subject in his *Panegyricus*, and this little exhibits some astonishing features. However, it is precisely these features in Trajan's career that we have to consider when attempting to understand the course of events in 97 and Trajan's presence at the right time in Germania Superior in October of that year.

8 Suggested by Syme 1971: 204–12, esp. 209; Fitz 1982: 319–31, esp. 320–1, 331 (with my objections to this reconstruction); Fitz 1993: 130. So too Birley 1997: 31; Franke 1991: i. 164 (in Moesia). Eck 1996; cf. too Bennett 1997.

9 Eck 1974; Birley 2000. It must be granted that the rules established by scholars were never absolutely binding and could at need be set aside; but this applies only when one can actually prove it. However, it is not legitimate to postulate posts in Trajan's career which are nowhere attested, merely because of this consideration.

Pliny will have it that the patrician youth spent ten years as military tribune with the army (*Pan.* 15. 3).[10] This is more than unlikely; it is rather a stylized picture drawn according to republican ideals, but one hardly attainable in the imperial age. That was already seen by Ronald Syme.[11] As a patrician *praetorius*, Trajan ought to have received a consulate from Domitian just a few years after the praetorship, which he must have discharged about 83/4. This did not happen. The reason for this anomalous behaviour on Domitian's part is unknown. The likeliest supposition is that Domitian's relations with Trajan's family were not without tension. The father had been one of Vespasian's and Titus' closest allies. Such senators did not immediately, if at all, enjoy Domitian's favour. It is thus easily comprehensible that the young Trajan's career was at first held back. All the same, in 88 at the latest, Domitian bestowed on Trajan, then 35 years old, the command of Legio VII Gemina; but commanders of this legion, so far as we can make out, had subsequent careers of no great significance. One could hardly attract much attention as a commander of this legion, stationed in northern Spain—a territory by that time already pacified.[12] To Trajan, however, this command supplied the chance to further his career: when in winter 88/9 L. Antonius Saturninus mutinied in Germania Superior, Trajan, with his legion, was among those summoned to the Rhine; in this way he was able to give proof of his absolute loyalty to Domitian. Pliny in his *Panegyricus* simply cannot give enough praise to Trajan's military competence as demonstrated on this march from Spain to the Rhine, although Trajan arrived too late to see any actual fighting (14. 2–5). If Pliny makes so much of the event as a way of showing off Trajan's *virtus imperatoria*—albeit that *virtus* served on that occasion merely to uphold Domitian's regime, so much detested by Pliny—this can only mean that there was no other material with which to show the future emperor commanding an army, already as a senator, and manifesting even then this *virtus* so crucial to leadership of the Empire and the army. To put it bluntly: judging by all the surviving evidence, Trajan was anything but the great military expert repeatedly so portrayed by Pliny, and also by modern

[10] Trajan is inferred from Pliny, *Pan.* 14. 1 to have spent these alleged ten years on the Euphrates and the Rhine; see e.g. Franke 1991: i. 162. But whereas the glory won on the Euphrates during his father's governorship is the result of having served there as a tribunus militum under his father, that won on the Rhine and connected with the title 'Germanicus' has nothing to do with a presumed tribunate there, and cannot serve as proof for his having served as tribunus militum in one of the Germanies.

[11] Syme 1958: i. 31.

[12] Alföldy 1969: 256. It is presupposed here that Trajan was born in 53 and not 56. Cf. too e.g. Syme 1958: i. 31.

scholarship.[13] Rather, this characterization, extrapolated by modern scholars from knowledge of the wars that Trajan later conducted, has nothing whatsoever to do with his senatorial career under Domitian and Nerva.[14] In fact, up to his command in Germania Superior in 97—so much taken for granted as the natural sequel to his career so far—Trajan had seen less service with the army and acquired far less experience in politics and government than was normal at that period for a consular governor. No one could have foreseen a man with his background as the governor of Germania Superior.

Nevertheless, that loyal conduct in 88/9 brought Trajan at the beginning of 91 the ordinary consulate, commensurate with his patrician rank, together with Acilius Glabrio, who belonged to a family perhaps made patrician already by Augustus. Pliny does not mention this magistracy, which confirmed Trajan's social and political standing, and which he owed entirely to Domitian; Pliny's failure to mention the consulate is not insignificant.

Trajan could hope for no more. That Domitian should entrust one of the consular provinces, that is, a province with several legions, to him was out of the question: the consul, then around 40, lacked the necessary prerequisites, delineated above, and in consequence the necessary experience in provincial administration. Thus there is no reason to suppose, in the absence of positive evidence, that towards the end of Domitian's reign Trajan governed Moesia Inferior or Pannonia as a consular legate.[15] Nor can Hadrian's legionary tribunate in Pannonia with the Legio II Adiutrix (*ILS* 308) support such a claim.[16] Why should Domitian have entrusted this

[13] e.g. Heuss 1964: 337; Christ 1988: 287. Garzetti 1974: 305, 'Trajan, who in any case enjoyed the favour of almost all the armies', and 306 'energetic and upright general'; Syme 1958: i. 31 with n. 6, on Trajan's failure to take part in Domitian's Dacian Wars from 85 on: 'Peculiar, given his ostensible military record.'

[14] e.g. Syme 1958: i. 34; Franke 1991: i. 163: 'Jedenfalls machte ihn (sc. Trajan) der langjährige Militärdienst zu einem hervorragenden Soldaten, wie seine späteren erfolgreichen Kriege gegen Germanen, Daker and Parther beweisen.' Ibid. 164: 'Bei seiner militärischen Erfahrung'.

[15] Cf. Pliny's words on Trajan at *Pan.* 44. 1: 'You lived with us, you shared the dangers, you were afraid: at that time such was the life of innocent men' (*Vixisti nobiscum, periclitatus es, timuisti, quae tunc erat innocentium vita*). That really makes sense only if Trajan had spent Domitian's last years in Rome.

[16] See nn. 4 and 8. Moreover, if Trajan is supposed to have taken his kinsman Hadrian to Pannonia as legionary tribune, he ought to have done the same on being transferred to Germania Superior. But this is precisely what he did not do. Hadrian's legionary tribunates cannot serve as the sole basis for conferring on Trajan an otherwise utterly improbable Pannonian governorship. Not even Pliny, *Pan.* 14. 5, 'when, after that march, you were judged worthy to conduct various campaigns' (*cum aliis super alias expeditionibus itinere illo dignus inveneris*), can be adduced as support for a consular governorship under Domitian; rather, Pliny is simply pointing out that Trajan, like Jupiter's son Hercules in front of King

province, in which four legions were already stationed, to a patrician without the necessary experience in provincial administration? There were other loyal senators with better qualifications.

The same reasoning should make us marvel at Trajan's appointment to the governorship of Germania Superior. Why send Trajan there? Nerva, the new emperor, was thoroughly familiar with the usual preconditions for award of these consular governorships; he had lived for a long time in the immediate entourage of Vespasian and Domitian and had no doubt exercised his influence, among other things, on personal appointments to the great military provincial commands. The criteria involved in these were entirely consistent with rational requirements. Why should he now, when he himself had the ultimate responsibility for taking such decisions, have departed from these criteria under normal conditions?

Yet the fact remains that in October 97 Trajan was stationed as governor in Germania Superior. He thereby commanded the nearest large army to Italy, aside from Pannonia, and was thus the man who could make the swiftest military intervention in the heartland of the Empire, should that prove necessary. The pressing question is therefore why Nerva sent Trajan to Germania Superior, and whether it happened by accident or in accordance with a prior plan for him to intervene from there in the internal Roman power struggle; and, if the answer to this last question is in the affirmative, then we must ask who was responsible: was it Nerva himself or others, working behind—or even against—him?[17] For even in imperial Rome policy was not made only by a single person, that is, the emperor, but by groups of people seeking to influence him. There were various factions in the Senate, often politically opposed to each other, although their internal power struggles are all too often concealed by the designation 'Senate', which we use, following in the steps of the ancient writers. That was the case in 97 too.

Since we have no direct information about who was there in Rome, in Nerva's entourage, who could have swayed the old emperor to adopt

Eurystheus, with whom Domitian is implicitly equated, through successfully discharging one task was deemed worthy of new ones. But Pliny cannot describe these *expeditiones* (unlike the legionary command in northern Spain in 88/9), because they were not real. Had they been, Pliny would not have neglected to portray them. It would have been far easier to describe military prowess on Trajan's part in fighting against, say, the Dacians than against Antonius Saturninus, that is in a civil war.

[17] See the striking formulation in Syme 1958: i. 14: 'The German command goes far to explain his elevation. The friends and allies who extorted that appointment from Nerva were not devoid of foresight.'

Trajan in October 97,[18] we must ask whether the circumstances that led in 97 to Trajan's adoption by Nerva may not be reflected in what happened in subsequent years.[19]

In the Roman political system service to the ruler was not only recognized, but very often rewarded by public distinction. There was a standard repertory of special honours, like the ones which Nero bestowed on those who had helped him detect the Pisonian conspiracy and afterwards. He had awarded the *ornamenta triumphalia* and triumphal statues, for instance, to the future emperor Nerva (Tac. *Ann.* 15. 72. 1). But the political helper could also, provided he was a senator, be rewarded by the grant of a second or third consulate. Marcus Agrippa, *consul iterum* and *tertium* in 28 and 27 BC, and Statilius Taurus, *consul iterum* in 26 BC, are clear examples of such distinctions under Augustus, as is L. Vitellius, *consul iterum* in 43 and *consul tertium* in 47 under Claudius. Can we identify in the early years of Trajan's reign men whose station and distinction at that period imply that they were already closely connected to him in 97 and had desired and worked for what he eventually attained?

Cornelius Nigrinus had supporters in Rome, not only among the praetorians, but also in the Senate; some of them are known, since Pliny mentions them in *Ep.* 9. 13. On Trajan's side, too, some may be recognized or inferred, above all from the consular *fasti* of the years following 97, and in particular in 98–100, which Trajan spent mostly on the Rhine and the Danube, before returning to Rome around October 99.

Almost all consuls for 98 and 100 are known by name; for 99 only some, but in sufficient number for us to discern the pattern of distribution, to detect the number of consuls, as well as to sense some unusual features. Our present knowledge allows us to reconstruct the *fasti* of those years as follows:[20]

98	K. Ian.	Nerva IIII, Trajan II
	Id. Ian.	Trajan II, Cn. Domitius Tullus II
	K. Febr.	Trajan II, Sex. Iulius Frontinus II
	K. Mart.	Trajan II, L. Iulius Ursus II
	K. April.	Trajan II, T. Vestricius Spurinna II

[18] The only direct reference in the sources, *Epit. de Caes.* 13. 6, applies to Licinius Sura, who is also repeatedly named in modern literature as Trajan's only direct collaborator in Rome. Cf. e.g. Garzetti 1950: 88: 'Altre influenze non è possibile scoprire' (It is not possible to discover another influence).

[19] For the following, see more generally Eck 2002.

[20] Details in Degrassi 1952: 29–30; Vidman 1982: 45–6; on the Fasti Ostienses see too now Bargagli and Grosso 1997.

	K. Mai	Trajan II, C. Pomponius Pius
	K. Iul.	A. Vicirius Martialis, L. Maecius Postumus
	K. Sept.	C. Pomponius Rufus, Cn. Pompeius Ferox
	K. Nov.	C. Pomponius Rufus, Cn. Pompeius Ferox
99	K. Ian.	A. Cornelius Palma, Q. Sosius Senecio
	(May–June)	Sulpicius Lucretius Barba, Senecio Memmius Afer
	(July–Aug.)	Q. Fabius Barbarus, A. Caecilius Faustinus
	(Sept.–Oct.)	Q. Fabius Barbarus, A. Caecilius Faustinus
	(Nov.–Dec.)	Q. Bittius Proculus, M. (Ostorius) Scapula[21]
100	K. Ian.	Trajan III, Sex. Iulius Frontinus III
	Id. Ian.	Trajan III, L. Iulius Ursus III
	K. Mart.	[—]cius Macer, C. Cilnius Proculus
	K. Iul.	Q. Acutius Nerva, L. Fabius Tuscus
	K. Sept.	C. Iulius Cornutus, C. Plinius Secundus
	K. Nov.	L. Roscius Aelianus, Ti. Claudius Sacerdos

Comparing this sequence of consuls with that attested for Domitian's last years, it can be seen at once that the number of consuls attested for each year between 98 and 100 is greater;[22] in Domitian's last years there were normally five or six *suffecti* (not more than three pairs at the most) per year. However, a smaller number of consular pairs may be observed again in the later years of Trajan's reign.[23] It is thus plain that at the beginning of his reign Trajan had to allow for more senators to be rewarded with a consulate. In other words, there were many claims for him to take into consideration: while he could not pass over those whose claim rested on their career (to make them wait longer might have led to tensions and discontent—the last thing Trajan could afford in his early years),[24] he had also to honour with

[21] On this pair of consuls see Eck 1993: 445–50 with *RMD* iii. 141; but cf. too P. Weiss 1999: 287–8, who doubts the dating on the ground that in that case we would have within a short span of time two *constitutiones* for auxiliary units in the same province. However, we should probably reckon with several *constitutiones* within a year for the same provincial army in far more cases than has been assumed up till now—above all if only few units were the beneficiaries of the citizenship bestowed in one of two (or more) constitutions. When a constitution related to only a few auxiliary units, the number of diplomas issued was considerably smaller and consequently also the chance that even a single one would survive. This is why such cases of survival of a diploma attesting a second constitution for the same province are extremely rare. For a new case of two, or rather three, constitutions for the army in the same province see *CIL* xvi. 41, *RMD* iii. 140 and the diploma referred to in n. 31 below.

[22] Degrassi 1952: 24–9; Vidman 1982: 43–5.

[23] Degrassi 1952: 31–5.

[24] Evidence for this is the case of Bittius Proculus, who till 97 had been *praefectus aerarii Saturni*, but on leaving office did not at once receive the suffect consulate he was entitled to expect. He definitely belonged to those senators who after Domitian's death did not desire a

the consulship those who had supported him in winning the imperial power. Domitian and Hadrian found themselves, at the beginning of their reigns, in the same predicament, and they too had recourse, in the early years of their rule, to shortening the length of the individual consulates, thereby admitting more people to the highest office in the state.[25] Nerva, as the list of consuls for 97 shows, had done the same: he named altogether ten *consules suffecti*, some of whom may already have been designated by Domitian.

And yet the *fasti* for 98–100 show very marked peculiarities, going beyond what has just been pointed out.[26] We are first struck in 98 by the series of four *consules suffecti* who held the *fasces* together with Trajan, and like him for the second time: Domitius Tullus, Iulius Frontinus, Iulius Ursus, and Vestricius Spurinna. Of those four, some, at least, must have rendered services to Trajan, not merely to Nerva; otherwise the long sequence of *consules iterum* would have appeared already in 97, not only in 98. And yet the overall picture of the *fasti* of the year 98 might still have been said to reflect Nerva's designs, were it not for what follows in the *fasti* of the year 100. The true political import of the *fasti* of 98 is disclosed for the first time in the fact that two of the iterate consuls of that year, Iulius Frontinus and Iulius Ursus, attain the consulate again as early as 100, now as *consules tertium*, together with Trajan, who also served then as consul for the third time. Such a rapid succession of second and third consulates, separated by only one year, is absolutely unique for a person not belonging to the imperial family.[27] Without doubt these two were of extraordinary political importance to Trajan; and this is also made quite clear by Pliny, who in his *Panegyricus* speaks at length about these two *consules tertium*. He refers to the extremely short interval between second and third consulates. It was clear to him, as to every other senator, that this constituted an absolute departure from normality. Likewise, he lays stress on the fact that only now did Trajan hold the *fasces* for the third time, that is to say he was on a par with his two colleagues (*Pan.* 60–2). Above all, however, he emphasizes that, unlike others who earned their distinctions as comrades in arms

total break with those marked out as Domitian's collaborators, and, therefore, he could hardly have belonged with those who from the start were determined to prevent Nigrinus from becoming emperor. Nevertheless Trajan could not, or would not, debar him entirely from the consulate. Proculus did not become suffect consul till 99, not 98, as was long believed; see Eck 1993: 448–9.

[25] Eck 1970: 55–76; Syme 1958: i. 58–9.

[26] On the following: Syme 1958: i. 16–17, 35.

[27] The only exception is Marcus Agrippa in 28 and 27 BC; he had won the decisive victories for Octavian over Antony. The reason for the extraordinary honours is thus plain.

(*bellorum . . . socii*), these two senators were treated by Trajan as 'having served you well and bravely, but as civilians' (*de te quidem bene ac fortiter, sed in toga meriti*); the *princeps* was indebted to the two for their *cura* and *vigilantia*.[28] They must therefore have exerted themselves on Trajan's behalf in Rome, not in a province. Since their services to Trajan were recognized and rewarded with a second consulate already in 98, the occasion for offering these services must have occurred before, namely in 97. Everything points in one direction: in some way the two had played a part in Nerva's decision to adopt Trajan. The question is simply how.

Before that can be discussed, another remarkable fact in the consular *fasti* must be noted. On 1 January 99 Cornelius Palma and Sosius Senecio entered upon the ordinary consulate. While we know nothing certain about Palma's origin and political career before 99, and therefore cannot draw any conclusion about his political attitude in 97,[29] Sosius Senecio is in all likelihood to be identified with the senator whose career is attested by an acephalous inscription from Rome.[30] From this text several important features emerge which make his ordinary consulate in 99 unusual, but at the same time comprehensible. Senecio seems to have been a *novus homo* who had already been significantly advanced by Domitian: he had been *candidatus principis* for the tribunate of the *plebs* and the praetorship. Some time after the praetorship he commanded the Legio I Minervia, stationed in Bonn in Lower Germany. He was swiftly promoted: his next office was the praetorian governorship in Belgica. The time of his governorship can be precisely determined. His predecessor in that province, Q. Glitius Atilius Agricola, had been installed there already under Domitian, and continued there for a while under Nerva, since he is attested as his legate in Belgica (*ILS* 1021, 1021a). However, Atilius Agricola's governorship ended at the latest in summer 97, since in September and October he held the *fasces* as *consul suffectus*.[31] Sosius Senecio could not have taken up his governorship in Belgica before spring or summer 97, hence clearly at the time, when, so far as we know, tensions in Rome connected with the praetorians and Cornelius Nigrinus had reached their peak. Merely a year and a half later

[28] *Pan*. 60. 5–6; Griffin 2000: 94.

[29] Perhaps his family came from the Etruscan town Volsinii, *PIR*² C 1412; but we cannot be certain. From the sequel it seems quite clear that he too must have been one of the very important members of Trajan's 'party'.

[30] *CIL* vi. 1444 = *ILS* 1022 = *CIL* vi. p. 4698; the attribution of this text to Sosius Senecio, now almost universally accepted, is due to C. P. Jones 1970: 98–106.

[31] Vidman 1982: 45. The name of his colleague is now attested in a fragmentary diploma as L. Pomponi[us Maternus]; the text is published by David John MacDonald (see now *ZPE* 138, 2002, 225 ff).

Sosius Senecio returned to Rome and received the ordinary consulate. Normally a praetorian governorship in an imperial province like Belgica lasted at least two or three years. Furthermore, a senator like Senecio who had begun as a *novus homo* did not in normal circumstances receive an ordinary consulate, but a suffect one. These considerations make it very likely that Senecio too had rendered extraordinary services to Trajan, so that in order to repay him adequately the normal rules of promotion were suspended.

The time of Sosius' governorship in Belgica, considered together with the geographical position of the latter, bordering as it is on the two Germanies, makes it highly likely that Sosius Senecio had played a key role in 97/8, when Trajan, then governor of Germania Superior, was adopted by Nerva and, after Nerva's death on 28 January 98, assumed sole rule over the Empire in Germania Inferior at the beginning of February.

It could be argued that it was merely by coincidence, not through a definite political plan, that Nerva (or whoever was behind the adoption of Trajan) sent Sosius Senecio to Belgica in summer 97. But two considerations tell against such a supposition. One arises from Sosius Senecio's family connections, and the other from a second appointment made with the same purpose in mind as that operative in Senecio's case.

To be sure, Sosius Senecio was a *novus homo*, but he was also the son-in-law of Sex. Iulius Frontinus, who, as pointed out above, played a leading role after Domitian's death in the internal crisis surrounding Nerva and the adoption of Trajan. True, such a relationship does not necessarily imply close political association; but since Frontinus and Senecio were clearly on the best of terms, it would be more than surprising if Senecio's posting in Belgica had not been made with the ulterior motive of having a loyal man, a relative, on the spot, who would safeguard Frontinus' political objects in 97.

The second appointment also concerned Belgica. It can support the view that it was no coincidence that Senecio was sent to that province in 97. It is all but certain that at the same time that Sosius Senecio was the praetorian governor of Belgica, the *eques* Sex. Attius Suburanus Aemilianus held the post of financial procurator there.[32] After the *praefectus praetorio* Casperius Aelianus, who had led the mutiny against Nerva, was summoned by Trajan

[32] His career in *AE* 1939: 60 = *IGLS* vi. 2785. Cf. also esp. Pflaum 1960–1: i. 134–5, who also shows very clearly that Suburanus undertook no other duties between his procuratorship in Belgica and his praetorian prefecture. So too Syme 1958: i. 56. The interpretation below is not affected by the possibility that he became Trajan's praetorian prefect immediately after the latter's adoption. Cf. Birley 1997: 319 n. 10.

to Germania Inferior at the end of 97, and executed, Suburanus was appointed to succeed him. Suburanus was close at hand; his headquarters as *procurator provinciae Belgicae* were in Augusta Treverorum (Trier), only some 140 miles from Colonia Claudia Ara Agrippinensium (Cologne). He had been in charge of finance in Germania Inferior and Superior: through his hands, above all else, passed the pay of the troops on the Rhine whom Trajan commanded first in Germania Superior, and then in Germania Inferior. In the delicate situation arising after the execution of Casperius Aelianus, Trajan was not going to appoint as *praefectus praetorio* anyone whom he did not fully trust (Aur. Victor 13. 9; Cassius Dio 68. 16; Pliny *Pan.* 67. 8). Trajan must therefore have become acquainted, and politically allied, with Suburanus, and this must have happened even before his own appointment to Germania Superior by Nerva in the course of 97; for it is not very likely that their alliance developed for the first time during the brief period they spent in neighbouring provinces. Furthermore, Suburanus was an old and close confidant of none other than Iulius Ursus, who, after Iulius Frontinus, held the *fasces* together with Trajan in 98 and 100 as *consul iterum* and *tertium* respectively. In the late 70s and early 80s, under Titus and Domitian, Suburanus had been Iulius Ursus' *adiutor* during the latter's *praefectura annonae* and *praefectura Aegypti*, when Suburanus was still a member of the equestrian order (only later was he adlected to the Senate).[33] At that time, such *adiutores* were still personally chosen by their superiors, a fact which leads one to suppose that there was a close relation of trust between the two. Again, we may regard Suburanus' appointment in Belgica as no more than a coincidence. But the old and close relationship between Suburanus and Iulius Ursus, whose services to Trajan in 97 are as good as attested in the consular *fasti* of 98 and 100, combined with Suburanus' appointment to praetorian prefect in late 97, tells strongly against such an interpretation. Iulius Ursus was behind Suburanus' appointment in Belgica no less than Iulius Frontinus was behind that of Sosius Senecio in the same province.

If one accepts the conclusions drawn so far, namely, that both Sosius Senecio and Attius Suburanus were sent to Belgica with a definite purpose at the initiative of Iulius Frontinus and Iulius Ursus, and that both men rendered services to Trajan in the course of 97, this creates a strong presumption that Trajan's dispatch to Germania Superior too was not the regular appointment of a governor on Nerva's part, but had a specific political goal, and that Iulius Frontinus and Iulius Ursus must have played a

[33] For dates see Pflaum 1960: 128–32.

decisive part here just as they did in the case of Sosius Senecio and Attius Suburanus. Why were they involved, and what part precisely did they play?

We must start from the fact that Nerva was put under pressure not only by the praetorians, but above all by Cornelius Nigrinus, who could employ the army in Syria to advance his ambitions. Nigrinus had undoubtedly been a loyal supporter of Domitian, and proved his military skills on the Danube, as his eight military decorations attest; but his military success led to political claims, above all after the death of a legitimate ruler like Domitian. Nigrinus was no doubt conscious of his merit and prestige, he could count on more than a few adherents in the Senate, above all on those whose careers had taken a turn for the better under Domitian, and who did not take part in his condemnation for fear of endangering their present status. In a Senate debate in the spring of 97 several of them let it be seen that they were thoroughly sympathetic to him (Pliny *Ep.* 4. 2. 4–6; 9. 13. 13; 19). Others in the senate were presumably appalled by the prospect of his attaining the purple. On what specific grounds they shrank from having Nigrinus for emperor is not recorded; perhaps they thought him too closely associated with Domitian's regime and with his closest confidants; they feared that the forms of rule of the last Flavian emperor would be revived and that his advisers would exercise great influence again. We should never underestimate the potency of competition and personal rivalries in the Roman Senate.

In all likelihood these dissenting senators included Iulius Frontinus and Iulius Ursus, who had both, in different ways, been disappointed by Domitian, and were realistic enough to recognize that Nerva could not hold out for long against Nigrinus and the praetorians. It was thus a question of time before Nerva was compelled to adopt Nigrinus or was himself disposed of at Nigrinus' behest. The threat of an outbreak of a new civil war as in 69 was real enough, and the supremacy of a group to which they did not belong was a certainty. They will therefore have looked for a way out or for an alternative candidate. That they themselves should succeed Nerva was impossible, if only on account of their age: if one of the problems with Nerva was that he was already 67 years old and childless, Frontinus could not have been much younger,[34] and Iulius Ursus was about 60. Furthermore, both were *novi homines*; they could not flaunt distinguished senatorial antecedents. Humble origins still counted against one at this period.[35] To

[34] Eck 1989: 47–62.

[35] True, Cornelius Nigrinus was also a *homo novus*, but his military glory in the past and his present control of a strong army both conspired to make up for his social inferiority.

forestall Nigrinus, they had to look round for a different candidate. Their choice fell on Trajan, then 44 years old, whose father had been a highly regarded consul in Vespasian's time and in 73/4 had even been adlected amongst the patricians. Like Nigrinus, he came from the Spanish provinces; he was from Baetica, Nigrinus' *patria* was Liria Edetanorum in Tarraconensis. The precise reason why their choice fell on him and what made him so attractive as a candidate against Nigrinus escapes us. But we can be sure that they knew him (as they did his father) and they obviously saw in him the appropriate candidate. Trajan for his part may have agreed with them that he was better suited than Nigrinus to occupy Nerva's place one day and rule the Empire. Frontinus and Ursus, no doubt in alliance with others, perhaps Licinius Sura, who later appears as Trajan's closest confidant,[36] must have reached the decision to thwart Nigrinus' claims and his praetorian support by having Nerva adopt Trajan. A precondition, however, was the presence of an army at hand, like that available to Nigrinus. Germania Superior with its three legions was, apart from Pannonia, the nearest province to Italy with a strong garrison. Trajan was successfully installed as legate of its army although he did not have all of the usual qualifications in his previous career. In an extraordinary situation this did not matter.[37]

Whether the plan that Frontinus and Ursus together with others wished to set in motion had already by then been coordinated with Nerva, who had to make the formal appointment of the legate in Germania Superior, is hard to decide. It need not have, but may well have been. In any case, Trajan's position in Germania Superior was reinforced by success in inducing Nerva to send Sosius Senecio, Frontinus' son-in-law, as governor to Belgica; at the same time the Emperor named Attius Suburanus, whom Ursus judged trustworthy, as financial procurator of Belgica and the two German provinces. A military coup, should that prove necessary, must above all not fail for want of money. How crucial in such a contingency loyalty in a procurator of Belgica was had been shown in the first days of 69, when the procurator there, Pompeius Propinquus, had opposed Vitellius (Tac. *Hist.* 1. 12. 1; 58. 1). This time nothing of the kind was to endanger the plans. Trajan's subsequent adoption showed that they had been well laid. Pannonia too seems to have been included in the preparations; Pompeius Longinus, who on 12 July 96 is still attested as governor in Moesia Inferior,

[36] *PIR*² L 253.

[37] It would be quite different of course if one started from the premiss that Trajan had already been intended for a consular governorship in Pannonia by Domitian, or by Nerva before the outbreak of the crisis in Rome.

was already in office in Pannonia on 20 February 98.[38] Later he was among Trajan's closest associates.[39] L. Iulius Ursus Servianus, Hadrian's brother-in-law, *consul suffectus* in 90, was also very close to the circle of Ursus and Frontinus. Ursus, who like Servianus hailed from Narbonensis,[40] made the latter his adoptive son.[41] Nor was it an accident that already in 97 Servianus succeeded Trajan as governor of Germania Superior.

Nerva's part in this complicated game is, as already indicated, hard to gauge. From what Pliny reveals in one of his letters, Nerva did not distance himself from those senators who had held leading positions under Domitian and had belonged to his closest circles of advisers (Pliny *Ep*. 4. 22. 4–6). Among these was Fabricius Veiento, *consul tertium* under Domitian. He, indeed, played a part in the session of the Senate in spring 97 when Pliny attacked Publicius Certus, one of the *praefecti aerarii Saturni*, for his role as a *delator* under Domitian (*Ep*. 9. 13. 13, 19). It is therefore possible that the senatorial coteries grouping around Frontinus and Ursus did not at first take Nerva into their confidence, and did so only later when they could be sure of success. Perhaps this happened only after Trajan, installed as governor in Germania Superior, held the necessary military and strategic strength; Nerva could now agree to act in his own interest, but had nothing more to decide.[42] Otherwise, it would have been easy enough to have Trajan adopted in Rome itself. Furthermore, it is noteworthy that Trajan shows no sign of especial gratitude to Nerva,[43] despite the many grand words that Pliny uttered about the close ties between Nerva, the father, and Trajan, the son. Trajan took over the *cognomen* Nerva, but not the *gentilicium* Cocceius; he remained Ulpius. That almost has the effect of distancing himself from his adoptive father. If the adoption had been made more or less under compulsion that would be less surprising.

Theoretically it is possible that the 'conspirators' had brought Nerva in early on, or even at the outset; but the few allusions in our sources do not allow us to indulge in any speculations of this sort. But to identify Frontinus, Ursus, and certain other senators, as the driving forces who set up Trajan as their candidate to succeed Nerva and installed him on the throne by means of a planned operation—these are no idle speculations.[44]

[38] Syme 1958: i. 15 with n. 3; Eck 1982: 326–7.

[39] *PIR*² P 263.

[40] Syme 1958: 536.

[41] *PIR*² J 631. The date of the adoption is not on record, but took place before 102, when Servianus became *consul iterum*. Cf. Syme 1958: i. 35.

[42] This would fit the brief notice in *Epit. de Caes*. 13. 6: Sura, through whose support he had seized power (*Surae, cuius studio imperium arripuerat*).

[43] Syme 1958: i. 12.

[44] Similarly Syme 1958: i. 13, but without specifying individuals, since he did not yet know the new order of the consular *fasti*, especially for 100.

Nerva was probably only a tool in their hands. They could rightly be pointed out to Trajan by Pliny as 'having served you well and bravely, but as civilians' (*de te quidem bene ac fortiter, sed in toga meriti*). The second and third consulates in 98 and 100 are proof that Trajan knew what he owed them.

Part IV

Philosophy and Religion

'Foolishness to the Greeks': Jews and Christians in the Public Life of the Empire

LOVEDAY ALEXANDER

One of my most enduring memories of Miriam's Roman History tutorials at Somerville was the way she encouraged (in an era when the interests of the Roman senatorial elite still tended to dominate the syllabus as well as the sources) a delighted and subversive exploration of the complex relationships between the public life of the Empire and the more marginal groups that flourished within its ecosystem; and the theme of this volume provides a welcome opportunity to pursue that exploration. If our common objective is to increase understanding of how and why philosophers were crucial to the conduct of public life among the Greeks and Romans, my purpose within this larger theme is to examine the hypothesis that the multifarious activities of philosophers created a philosophy-shaped hole, a template within the structures of imperial public life, ready to be exploited by Jews and Christians who were themselves excluded from the normal channels that facilitated exercise of power within those structures. Advising rulers, seeking to attract the interest of elite citizens, inspiring resistance, and discoursing on the nature, forms, and exercise of power: all of these modes of connection between philosophy and power can be paralleled within the discourses of self-presentation constructed by Jews and Christians. Here I intend to look chiefly at the narrative of Paul's mission in the Acts of the Apostles, particularly at the way in which it constructs the task of evangelizing the cities of the Empire through the use of public and private space, and at some of the contested ways in which the paradigm of the resistant philosopher is used to explore the limitations of power.

A PHILOSOPHY-SHAPED HOLE

When the author of Acts sets out to depict Christianity making an impression on the city which epitomizes Greek culture (in image if not in fact), he has his hero visit Athens and talk with Epicurean and Stoic philosophers:

first in the street, then in public debate on the Areopagus, a public venue inextricably associated with the trials of philosophers.[1] The whole scene has a distinctively philosophical flavour. Paul conducts daily 'dialogues' (διελέγετο) in the *agora* 'with the passers-by (πρὸς τοὺς παρατυγχάνοντας)'. This is a recognizably Socratic mode of discourse, and its Socratic character is underlined by the comment (quizzical rather than actively hostile) of the philosophers: 'he seems to be a preacher of strange divinities (ξένων δαιμονίων)'. In the New Testament, the word δαιμόνιον normally means an evil spirit: here, uniquely, it has a neutral or positive referent (what Paul was actually preaching was 'Jesus and the resurrection'), and must surely evoke, in Athens of all places, the Socratic charge of advocating new deities (καινὰ δαιμόνια) which the city does not believe in (Alexander 1993: 59; Sandnes 1993).

This is the only place in the New Testament where the word 'philosopher' occurs; and Luke's picture of the apostle engaged in dialogue with Stoics and Epicureans might seem *prima facie* to be contradicted by the apparently anti-philosophical stance adopted by Paul himself in the letter to the Corinthians, where the apostle insists that the gospel message he preaches is 'foolishness to the Greeks' (1 Corinthians 1: 23).[2] Nevertheless, as Barnes shows elsewhere in this volume (pp. 293–306), many Christians from the second century onwards were happy to accept the label of philosopher; and there is evidence from the first century that the philosopher was seen by Jewish writers as an acceptable model for understanding the role of Jews in the society of the Empire. Josephus and Philo seek to promulgate the view that Moses both anticipated and outclassed Plato as a wise lawgiver whose writings continue to inspire the present-day Jewish community (Gager 1972: 25–79):[3]

That the wisest of the Greeks learnt to adopt these conceptions of God from principles with which Moses supplied them, I am not now concerned to urge; but they have borne abundant witness to the excellence of these doctrines, and to their

[1] Acts 17: 16–34. There is a decidedly novelistic flavour in Luke's depiction of the city of Athens. Compare Chariton, *Callirhoe* 1. 11. 6. For the common perception of the Areopagus as a trial location (whether or not it corresponds to the actual facts of 1st-cent. Athenian civic life), cf. also Diog. Laert. 2. 101, 116, 7. 169.

[2] Paul's words were so taken at least as early as Celsus: cf. Origen, *Contra Celsum* 3. 47–8. For a rather different estimate, see Alexander 2001.

[3] Cf. Philo *Spec. Leg.* 1. 59, 'the most holy Moses . . . loves and teaches the truth which he desires to engrave and stamp upon all his disciples, dislodging and banishing false opinions to a distance from their understanding'; *Op.* 8 'Moses, both because he had attained to the very summit of philosophy, and because he had been divinely instructed in the greater and most essential part of nature's law . . .'. For a contrast with Greek philosophy, cf. e.g. *Leg. All.* 2. 14, *Op.* 131: 'Other philosophers say . . . but Moses . . .'.

consonance with the nature and majesty of God. In fact, Pythagoras, Anaxagoras, Plato, the Stoics who succeeded him, and indeed nearly all the philosophers appear to have held similar views concerning the nature of God. (Jos. *Ag. Ap.* 2. 168; cf. *Ag. Ap.* 2. 279–81)

For Philo, studying philosophy is not an elite activity limited to his own rather esoteric Middle Platonic circles, but something all Jews do on sabbath:

For the law bids us to take the time for studying philosophy (φιλοσοφεῖν), and thereby improve the soul and the dominant mind. So each seventh day there stand wide open in every city thousands of schools (διδασκαλετα) of good sense (φρονήσεως), temperance (σωφροσύνης), courage (ἀνδρείας), justice (δικαιοσύνης) and the other virtues,[4] in which the scholars sit in order, quietly, with ears alert, and with full attention, so much do they thirst for the draught which the teacher's words supply, while one of special experience rises and sets forth what is the best and sure to be profitable and will make the whole of life grow to be something better. (*Spec. Leg.* 2. 61–4; cf. also *Hypothetica* 7. 10–14)

Josephus makes a similar claim:

All schemes of education and training (παιδείας) fall into two categories: instruction is imparted in the one case by precept, in the other by practical exercising of the character. . . . Our legislator, on the other hand, took great care to combine both systems. . . . For ignorance he left no pretext. He appointed the Law to be the most excellent and necessary form of instruction, ordaining, not that it should be heard once and for all or twice or on several occasions, but that every week men should desert their other occupations and assemble to listen to the Law and to obtain a thorough and accurate knowledge of it, a practice which all other legislators seem to have neglected. (Jos. *Ag. Ap.* 2. 171–5)[5]

The implication seems to be that, since the Torah is binding on all Jews, all Jews are (potentially at least) students of philosophy, committed to a morally demanding lifestyle which requires study and the kind of commitment normally expected of adherents to a philosophical school.[6]

Clearly there is a propaganda point being made here by both Philo and Josephus. But that is not the point. What is interesting from our point of view is that both clearly feel that ethnicity by itself cannot provide an adequate definition of what is entailed in being Jewish in the Graeco-Roman

[4] Cf. Josephus, *Ag. Ap.* 2. 170 on the four philosophical virtues as 'departments of religion'.

[5] Cf. *Ant.* 16. 43: 'We give every seventh day over to the study (μαθήσει) of our customs and law, for we think it necessary to occupy ourselves, as with any other study (μελέτην), so with these through which we can avoid committing sins.'

[6] Cf. Philo, *Hypoth.* 7. 14: 'Any one of them whom you attack with inquiries about their ancestral institutions can answer you readily and easily.' Compare Josephus, *Ag. Ap.* 2. 178: 'Should any one of our nation be questioned about the laws, he would repeat them all more readily than his own name'.

world. The experience of belonging to an alien *ethnos*, owing emotional allegiance to an alien *metropolis*, was after all common enough within the complex social structures of the Empire's cities (Momigliano 1975). Being Jewish involves something more, something to do with loyalty to a way of thinking, a system of values, that seems most easily categorized by calling it a kind of philosophy. It also involves a form of social activity, meeting once a week to study ancient laws and listen to moral exhortation: and for many ancient observers (both insiders and outsiders) the most convenient pigeon-hole for this kind of activity was the philosophical school.[7]

Both writers also use the template of philosophy as a metaphorical framework for analysing the multi-strandedness of first-century Judaism. This is not a monolithic system of thought but a complex intellectual structure which can accommodate a diversity of value-systems: and for such diversity-within-coherence, the model of the philosophical *hairesis* seems to provide the flexibility needed. Philo's description of the Therapeutae is already an idealized (and perhaps utopian) description of a philosophical community of the Pythagorean type.[8] Josephus, more comprehensively, characterizes the four major political groupings of pre-war Judaea as *haireseis*, that is, as philosophical sects. The term (like its English counterpart) is apt precisely because it allows for an element of personal choice, and even perhaps a certain amount of mutual toleration, within a larger overarching system: to be a Pharisee, or an Essene, was not to cease to be Jewish but to take on an additional, intensified loyalty within Judaism. That the term was so understood within Greek culture is evident from the passionate second-century debates enshrined in some of Galen's introductory writings: both philosophy and medicine have sects, among which the novice is expected (unwisely, in Galen's view), to choose. Thus Josephus' comparison need not be dismissed as unrealistic cultural apologetic: it can be seen as 'part of a linguistic struggle to find mutually comprehensible categories to describe parallel social systems', arguably at least as apposite as the anachronistic (and equally cross-cultural) model of the political party.[9] But it is interest-

[7] This position (based largely on functional parallels) is argued more fully in Alexander 1994, 2001. See also Stowers 2001; and for a more thoroughgoing treatment of conceptual parallels between St Paul and contemporary philosophy, see Engberg-Pedersen 2000.

[8] Cf. Philo *On the Contemplative Life*, *passim*. Cf. e.g. §2 'The vocation of these philosophers is at once made clear . . .'; §26 'many when asleep and dreaming give utterance to the glorious verities of their holy philosophy'; §28 'they read the Holy Scriptures and seek wisdom from their ancestral philosophy by taking it as an allegory'. Cf. also, more generally, the philosophical cast Philo gives to the few 'who practise wisdom, either in Grecian or in barbarian lands' and who 'in the delight of their virtues, naturally make their whole life a feast': *Spec. Leg.* 2. 44–6.

[9] Alexander 2001. Cf. also Goldin 1965: 10 (= Fischel 1977: 375) on the careful way in which Josephus sets up the comparison.

ing that Josephus (unlike Origen, who sees a parallel to Christian sectarianism in both philosophical and medical sects: *C. Cels.* 10) conceives the choice of sect within Judaism very specifically as a *philosophical* choice. The Pharisees and Sadducees are distinguished as holding characteristically philosophical patterns of thought (for example, on the immortality of the soul); the Essenes and the Zealots display characteristically philosophical behaviour (for example, contempt of death). Josephus' near contemporary Luke uses the same term *hairesis* for both the Pharisees and Sadducees and the Christians.[10] It is unlikely (though not impossible) that Luke knew Josephus' writings (the *Antiquities* at least is almost certainly too late), or that he had combed the *Jewish War* to extract this one metaphor from it while ignoring (or misunderstanding) the vast bulk of its contents. Certain points of overlap may suggest some kind of common source or tradition between Luke and Josephus (Schwartz 1990: 145–9); but it probably makes more sense to see their common use of *hairesis* not as proof of dependence (in either direction) but as testimony to the readiness of educated Jewish writers in the first century, moving in socially distinct but not dissimilar circles in Palestine and Rome, to plot the complex sectarian groupings of first-century Judaism on to a philosophical grid.

Public Space: The Philosopher on the Streets

There are many possible ways of exploring the value (and the limitations) of philosophy as a cross-cultural model for understanding the role of Judaism and Christianity within the Empire, and I have pursued some of them at greater length elsewhere (Alexander 1994, 2001). Here I am considering how it may help us to appreciate some of the ways Jews and Christians locate themselves—and how they are perceived—in relation to the public life of the Empire; and the first question we have to ask is about the use of public space. How public is public space? Who can use it? Who feels at home in the public spaces of the Greek or Roman city, and what activities are excluded?

The unique scene Luke creates of St Paul's encounter with the philosophers in Athens demonstrates the need for the missionary to find a mode of entry into the institutional life of the *polis*. The problem is highlighted at the conceptual level in the Areopagus speech itself (Acts 17: 22–31). Paul's sermon is a masterly demonstration of cultural bridge-building, taking its

[10] Acts 5: 17, 15: 5, 24: 5, 14, 26: 5, 28: 22. The term is used more negatively (but apparently without philosophical connotations) in Gal. 5: 20, Titus 3: 10; ambivalently in 1 Cor. 11: 19.

aphorme from the religious monuments of the host city with the allusion to the 'Unknown God' and weaving a skilful net of literary and philosophical links with this (presumably) cultured Athenian audience. The fact that many of these links were already in place in Hellenistic-Jewish apologetic does not in any way detract from their force. Luke is clearly drawing on a long-standing tradition of cultural appropriation which uses semi-popular tags of philosophical poetry as a point of contact for religious dialogue with Greek audiences. This kind of material is relatively scarce in the New Testament (and notably lacking in Paul's own letters), but is well represented in the apologetic literature of Diaspora Judaism.[11] What is significant here is precisely the location Luke gives it: a formal discourse on the Areopagus, sparked by street-level dialogue with Stoics and Epicureans, within the city of Athens, symbolic home of Greek culture and especially of Greek philosophy.

Within this context, the physical locations of this highly symbolic missionary discourse take on an added significance. In most of the Greek cities he visits (at least according to Acts), Paul's public speaking takes place in the synagogue, the public space of the local Jewish community. Only in Athens does he voluntarily augment this pattern by actively initiating debate in the *agora*, utilizing the public spaces of the Greek *polis* in characteristically Socratic fashion.[12] The Athenian episode has popularly been taken as paradigmatic for the Pauline mission (indeed, for early Christian missionary activity) in general; but, as Stanley Stowers demonstrated in an important article some years ago, this episode is actually the exception rather than the rule (Stowers 1984). Elsewhere, Paul's normal custom (17: 2) is to makes his pitch in the synagogue: in Cyprus (13: 5), in Antioch of Pisidia (13: 14), in Iconium (14: 1–44), in Thessalonica (17: 1–2), in Beroea (17: 10), in Corinth (18: 4), and in Ephesus (18: 19, 19: 8; cf. also Apollos, 18: 26). Where Luke has Paul deliberately move outside the synagogue it is because he is pushed out (14: 26, 18: 6–7, 19: 9) or because no synagogue exists (cf. 16. 13: Philippi has a *proseuche* by the river outside the city). This is not to say that Paul does not on occasion find himself provoked into speech in the public spaces of the cities he visits; but these are not formal missionary speeches. They are improvised reactions to street-level events sparked off by others: for example, the exorcism in the streets of

[11] Acts 17: 28 includes a citation from Aratus *Phaenomena* 5, which also appears in a fragment of Aristobulus (Eusebius, *Praep. Evang.* 13. 12. 6). On the whole passage cf. Fitzmyer 1998: 599–617, with bibliography.

[12] The only other *agora* mentioned by Luke (16: 19) is a hostile environment, the forum of the Roman colony of Philippi, where Paul is hauled before the magistrates (who give him no opportunity to speak). *Agoraioi*, similarly, is elsewhere used negatively (17: 5, 19: 38).

Philippi (16. 16–18), or the impromptu sermon at the city gates at Lystra (14. 8–18). City streets are not presented as the normal location for proselytizing activity in Acts.

Whether this pattern reflects Luke's perception or Paul's own experience, it draws attention to a real problem for a group whose self-construction was as relentlessly missionary as that of the Christians seems to have been. Where could such missionary activity legitimately take place? Socrates was a citizen of Athens, and so could claim a legitimate right to converse with fellow citizens in the *agora* (though even he eventually got into trouble for using this civic space for activities which the restored democracy deemed un-Athenian). Paul, as an outsider, could claim no such right.

> The public spaces of the city were not places which no-one happened to own; they were owned by 'the public', that is by the sovereign people of the city—which sometimes had designated areas created precisely for the purposes of philosophical teaching. . . . A stranger from a different city could not automatically assume the right to teach there. (Alexander 1994)

'The gymnasiarch was responsible for receiving these speakers and had the obligation to expel any who caused trouble or were considered to be a bad influence' (Stowers 1984: 78). This is a problem that does not arise for the Christian sect on its home ground, in Jerusalem or Galilee or Samaria; there, public space is effectively legitimate territory (until you offend the authorities: cf. Mark 11: 28; Acts 4: 1–20, 5: 25–9). Seen in this light, the pattern of the Pauline mission depicted in Acts in fact makes excellent political sense: the synagogue, as community centre and meeting-place for the local Jewish community, would be the natural first port of call for Paul, and its sabbath meetings provide (until he is thrown out) a legitimate platform for expounding his theological vision.[13] From there he has the option of retreating to the hospitality of a private house (building on contacts made through the synagogue: Acts 16: 15, 18: 5), or of moving to an alternative venue.

The only other public venue actually used by Paul in Acts is the 'school (σχολῇ) of Tyrannus' which Paul uses as a base for a two-year mission after being expelled from the synagogue in Ephesus (Acts 19: 9). This was probably an auditorium used for lectures by visiting philosophers or rhetors, perhaps for regular classes; the name suggests that it was privately owned rather than a civic building. How Paul got the use of it is not stated. Did he

[13] Although the narrative pattern described depends on Acts, the importance for Paul of the platform provided by the synagogue is reinforced by his own admission that he had received the thirty-nine lashes (a synagogal disciplinary measure) no less than five times (2 Cor. 11: 24): why, unless he kept going back?

(or a wealthy supporter) hire it for the duration? Did he get it cheap for use in siesta hours, as implied by the Western reading which states that he taught there 'from the fifth hour to the tenth'? However it operated, this rather unglamorous venue seems to be the basis for Luke's claim that during Paul's two-year stay in Ephesus 'all the residents of Asia heard the word of the Lord, both Jews and Greeks' (Acts 19: 10), and for the 'public' side of the claim in Acts 20: 20 that Paul had taught 'both publicly (δημοσίᾳ) and from house to house'. There are glimpses, however, of wider ambitions. When the rioting silversmiths of Ephesus seize Paul's companions and drag them into the theatre, Paul, ever the opportunist, is all set to grab this chance to participate in an assembly in a much more public venue, at the heart of the city's public life (Acts 19: 28–41). The scene recalls the Greek novel, where the theatre has become the standard venue for civic assemblies, regular or impromptu, and thus the prime location for hero (and, on occasion, heroine) to demonstrate the power of love to the assembled *plethos* of the city (cf. e.g. Chariton 3. 4. 4, 8. 7. 1). In Acts, by contrast, the episode only serves to underline the powerlessness of Paul and his associates, and the distance that separates them from the real sources of civic power. Paul has powerful friends (19. 31), but even they can only beg him not to venture in among the *demos*; their caution is vindicated when an unknown Alexander, attempting to speak to the *demos* on behalf of the Jewish community, is identified as a Jew and shouted down in a frenzy of religious xenophobia (19: 33–4).

Luke's depiction of the beginnings of the Christian mission, then, presents a movement which has a legitimate and natural base of operations in the meeting-places of the Jewish communities of the Diaspora, and plays out most of its debates within the framework of the Jewish community. Only occasionally and with reluctance does Paul venture outside that framework; and when he does so, his options for using public space to influence the sources of civic power are strictly limited. Street-level encounters provide rare occasions for the display of spiritual power, but little opportunity for extended public speech; outside the Jewish community, Paul seems to be always in imminent danger of expulsion from the city (13: 50, 14: 5–6, 14: 19) or of a highly charged confrontation with the *demos* (17: 5–8) or with Roman authority (18: 12).

Where the apostle does achieve some kind of successful engagement with the life of the *polis*, he seems to be following a cultural template created by the activities (real or imagined) of philosophers. Whatever the exact mechanisms involved, Paul's use of the 'school of Tyrannus' as a base for the two-year mission in Ephesus implies that the most likely physical location for Christian teaching within the *polis* was a scholastic one: and this reflects a pattern which came to be widely accepted as the Church established itself in the cities of the Empire (cf. Barnes in this volume: 293–306). How far this pattern should be called truly *public* is another point altogether: there is no suggestion that Paul had (or needed) any kind of official licence for this activity, and the obvious inference is that it fitted the widely accepted paradigm of philosophical (and other) teaching taking place in private premises (Stowers 1984: 71–3). With the Athens episode, on the other hand, we are faced with a type-scene envisaged as full-fronted engagement with the public life of the *polis*: and here we must look to a literary paradigm. The model of Socrates must surely lie somewhere (consciously or unconsciously) behind Luke's picture of Paul's dialogue with passers-by in the *agora*, the pointed but not unfriendly confrontation with Stoic and Epicurean philosophers, and the showpiece speech of philosophical apologetic before the Areopagus. Certainly, for many of Luke's contemporaries, Acts' depiction of a God-given mission conducted in the streets and public spaces of the city would irresistibly recall the model of Socrates (Alexander 1993). Dio Chrysostom bases his own mission on 'some ancient discourse, said to be by a certain Socrates, which he never ceased proclaiming, shouting and raising his voice everywhere and before everybody, both in the palaestras and in the Lyceum and before the law courts and in the market-place, like a *deus ex machina*, as somebody said' (*Or.* 13. 244. 17–22).

This is a powerful and influential social template, as a number of texts from the first and second centuries bear witness (Epictetus, the Cynic Epistles); but it is essentially a literary construct, based on texts and traditions derived ultimately from fifth-century Athens. How far it relates to the realities of imperial life in the first century is a debated question. For all his philosophical aspirations, Dio himself could rely on wealth and social status (as well as rhetorical reputation) to win him the right to speak in public in any city he visited: Paul, as a Jew and a leather-worker, could not (Stowers 1984: 74–5). Among the philosophers of the Roman period, it was above all the Cynics who claimed to keep alive the Socratic tradition of philosophizing in the streets: but Epictetus, who claims to have tried this out, does not recommend it as a practical method of influencing the rich and powerful on the streets of Rome: 'if you persist in annoying him, he will lift up his fist and give you a blow' (2. 12. 14–25; Stowers 1984: 79). Cynic beggars may have been a common sight on the streets of the Empire's cities, but they had little access to the seats of power: 'most Cynics lived not in Rome or the West, but in the Greek-speaking cities of the East. . . . Socially their status had been extremely mixed from the beginning, but as a rule they were not the associates of men of wealth and power such as Seneca the Younger.'[14] By the time of Philostratus, writing about a first-century philosopher a couple of centuries later, access to public space is seen as something very much within the control of the powerful. Apollonius of Tyana, approaching Rome, is warned that the Emperor Nero does not like philosophers. On arrival in the city, he is summoned and cross-examined by the consul Telesinus. Telesinus is impressed by Apollonius' un-Cynic appearance ('holy and not at all like beggars'), and issues a concession:

'You may visit any shrine. I will write to the priests telling them to welcome you and to adopt your improvements.'

'If you don't write,' said Apollonius, 'will they not welcome me?'

'No,' said Telesinus; 'that is in my power.'[15]

Private Space: The Philosopher in the Home

Public space, then, whether of the city or of the Jewish community, quickly becomes a dangerous and contested location for the preaching of the Christian gospel. What alternatives are open to the apostle? Paul in effect has two options: to use his own premises (and those of his associates) as a base for teaching, or to seek the support of a patron. There is ample evidence for both in Acts and the Epistles. Paul is depicted as working as a tentmaker in Corinth in partnership with Aquila and Priscilla (Acts 18: 1–3), probably in a rented workshop; when the same couple turn up in Ephesus a few years later, there is no hint that the location they use for giving private instruction to Apollos is anything grander than their own shop (Acts 18: 26: cf. Reimer 1995: 199–208). Paul himself speaks of 'the church in their house' (Rom. 16: 3–5, 1 Cor. 16: 19). Attracting the support of householders able to offer hospitality to the missionaries is an essential component in the mission's success: cf. Lydia's role in Philippi (Acts 16: 15), and Crispus' in Corinth (Acts 18: 8). The latter is described as an *archisynagogos*, which implies that he was a wealthy patron and supporter of the synagogue (Rajak and Noy 1993): there is no reason to suppose he withdrew from this useful role when he became a Christian. The Pauline epistles mention other hosts whose hospitality and patronage provided a base for Paul's missionary activities: Phoebe, described as a *προστάτις* (Rom. 16: 2); Gaius, who acts as host (*ξένος*) 'to me and to the whole church', and

[14] Branham and Goulet-Cazé 1996: 13–14. Miriam Griffin explores the ambiguities and selectivity of the Roman appropriation of Cynicism (a function more of the literary image of the Cynic than of any acquaintance with street preachers) in the same volume (1996: 190–204).

[15] Philostratus, *Life of Apollonius* 4. 35–40; tr. C. P. Jones and G. Bowersock 1970.

therefore presumably has a house large enough to accommodate a gathering of all the separate house-churches in Corinth (Rom. 16: 23); Philemon and his wife, who host a church in their house (Philemon 1). Acts in fact gives the impression that Paul could call on a network of safe houses across the eastern Mediterranean: besides those mentioned, cf. 20: 9 (where the third-floor rendezvous suggests a room in a tenement block), or the nameless disciples who put Paul up in Tyre (21: 4) and in Ptolemais (21: 7). And at the end of the book, Paul, though technically a prisoner, is depicted using his own lodgings as a base for mission and for debates with the leaders of the local Jewish community (Acts 28: 30).

Both the private house and the workshop have precedents as locations for philosophical discourse. Paul's practice of supporting himself by working with his hands (Acts 18: 1–3) has obvious echoes in the practice of the rabbis (Bruce 1990: 391); but it is equally well-rooted in the anecdotal traditions which carry and form the Greek template of the philosophical life. A small but significant minority of Greek philosophers chose to work for a living, and are shown in tradition conducting philosophical debate in the context of workshop or field. Some Hellenistic authorities traced this pattern of activity back to Socrates himself and his immediate circle:

Duris makes him out to have been a slave and to have been employed on stone-work, and the draped figures of the Graces on the Acropolis have been by some attributed to him. (Diog. Laert. 2. 19)

Demetrius of Byzantium relates that Crito removed him from his workshop and educated him, being struck by his beauty of soul; that he discussed moral questions in the workshops and in the market-place, . . . and that he claimed that his inquiries embraced, 'Whatso'er is good or evil in a house'. (2. 20–1)

Aeschines was the son of Charinus the sausage-maker. (2. 60)

Simon was a citizen of Athens and a cobbler. When Socrates came to his workshop and began to converse, he used to make notes of all that he could remember [*or better*, of the remarks he (Socrates) used to make: ὧν ἐμνημονέυεν]. And this is why people apply the term 'leathern' to his dialogues. (2. 122)

Ronald Hock (1980) has shown that these apparently accidental notices form part of a broader debate about the proper means of support for a philosopher, carried out both in the anecdotal tradition (to which Diogenes is largely indebted, at least for the Socratics) and in the pseudonymous Cynic Epistles (cf. e.g. Malherbe 1977: 219; 245). Working for a living became emblematic of a desire to preserve intellectual freedom: 'When Pericles promised to support [Simon], and urged him to come to him, his reply was, "I will not part with my free speech (παρρησίαν) for money"' (Diog. Laert. 2. 123). In the Socratic tradition, refusing such offers (especially from tyrants) becomes part of the template of proper philosophical behaviour: 'Ptolemy Soter, they say, made much of [Stilpo], and when he had got possession of Megara, offered him a sum of money and invited him to return with him to Egypt. But Stilpo would only accept a very moderate sum, and he declined the proposed journey, and removed to Aegina until Ptolemy set sail' (Diog. Laert. 2. 115). The philosophical ideal of self-sufficiency (*autarkeia*) and simplicity of lifestyle was in part a necessary defence against the temptations posed by such invitations: cf. Diogenes Laertius 2. 24–32 on Socrates, esp. 24 and 25:

> He showed his contempt for Archelaus of Macedon and Scopas of Cranon and Eurylochus of Larissa by refusing to accept their presents or go to their court. . . . [27] He could afford to despise those who scoffed at him. He prided himself on his plain living, and never asked a fee from anyone. He used to say that he most enjoyed the food which was least in need of condiment, and the drink which made him feel the least hankering for some other drink; and that he was nearest to the gods when he had the fewest wants.

His disciples followed suit:

> Again, when Demetrius, the son of Antigonus, had taken Megara, he took measure that Stilpo's house should be preserved and all his plundered property restored to him. But when he requested that a schedule of the lost property should be drawn up, Stilpo denied that he had lost anything which really belonged to him, for no one had taken away his learning, while he still had his eloquence and knowledge. (Diog. Laert. 2. 15)

Some of the same tensions can be seen in Paul's relationships with his hosts and would-be patrons in Corinth and Philippi. Paul's evident reluctance to accept financial support from the Corinthian church (despite an elaborate theological defence of his right to such support in 1 Cor. 9) may well reflect a refusal to entangle himself in the web of patronage obligations that such support would implicitly entail: cf. Paul's use of the very philosophical term αὐτάρκης (a loaded term when thanking one's benefactors) in Philippians 4. 11. Something of this pride in maintaining financial and emotional independence (and with it the ability to be a benefactor to others) comes across in the farewell speech to the elders of the Ephesian church:

> I coveted no one's silver or gold or apparel. You yourselves know that these hands ministered to my necessities, and to those who were with me. In all things I have shown you that by so toiling one must help the weak, remembering the words of the Lord Jesus, 'It is more blessed to give than to receive'. (Acts 20: 33–4)

Working for a living, however, was always a minority pursuit among philosophers: and, whatever its impact on democratic Athens in the fifth century BC, a workshop-based teaching mission was unlikely to have much influence on the seats of power in the more status-conscious world of the Roman Empire (Stowers 1984: 74, 81–2). Much better attested (and much more influential) is the practice of using the private houses of patrons as a semi-public base for philosophical teaching, a practice which goes right back to the time of Socrates and the sophists. For the sophists, many of whom were non-Athenians, local patronage provided an entrée into the public life of the city, offering a form of *proxenia* for the visitor as well as material support and a venue for meetings; but many of the Socratic dialogues too are set in private houses. The semi-public nature of these gatherings is well illustrated by Epictetus' ironic reference to a contemporary would-be Cynic: 'But no, your idea of [Socrates], no doubt, is that, as he was taking them along, he used to say, "Come around today and hear me deliver a discourse at the house of Quadratus"' (3. 23. 23). The dining quarters of a Greek house, like the atrium of a Roman house, were more than half in the public domain, clearly demarcated from the private women's quarters at the back of the house, and used not only for privately invited dinner-guests but for the bustle of clients and petitioners who regularly hung around any houseowner of substance in the ancient city. A similar blurring of the public–private distinction is evident in Paul's references to the house-church meetings in Corinth (1 Cor. 14: 23–5). It is assumed here that 'outsiders [ἰδιῶται] or unbelievers' may wander into such a meeting. This assumption provides the grounds for Paul's argument that in this case prophesying is a more effective mission tool than *glossolalia* because the outsiders will be 'convicted' and 'called to account' by what they hear. The argument seems to presuppose that Paul himself (if not his Corinthian addressees) still saw such gatherings as having a missionary function: but it is also intriguing that Paul uses the philosophical term ἐλέγχεται for the effect of such an experience, though here it is the whole assembly that takes on the very Socratic role of 'testing' in order to bring about a change of heart (Stowers 1984: 69).

Having a tame philosopher as part of your entourage became fashionable among the Roman dynasts of the late Republic (Rawson 1985: 66–99); Philodemus is an obvious example, ensconced in Piso's luxurious villa with library and garden at his disposal, and encouraged to use the whole place (apparently) as a base for an intimate Epicurean coterie (Gigante 1995). Paul's patrons in Acts tend to be of humbler status, but we do get glimpses of a Christian attempt to secure this kind of influence on Cyprus, where

Paul (here a wonder-working philosopher of the Apollonian type rather than a Socratic teacher) uses the power of miracle to maintain an influence over the proconsul Sergius Paulus (13: 6–12); and again on Malta, where a fortuitous healing secures the good offices of Publius, the 'chief man' (τῷ πρώτῳ) of the island (28: 7–10).[16] The advantage of such an arrangement for the philosopher was not only that it gave him a legitimate base for operations in the life of the city, but that it gave him an entrée into the circles of power. As an honoured guest and member of the household, he could expect to meet—and therefore had the opportunity to influence—elite citizens at a level no amount of street preaching could ever reach. This of course had been the theoretical justification for 'eating at Sicilian tables' ever since Plato's move to the court of Dionysius: the case is made with elegance and passion in the second and seventh Platonic Epistles. It is interesting to reflect that the perennial philosophical aspiration to exercise a beneficial influence on political dynasts may have come to its closest realization in the Pisonian circle in republican Rome.

The dangers attendant on such a relationship were equally obvious, and the tension between the two informs much of the debate in the Hellenistic anecdotal tradition recorded by Diogenes Laertius as well as in the Cynic Epistles (a fact which in itself suggests that the issue was a live one in the first century). Other, more mundane, disadvantages are satirized by Lucian in *On Salaried Posts in Great Houses*: his household philosopher, who starts life with great hopes of the influential position he will hold in the household he has been invited to join, finds himself condemned to a miserable existence not unlike that of the governess of nineteenth-century English fiction: despised by master and servants alike, underpaid, underfed, totally lacking in authority, and expected to be grateful. The theme is endemic to the narrative construction of the philosophical life. One of the major interests of Philodemus' *History of the Academic and Stoic Philosophers*, as Clay points out, is 'the theme of the philosopher and his ambiguous and dangerous relation to the powerful' (1998: 118). Philodemus, like the Cynics, shows a particular interest in Plato and the court of Syracuse, 'because a philosopher's autonomy and freedom of speech are tested and maintained in such contacts as these' (Clay 1998: 114–15). The moral ambivalence of the court philosopher's position is well illustrated by Miriam Griffin's study of Seneca (1976). Nevertheless, the idea that philosophers could exercise power by gaining personal access to the power-

[16] Cf. also the constant stress in Acts on the importance of having high-status friends: 13: 50 ('devout women of high standing'); 17: 4 ('leading women'); 19: 31 (Asiarchs as friends of Paul).

ful remained an enduring ideal, all the more attractive in the Hellenistic world as power seemed to be leaving the democratic city-states and becoming concentrated in the hands of the Hellenistic monarchs and then of the Roman dynasts.

Parrhesia: The Philosopher on Trial

The key term for exploring this relationship is *parrhesia*, the subject of Philodemus' treatise *Peri Parrhesias*. *Parrhesia* is the ancient civic virtue of 'freedom of speech', that is, an independence of moral purpose which allows the philosopher to speak as freely and frankly to tyrant as to friend, without fear or favour. *Parrhesia* was highly valued by the Socratics and Cynics (as we have seen), as the virtue which allowed the philosopher to maintain his autonomy by refusing to accept favours from the powerful. But it was also an Epicurean virtue which encouraged the practice of 'frank criticism' as a means to mutual character-building between friends within a philosophical community. Allowing a friend to administer frank criticism of any aspect of one's own moral life was a highly recommended tool for self-improvement among ancient philosophers: Galen commends that as a cure for enslavement to the passions you should 'let the door to your house always stand open and grant your close friends the right to enter at any time'.[17] But if one 'friend' was a humble philosopher, and the other a powerful patron or monarch, the exercise of such frankness called for a particular kind of courage—one perhaps best exercised from outside the dependent position of the household philosopher.

Thus, for many ancients, the quintessential position for exercising *parrhesia*—and thus in effect the quintessential location for philosophizing—was the trial. The trial scenario, whether formal or informal, was one of the few places where the philosopher could count on face-to-face confrontation with the sources of power and where, if he stood firm, he had a unique opportunity to make a public statement of the philosophy he had staked his life on. If he was prepared to face death for that philosophy, so much the better (Rajak 1997: 59). Anecdotes of philosophers facing up to tyrants are central to the philosophical paradigm in antiquity, from Socrates onwards: first-century exemplars are as varied as the 'Stoic opposition' led by Thrasea Paetus and Helvidius Priscus, the so-called 'Alexandrian martyrs', Apollonius of Tyana imprisoned by Nero, or Secundus the Silent Philosopher refusing to speak to Hadrian. The ability to philosophize in such a situation—that is, to administer fearless advice to

[17] Galen, *On the Diagnosis and Cure of the Soul's Passions* 3: Harkins and Riese 1963: 45.

the person who appears to have you in his power—was a widely admired form of *parrhesia*.[18] So it is not without significance that when Paul finally enters the imperial city, at the end of Acts, it is not as street preacher or as household teacher but as a prisoner, on course (though the book never narrates the denouement) for a trial before the face of Caesar himself. In fact the last quarter of the book shows Paul as a prisoner, his readiness to face death for the cause he believes in clearly laid out (20. 22–4, 21. 12–14) and farewells said in thoroughly Socratic fashion (Alexander 1993: 60–3). The apologetic speeches from the trial chapters display a recognizably philosophical agenda as Paul argues with Felix about 'justice (δικαιοσύνης) and self-control (ἐγκρατείας) and future judgement' (Acts 24: 25), or discourses calmly about 'the Way' with Agrippa (Acts 26). Luke's abundant use of the noun παρρησία and its cognate verb παρρησιάζομαι (unique to Acts in the New Testament), as well as the numerous subtle echoes of the Socratic paradigm in Paul's final voyage, all suggest that the template of the philosopher is helping to shape Luke's presentation of his story for a Graeco-Roman audience.

It is in fact in the ability to inspire resistance to tyranny—and to sustain that resistance in the face of torture and death—that ancient writers were most inclined to identify the Jewish and Christian sects as 'philosophical'. The connection between philosophy and Jewish resistance and martyrdom is made explicitly by Josephus. He uses the term σοφιστής both for those who inspired the young men of Jerusalem to tear down the eagle from the Temple gate in 4 BC (*Jewish War* 1. 648–50) and for Judas the Galilean, leader of the revolt against the census of Quirinius (*Jewish War* 2. 118). The heroic ability to despise death for the sake of the Law is also an important aspect of the 'philosophy' of the Essenes:

> Racked and twisted, burnt and broken, and made to pass through every instrument of torture, in order to induce them to blaspheme their lawgiver or to eat some forbidden thing, they refused to yield to either demand, nor even once did they cringe to their persecutors or shed a tear. Smiling in their agonies, and mildly deriding their tormentors, they cheerfully resigned their souls, confident that they would receive them back again. (Josephus, *Jewish War* 2.150–3)

Josephus did not need to look to Greek tradition to find a way of articulating this particular ideal: the ideal of the martyr is firmly rooted in biblical and post-biblical Jewish tradition (Fischel 1946). What is interesting here is that when he wants to find a way to describe that ideal for a Roman audi-

[18] Secundus' refusal to break his moral resolve by speaking to the emperor may be regarded as a paradoxical form of *parrhesia*.

ence, it is the language of philosophy that seems most appropriate. The spectacle of the zealot prepared to die for a cause activated not merely the ancient military-patriotic ideology of courage and steadfastness in the face of death, but a whole complex of ideas (selfless devotion to a way of life; belief in the immortality of the soul) which irresistibly evokes description in philosophical terms:

This [eagle] it was that these doctors (σοφισταί) now exhorted their disciples to cut down, telling them that, even if the action proved hazardous, it was a noble deed to die for the law of one's country; for the souls of those who came to such an end attained immortality and an eternally abiding sense of felicity; it was only the ignoble, uninitiated in their philosophy (σοφίας), who clung in their ignorance to life and preferred death on a sick-bed to that of a hero [lit. δι' ἀρετῆς]. (*Jewish War* 1. 650)

On the face of it, this is an odd link between intellectual/teaching activity and acts of heroic resistance: the ordered and contemplative Essenes look much easier to accommodate to a philosophical mould than the Zealots (cf. *Jewish War* 2. 154–8 for a thoroughly philosophical and explicitly Greek description of Essene views on immortality). But Josephus' disapproval of the 'folly' (ἀνοίᾳ) of the Zealots does not prevent him including them under the rubric 'philosophy' (*Antiquities* 18. 23–5)—an ambivalence with which we might parallel Graeco-Roman attitudes to the *mania* of the Cynics (Krueger 1996).

It is not only insiders who identify this aspect of Jewish and Christian behaviour as philosophical. Two second-century observers, looking from outside at the readiness of Jews and/or Christians to face death for the sake of their beliefs, independently identify this behaviour as in some way 'philosophical'—though they have their reservations. Epictetus, writing on freedom from the fear of tyrants, points out that one way to cure oneself of fear is to cultivate a cast of mind which allows one to 'set the will neither upon dying nor upon living at any cost, but only as it is given one to live' (4. 7. 6). The same effect can be produced by 'madness' (μανίας), and also by 'habit' (ἔθους), 'as with the Galileans'.[19] In a not dissimilar passage, Galen notes the 'philosophical' behaviour of some followers of Christ, who are able to achieve a laudable degree of detachment from material things and willingness to die for their beliefs:

Most people are unable to follow any demonstrative argument consecutively; hence they need parables, and benefit from them—and he [Galen] understands by parables tales of rewards and punishments in a future life—just as now we see the

[19] Fischel (1946: 267 n. 8) suggests that Epictetus may be referring to a memory of the Galilean Zealots going back to the Jewish War some fifty years earlier; but Stern (1974: i. 541 n. 1) takes the passage as a reference to Christians.

people called Christians drawing their faith from parables [and miracles], and yet sometimes acting in the same way [as those who philosophize]. For their contempt of death [and of its sequel] is patent to us every day, and likewise their restraint in cohabitation. For they include not only men but also women who refrain from cohabiting all through their lives; and they also number individuals who, in self-discipline and self-control in matters of food and drink, and in their keen pursuit of justice, have attained a pitch not inferior to that of genuine philosophers. (Walzer 1949: 15–16)

These observations show something of an advance on earlier pagan references to Christians (like those of Tacitus *Ann.* 15. 44, and Pliny, *Ep.* 10. 96, who merely note and disapprove of their *pertinacia*). Nevertheless, they are distinctly ambivalent. Both seem reluctant to award the name of 'philosopher' to the Jewish and/or Christian groups they have observed, despite the fact that, for both, there is something about the groups' behaviour for which 'philosophical' is the only appropriate label. For Galen, the problem is that (as he explains elsewhere) the 'followers of Moses and Christ' rely on faith rather than reason to attain their otherwise admirable conclusions (Walzer 1949). For Epictetus, it is their reliance on 'habit'—perhaps another way of saying the same thing. Either way, we sense in these writers an element of resistance to using the philosopher as a cross-cultural model. It seems to work, but only on the phenomenological level: the effects are the same, but the causes are different. And their contemporary Marcus Aurelius, implicitly entering the same debate, refuses to allow any philosophical credibility at all to Christian martyrs: the martyr's resolve, to be truly admirable, 'must arise from a specific decision, not out of sheer opposition, like the Christians, but after reflection and with great dignity and so as to convince others, without histrionic display' (*Med.* 11. 3).

It is interesting, then, to find at least two early Jewish texts which explicitly make the point that the ability of the martyrs to choose death in preference to life is precisely the product of reason, and thus is truly philosophical. The first is the speech of Eleazar in Josephus' account of the fall of Masada (*Jewish War* 7. 341–88). This is the point where the remaining Zealots, barricaded into Masada and seeing the imminent fall of the stronghold to the besieging Romans, determine on mass suicide as preferable to surrender or capture. Eleazar's first speech (7. 323–36) is largely theological (God is on the side of the Romans, a favourite Josephan theme) and heroic (we prefer death to slavery). His second, however, is much more explicitly philosophical, based on the argument of reason (§343) 'that death gives liberty to the soul and permits it to depart to its own pure abode'. This is supported by a proof (τεκμήριον, §349), supplied by the analogy of sleep, and by a familiar philosophical *exemplum*, the σοφίαν of the Indians (§351). The whole thing is presented as a *paideia* based on *logoi* (cf. §358 λόγους ἐπαιαδεύθημεν): in other words, the Torah provides a reasoned foundation for life (and, if necessary, for death) comparable to the best of the 'barbarian' philosophers.[20]

The second is the so-called Fourth Book of Maccabees, a Jewish-Greek text dating from the first or second century AD, which gives an impassioned and highly rhetorical account of the deaths of the old man Eleazar (a different Eleazar) and the nameless woman and her seven sons at the time of the Maccabean revolt. The narrative is based on the story told in 2 Macc. 6: 18–7: 41, but is cast in the form of an elaborate philosophical argument: 'Highly philosophical is the subject I propose to discuss, namely, whether reason is absolute master of the passions, and I would strictly counsel you to give earnest attention to my philosophical exposition' (4 Macc. 1: 1). The deaths of the martyrs are adduced as an unanswerable demonstration of this general truth:

> I could prove to you from many and varied sources that reason is absolute master of the passions, but by far the best example I could furnish is the heroism of those who died for virtue's sake, namely Eleazar and the seven brothers and their mother. Taking no account at all of the sufferings that brought them to their death, they all proved that reason is lord of the passions. (4 Macc. 1: 7–9)

The confrontation between Eleazar and Antiochus is explicitly constructed as a confrontation between tyrant (τύραννος 5: 1) and philosopher. Eleazar, a man distinguished for his ἐπιστήμην (5: 4), is taunted by Antiochus for his fidelity to Jewish religious practice (θρησκείᾳ), which 'makes you anything but a philosopher (φιλοσοφεῖν) in my eyes' (5: 7). This is precisely the challenge that Eleazar takes up in his response: Jews live 'in accordance with the divine Law', he says (5: 16), and fidelity to this belief (even if it should turn out to be unfounded) is truly philosophical:

> You mock at our philosophy as though our living under it were contrary to reason. On the contrary, it teaches us temperance (σωφροσύνην) so that we are in control of all our pleasures and desires; and it gives us a thorough training in courage (ἀνδρείαν) so that we willingly endure all hardship; and it teaches us justice (δικαιοσύνην) so that whatever our different attitudes may be we retain a sense of balance; and it instructs us in piety (εὐσέβειαν) so that we most highly reverence the only living God. (5: 22–4)

Eleazar's claim to the philosophical high ground is vindicated by his *parrhesia*: far from being silenced in the face of physical coercion, he is able

[20] For the Platonic background to this speech, cf. Droge and Tabor (1992: esp. 92–6) and especially Luz 1983.

to show that Antiochus, by his insistence on forcing a pious old man to abandon his philosophical way of life, clearly brands himself as a tyrant: 'Tyrannize as you will over the ungodly, but you will never lord it over my thoughts on the subject of true religion, neither by your words nor through your works' (5: 38, cf. 5: 27).

This classic trial scene thus encapsulates a number of key strands in the long-running and complex relationship between philosophy and power. Within the structured and hierarchical society of the Empire, the trial scenario, real or imagined, provides one of the few avenues for direct access to the seats of power. The trial is a unique opportunity to make the powerful listen, to expound the principles for which the martyr is prepared to stake his or her life: hence the tendency in trial apologetic to blur the distinction between *apologia* proper (defence against specific charges) and apologetic propaganda (speech in support of an ideology). This blurring is a notable feature of Paul's apologetic speeches in Acts, which Luke presents as having precisely the reasoned and persuasive effect that Marcus Aurelius was looking for (Acts 24: 24–5; cf. esp. 26: 28: 'You almost persuade me to be a Christian!'). It also appears in the way Paul sees his own imprisonment as giving scope for both *apologia* and 'confirmation of the gospel' (Philippians 1: 7). But it is a high-risk strategy: only by maintaining their *parrhesia* in a potentially life-threatening situation will the martyrs be able to exploit the opportunities presented to them (hence Paul's request for prayer in Philippians 1: 19–20; cf. the importance of *parrhesia* in Acts 4: 13, 29, 31, and of Jesus' promise to his disciples that 'I will give you a mouth and wisdom, which none of your adversaries will be able to withstand or contradict' in Luke 21: 12–19). And an essential element in that *parrhesia* is freedom from the fear of death, which in its turn relativizes all other kinds of power. When Jesus says, 'I tell you, my friends, do not fear those who kill the body, and after that have no more that they can do; but . . . fear him who, after he has killed, has power to cast into hell' (Luke 12: 4), he is presumably bolstering his teaching with the kind of 'parables' that Galen (or his Arabic interpreter) saw as characteristic of Christian philosophy. Epictetus employs a more abstract argument, but the practical effect is much the same:

> 'But it is now time to die.' Why say 'die'? Make no tragic parade of the matter, but speak of it as it is: 'It is now time for the material of which you are constituted to be restored to those elements from which it came.' And what is so terrible about that? What one of the things that make up the universe will be lost, what novel or unreasonable thing will have taken place? Is it for this that the tyrant inspires fear? Is it because of this that his guards seem to have long and sharp swords? Let others see

to that; I have considered all this, no one has authority over me. I have been set free by God, I know his commands, no one has power any longer to make a slave of me, I have the right kind of emancipator, and the right kind of judges. 'Am I not master of your body?' Very well, what is that to me? 'Am I not master of your paltry property?' Very well, what is that to me? 'Am I not master of exile or bonds?' Again I yield up to you all these things and my whole paltry body itself, whenever you will. Do make trial of your power, and you will find out how far it extends. (4. 7. 15–18)

More than anything else, it is this freedom that not only liberates the philosopher from fear of the tyrant but turns him into a living exemplar of the philosophy he preaches. The confrontation between philosopher and tyrant becomes a 'narrative demonstration' (4 Macc. 3: 19) which itself calls into question both the efficacy and the legitimacy of the tyrant's power (cf. John 19: 10: 'You would have no power over me unless it had been given you from above'):

You imply, then, that Socrates did not fare badly?
—He did not; it was his judges and accusers who fared badly.
Nor Helvidius at Rome?
—No, but the man who put him to death. (Epictetus 4. 1. 123)

Jews and Christians here could draw on a long narrative tradition of fearless prophets outfacing kings, going back to the book of Daniel and beyond (e.g. Daniel 3. 16–18). But when the story of Jewish or Christian martyrdom is written in the cultural script of the Graeco-Roman world, it is inevitably the philosopher who provides the template.

Old Philosophy and New Power: Cicero in Fifth-Century North Africa

MARGARET ATKINS

On 26 May 51 BC, soon after the *De Republica* was completed, Cicero's friend Caelius wrote to him to congratulate him: 'tui politici libri omnibus vigent' ('your political books'—as Shackleton Bailey translates (1977: 384)—'are all the rage' *Fam*. 8. 1. 4). Some time around the beginning of the eighth century an unnamed monk scrubbed down a version of the same text (dating from the fourth or fifth century) in order to copy onto it Augustine's *Commentary on the Psalms*. This was the manuscript discovered in 1819 by Cardinal Mai in the Vatican Library. We have only brief glimpses of how the text was used in the 750 years between Cicero and the nameless scribe, and we know very little of how non-Christians used the text. In AD 408, however, it surfaces briefly in some letters between Augustine and a non-Christian called Nectarius.[1] The trigger is a riot in Calama, a small town about 40 miles south-west of Hippo. Nectarius writes to Augustine to persuade him to use his influence to minimize the punishment of those held responsible. Both sides in this exchange quote the *De Republica*, in the heat of an actual political debate with serious consequences. Yet the political and religious context has changed drastically since Cicero's day. The appeal to Ciceronian ideas, I shall argue, is successful where these ideas can be integrated effectively into a new world-view; ironically, it is the Christian Augustine, rather than the semi-pagan Nectarius, who achieves this more smoothly. Reflection upon their exchange suggests, moreover, that the mangled textual history of *De Republica* is not entirely due to chance: some

It is a delight to be able to contribute to this volume; as all her friends know, the privilege of learning from Miriam is only outweighed by the sheer enjoyment of her company! I should like also to thank Peter Garnsey, Jonathan Powell, and the editors for kindly reading and commenting on this piece at short notice.

[1] *Epp*. 90, 91, 103, and 104 (numerical references alone refer to these letters). The text is in Goldbacher 1898: 426–35, 578–95. Translations in Atkins and Dodaro 2001: 1–22, with nn. at 251–6. For discussion see Lepelley 1981: 90–103; Dodaro 2000. On Augustine's use of *De Republica*, see Hagendahl 1967: 112–31, 540–53. For *De Republica* I refer to the text of Ziegler (1958).

of the book's ideas might be given new life in a later context, whereas much of it was rendered redundant by events almost as soon as it was written.

The town of Calama was religiously mixed. It included a strong Donatist contingent, some of whom had once ambushed the Catholic bishop, Possidius (Augustine's future biographer), with the intention of killing him. We can only guess how far the tension between pagans and Christians was exacerbated by the presence of the Donatists. Non-Christians[2] were still in the majority in 408, long after Theodosius I had officially banned their worship in 391 (*Cod. Theod.* 16. 10. 10); they were also committed enough to fund and celebrate an annual festival, and confident enough to risk the Christians' wrath in doing so publicly. Clearly the active, or at least passively supportive, pagans included many of the wealthy and influential. Initial Christian attempts to make official complaints on record about violence by pagans were frustrated, which suggests a non-Christian majority on the town's council. At any rate, the Christians certainly believed that influential pagans would have been in a position to put an end to anti-Christian rioting had they so wished.

The rioting, according to Augustine, had happened in this way: on 1 June 408 the pagans had celebrated their annual festival by, among other things, having a troupe of dancers process right up to the Christian church and dance in front of it.[3] The clergy tried to prevent them, and were stoned by the crowd. The bishop responded by appealing to the authorities to implement the recent laws of the Emperor Honorius, which banned pagan religious ceremonies, giving Catholic bishops the right, and magistrates the obligation, to enforce this (*Cod. Theod.* 16. 10. 19 (15 November 407), cf. *Sirm.* 12). This triggered a second round of stoning; moreover, the Christians were denied the right to give evidence on record. A mob then stoned the church for the third time and set it on fire. They killed one of the escaping clerics and began a hunt for the bishop, with the intention of killing him if they found him. Soon after this Augustine visited Calama and

[2] I use the term 'non-Christian' interchangeably with 'pagan' throughout (with apologies to the Jews) to signal the unsatisfactory nature of the second category, forged by Christian, rather than non-Christian, self-definition (Chadwick 1985: 9; Athanassiadi and Frede 1999: 1–20). In particular, the conflation of several different types of practical religion and of several different theories of religion, makes it harder to see how in fact these were related among themselves.

[3] Were they simply being provocative? Perhaps the Christian church had been built on or next to ground sacred to the relevant god, and the procession traditionally involved dancing through this area (on temple conversions see Trombley 1993: 108–22). Trombley also provides a detailed account (based on Mark the Deacon) of a riot in Gaza in 407, related to the destruction of the temple, which provides an interesting parallel with the incident in Calama (1993: 201–3; Grégoire and Kugener 1930: 95–9).

discussed matters with the Christians and, at their request, with some of the pagans, with whom he engaged in a lengthy discussion about the relative merits of the two religions. It was about then that Nectarius wrote his first letter to Augustine and Augustine replied. At this point Possidius was staying with Augustine (he appears to have acted as postman for Nectarius' letter) *en route* to the imperial court in Ravenna where he was travelling to report the incident and request legal support. This was in August. It was not until 27 March of the next year that Augustine received a second letter from Nectarius. Augustine speculates that the reason for this is that Possidius has by now received imperial support to enable him to enforce fines imposed upon the leading citizens. In theory, the fines were for failing to prevent the religious ceremonies. In practice, as Augustine suggests, it was the subsequent violence which persuaded the Christians to resort to law. In the tense environment of the divided cities of North Africa, there was often a fine line between celebration and riot (Chadwick 1985).

Nectarius' letters are both brief appeals, the first for Augustine to defend those 'not responsible' (*innoxius*, *innocentes*) and to limit any penalty to damages rather than criminal punishment. The second pleads with Augustine not to press for fines, to avoid inquisitorial torture, and to drop charges against those 'whom everyone agrees not to have been involved in the crime' ('quos a crimine constat esse discretos', 103. 4).

Augustine's replies are more substantial, running to eight and thirteen pages respectively of Goldbacher's *CSEL* text. In the first, he distinguishes the heavenly *patria* from Nectarius' earthly one and expresses hope that Nectarius will one day become also a citizen of the former. He then picks up Nectarius' reference to Calama 'flourishing' (*florentem*) and argues that true flourishing requires virtuous rather than riotous behaviour from its citizens. Paganism, exemplified by a wall-painting of Jupiter committing adultery described by Terence, and by the festival of the goddess Flora, honoured in particular by prostitutes (a favourite target of Augustine's, in part, perhaps as a result of its renewal in Rome in 394 by Nicomachus Flavianus (Matthews 1970)), can only foster vice in its adherents. Calama will not flourish until its citizens abandon such things and turn to Christianity. After describing the events following 1 June, Augustine concludes by arguing that Christians must both preserve gentleness and moderation and, at the same time, employ such measures as might lead to the reform (including the conversion) of the culprits.

Augustine's second letter deals at some length with Nectarius' appeal to two points of philosophy. (I shall discuss these further below.) He elaborates here his own understanding of the purpose of punishment as corrective.

Augustine is concerned to foster repentance in the inhabitants of Calama because, he argues, only conversion to the true God will bring them true happiness. He, like Nectarius, is motivated by love for them; the difference, he states flatly, is that Nectarius' love is misguided.

Finally, Augustine gets down to the concrete political issue: who should be punished? He repeats a set of distinctions he had already made in the previous letter between those who actually committed the crimes, those who instigated them, and those who wanted them committed. (In the previous letter he had excused as minimally guilty those who had wanted to help prevent the riots but had failed to do so out of fear.) Nothing is said of the punishment of the actual perpetrators: this seems to have been dealt with long before. Those Christians who had confessed to, and repented of, either failing to help when the church was burning or taking part in the general looting, had been treated mercifully (103. 4, 104. 9). The next most guilty group are the instigators, but they could only be identified by securing evidence under torture, something that Augustine refuses to request on the grounds of its incompatibility with Christian gentleness.[4]

The point of dispute with Nectarius was the treatment of the third group, those who, as Augustine puts it, 'were willing for the crime to be committed' ('qui hoc committi voluerunt', 104. 17). Augustine's argument was that the leading (pagan) citizens of Calama had made no effort to put an end to the rioting, which followed religious celebrations that they ought to have used their influence to stop. (Indeed, the one person—a foreigner—who had tried to intervene in the violence had had a significant effect.) It was proper, therefore, Augustine argued, that they should be held responsible and be fined in accordance with Honorius' provisions. The accountability of the civic administration to the emperor for the behaviour of the citizens is, of course, a consequence of imperial rule (cf. A. H. M. Jones 1964: 406–10): how else can the laws be enforced except by penalising negligent magistrates? The law corresponds to Augustine's sense of the responsibility of political office (cf. Cic. *Off.* 1. 23 on the 'negative injustice' of failing to prevent injury). In Nectarius' view the same group, even if guilty in strict law, were clearly innocent with regard to the riot and ought to be protected from punishment by Augustine.

My specific interest in this debate is in the way in which Nectarius and Augustine make use of philosophical references, in particular from Cicero. Nectarius exploits his knowledge of Cicero for both rhetorical and philosophical purposes. He begins his first letter by defending (and displaying) his patriotism in Ciceronian language, and by appealing to Augustine as 'a

[4] This a common theme: see Index of Topics, 'Gentleness', Atkins and Dodaro 2001: 297.

man who is thoroughly well educated' ('instructum disciplinis omnibus virum', 90. 1). He and Augustine, he seems to suggest, share an intimacy proper to those who can drop or spot a Tullian quotation. The second letter begins also with an attempted *captatio benevolentiae*, this time elaborately developed, with implicit reference to the *De Republica*'s theme of the importance of putting philosophy into practice (for contemporary Greek use of the same *topos* see Fowden 1982: 54–9). While reading Augustine's reply, Nectarius had seemed to see before his eyes not some mere quibbling and sceptical Greek philosopher 'sitting in some dark corner' (cf. *Rep*. 1. 2, Plato, *Gorg*. 485d), but the great Roman orator himself, who

redirected his clarion, that sonorous voice and the tongue with which he had blasted guilty criminals and the parricides of his republic, and panting with the breath of righteous indignation flung back his toga itself, imitating the appearance of the folds of the Greek pallium in his flowing pages.

tubamque illam canorae vocis et linguae, quam in criminum reos et rei publicae parricidas spiritu iustae indignationis flaverat anhelus, inverteret togamque ipsam rugarum paginis resolutis palliorum imitatus speciem retorqueret. (103. 1)

I fear that Nectarius misjudged his correspondent: Augustine was not the man to be impressed by florid flattery, particularly if the arguments that accompanied it lacked rigour. Nor was he swayed by Nectarius' peroration, which employed the Ciceronian technique of arousing pity: imagine the grief and shame of the defendants, scarred by the torturer (cf. e.g. *De Or*. 2. 21: of course the method is more effective in a lawcourt than in a letter!). Augustine had already made it clear, as he reminds Nectarius a little impatiently, that he opposed both inquisitorial torture and physical punishments (91. 9, 104. 5).

So much for the Ciceronian style of Nectarius' plea. What of its substance? Nectarius discusses three philosophical *topoi* in the course of his two letters: the good of patriotism, the indifference or otherwise of death and poverty, and the Stoic paradox 'all sins are equal' (103. 3). Patriotism is introduced in the first place in order to justify his intervention with Augustine. Patriotic love alone can take precedence even over affection for parents (cf. *Off*. 1. 160, *Rep*. 1. 1a, 6. 16). It has no 'limit or terminus' ('cui si ullus esset consulendi modus aut finis bonis', 90. 1), and therefore even an old man like him ought still to be responding to the summons of his hometown. (Augustine takes this as a direct reference to *De Republica* here ('ipsos de re publica libros', 91. 3); we need not, however, assume a precise quotation.) In his second letter, Nectarius is forced by Augustine's mention of the heavenly *patria* to expand upon this theme. He distinguishes three cities: the physical one, the international 'city of the wise' beloved of philosophers, and Augustine's 'heavenly' city. The third, he claims, is the object of 'all laws . . . by various paths and ways' and he argues that it should be 'our principal goal and our principal love' ('omnes leges diversis viis et tramitibus . . . haec ergo licet principaliter appetenda atque diligenda sit', 103. 2). However, he goes on, this should not undermine our local earthly patriotism: for (so the *doctissimi* say) the gods reward loyal servants of their native cities with heaven. This looks like an explicit reference to *De Republica* 6.13, where Scipio's grandfather tells him in the dream that:

> for everyone who has saved and served his country and helped it to grow, a sure place is set aside in heaven where he may enjoy a life of eternal bliss. To that supreme god who rules the universe nothing (or at least nothing that happens on earth) is more welcome than those companies and communities of people linked together by justice that are called states. Their rulers and saviours set out from this place, and to this they return. (Rudd 1998: 88)

> omnibus, qui patriam conservaverint, adiuverint, auxerint, certum esse in caelo definitum locum, ubi beati aevo sempiterno fruantur; nihil est enim illi principi deo, qui omnem mundum regit, quod quidem in terris fiat, acceptius quam concilia coetusque hominum iure sociati, quae civitates appellantur; harum rectores et conservatores hinc profecti huc revertuntur.

Cicero is a wise choice for a defender of patriotism; on the face of it, moreover, he and Nectarius seem to share much common ground. They are both political servants of the Empire of Rome, and concerned with the problems of its administration. They are both non-Christians, who at least pay lip-service to religious belief, and who wish to hold together a philosophical faith in the supreme God with respect for local civic religion. On the other hand, the government of the Empire has changed dramatically in the intervening centuries, from a relatively loose federation of unequal allies, administered by the aristocrats of Rome, to a unified, centralized monarchy.

Cicero has no doubt where his loyalties lie. In a nostalgic moment in the preface to *De Legibus* 2, he describes Arpinum as his second *patria*, but the priority of his commitment to Rome is unquestioned; or rather, there is no tension between the two, because the one contains the other (*Leg*. 2. 5). In *De Republica* he is notably concerned with questions of justice between cities, but they are different questions from the ones that will be most pressing in the early fifth century. His discussion of international justice is focused on warfare and taxation, that is, on the external relations between the metropolis, on the one hand, and her allies and enemies on the other. By

Nectarius' time, the laws that govern relations between Rome and North Africa are no longer international laws; they are internal to the Empire. Moreover they govern not only the external, but also, in a far more detailed and systematic way, the internal, activities of towns like Carthage and Calama. Does justice demand obedience to the emperor's laws? Does it require subordinating the good of Calama, and the wishes of its citizens, to the needs and dictates of the Empire, even in matters that affect no one beyond its own walls? The answer Nectarius has to assume to both of these questions is yes; but it is an answer that radically restricts his freedom of argumentative movement.

Religious laws in themselves are no novelty; the new problem for Nectarius is that he is simultaneously committed to the laws of the Empire and the customs of his home-town. Indeed, it has been cogently argued that he was considered powerful enough to intercede as patron of Calama precisely because he was not actually a resident town-councillor, but an agent of the Empire, of at least the rank of proconsul or *vicarius*, whose successful career had made him an expatriate (Huisman 1956: 9–20; cf. Dodaro 2000: 252 n. 2). The unified patriotism of Cicero's *De Republica* has fragmented under the pressure of new questions: is true patriotism local or imperial? Does justice require observance of imperial law or of local policy where they conflict? Even, perhaps, does political service require one to leave home in order to further one's career? In practice, Nectarius answers in favour of the Empire, but that leaves him with no coherent defence of his fellow citizens.

The relation between political and religious ideas has also changed. In *De Republica*, although heaven is seen by Scipio as the reward for a patriotic life, religion does not shape the meaning of patriotism; it merely provides extra encouragement. Jonathan Powell's reminder (1996) that the pious Scipio is a character in his own right and not a mere mouthpiece for Cicero can only strengthen this point. Nectarius, however, agrees with Augustine's claim that the supreme goal of life is God. Perhaps he does so simply under the pressure of the latter's attack, but the religious seriousness of contemporary intellectual paganism would have influenced him in the same direction. Consequently, neither the purpose nor the content of patriotic behaviour can remain insulated from religious considerations. It may be worthwhile to help Calama as part of a life dedicated to God, but this will be of no avail to Nectarius unless his beliefs about God are in order. Furthermore, what counts as helping Calama to flourish is now contested; Christianity makes moral claims that are at odds with at least some popular pagan practice. Nectarius clearly wishes to avoid the issue of religious truth; if he had stuck with Cicero's emphasis on justice for its own sake he might have succeeded in doing so. Once he acknowledges that justice should be subordinated to piety, he can no longer deflect Augustine's insistent question: what, then, counts as true piety? But that is a question that Nectarius clearly prefers not to answer in public.

It may seem unfair to read too much into the very little that Nectarius does say. However, his appeal to philosophy suggests that he would be prepared to use the arguments available to him. It is striking how many arguments he in fact fails to use. He does not defend the value of the pagan ceremony on the grounds of religious truth, by arguing (along with both Symmachus and the pagans who will soon provoke *De Civitate Dei*) that events prove the dangers of abandoning the gods. He does not plead for the preservation of ancestral tradition. (In fact, we only know from *Augustine*'s letter that a festival was the cause of the trouble, and he tells us too little for us to identify it.) Nectarius does not criticize the prevention of the celebration on the grounds of freedom of worship. He does not question the justice of imperial laws, which ban long-standing civic practice against the wishes of the town's inhabitants. He does not argue against either the truth or the political role of Christianity.

For some of these points—the importance of polytheistic civic religion, the value of tradition, the appropriateness of civic government by a council of leading citizens, the dangers of monarchical rule—he might have adapted Ciceronian arguments. He does not do so: the constitutional debates of *De Republica*, the arguments about international justice, and even, it seems, the account of the education and character of the ideal statesman, are of little use now; the historical narrative is better found elsewhere (cf. Markus 1974: 11, on Livy): only a few platitudes about justice and patriotism are worth superficial allusion.

It makes some sense for Nectarius to appeal to Cicero on patriotism, despite the changing context. His second (apparently) philosophical appeal is more puzzling. He claims that it often says 'in literature' ('quod frequentatum in litteris nosti') that 'death entirely removes our perception of evil while a life of poverty produces endless misfortune'. He goes on: 'It is a more serious matter to live a life full of evils than to put an end to those evils by dying' ('mors malorum omnium auferat sensum, egestosa vita aeternam pariat calamitatem; gravius est enim male vivere quam mala morte finire', 103. 3). Nectarius' literary allusions are puzzling (as Augustine will note: 104. 3). The Epicureans in particular indeed held that death removed all perception of evil, and was not therefore itself evil. The Stoics argued (albeit with some tactical redefinition) that neither death nor poverty were true evils. No philosophical school, however, claimed that 'a life of poverty produces endless misfortune': philosophers of all shades were united in their relative disdain for material comforts. Is Nectarius alluding to the Stoic use of poverty as a justification for suicide (Griffin 1986: 73)? It is possible, but our only definite evidence for the Stoics' mentioning this argument comes from late Greek sources (Westerink 1973: 49–51). Or is he referring to an oratorical, rather than philosophical, *topos*: Sallust's Caesar, arguing against the death penalty for Catiline's conspirators, suggested that death would be a release rather than a punishment.[5] The parallel would not help Nectarius' friends greatly: Caesar was proposing as an alternative punishment exile, the confiscation of all goods, and life imprisonment. At any rate, Nectarius' attempt to bolster this argument about poverty by appealing to the Christian practice of assisting the poor seems strained.

From the puzzling to the seemingly perverse. Nectarius' final philosophical ploy is to propose the Stoic paradox 'all sins are equal'. There can have been few precedents for his appeal to this Stoic paradox in the heat of practical and urgent debate (cf. Cicero, *Parad.* preface). Nectarius' argument is this: if all sins are equal, then violating churches is no worse than, say, mild rudeness. Rudeness is easily pardoned; so therefore should be the unruly (and even murderous) citizens of Calama. The Stoics, of course, used the paradox to emphasize the gulf between the wise man and the rest. Nectarius again gives a Christian twist to an argument drawn from philosophy by using it instead to defend forgiveness. Once more his ideas lack coherence, and it is not a surprise when Augustine dismantles them with ruthless speed.

'All sins are equal': the claim is hardly likely to impress a clear-headed non-Stoic, especially when, as Augustine points out, it is unsupported by argument (104. 14, 17). But Augustine has more to say on this: the Stoic paradox is a part of Stoic *duritia*; the Stoics count mercy as a vice. What Nectarius has need of is not Stoic rigour, but Christian mercy; Augustine therefore elaborates on the proper relation between repentance, reform, punishment, and forgiveness to explain fully and precisely why he thinks it appropriate for those leaders of the community who are not Christians to be fined because of the riot (104. 9, for theological reflection on this see Dodaro 2000). Augustine's illiberal conclusion that repentant non-Christians should be treated differently from repentant Christians is dangerous because of, not despite, its coherence. He needed a more penetrating critic than Nectarius to explain why an even-handed application of the law was at

[5] 'aerumnarum requiem', *Cat.* 51. 20, cf. 52. 13, Cicero, *Cat.* 4. 7–8: I owe these references to Miriam Griffin.

least as important as the pastoral or corrective use of it (not a straightforward thing to argue in a context where the right of a judge to exercise mercy was taken for granted; cf. Atkins and Dodaro 2001: pp. xviii–xix).

Augustine finds it equally easy to deal with Nectarius' arguments about poverty and death. He explains the Christian attitude by setting both in the context of eternal life: the misfortunes of earthly poverty itself cannot be 'endless', for we die; but the post-mortem consequences of sin or virtue will indeed be endless. This does not, however, lead Augustine to the indifferentism of a Cynic or of a Stoic such as Ariston. There is a qualitative difference between necessities and luxuries; the absence of necessities causes genuine, albeit temporal, suffering, which Christians rightly aim to avoid or alleviate. Human beings have three benefits: health, the means to life, and the resources to live luxuriously (or, as Augustine puts it, 'badly'). Augustine does not approve a punishment that would either threaten health or cause poverty. The fines he is willing to support will merely reduce the freedom for luxurious living (including, for example, the making of silver statues of the 'false gods'; cf. *Ep.* 138. 14). Augustine is developing here the standard Hellenistic division of goods as mediated through Cicero and Varro: spiritual, bodily, and external. His subdivision of externals into necessities and luxuries has, of course, pre-Christian precedents in Cynicism, in Epicurus' division of desires into natural and non-natural, in eclectic Stoics such as Seneca, and in Roman *frugalitas* (he cites in his support Cincinnatus and Fabricius, and the case of the consul Rufinus, who was criticized for owning 10 pounds of silver: 104. 6). However, when Augustine selects and integrates this particular Graeco-Roman tradition, his reasons are Christian: the Jewish and New Testament suspicion of wealth and respect for the poor, which was subsequently incarnated in the tradition of monasticism of which Augustine is part. His understanding of punishment, therefore, is one piece locked into a bigger jigsaw of ideas.

The remaining philosophical *topos* is devotion to one's *patria*. Augustine's allegiance to the heavenly city does not require him to reject local patriotism: in fact, he is able to integrate Cicero's ideas more coherently with his theology than Nectarius succeeded in doing. There were indeed striking contrasts between him and Cicero. For Augustine, the true *patria* was not Rome, but heaven;[6] therefore religion should not be shaped by civic patriotism but vice versa. Cicero's saint is loyal to his city and ends up in heaven; Augustine's is loyal to heaven but happens to live in his physical city. Ciceronian virtues are shaped by the needs of the *res publica*;

[6] He does not use here the more complex idea of the *civitas Dei*, which includes the living faithful.

for Augustine, true justice can be defined only with reference to the city of God. (Consequently pro-Christian legislation can be justified, while pagan religious rituals must be unjust.) Despite the differences, though, Augustine manages to adapt Cicero's belief that certain men at least have been given a duty to govern by the gods. Officials do indeed have a responsibility for the people, one captured precisely in two metaphors he uses regularly: the pastor and flock, and the requirement to render an account (*rationem reddere*; Atkins and Dodaro 2001: 274 n. 13) at the last judgment. Civic responsibility, as with Cicero, is for the moral as well as the material welfare of the populace. *De Republica* had argued that political reform was based on ethical reform. Augustine appropriates the theme, and quotes Cicero in doing so. In *Letter* 91 he appeals to *De Republica*'s advocacy of *frugalitas*, *continentia*, and marital fidelity, along with 'casti . . . honesti ac probi mores' in general, and to its criticism of the corrupting effects of comedy (91. 3–4, cf. *De Civ. Dei* 2. 9–14). In *Letter* 104. 7, he cites the saying: 'Don't give a boy a sword', and quotes Cicero as adding: 'You wouldn't give one even to your own son.' The source and context of the quotation are unknown, though Augustine claims that Cicero was talking about wealth. Augustine is able, in other words, to recycle Cicero's arguments for a paternalistic control of others' wealth, and use them once again to defend the fining of the citizens of Calama, allegedly for their own good. Augustine drives home the point by quoting Cicero again: the 'rector patriae' is praised for consulting his citizens' *utilitas* rather than their *voluntas* (Cic. *Sull.* 25).

Cicero's concern with political ethics in *De Republica* is direct: the problem is to prevent political decline and the solution is moral reform. Augustine's concern is indirect: the goal is to live as good Christians. However, good Christians will turn out to be good citizens, and paganism, conversely, will lead to uncivic and unjust behaviour. Therefore the goal of political flourishing in itself justifies measures to suppress pagan ceremonies. Once again, Augustine succeeds in turning Nectarius' learning against him by the judicious selection of Ciceronian themes and integration of them with his own philosophy.

Integration requires development, and it is the notion of responsibility which Augustine develops most notably. Cicero saw himself as a *rector rei publicae*, one of the elite (Powell 1994); Augustine considered himself a pastor. The metaphors are revealing. Cicero wrote as an aristocrat about aristocrats and for aristocrats. His theme was 'the best state of the republic and the best citizen' ('de optimo statu civitatis et de optimo cive', *Q. Fr.* 3. 5. 1). The best citizen, it is taken for granted, will be a republican senator.

While the mangled text of *De Republica* will not allow us to be sure, it seems unlikely that the book showed much interest in the mores of the common people, except in so far as they might function as a potentially dangerous mob. When Cicero quoted Ennius' words 'moribus antiquis res stat Romana virisque' (Rome stands by her ancient customs and her men, *Rep.* 5. 1) he meant the *mores* of its leaders, the *optimi* whose special function is the making of political decisions (Atkins 2000: 491–2). An interesting discussion in *De Legibus* of the law that the senate should 'be a model for the rest of the citizens' ('ceteris specimen esto', 3. 10, 30–2; cf. *Rep.* 1. 69) makes it clear that the example of a few notable men can edify or corrupt 'the rest' of the citizens, but it is clear that Cicero means those wealthy enough to be corrupted by luxury. Certainly, he cannot have expected anyone outside an elite group to have read his books: the age of mass-publication was far in the future.

The age of the sermon, however, was nearer. Augustine's role as a pastor required him to teach his flock morals. The mob had rioted at Calama; but the mob consisted of individual souls, for each of whom the bishop, Augustine's friend Possidius, was potentially responsible. Ethics was no longer the preserve of the intellectual or cultural elite; everyone was called to a life of virtue. Educated bishops like Augustine and Possidius acted as channels of philosophical wisdom to the ordinary people. Christian intellectuals succeeded where pagan intellectuals had failed for centuries, both in transmitting their theories to the masses and in sharing the beliefs of the masses (Momigliano 1977: 155).

Momigliano argues that the 'two-tier' system of beliefs of a century or two previously has collapsed into one: there are no longer, by the late fourth century, distinctively 'popular' or 'elite' religious beliefs, for either pagan or Christian. He does not examine closely the mechanisms of this shift, in so far as it existed. The sermon, however, in one direction, and in the other the process of pastors listening to, and even learning to admire, the humbler members of their flock, must have been important channels for unifying culture. Momigliano also seems to me to downplay the continuing debate, both conflictual and creative, required to sustain a 'one-tier' system of beliefs across all levels of education (and religious commitment) within society. He continues: 'The Christian abolition of the internal frontiers between the learned and the vulgar had clear implications. . . . For the vulgar and uncultivated it meant appreciation, to the point of fanaticism, of the importance of theological controversies and consequent participation in these struggles' (1977: 155). Leaving aside the question of theologically inspired riots, we should not underestimate the achievement of persuading the 'vulgar and uncultivated' to think about, let alone care about, subtle theological doctrines. Is it too much to hope that such education made some of them less 'vulgar and uncultivated'? It is likely, for instance, that at least a few of Augustine's congregation marked and inwardly digested his distinction between legitimate force and mob violence, explained in a sermon given the day after the local crowd had lynched an imperial official (*Serm.* 302; Lambot 1950: 100–11). At any rate, Augustine certainly claimed that sermons were educational: virtuous behaviour, he told Nectarius, 'is being taught and learnt in the churches that are springing up all over the globe, like sacred lecture-halls for the peoples of the world' ('hi autem mores in ecclesiis toto urbe crescentibus tamquam in sanctis auditoriis populorum docentur atque discuntur', 91. 3, cf. *Ep.* 138. 10–12).

Indeed, Augustine saw intellectual accessibility as one of the strengths of Christianity. In his letter to Dioscurus (dated to 410, a year or so after his exchange with Nectarius) he argues that while Epicureanism, and even Stoicism, can be made intelligible and attractive to a wide audience, Platonism, although its conclusions come close to the truths of Christianity, is too esoteric except for a few very clever philosophers. The Platonists use arguments that the many could not follow, and had no other authority with which to persuade them; consequently, 'they chose to hide their opinions' (*Ep.* 118. 20). Christianity, through the humility of Christ, was able to present divine truths in a bodily manner accessible to all, and backed by the authority which could command assent without relying on abstruse arguments: 'so that not just a few, but even whole peoples, who are not able to decide these things by reason, believe by faith' ('ut non pauci, sed populi etiam, qui non possunt ista diiudicare ratione, fide credant', *Ep.* 118. 32). Whatever the theological merits of Augustine's respect for non-rational faith, there can be no doubting the urgency of his insistence that truth should not be the preserve of the minority. A two-tier system of beliefs is an offence, because the truth is salvific, and because leaders have a responsibility for the individuals in their care. Education has become a theological imperative. It is no coincidence that, whereas Cicero's philosophical works contrast sharply with his forensic in both tone and content, Augustine's vast range of writings, aimed at a variety of audiences, remain (allowing for chronological development) remarkably consistent in their arguments (cf. Brown 1972: 279–300).

What Christianity gave its devotees, in their confrontation with classical philosophy, was a criterion of choice, an ultimate principle by which to choose the various doctrines philosophy had to offer. In this Christianity was like a living organism, digesting or rejecting the food it is offered according to a principle within itself, a principle which tests the food on the basis of the question, 'will it help me or harm me?' (A. Murray 2000: 243)

By the early fifth century, it was as true of paganism as of Christianity that classical texts needed digesting to be of use. My story has been one of an unsuccessful attempt at the reappropriation of Cicero by Nectarius, and the far more effective adaptation of his ideas by Augustine. Nectarius attempted to exploit three philosophical *topoi*, but failed because he could not integrate them into his wider system of thought. In Augustine, Cicero's ideas took on a new life, because he was able to connect them coherently with a network of ideas. If doctrines are foods, then books are deep freezes. Ideas are preserved in unyielding chunks, which need careful selection and defrosting in order to become digestible. A skilled cook understands the meal as a whole and can see how the frozen food will fit into it. Before that, however, it must be defrosted and subtly reshaped in the process. Augustine can successfully reuse philosophical ideas because he is quite clear about how they mesh with his understanding of Christian charity, of asceticism and of corrective punishment, and knows therefore how to develop the *topos* in question. He is able to explain the proper place of local patriotism without compromising the heavenly *patria* because he redefines what counts as flourishing for a city, and in the process draws into his argument a second Ciceronian theme, that of paternalistic responsibility (once again appropriately remodelled). On the other hand, he wastes no time in rejecting the claim that 'all sins are equal': he is absolutely clear that this cannot be developed in a way that makes it compatible with either mercy or the gradual process of sanctification. Augustine, in short, knows his own mind. That is why his arguments possess 'the consistency that can alone give ideas a force of their own' (A. Murray 2000: 394).

There may be a grim fascination in watching a cat playing with a mouse, but does it tell the observer anything except that the cat is the bigger and stronger? Augustine is intelligent, articulate, influential, and backed by imperial legislation. Nectarius appears frivolous, indecisive, and muddled; in any case, the laws are against him. Is he too weak a character, then, to teach us anything interesting about late paganism? Possibly; but for every Symmachus there were many Nectarii; his very weaknesses may be informative. The most striking thing about Nectarius is that he does things by halves. He makes the effort to appeal to Augustine in a grave and tense situation; yet he resorts to empty flattery, and when Augustine uses word-play to make a serious point, he misinterprets this (to Augustine's annoyance) as a mere joke (103. 2, 104. 17). He remains outside the Christian fold, but he appeals to the role of the Christian bishop. Although he is normally described as a pagan intervening on behalf of his fellow pagans, he never uses 'gods' in the plural; in fact, he is careful to accept the language of monotheism and of the priority of the heavenly homeland.

At first sight, Nectarius' claim that 'all laws . . . by various paths and ways' aim at the heavenly city seems reminiscent of Symmachus' appeal for religious tolerance on the grounds that no one route would be enough to 'so great a mystery' (*Relat.* 3. 10). But Nectarius does not say 'all cults'; he says 'omnes leges', in a context when the laws most immediately relevant are the imperial laws against pagan worship: his language is ambiguous at least. In fact, he never questions the strict justice of punishing the rioters, nor argues for their right to celebrate their festival. Indeed, he goes so far as to praise Augustine's attack on pagan cult just before introducing the flattering comparison with Cicero. In short, Augustine's hope that he will follow his father and convert before his death does not seem wildly unrealistic. Nectarius is not so much a 'païen convaincu' (Lepelley 1981: 102) as something approaching one of the semi-Christians described by Gerald Bonner, 'persons well disposed towards the Christian faith and to the Church, who could even adhere to them quite firmly, but who nevertheless still clung to the old faiths to a greater or lesser degree' (1984: 348). Of course he was a 'pagan' in Augustine's eyes, because he was uncommitted and still far from baptism. To others, he might have seemed a more ambiguous figure (and for that reason, perhaps, all the more suited to mediation).[7]

Nectarius' intellectualism is equally half-hearted. When he contrasts the 'Ciceronian' Augustine with a Greek philosopher his description of the philosopher is too confused to be identified (Atkins and Dodaro 2001: 253 n. 1). His incoherent combination of Christian and Stoic themes and his clumsy appeal to the Stoic paradox have been noted. His suggestion that poverty is worse than death seems particularly inept: surely the convicted citizens of Calama would prefer fines to execution! Nectarius' original motive for intervening, it seems clear, was a social one, and not religious or political principle. Leading citizens of Calama, men of his own class, linked to him (one presumes) by ties of friendship and perhaps of family, were being held liable for the riots, even though they did not actually take part. Nectarius wants to help only them off the hook; he shows no interest in defending the actual rioters (who were probably lower in the social scale) or the pagan festival itself. Moreover, he does not wish to debate the issue for

[7] Attempts to categorize him ought perhaps to be set in the context of the thesis of the essays in Athanassiadi and Frede (1999), albeit based largely on Eastern evidence, that pagan monotheism flourished independently of Christianity and that this facilitated syncretistic and cooperative religious practice.

its own sake: he ignores Augustine's first reply for several months until, it seems likely, further political developments trigger his response (104. 1).

Semi-serious, semi-pagan, and semi-intellectual: it is Nectarius' lack of conviction as much as his lack of intellect that exposes him to Augustine's replies. On the other hand, it is not hard to sympathize.[8] To attempt to justify the procession would have required open criticism of imperial laws. Some people believed deeply enough in the necessity for pagan ritual to defend it by force (or, as the history books put it, 'riots'); the intellectuals, however, would have described the concrete ideas of this group as 'vulgar'. The philosophers themselves could defend their religion articulately, but they did not have to insist, in the face of oppressive laws, on sharing in public celebrations: their religious needs could be satisfied more privately. The most vulnerable part of the artificial unity called 'paganism' was the link between its popular and its philosophical expressions. Intelligent Christians had demolished the fragile theoretical defences of the former and expropriated much of the sophisticated theology of the latter. Nectarius was caught between the two, attempting, in true Ciceronian spirit, to defend practice with theory; sadly, however, it was too late for Cicero to help him now.

Nectarius' superficial use of *De Republica* suggests a wider question: how far was it still a living text? Could its ideas and arguments play a part in serious ethical and political debate in the way in which *De Officiis* could in the hands of Ambrose? Alan Cameron has argued that the antiquarian learning of the pagan aristocrats of Rome in the late fourth century has been overrated, and that it was Christians rather who were using these texts with creativity and vigour (on *De Republica*, see Cameron 1977: 25). The exchange of letters with the young Dioscorus is also revealing. The latter had come to Carthage to study, and has had to consult Augustine on the meaning of difficult passages in Cicero's philosophical works; he is about to travel to the East and is afraid of making a fool of himself by appearing ignorant. Augustine replies that he need not worry, because no one studies Cicero seriously any more in Rome or in Africa, let alone in Greece (*Epp.* 117 and 118). James O'Donnell (1980), in the course of warning against the temptation to overestimate Augustine's fresh knowledge of classical literature, concludes that Augustine himself began to reread *De Republica* with care and attention only for the purpose of writing *De Civitate Dei*.

A close reading of the surviving quotations from *De Republica* will

[8] For a far more generous interpretation of him as 'homme de grande culture', as the last defender of 'l'idéal patriotique municipal', and as having the better of Augustine precisely on the question of patriotism, see Lepelley 1979: 293–4, 357–8; 1981: 97–101.

corroborate the impression of its neglect by pagans and also suggest that even Christians were able to exploit the text only to a limited degree. It is striking that the vast majority of quotations from non-Christian writers are from the grammarians. Already in the second century Aulus Gellius cites the text only for points of vocabulary or style; by the fourth century a range of grammarians are using it extensively for illustration. Cicero, the author set for every school student to read, is worthy of comment for his language rather than his thought. There are no explicit references by a non-Christian author to any substantial point of the thought of *De Republica* after Seneca. As Seneca himself put it, with characteristic pithiness, 'itaque quae philosophia fuit, facta philologia est' ('therefore what was philosophy has become philology', *Ep*. 108. 23).

Seneca's letter reveals that philosophers were well aware of the problem. He describes at some length the fashion for using books which would yield valuable philosophical guidance—he mentions specifically *Aeneid* and *De Republica*—merely as a quarry for grammar or philology. The point of such texts is to inspire deeds not preserve words:

> I advise that listening to and reading the philosophers should be directed at the goal of a happy life, for us to track down not ancient or made-up words, or rare metaphors or figures of speech, but rather beneficial precepts and inspiring and spirited sayings, which can quickly be translated into reality. Let us study these things in such a way that what were words become deeds.

> illud admoneo, auditionem philosophorum lectionemque ad propositum beatae vitae trahendam, non ut verba prisca aut ficta captemus et translationes inprobas figurasque dicendi, sed ut profutura praecepta et magnificas voces et animosas, quae mox in rem transferantur. sic ista ediscamus, ut quae fuerint verba, sint opera. (*Ep*. 108. 35)

At the same time, Seneca's explicit reference to *De Republica* gives away perhaps more than he intends. He takes about a page to explore his examples of the treatment of the book by philologist or grammarian (and indeed apologizes for the length at which he does so). Of the philosopher, however, he says only this: 'the philosopher is amazed that so much could be found to say against justice' ('philosophus admiratur contra iustitiam dici tam multa potuisse', *Ep*. 108. 30). When he thinks of *De Republica* he remembers not the discussion of constitutions, not the history, not even the account of the statesman's education and character; it is Carneades' sceptical arguments against justice that spring to his mind. Already the serious questions of political theory have drastically changed (Griffin 1988).

The handful of non-Christian *testimonia* that Heck (1966) has carefully garnered contain only the barest hints that the political content of *De Republica* was examined seriously after Seneca's day. Tacitus *Annals* 4. 33. 1 is plausibly understood as a reference to Cicero's theory of the mixed constitution (see especially *Rep.* 3. 34 = *De Civ. Dei* 22. 6); Tacitus mentions it, however, only to dismiss it with equal brevity:

For all nations and cities are ruled by either the people or the aristocrats or individuals. The form of *res publica* selected and combined out of these finds praise more easily than existence, and if it should come to exist, it cannot last forever.

nam cunctas nationes et urbes populus aut primores aut singuli regunt. delecta ex iis et consociata rei publicae forma laudari facilius quam evenire, vel si evenit, haud diuturna esse potest.

The *Historia Augusta* contains a tantalizing mention in the life of Alexander Severus, who, it is alleged, read Plato's *Republic* and Cicero's *De Officiis* and *De Republica* more than any other books (30. 2). If this is true, it would be fascinating to know more of what a third-century emperor might have made of the texts of an aristocratic republic. If not, at least we can deduce that a fondness for *De Republica* still, in the late fourth century, seemed appropriate reading for an emperor with an ostentatious accessibility, respect for the Senate, and commitment to justice.[9]

The most extensive fourth- and fifth-century *testimonia* come, of course, from the pens of Lactantius and Augustine. Both of them allude to a range of topics from the text, but their coverage is notably uneven. Lactantius is particularly interested in exploiting the Carneadean discussion of justice for the apologetic purpose of casting doubt on the claim of philosophy to deliver moral truths. Augustine's fullest explanation of any passage from *De Republica* is the well-known discussion of the definition of *res publica* in *De Civitate Dei* 2 and 19, where he also makes use of the debate from Carneades. His strategy is similar to that of Lactantius: to undermine Roman claims this time not by exploiting scepticism, but by allowing religious questions to redefine justice. Lactantius also shows some interest in the themes of philosophy versus practical politics and of the origins of social life, while Augustine uses book 2 to illustrate his historical theme of the pre-Christian decline of Rome, and book 4 for his moral theme of the dangers of theatre. Finally, the Christian impulse to pacifism (in Lactantius) and to suspicion of war mongering (in Augustine) lead both to rediscover Cicero's questions about the justice of war. The mixed constitution and the nature of its constituent parts, and the character of the ideal statesman, two funda-

[9] Heck (1966: 57) also attributes a quotation from Ammianus Marcellinus (30. 4. 10) on the evils of corrupting judges by eloquence to *De Republica*; the evidence is not strong.

mental themes of the original book, unsurprisingly prove of no direct interest to the Christian writers.

By the early fifth century, the *De Republica* has long ceased to be popular as a political text. The final confirmation of this is provided by the two authors, Macrobius and Favonius, who wrote commentaries on the *Somnium Scipionis* in the late fourth or early fifth centuries (for dates, see Cameron 1966; van Weddingen 1957: 7–9). First, both chose to treat the dream separately from the rest of the text, thereby initiating a long tradition of spiritualized interpretation. The episode that seems to modern interpreters a tailpiece to the text is for Macrobius its climax: 'ipso consummati operis fastigio' (1. 1. 8); at the end of the commentary he praises the subject-matter of the *Somnium* (which he calls 'hoc opere') precisely as if it were an independent work. Secondly, the political content of the dream itself, which, it can be argued (see Powell 1996), connects tightly with the practical and political focus on the earthly city of Rome, is either ignored altogether (by Favonius) or turned upside down. Macrobius spends almost no time on the political references, expanding instead on such themes (incidental in Cicero) as the number of revolutions of the planets. More importantly still, political virtue, the fostering of which was the purpose of *De Republica*, is demoted to the bottom of a ladder with three rungs of philosophical virtues above it. Its role is as a mere stepping stone to higher things. The accounts of the 'political' versions of the four cardinal virtues are highly general and with no specifically political content (1. 8). Scipio's own political justice, to take a related example, is exemplified by his dutiful affection for his family ('pietate et nimio in suos amore', 1. 10. 3) in fearing his relations' treachery. For 'political' read simply 'social'. In book 1 of *De Republica* Laelius had called the discussion away from astronomy to the real business of politics. In Macrobius, the wheel comes full circle, and Scipio is requisitioned to serve for centuries as the dreamer of the music of the spheres. The passage can be reread thus by future generations precisely because it is empty of contemporary reference (for the later medieval rediscovery of its political themes, see Kempshall 2001). In 51 BC *De Republica* had seemed 'all the rage', to the naïve, nostalgic, or free-spirited at least, because it seemed to diagnose the ills of the current political situation. Its immediate popularity was the other side of its imminent neglect. Only its timeless, and incidental, subthemes would endure.

The Creation of Orthodoxy in Neoplatonism

POLYMNIA ATHANASSIADI

He did not want to compel either himself or his pupils to pursue the invisible truth through reasoning alone, herded together by syllogisms along a single road like the blind whom one guides on the right path. But he always strove to persuade them by placing eyes in their soul, or rather cleansing those which were already there.

Nothing could be more appropriate for describing Miriam's teaching ethos than the above lines, in which Damascius pays tribute to the man who converted him to philosophy—the Alexandrian Isidore. And nothing could be more alien to her mentality than the notion of orthodoxy, which thrives on exclusion and suppression. For what follows, however, Miriam *is* responsible—albeit indirectly—for it was after an interview with her that in October 1972 Somerville offered me a place to do graduate work at Oxford. Wisely though, Miriam limited herself—as she often reminds me—to the role of moral tutor.

THE CHANGING SCENE: *αἵρεσις*: FROM CHOICE TO HERESY

The Roman Empire was a pluralist world. Many cults, religions, theosophies, and philosophies mingled to create its spiritual landscape. What is more, these alternative ways to God were not mutually exclusive, but formed an organic synthesis. Were we to represent them schematically, they would appear as converging lines on a pyramid or a cone, the apex of which symbolizes the end of the search for truth. But if all roads led to the same goal, it was possible, and even desirable, for the individual seeker to stray away from his path, so long as he did not lose sight of his destination. Rather such detours were encouraged in a society where toleration of other creeds was not a passive principle, but an active drive which produced through cross-fertilization syncretistic structures of often vertiginous complexity.

I would like to thank Michael Frede who read an earlier version of this paper. I have made several changes on the basis of his comments. Thanks are also due to Paul Kalligas who read the final proofs and suggested amendments.

In this climate of spiritual promiscuity one religion, Judaism, stood apart in claiming a monopoly of God. Its self-righteousness was, however, not of the aggressive type, and proselytism of the religiously inferior 'nations' was not encouraged (Goodman 1994). As an offshoot of Judaism, Christianity also claimed exclusive knowledge of God, but at the same time recommended missionary activity as an obligation of the believer. Converting 'the nations' to the one true creed, and thus saving humanity from spiritual ignorance, was a duty for the good Christian.

The intolerance professed by the Christians as a principle of religious thinking and behaviour was not so much a new attitude in the multicultural world of the Mediterranean as a dynamic manifestation of latent trends. Yet however one defines it in sociological terms, spiritual intolerance led to tension and reaction: the Christians were persecuted, at first sporadically and from the mid-third century systematically,[1] while on the intellectual level their social and physical persecution was complemented by polemic. A climate of litigiousness and aggression spread, affecting society at large. Slowly but surely, intolerance permeated mentalities, and by the early fourth century it was not only the Christians who thought in terms of one single truth and, more importantly, of a universal way of reaching this truth.

These developments are faithfully mirrored in the word *αἵρεσις* and its changing fortunes during the centuries which lead from the 'open' world of the classical city-state to the 'oecumenicity' of the late Empire. From its broad classical meaning of 'choice' and 'election', the word *αἵρεσις* came in Hellenistic times to designate a system of philosophical principles and also the group of individuals professing such a school of thought and way of life—the Epicurean, the Stoic, or the Cynic, to mention only the most obvious. For pagan intellectuals this was still the prevailing meaning of the word in the fourth century, when their Christian contemporaries were already using it with the same semantic value that we now attach to the term 'heresy'. For the Christians, in philosophical and theological matters there was one truth only (the *ὀρθὴ δόξα*), to be pursued by one sole path.

The *ὀρθὴ δόξα* was not a totally novel concept for late antique men, but a notion with firm roots in Plato, for whom it signified a cognitive landmark reached through inspiration or by empirical means. Moreover, the path leading to the *ὀρθὴ δόξα* was an individual process of free enquiry and not a single public road imposed by dogma. To the Christian Fathers, by contrast, the one true faith could only be reached by one sole path. All other

[1] On the dynamic nature of anti-Christian persecution, see the dialogue between Sherwin-White (1952, 1964) and de Ste Croix (1954, 1963, 1964).

ways were deviations from the true road, indeed 'heresies'—the wrong kind of choice. This way of thinking was so well entrenched in the Christian mind that as soon as Christianity became a *religio licita*, oecumenical councils were convened under imperial patronage with the intention of defining dogma not only positively, by the formulation of a 'creed', but also apophatically, by the condemnation of heterodoxy.

The polarization between a pagan and a Christian use of language as reflected in the usage of the word αἵρεσις does not necessarily illustrate two conflicting ways of perceiving reality. People did not live in watertight compartments, though many of those engaged in sectarian fighting pretended, or even fooled themselves, that they did. As a comment on the above and by way of introduction to the main themes of this paper, one may quote a phrase of the Emperor Julian from a letter to the inhabitants of Bostra: talking of the religious policy of his predecessor, Julian refers in a condescending manner—almost with repugnance—to 'the so-called heretics', τῶν λεγομένων αἱρετικῶν (*Ep.* 114. 435d). The meaning of the participle τῶν λεγομένων in Julian's phrase is clear enough; it suggests that the author is forced to use a familiar word with the semantic hue that it has acquired in the jargon of people with whom he has nothing in common. One of the aims of this paper is to discover how alien the categories (in contradistinction to the actual words) 'orthodoxy' and 'heresy' were to the pagan intellectuals of late antiquity as they revised their spiritual heritage. A second objective is to examine the extent to which the orthodox (or politically correct) understanding of the way to God was used by them as an instrument and a pretext for wielding worldly power.

The Origins of Neoplatonism

The Precursor: Numenius

For the historian of philosophy the founder of Neoplatonism is Plotinus, with the nebulous figure of Ammonius Saccas lurking in the background. But this is the dispassionate verdict of outsiders. To those who were themselves part of the movement, the pivotal figure of regenerated Platonism was indisputably Iamblichus. To answer the question 'why Iamblichus and not Plotinus?', one must concentrate on what the Neoplatonists considered fundamental in their thought-world, and try to detect its historical roots. Such a search might well leave us with the unexpected answer 'neither Plotinus nor Iamblichus!' But let us start at the beginning.

In the second century AD Numenius of Apamea made two large claims: that in order to understand Plato one must revert to Pythagoras, and additionally that 'those initiations, dogmas and rituals that the Brahmans, the Jews, the Magi and the Egyptians hold in accordance with Plato' should be seen as the touchstones of truth. Indeed that Plato's truth, which was lost to the Greeks, was preserved by 'the thriving nations' (τὰ ἔθνη τὰ εὐδοκιμοῦντα: fr. 1a).[2]

Numenius, whom his contemporaries and immediate successors invariably describe as a 'Pythagorean philosopher',[3] is a mysterious figure, as too little of what he has produced survives; yet the impression created by the fragments of his works, that he was a boldly revisionist thinker, is corroborated by a cluster of outward testimonies. His connection with the new revelation of the age—the Chaldaean Oracles—though obscure, is beyond doubt; indeed for E. R. Dodds, Numenius constitutes the missing link between the Oracles and Porphyry (1960: 11).[4] More importantly, his influence on Plotinus was felt to be so great that the latter had to be formally defended against the accusation of plagiarism (Porphyry, *V. Plot.* 17.1). And though on the evidence of what survives it is not possible to assess Plotinus' debt to Numenius, it is nevertheless clear that the two men shared a breadth of vision transcending scholastic boundaries and a comparable revisionist insight into Plato's thought which served them as the basis for the formulation of revolutionary theories and methodologies.[5] Porphyry

[2] It must be pointed out that the dependence of Plato on Pythagoras had already been put forward, and in rather aggressive terms, by Moderatus of Gades.

[3] Among others Origen, Eusebius of Caesarea, Nemesius, and Calcidius. Cf. Dodds 1960: 11, who calls him 'a Pythagorean rather than a Middle Platonist'. On the psychology and theology of Numenius, Frede 1987: 1034–75.

[4] This judgement was later modified by Dodds 1961: 271. For the more balanced view that 'both the Oracles and Numenius are influenced by the same currents of thought, Pythagorean, Gnostic and Hermetic', Dillon 1977: 364, cf. 393. My recent involvement with the Chaldaean Oracles leads me to the hypothesis that Julian the Theurgist, to whom we owe the poem, and his father, Julian the Chaldaean, who was instrumental in the editing of the divine revelation, belonged to a priestly caste linked with the temple of Bel at Apamea. Both men must have moved in the circle of Numenius, influencing him and at the same time taking in his own ideas. And it was this mutual and long-term give and take that gave shape to both the Chaldaean revelation and the system of Numenius, which was born in conjunction with the Oracles and developed in close interrelation with them.

[5] As E. R. Dodds put it epigrammatically in the discussion following his paper: 'The ghost of Numenius haunted Plotinus all his life because they were the same unsettled and in the end insoluble problems which both men attempted to deal with' (1960: 59). Significant evidence linking the two men is provided by their ardent admirer, the literal-minded Amelius, who, having collected and copied out all of Numenius' works, learned almost all of them by heart, while in the course of the twenty-four years that he spent at Plotinus' feet, he produced no less than a hundred books of notes based on the master's seminars (Porphyry, *V. Plot.* 3. 38 ff.; cf. 14. 13 for Plotinus' use of Numenius' works). Then, as he saw his place as favourite pupil and spokesman for the circle devolve to the newly arrived Porphyry, Amelius left Rome for Apamea where he spent the rest of his days, probably as head of a circle which propagated the doctrines of Numenius. The formation of a 'Numenian' circle by Amelius, which may in due

too, as it now emerges from recent research, was crucially influenced by Numenius before becoming himself an inspiration to later Platonists both pagan and Christian (P. Hadot 1996; Tardieu 1996), a fact fully realized by Eusebius, who not only singled out Numenius as a dangerously original theologian, but, following Origen, identified him with the critical turning-point in the history of Platonism.[6]

As the self-appointed arbiter of Plato's thought, Numenius denounced the *diadoche* (succession) of Plato as spurious and called for a new beginning. He then defined Platonic orthodoxy by mustering criteria of selection consisting in methodologies both of inclusion and of exclusion. To this end he rewrote the history of the school as doctrine and prosopography, accepting as genuinely Platonic much of the contemporary 'Oriental wisdom', while charging every single diadoch with the betrayal of the Platonic dogmas.[7] A first attempt at defining Platonic orthodoxy!

A New Beginning: Iamblichus of Apamea

The common spring from which Plotinus, Iamblichus, and Porphyry drank, the elusive Numenius saw himself, and was seen by his immediate successors, as a landmark in the spiritual history of the age; but, as is often the case with exceptionally original thinkers, a screen was raised between himself and posterity: his innovations had to be digested by the following generation and spelt out to the world according to the understanding of individual interpreters. Paramount among these was Iamblichus, the boundaries of whose originality in defining Platonism and setting out the norms by which it can be assessed clearly lie in Numenian terrain. Yet, while suspecting the magnitude of his debt to his Apamean predecessor, all we can do today is concentrate on the concept of orthodoxy that Iamblichus himself created, and go on to study its transfiguration at the hands of his epigoni who used it as a means of wielding social and spiritual power.

Already in the consciousness of his contemporaries Iamblichus was a major religious reformer, endowed with all the formal and essential characteristics of a prophet, 'as if appointed for the salvation of the entire human

course have been instrumental in attracting Iamblichus to Apamea, is corroborated by the title of one of Iamblichus' works addressed *πρὸς τοὺς ἀμφὶ Ἀμέλιον καὶ Νουμήνιον* (Proclus, *In Tim.* 2. 277. 28–30); for Amelius' circle, cf. Syrianus, who seems to dislike him, finding him merely *ἐλλογιμώτατον* (*In Met. CAG* vi: Kroll 1902: 119. 14 and 147. 6: *τοιαύτα γὰρ οἱ περὶ Ἀμέλιον τὸν Πλωτίνειον νεανιεύονται*). Cf. also Kalligas 1991, 115–16, 94, 109. For Amelius in general, Brisson 1987.

[6] *Praep. Ev.* 11. 9. 8, 11. 17. 11, 14. 4. 16; Origen *CC* 5. 57, 1. 15.

[7] The work, which survives in fragmentary form (frs. 24–8), was entitled *On the Dissension of the Academics from Plato.*

race' (Ps.-Jul. *Ep*. 187. 406c). An acute sense of cosmic divinity and a sure instinct for what was significant in tradition irrespective of origin enabled him to become an oecumenical exegete and a holy man of wide fame, who performed miracles if put under pressure but, more importantly and more durably, allied the newly structured Platonic and Pythagorean system of thought with the authority of revelation. Returning to his native Syria after long years of peregrination in Egypt and Italy, and significantly enough settling in Apamea, the Chalcidian Iamblichus injected Platonism with Hermetic wisdom, of which he seems to have been himself for many years an authoritative exegete (Athanassiadi 1995: 245–6), and carried out the immense task of sanctioning the recently revealed Chaldaean Oracles as the holy book of Hellenism.[8] Moreover, in tune with the spirit of the age, he established a canon of texts to be read in a specific order and manner: his selection of Platonic dialogues became, as it were, the Old Testament of Hellenism, with the Chaldaean Oracles functioning as the New Testament of the new faith. In all these respects Iamblichus distanced himself from Plotinus, who had ignored, or even attacked, recent theosophical wisdom, drawing his material for discussion exclusively from the store of Greek philosophical literature, where he did not limit his choice of texts to a set curriculum, but gleaned through the entire tradition in a manner that was perhaps too liberal and unprescriptive to be followed by disciples of lesser ability. More significantly, Plotinus did not believe in the primacy of grace. Following on the tradition of Greek rationalism, he founded his exegesis on minute argument and discussion (*V. Plot.* 13), presenting the mystic union not as a matter of divine intervention but as a result of intense personal effort in the intellectual and the moral spheres.[9]

Like Plotinus, on the other hand, Iamblichus was a systematic theologian and a gifted teacher. Yet if his immediate appeal proved so much stronger, this is only because he was also a hierophant who gave meaning, and even depth, to ritual (Athanassiadi 1993*a*: 119–20). Seeing himself as the pedagogue of mankind in spiritual matters,[10] he painstakingly mapped out a way—indeed, *the* way—to perfection, with all its practical and theoretical milestones. He thus established a canon of texts, which remained unaltered throughout late antiquity, and propagated the use of the structured com-

[8] For my hypothesis that the Chaldaean Oracles were produced, codified, and kept in the temple of Bel at Apamea, see Athanassiadi 1999*b*: 153–6. Iamblichus' *Commentary on the Chaldaean Oracles* numbered at least twenty-eight books (cf. Damascius, *De princ.* 2. 1).

[9] 'To set oneself above the mind, is to fall away from it.' Enn. 3. 9.

[10] Cf. the expressions 'universal blessing of the Hellenes' and 'saviour of humanity as a whole' used by one of Iamblichus' pupils on his account: Ps.-Jul., *Epp*. 187. 406e and 181. 449b respectively.

mentary as the only method of research and teaching for that curriculum. At the same time, using Pythagorean numerical symbolism, he divided the path to God into ten stages, which are mirrored with exemplary clarity in the ten books of his substantially extant *Συναγωγὴ τῶν Πυθαγορείων Δογμάτων* (O'Meara 1989: 30–105).

Pupils flocked to 'the sacred hearth' of Apamea from all over the Mediterranean world (Ps.-Jul. *Ep.* 187. 405d) to share a life which combined in a traditional manner the notions of παιδεία and παιδιά—one where pleasure went hand in hand with the pursuit of wisdom and the practice of a pious routine.[11] The incidental information provided by Eunapius on the circle's daily activities, when read against the background of Iamblichus' *Pythagorean Life*, suggests an atmosphere of philosophical and human intimacy, which seems consciously to reproduce Pythagorean models. Master and pupils lived together. They discussed philosophical issues formally, but also at their evening gatherings, while drinking their wine; they took long walks to holy sites in the Syrian countryside, and also more secular excursions to bathing stations. The pupils were teased by Iamblichus' slaves for their belief that their teacher was divine and they in their turn pestered the master for miracles and other tokens of his sanctity. The surviving letters of Iamblichus to his friends and pupils, and the correspondence of a pupil—a certain Julian who seems to have been a high official at Licinius' court—allow us further insights into the ambience of the circle, the diversity of its concerns, and the dominant ideology which animated it.[12] In one of his addresses to his beloved master, Julian puts his finger on a point of cardinal importance: Iamblichus' systematic sanctification of Greek letters. 'Just as in a lyre the harmonious combination of various notes achieves musical perfection, in the same way you have succeeded in uniting not just Pindar or Democritus or the most ancient Orpheus, *but the entirety of that Hellenic spirit which is on record as having reached the very summit of philosophy*' (Ps.-Jul. *Ep.* 187. 405d).

Here we have the first clear formulation of what the Emperor Julian was to express in negative terms in his edict on education and his pastoral letters: that Greek culture as defined by Iamblichus was sacred, that what he had left out was profane, despite its antiquity and other philosophical

[11] A detail worth noting in this connection is that Iamblichus celebrated Pleasure as a goddess: Damascius, *In Phil.* 19. 5. For the traditional mode, cf. the expression of Iamblichus' pupil Julian who describes the circle as being τοῦ παλαιοῦ κόμματος (*Ep.* 187. 406d).

[12] For the identification of Julian, T. D. Barnes 1978: 99–106. I find the newly advanced hypothesis by Vanderspoel (1999) that the epistolographer may be the maternal grandfather of the Emperor Julian, Julius Julianus, lacking in probability.

credentials, whereas what he had sanctioned from even the most recent 'wisdom of the Barbarians' represented the highest form of spirituality. As presented by Iamblichus, the ingredients of the new paganism were a set number of texts, a given hermeneutic methodology, and a ritual framework. Its authorized language was Greek, while the vehicle through which its message would reach the world was the circle of disciples who gathered around the Exegete of the divine mysteries. The need for a 'metropolitan' theology expressed only in Greek was firmly launched by Iamblichus, and in the following centuries every effort was made to integrate all local gods, cults, and myths in a systematic thought-world which bore the formal name of *Ἑλληνισμὸς*, in response and open challenge to the term *Χριστιανισμός*.

The Rift

Both during Iamblichus' own lifetime and after his death, some of his spiritual heirs went away to wield worldly power,[13] while others embraced an academic career in the traditional centres of learning of the Eastern Mediterranean (Eunapius *V. Phil.* 6. 2. 1). As holy men and scholars they spread the teaching of their master widely, each according to the way in which he had imbibed it. Thus the Cappadocian Aedesius, who was recognized as Iamblichus' direct successor (6. 4. 1), seems to have inherited, together with his master's breadth of outlook, his qualities as an affable man, a cool-headed philosopher, and a diviner in intimate contact with the cosmic powers (6. 4. 5; 9. 2; 4. 1–4). Unfortunately, so full and balanced an attitude was not displayed in the generation that followed and, of the four most prominent pupils of Aedesius, Eusebius and Priscus were noted for their combative rationalism, whereas Maximus and Chrysanthius became famous as manipulators of the divine hierarchy (7. 2. 1), not least through their connection with the Emperor Julian.

The rift thus occurred within a few years of Iamblichus' death, but what is of interest for present purposes is that, to judge from the available evidence, the rationalists did not claim descent from Iamblichus. Another figure from the recent past, Theodore of Asine, emerges as their mentor. His followers, 'the Theodoreans', disparaged Iamblichus as an ambitious showman, rejected the authority of the Chaldaean Oracles, and equated philosophical research with dialectics (Julian, *Ep.* 12). Indeed Priscus, whom Julian beseeches to shut his ears against the propaganda of 'the

[13] An extreme case is that of Iamblichus' favourite pupil, the Apamean Sopater, who, after becoming Constantine's mentor, fell from grace as a result of court machinations, and paid with his life for the influence that he had exerted upon the emperor: Eunapius, *V. Phil.* 6. 2.

Theodoreans', denigrated Aedesius to his face as a 'traitor' to philosophy (*V. Phil.* 8. 1. 9).[14]

But the key figure in this debate in more than one respect is the Emperor Julian; for he seems to have both precipitated and exacerbated developments which were latent in Neoplatonism before his appearance at Pergamon in 351. No sooner had he been introduced to the two methodologies than he knew where his heart lay. This moment is caught in a famous exchange between master and pupil: when the sober Eusebius, who, with reference to Maximus of Ephesos, warns Julian against 'the tricks and impostures of conjurers which deceive and beguile the senses', indeed against 'madmen who are led astray by material powers' (7. 2. 3), Julian retorts with sarcasm: 'I am off! Stick to your books; as for me, you have shown me the man I was looking for!' (7. 2. 12). Converted to Maximus' 'violent way' of dealing with the supernatural,[15] the impulsive and uncompromising Julian used word and action in his campaign for orthodoxy. In fact he stands as the first clear landmark in Hellenism of a choice to be made between the one right way and numerous blind alleys.

From his position as worldly and spiritual leader of the Roman Empire—at once *basileus* and *pontifex maximus*—Julian defined the content of Hellenism, a term that he did not coin but to which he gave new weight and universal currency (Athanassiadi 1992). To disseminate his idea of Hellenism as the indivisible spiritual, cultural, and political force which would cement the oecumenical state that he now ruled by God's grace, Julian had recourse to all the practical and intellectual weapons at his disposal: formal legislation, encyclical letters to the priesthood of which he was the hierarchical chief, systematic polemic, and finally dogmatic or canonical writings which reflect his own view of Iamblichanism. As he confessed, 'I am mad (*μέμηνα*) about Iamblichus in philosophy and my namesake in theosophy' (*Ep.* 12).[16]

If the extent to which Iamblichus would have recognized his own teaching in Julian's Hellenism is a matter for speculation, what is important for us at this stage of the argument is that, to Julian's mind, his programme was

[14] On the rift between the two schools of paganism, see my analysis (with new prosopographical data) 1991: 271–8.

[15] To Chrysanthius, who at the sight of inauspicious signs is reluctant to go along with helping Julian in his religious campaign, Maximus puts across as a principle that one must compel the divine nature until it bends towards the servant (*ἐκβιάζεσθαι τὴν τοῦ θείου φύσιν ἄχρις ἂν ἐπικλίνῃ πρὸς τὸν θεραπεύοντα*: 7. 3. 12).

[16] The namesake is Julian the Theurgist, to whom the authorship of the Chaldaean Oracles was attributed. In his *Hymn to King Helios* Julian admits that his treatment is entirely based on Iamblichus (150d), an acknowledgement that he makes a point of reiterating at the end of the oration (157d).

the very embodiment of Iamblichus' spirit. His educational absolutism, as expounded in his edict on education which prohibited the Christians from teaching what they did not consider holy—that is, the entirety of Greek letters—his definitive banishing of the Epicureans and the Sceptics from the province of Greek letters, and finally his denunciation of latter-day Cynics as heretics are the first indications of a new conception of intellectual protectionism that we do not find fully articulated before the era of Justinian.[17]

Back in the time of Julian the battle between rationalists and visionaries was still undecided, though the balance was already tilting towards the latter. The dogma of the agreement of Plato with Aristotle enunciated by Ammonius Saccas (Hierocles ap. Photius, *Bibl.* Cod. 214. 172a) and endorsed by Iamblichus had not yet acquired universal value, and for the best part of the fourth century the influential and long-lived Themistius continued commenting on Aristotle in a distinctly untheological manner, and advising Court and Senate on political ideology and social behaviour. As well as old-fashioned Aristotelians, the Cynics and the Epicureans led a campaign against oracles, which explains the rage with which Julian attacks them (Eus. *Praep. Ev.* 4. 3. 14; Julian *Ep.* 89b. 301b–c). By the end of the fourth century, however, the direction in which Greek philosophy was to move had been settled. After a long interval of dissociation from Plato, Athens emerged as the authorized seat of Platonic studies,[18] yet this time the road passed through Apamea.[19] The nebulous figure of the Eleusinian hierophant Nestorius with his well-attested Chaldaean connection and the clear-cut figure of his son, the Platonic diadoch Plutarch, were the men who set the firm bases for the perpetuation of the Iamblichan philosophical model in Athens, not just as theory but also as a practical way of life.[20]

Invariably described as 'divine', Iamblichus became the one unchallengeable authority, the sole guide on the path to philosophical and spiritual perfection for all the official exegetes who flourished in Athens and

[17] Iamblichus, in the tradition of Numenius and Amelius, was a tolerant man.

[18] There was never an Alexandrian school of Neoplatonism as such: see I. Hadot 1978.

[19] Justifiably Dillon calls the Athenian school of the 2nd cent. AD 'an empty name' (1977: 265). And the fate of Longinus, who dominated the Athenian scene in the middle of the 3rd cent., is a perfect example of the *damnatio memoriae* suffered by those who did not adopt 'the correct approach' to Plato. Remembered simply as a 'living library and walking museum' (*V. Phil.* 4. 1. 3), he was totally ignored by the genealogists of the Platonic succession (cf. Hierocles ap. Photius, *Bibl.* Cod. 214, 173a ad fin.), for whom Plotinus' aphorism 'Longinus is a scholar but certainly not a philosopher!' (Porphyry, *V. Plot.* 14. 19–20) provided the definitive verdict.

[20] On the identity of Nestorius, and his connection with Iamblichan Neoplatonism see Athanassiadi 1999*a*: 173, 355.

abroad until well into the sixth century. He was the norm of orthodoxy at a time when the struggle to define dogma had become the main task both of the Christian Church and of the Neoplatonic *Diadoche* (Athanassiadi 1993*b*: 11–12). Chiefly responsible for this development is the man who dominated the international philosophical scene for the best part of the fifth century, the Athenian successor Proclus, who seems to have played for Neoplatonism the combined roles of an Athanasius and a Cyril.

Proclus as Defender of Iamblichanism

The Succession

Proclus was in his early twenties when in 432 he arrived in Athens from Alexandria and was adopted by Plutarch and Syrianus as their spiritual offspring (Marinus, *V. Procli* 11). He went on to inherit the *diadoche* and, more importantly, shape and dominate the Neoplatonic scene at home and abroad. A compulsive writer, an exemplary saint, sage, and leader of the pagan community, as he emerges from Marinus' biography and Damascius' *Philosophical History*, Proclus had no difficulty, through his daily pious routine, systematic teaching, and voluminous writings, in propagating his own view of Iamblichan Platonism as the authorized version.

Proclus died in 485 at the age of 75. In the last five years of his life he was progressively struck by senility, yet by that time he was such a venerable figure that not only did he keep his post as diadoch, but he was actively involved in the complicated (and often vicious) struggle for the succession. This fascinating contest is reported in all its recondite detail by the last holder of Plato's chair; in his *Philosophical History* Damascius tells us that, 'fearing that the golden chain of Plato might forsake Athens' (fr. 98e), Proclus drew up a list of successors, choosing his candidates among a chorus of pure Platonists (*τῷ ἀκηράτῳ χορῷ* fr. 152). Though we have no sure way of reconstructing this list in its entirety, Damascius provides sufficient evidence as regards both the personalities participating in it and the criteria of their selection.

The heir apparent had for many years been Zenodotus, 'the only man thought worthy of the nickname "the darling of Proclus"' (fr. 99b). Though certainly of the orthodox persuasion (since we find him in the early 490s teaching Damascius theoretical philosophy),[21] Zenodotus seems not to have been unimaginative enough to be selected to carry the torch upon

[21] Photius, *Bibl.* Cod. 181 and Athanassiadi 1999*a*: 43–4 and 341 with nn. for clarification.

Proclus' death. This task fell on Marinus, a convert to Hellenism, who 'through hard work and tireless effort, . . . succeeded in burying with his own name the reputations of many people more gifted and also older than himself' (fr. 97c). A literal-minded, fearful and malleable man, with fragile health and minimal self-respect (frs. 38a, 97j), Marinus was chosen by Proclus to write his authorized biography, indeed to personalize and simplify through a neatly structured hagiographical text the norms of scholarship and sanctity valid in the school.[21a]

But there were others too: the ingenious Asclepiodotus, and the eccentric Isidore. The first, to whom Proclus had dedicated his commentary on the quintessentially theological Neoplatonic dialogue, the *Parmenides*, was, according to Damascius (fr. 80), 'the sharpest and most learned of all his contemporaries', yet his final verdict on him is that he was of 'uneven intelligence, especially when it came to divine matters—the invisible and intelligible essence of Plato's lofty thought' (fr. 85a). For this reason, despite the enormous and many-sided pressure that he exerted on Proclus, not least through his influential father-in-law (Athanassiadi 1999*a*: Appendix II: 348–9), Asclepiodotus was not included in the final list.

Isidore, on the other hand was the opposite of Asclepiodotus, as Damascius notes in a passage of clear polemical intent:

> His senses were moderately acute, merely serving his needs; and not only the senses, but also the wax mould which is the imagination did not surpass the average as regards its memory nor was it altogether free of forgetfulness. For it seems that God wanted to show that he was a soul rather than a combination of soul and body, and that he had not deposited philosophy in this combination but had established it in the soul alone. (*PH* fr. 14)[22]

Unlike the innovative Asclepiodotus, Isidore was a staunch defender of the Iamblichan view of the history of philosophy.

> Among the ancient philosophers [Isidore] worshipped as divine Pythagoras and Plato [considering them] to be among those winged souls who dwell in the supra-celestial regions, in the plain of Truth, in the meadow of divine forms. But after Plato he particularly devoted himself to Iamblichus and his friends and adepts, the best of whom he claimed was his own fellow citizen Syrianus, the teacher of Proclus. (fr. 34d)

[21a] See now the translation and commentary by Edwards 2000; the new Budé edition (H.-D. Saffrey and A.-Ph. Segonds, Paris, 2001) has little of substance to add.

[22] What follows is an open attack on Asclepiodotus: 'I have indeed chanced upon some who are outwardly splendid philosophers in their rich memory of a multitude of theories; in the shrewd flexibility of their countless syllogisms; in the constant power of their extraordinary perceptiveness. Yet within they are poor in matters of the soul and destitute of true knowledge.'

This insistence on what constitutes Neoplatonic orthodoxy—clearly in the face of opposition—must have been one of the main reasons for which Proclus looked upon Isidore as a worthy successor.

By the early 480s, however, when Proclus was putting pressure on him to accept the succession, Isidore was already an acclaimed teacher in Alexandria. His mentor, as it appears from Damascius' account, was not so much Proclus as the holy Sarapio, an urban hermit who spent his days in absolute solitude 'meditating in silence. A seeker of the Truth and a man with a theoretical cast of mind, he could not bear to occupy himself with the technicalities of philosophy, but immersed himself in those vigorous concepts which fill one with God' (fr. 111). Unlike Proclus, who emerges as a great master of analytical thinking, Sarapio had a wholly negative view of learning that he bequeathed, alongside his 'two or three books' (the Orphica), to Isidore and through him to Damascius (fr. 111).[23]

It may indeed be argued that in his obstinate refusal to assume the Platonic succession, or even be included in 'the list' (frs. 98c–d), Isidore was not solely led by his reluctance to shoulder the burdens of a post which combined academic and spiritual duties with a heavy administrative load. The example of his admired Sarapio may not have been unconnected with his choice to remain in Alexandria, where he already enjoyed universal fame at a time of reasonable security (fr. 106b). Conversely the hovering around the ailing Proclus of two tycoons—Asclepiodotus of Aphrodisias and Theagenes of Athens, respectively scheming on account of a son-in-law (the younger Asclepiodotus) and a son (Hegias)—must have confirmed Isidore in his decision to keep away. The climate in Athens in the early 480s was particularly insalubrious and Marinus who is lumped together with Isidore as a 'true philosopher' for the purpose of a contrast with Asclepiodotus 'who was equipped with all the things which give glamour to this life' (fr. 103b), had to leave Athens for a period 'as he suspected that plots were being directed against his very life' (fr. 101c). Finally Theagenes seems to have reached a compromise by persuading Proclus to include Hegias in the list of diadochoi (fr. 145); while the pressure brought by Proclus and Marinus on Isidore (frs. 98c, 103c) eventually bore fruit and he accepted, however reluctantly, 'the vote on the succession' (frs. 103e, 148c).

The Holy Life

Iamblichus' pupils shared a common life with their master. They took their meals together, drank their wine while discussing the mysteries of being, and made excursions to holy places thus allying pleasure with piety. They

[23] Cf. fr. 35a for 'the noisy babble of books'.

even insisted on communal prayer, denying their master any privacy (*V. Phil.* 5. 1–2). From the information that we possess there emerges the picture of an informal circle rather than a school, bathing in an ambience of mild asceticism. Proclus' establishment, on the other hand, had more the air of an institution than that of a circle, where the rules of an ascetic life were enforced by a superintendent who taught at the Academy alongside with Proclus. This was Salustius, an old-fashioned Cynic who went round at all seasons barefooted (*PH* frs. 66b–c). No great lover of humanity, he was endowed with a sharp sense of the ridiculous and a sarcastic sense of humour which he used in order to make fun of self-important people, attack the wicked, and terrorize the not-so-bright (frs. 66a, 66b, 66e). When candidates applied for admission to the Academy, Salustius set them a series of tests, which to Damascius' mind were traps rather than a straightforward exam. Having had their nervous system and intellectual ability tested 'like gold in fire' (fr. 66f), once admitted to the Academy, the students went on to hear on a regular basis that they should give up philosophy as a calling beyond their abilities (frs. 66a, 66e).

On a more mundane note, 'Salustius went in and out of the students' dwelling place [and] saw that the cooking pots were absolutely immaculate and free from smoke, as if they were on display for sale in the market-place; for he laid particular stress on adhering to a diet of uncooked food for a long time' (fr. 66d). This culinary philosophy was in tune with Proclus' well-attested ascetic tastes and his insistence on a pure life.[24] Where the two men differed, however, was their attitude to good form. In genuine Cynic fashion, Salustius only cared about inner discipline, 'knew how to get to the core of things' (fr. 66a), and never missed an opportunity of decrying social convention even in its most innocent aspects. Proclus, on the other hand, was a great believer in decorous behaviour over the tiniest things. He was shocked, for instance, by Isidore's charming habit of reproducing the cries of birds, and even more by his 'imitation of sparrows and hens and other birds fluttering their wings as they rouse themselves for flight' (fr. 59f)—a performance that Isidore chose to give during the solemnity of the Chaldaean rituals. An even more telling illustration of Proclus' attachment to form concerns his order to the young Isidore to assume a coarse cloak as an indication that he had adhered to 'the better life' (fr. 59b). While attempting to argue that a taste for asceticism should normally follow rather than pre-

[24] The Antiochene Hilarius is not admitted by Proclus to read philosophy on account of 'his customary hedonism' (41ab); on Proclus' emphasis on virginity as a philosophical characteristic, Marinus, *V. Procli* and *PH* frs. 56, 97b, 59e, 59a, 59d. Marinus reports that the ascetic feats of the young Proclus were such that Plutarch and Syrianus feared for his life (*V. Procli* 12).

cede one's decision to embark on the study of philosophy (fr. 59d), Isidore—perhaps with some encouragement from Salustius too—ignored this injunction; and, when at some point in the 470s Salustius had a definitive quarrel with Proclus and left for Alexandria, Isidore went with him (fr. 60).[25]

An important item of Iamblichanism was the profession of cult and ritual. As 'the hierophant of the entire world', Proclus did not tire of expressing both in private and in public his religious fervour towards both the traditional Graeco-Roman gods and the ethnic deities of the Hellenistic *oecoumene*. He prayed every day at dawn and dusk, visited the shrines of the gods on appointed days, dedicated religious hymns to universal and regional gods alike, and revived local cults at home and abroad (*V. Procli* 15, 19, 29, 32, 36). In promoting pagan oecumenism through an intense and dangerous personal campaign, he certainly upheld the Iamblichan model of piety. His example was followed by both Isidore and Damascius. The latter in particular boosted the Proclean programme by harking back to Iamblichan methods of popularization (Athanassiadi 1999*a*: 46).

But the objective circumstances were so inimical that, far from investing the philosopher with power, the promotion of 'pagan holiness' hampered his public image.[26] Increasingly marginalized in social and political terms, the pagan philosopher realized that the only power he could wield in society was of a spiritual order, and that the seeds of this power could only be sown in the classroom and in the solitude of the study. The fruit of his efforts would thus reach posterity by the twin avenues of orality and of the written word, and the only sure way of achieving this objective was, as Iamblichus had decreed, hermeneutics.[27]

[25] Whether the influence of Salustius on Isidore served him as a stepping stone for his adherence to Sarapio is a question worth exploring, especially as some of the qualities that Isidore cultivated under this dual influence may have been instrumental in shaping Damascius' attitude to philosophy.

[26] The case of Hegias, who seems to have been the diadoch of the Academy in the 490s is telling: 'Aspiring to be the most pious of men, he completed work on the shrines of his relatives all over Attica, secretly, for he did not have their approval, and restored many holy places which had been lying in ruins for a long time, with an enthusiasm which was more indiscreet than pious. Thus he became notorious among his compatriots, attracting to himself dangerous enemies, of whom some desired the huge fortune that he possessed, and others conspired against him with the backing of the established order' (*PH* fr. 145b).

[27] A symbolic illustration of this is to be found in Marinus, *V. Procli* 30: when, towards the end of Proclus' life, 'those who move the immovable' took away from the cella of the Parthenon the cultic statue of Athena, the goddess, in the guise of a venerable lady, came to the doorstep of the philosopher and asked him if she could reside with him. This piece of Neoplatonic mythology, which mirrors the mood of the circle immediately after Proclus' death, also carries unequivocal messianic undertones for the adepts of the Platonic theology: repudiated from all official places, wisdom and learning went into hibernation in anticipation of more propitious times.

Interpreting Plato

Neither the curriculum of undergraduate and graduate studies nor the methodological approach decreed by Iamblichus were in any way questioned by the generations of scholars who taught at the Academy, but the authority of Iamblichus as the indisputable interpreter of Platonic theology did not go unchallenged: 'We see and hear not a few among those who philosophize, having the opinion, some that Iamblichus is utterly inaccessible, others that he glorified in wilful grandiloquence rather than the truth of things' (*PH* fr. 34b), reported Damascius, while Isidore had to reiterate his devotion and loyalty to Iamblichus in the face of constant provocation (fr. 34d). The significant detail in Isidore's view of the school's progress is that Syrianus, and not Proclus, was the best of the Moderns. In this connection it is worth recalling that at a relatively early stage in the history of Athenian Neoplatonism Syrianus wrote a didactic work on the agreement between Orpheus, Pythagoras, and Plato, which must have reproduced the main lines of Iamblichan syncretism both as ideology and method (*Suda* 4. 479. 1–2). But the most revealing comment of Damascius comes in the guise of a damning general criticism on the teaching of philosophy, presumably as practised by Proclus. Isidore 'did not want to compel either himself or his pupils to pursue the invisible truth through reasoning alone, herded together by syllogisms along a single road like the blind whom one guides on the right path. But he always strove to persuade them by placing eyes in their soul, or rather cleansing those which were already there' (fr. 38b).

Such was not Proclus' way. Indeed we have sufficient evidence on his methods of constructing orthodoxy: they consisted in guiding those who were prepared to listen by commenting on the prescribed texts, and in silencing any opposition by means of exclusion, or even slander. For his authority did not go unchallenged. 'The best of Proclus' pupils', Asclepiodotus, had in the end to be excluded from the Succession because he was impossible to control. 'He delighted in new ideas because of his extraordinary intelligence' (*CAG* ix. 795. 13–17). This judgement is passed on to us by one of the epigoni, Simplicius, who is clearly repeating what he heard from his own master, Damascius. One may note in passing that nothing of what 'the extremely sharp and erudite' Asclepiodotus wrote survives—a circumstance which might not be irrelevant to Proclus' ability to control orthodox thinking.

An even more interesting case than Asclepiodotus—indeed one of outright *damnatio memoriae*—concerns Domninus, the gifted fellow student of

Proclus and one on whom the status of diadoch had been conferred, possibly by Syrianus.[28] Domninus went down in history as 'a rather superficial' philosopher, since 'he distorted many of Plato's doctrines by introducing his own views. However, he was held to proper account for this *falsification* at the hands of Proclus, who wrote against him a whole treatise "purificatory" as its title indicates "of Plato's doctrines"' (*PH* fr. 89a).[29] But that was only half of Domninus' crime. He also transgressed on the norms of a pious life and ate meat every day, insisting that he had to do so for medical reasons, and interpreting in a far-fetched way the Pythagorean prohibitions on a meat diet to suit his purposes, so that it would appear that 'in his way of life he did not display that perfection that would entitle him to be called a true philosopher' (fr. 89a).

If we did not have the fragments of Damascius' *Philosophical History*, we would not know anything about Domninus' condemnation or Isidore's liberal teaching methodology and unconventional personality; or any other non-mainstream attitudes and behaviour among the men of Proclus' circle. As it is we know that Isidore (who significantly enough seems to have written nothing) was a difficult teacher, one who often 'spoke too profoundly for his pupils' understanding', and gave them insoluble problems to deal with (frs. 37b, 37c). His manner was far from clear as a result of personal deficiencies, at once intellectual and personal, which Damascius—possibly reproducing his master's point of view—turns into virtues. For example we learn that

> when lecturing, he lacked the linguistic skill necessary to present his views satisfactorily. And yet, not being unaided in this respect either by nature or by training, he still made zealous efforts at clarity. Leaving to others the graceful display of words, he occupied himself with revealing the thing itself, pronouncing concepts rather than words, or rather not even concepts as he brought to light the very essence of the things themselves (fr. 37d).

A man 'who had not read many books', but who, 'in the infinite rapture of his yearning after God resembled a seer who divined the truth by instinct' (fr. 37e), Isidore was a true *bacchus*, who through his passionate enthusiasm could *convert* people to the philosophical life. Indeed we know of at least two 'technicians', the Aristotelian Dorus (fr. 134a with note in Athanassiadi

[28] For a possible interpretation of the term *diadochos*, see Athanassiadi 1999*a*: 43.

[29] As is clear from many passages in Damascius' *Philosophical History*, by the time of Proclus there was only one orthodox way of interpreting Plato, and heretics were duly dealt with. Those who wished to remain within the Orthodox mainstream and receive the approval of their contemporaries and posterity had to destroy any of their own works which deviated from the dogmatic norm: cf. the case of Marinus, frs. 38a, 97j.

1999*a*) and, most importantly, the rhetorician Damascius (Athanassiadi 1999*a*: 32–6), whose soul Isidore 'unfurled for sailing on the vast sea of truth' (*PH* fr. 134a).

The Irreverent Damascius

It was through Proclus' triple activity—oral teaching, writing, and divine worship—that recognizable standards of orthodoxy were finally established for Hellenism, with the Athenian Academy acquiring all the formal and essential characteristics of a late antique theological college. Nor was his an achievement of one place and one time only. As a token of his lasting reputation, we possess the bulk of Proclus' writings, transmitted and preserved throughout the Christian centuries; this voluminous output establishes him as the supreme exegete of Plato, the transmitter of and quintessential commentator on Iamblichus—now co-terminous with orthodoxy—and consequently the indisputable authority on late pagan theology.[30] To such an extent was Proclus seen as the elucidator of Iamblichus' thought that, instead of battling with the Syrian's intractable text, people read his Athenian popularizer and exegete. The ultimate consequence of this was the loss of Iamblichus' systematic writings, such as his commentaries on the Platonic dialogues of the curriculum and on the Chaldaean Oracles, so that our view of them depends primarily on the references which are to be found in Proclus' works.[31]

Since Proclus was an intelligent, diligent, and honest reader who genuinely admired his Syrian predecessor, it is reasonable to assume that the way he represents him faithfully mirrors the true Iamblichus. For many decades such a supposition was treated as tantamount to certainty, but recently, since the work of the last diadoch of the Platonic Academy, the Syrian Damascius, with its abundant reference to Iamblichus, began to be studied, scholars are beginning to discover with a certain amount of surprise and unease that Damascius not only contradicts Proclus on important theological issues, but also bases his metaphysical theories on an interpretation of Iamblichus which goes totally against the Proclean view. Indeed,

[30] As the crowning achievement of a life devoted to Plato, Proclus wrote a *Platonic Theology* in many volumes; for the history of the text Saffrey and Westerink 1968: pp. cl–clx. Psellus' attitude to Proclus is indicative, if not characteristic, of the respect that the Byzantines paid to their late antique forebear: for references to Proclus in Psellus, cf. the *index locorum* in his *Philosophica Minora* i and ii (ed. J. M. Duffy and D. J. O'Meara).

[31] It is by no means coincidental that out of the ninety fragments which have been preserved from Iamblichus' *Commentary on the Timaeus*, eighty-eight have been transmitted by Proclus alone.

as his own pupil, Simplicius, states 'Damascius did not hesitate to oppose many of Proclus' doctrines because of his taste for hard work and also *his appreciation of Iamblichus' theories*' (*CAG* ix. 795. 15–17).

What Simplicius reproduces here is clearly Damascius' own point of view, a proposition that the last head of the Academy must have reiterated in his formal lectures and private conversations in a multitude of ways. The implication is that Proclus had failed to understand Iamblichus and misrepresented him, so that, in the name of Platonic orthodoxy, the new holder of Plato's chair had to take corrective action. Judging from his surviving works, and especially his systematic work *On the First Principles* and his no less systematic *Commentary on the Parmenides*, Damascius fulfilled this task with ferocious methodicality: in both these works he systematically questioned Proclus' authority as the exegete of Neoplatonic metaphysics, while affirming his own link with Iamblichus. It is true (and of the utmost significance for the argument of this paper) that, under the pretext of interpreting Iamblichus, Damascius expounded a personal theological system which nevertheless proved too difficult to grasp as a theoretical structure and too vague to follow as a practical way—indeed, a system which, by being too critical and too liberal, confused people rather than guiding them.

The extent of Iamblichus' responsibility for Damascius' formidable metaphysics may be an unanswerable question. However, a common Syrian origin (which meant that the two men were exposed during their formative years to the specifically Semitic conception of God as wholly transcendent)[32] may not be irrelevant in this connection, and may well constitute a suitable starting-point on the right path for investigating the sources of Damascius and the breadth of his originality. What is important, however, for the present argument is that Damascius based his authority as the head of the regenerated Academy on the claim that he understood Iamblichus. To his mind this empathy with the 'second founder of Platonism' enabled him to relaunch the ship of faith on its right course from which it had drifted away as a result of Proclus' inexpert steering.

Such, however, was not posterity's view. And while Proclus was seen, in Psellos' phrase, as 'the ultimate harbour from which all science and precise understanding could be obtained' (*Chronogr.* 6. 38), Damascius was held responsible 'for the shipwreck of Neoplatonism'.[33] To be fair, the two men

[32] For the recognition of the fact, Damascius *De Princ.* 2. 100 with Combès 1986.

[33] Zeller's famous phrase (Zeller and Mondolfo 1961: vi. 218) not only encapsulates the mood of the generations between the 6th and the 19th cents., with very few remarkable exceptions, but seems also to have worked as a binding charm on scholarship for over a century after it was written.

had their share in the creation of their respective images. Proclus' attitude to himself and to the world was a balanced attitude, inspired by modesty and good will. His basic optimism and his need and ability to communicate his thought to others carried his uncomplicated understanding of the Platonic theology down to the present day with exemplary clarity. Conversely, Damascius' deeply pessimistic view of man and the world earned him the charge of misanthropy in his capacity as a social historian,[34] and of nihilism in theology.[35]

Indeed, Damascius' acute sense of the tragic condition of mankind makes him express himself like a philosopher of the absurd *avant la lettre*, a style that one would not have expected his Byzantine descendants to appreciate. If his craving for the absolute was fully in tune with the spirit of the age in which he lived, the irreverent manner in which he systematically exposed relativity in society and in the human soul, and the undignified way in which he wept over 'the compulsion of our miserable nothingness' (*De Princ.* 3. 141), were features that met with angry incomprehension from posterity. Indeed his overcritical attitude towards everything and everybody is still a cause of mystification among scholars. For Damascius revolts against God in the manner of a modern existentialist while at the same time deriding and scorning reason and intellectual achievement in the manner of a Byzantine holy man.

The most direct reason, however, for Damascius' lack of appeal among his contemporaries and immediate successors may be sought in his very understanding of Iamblichus. Proclus had established, in Iamblichus' name, an orthodoxy which was a good mix of all the ingredients required for the creation of a successful system.[36] His theology was sufficiently exotic to intrigue without shocking, with a ritual aspect that was at once attractive and respectable, and a hierarchical structure that was eminently logical and therefore easy to comprehend. But above all the Proclean vision was human, even benign, with the elements of hope and love paramount, and in this respect at least Proclus' understanding of Neoplatonism was true to the Iamblichan psychology.[37] By contrast, Damascius concentrated

[34] Cf. Photius' damning comments on the *Philosophical History*: *Bibl.* Cod. 181.

[35] One comes back to Zeller's angry comment (n. 33), which concludes an analysis portraying Damascius as a 19th-cent. nihilist.

[36] For belief among the epigoni in Proclus' infallibility in the understanding of Iamblichus, see the note that Simplicius scribbled in the margin of Proclus' *In Timaeum* (Proclus, *Théologie Platonicienne* I, Paris 1968, p. CLIII): *Σιμπλικίου πόνος οὗτος· Ἰάμβλιχε δῶτερ ἐάων, ἵλαθι νικηθείς, ἀλλ' ὑπὸ σῶν ἐπέων.* (This is the work of Simplicius. Iamblichus, giver of good things, | Be gracious in defeat—since it came through your own words.)

[37] See the good analysis of Iamblichus' innovations in the domain of psychology by G. Shaw, *Theurgy and the Soul*, Pennsylvania 1995, *passim*.

on Iamblichus' metaphysics, stressing the system's 'hard monotheism' and, over and above that, viewing it in the light of his own despair and putting it into words too soon and in too complicated a philosophical idiom. Like his master, Isidore, he respected his readers' critical faculty too much to offer his ideas in a dogmatic form. Yet by doing that, he was neither convincing enough nor sufficiently reassuring at a time when people sought unequivocal answers to the difficult questions.

A more careful reading of Damascius may—or may not—lead to a drastic revision of our appreciation of his contribution to philosophy. What is of essence to the present argument however is that, with all his originality and independence of mind, Damascius accepted the premise of a spiritual orthodoxy which was co-terminous with Iamblichus' understanding of Plato. His negative theology is put forward primarily as the correct reading of Iamblichus and therefore as the orthodox Platonic way from which his predecessors had deviated.

Select Bibliography of Sources

Damascius, *The Philosophical History* (= *PH*), P. Athanassiadi (ed.) (Athens 1999).
Eunapius, *Vitae Sophistarum*, J. Giangrande (ed.) (Rome 1956).
Julian, *Epistulae, Leges, Poematia*, J. Bidez and F. Cumont (eds.) (Paris 1922).
Numenius, *Fragments*, E. des Places (ed.) (Paris 1973).

Ancient Philosophers

JONATHAN BARNES

Magnilla, a philosopher: daughter of Magnus, a philosopher: wife of Menius, a philosopher. (*IGRR* 125)

This stone apart, Magnilla and her family are unknown; and their names are not found in any philosophical history.

Condemned to the mines, Aedesius led a philosophical way of life, dressed in the cloak—for he had gained more education than his brother and was inspired by philosophical studies. (Eus. *Mart. Palaest.* 5. 2).

Aedesius has left no mark in the annals of philosophy.

When Rome ruled the civilized world, philosophy and philosophers played a prominent part in public life. No scholar has done more to analyse and to explain this phenomenon than Miriam Griffin.[1] In particular, and unlike many historians, she has always been keenly aware that philosophy, even in its public context, is not to be reduced to ethics, let alone to 'practical ethics' or sermonizing. If one of the two philosophical emperors thanked the gods that he had not wasted his time on syllogisms (Marc. Aur. *Med.* 1. 17. 22), the other was called upon to umpire a dispute among the professionals on a technical point in Aristotelian logic (Julian: Ammon. *in An. Pr.* 31. 11–22).

Philosophy was prominent. It was also popular. When Stilpo came to Athens, the artisans left their workshops to hear him discourse—doubtless on logical paradoxes (Diog. Laert. 2. 119). Theophrastus' lectures attracted 2,000 students (Diog. Laert. 5. 37). Such anecdotes should be treated with suspicion; and in any event they refer to the golden past. But they did not seem absurd to an age in which a chef might be expected to recite Plato while he served the roast peacock (Ath. 381f–382a). Philosophy was a part

[1] It would be enough to refer to two classic pieces: *Seneca: a Philosopher in Politics* (1976), and 'Philosophical Bandinage in Cicero's Letters' (1995*b*); but I shall not refrain from mentioning the two volumes of *Philosophia Togata*.—From an abundant literature on the general topic of 'philosophy and society', I pick out—for their different and complementary approaches—Hahn 1989 and Zanker 1995.

of general culture, the third element—after grammar and rhetoric—of a normal education. There were schools and teachers of the subject everywhere. It was in remote Oenoanda in southern Lycia that the Epicurean Diogenes set up his massive philosophical inscription, so that citizens and tourists might read the truth and discover happiness.[2]

Some philosophers, it is true, laid claim to an esoteric knowledge which was not for the ears of hoi polloi; and it was not uncommon to suggest that great thinkers—Aristotle as well as Heraclitus—practised a deliberate obscurity.[3] But whatever may be made of this curious notion, most philosophers were presumably content to be popular.

I

Menius, Magnus, and Magnilla offer particular illustration of these general truths. Magnilla had philosophical sisters—thus Aurelia Oppia, 'daughter of the most philosophical Callias', was herself 'most philosophical and modest' (*IG* v. 1. 598). Or again from Rome, and in a limping Latin hexameter: 'Euphrosyne: pious, instructed in the nine muses, philosopher: she lived for twenty years' (*ILS* 7783).

There are a dozen other cases—but of course inscriptions show more men than women. Here is a handful of examples. A stone cut in the second century and found at Claudioupolis in Asia Minor honours a sound local citizen:

> Good fortune: Julius Nicetas—philosopher, Caesarian, patriot. By the Augustan tribe. At private expense. (*Inschr. Claud. 67*)

In 217/18, at Ephesus, Marcus Aurelius Daphnus, an Asiarch and generous giver of games, honoured a man whom he described as his own benefactor and 'the benefactor of everyone in his country'. The benefactor was

> Appius Alexander: most excellent procurator of our lords Opellius and Diadumenianus,[4] frequently ducenarius, philosopher, pious and just and adorned with all virtue. (*Inschr. Eph. 616*)

[2] The fragments of Diog. Oen. are in M. F. Smith 1996, 1998.

[3] On deliberate obscurity see e.g. Harl 1982; Erler 1991; Mansfeld 1994: 149–61. For Heraclitus see e.g. Diog. Laert. 9. 6; for Aristotle, see his exchange of letters with Alexander the Great in Aul. Gell. *NA* 20. 5. 7–12. Note also e.g. Gal. *in Hipp. Off.* 18A 665K (doctors); *Suda* s.v. *Καλλίμαχος* (poets).

[4] i.e. Macrinus and his son (hence the dating). The two names have been scratched out on the stone: Macrinus and Diadumenianus suffered *damnatio memoriae* (Cassius Dio 79. 2. 6).

From the later third century a fulsome inscription from Selge thanks Publia Plancia Aurelia Magniana Motoxaris, who had lavished money on the city (*Inschr. Selge 17*). Plancia's father, Magnianus Xenon, had held the highest local offices—he was also 'a patriot, adorned with all virtue'. Her brother, Magnus Aelianus Pericles Arrius was an honest orator—'first in character and in discourse'. Her husband, Caius Valerius Eugenes, is described thus: 'patriot, adorned with all virtue, founder and sustainer of the city, philosopher'.

Philosophers were not only flattered on their tombstones and honoured in their home-towns: they won distinction abroad. An example from Delphi, from the end of the first century:

> Good Fortune. The Delphians honoured Publius Cornelius Lupus of Nicopolis, Amphictyon and philosopher, with citizenship, the right to front seats, and the other honours which are granted to men of nobility and virtue. In the magistracy of Tiberius Julius Agathon. (*FD* iii. 115)

To be sure, the Delphians also honoured a tight-rope walker (*FD* 226).

The intellectual affiliations of most of these philosophical honorands are unrecorded. But many inscriptions bawl allegiance to a sect. The Platonists are, unremarkably, the most numerous—men like Secundinus of Tralles (*Inschr. Eph.* 4340), or A. Mestrius Autobulus, a descendant of Plutarch (*SIG*[3] 844), or Isidore of Thmous, whom the Delphians made a citizen and a councillor (*FD* iii. 116). There is a good scattering of Stoics—among them the 'Stoic successor' Titus Coponius Maximus (*IG* ii[2]. 3571) and Titus Avianus Bassus Polyaenus, member of a philosophical family in Prusa (*Inschr. Prusa* 17). There are a few Peripatetics—for example, Epicrates of Heracleia (*SEG* i. 368); and a few Epicureans—for example, Caius Julius Amynias, son of Sosigenes and known as Isocrates (*IGRR* iv. 997). There is the odd Pythagorean, like Sextus Claudius Aurelianus of Smyrna (*FD* iii. 203). There is a solitary Pyrrhonist—Menecles of Cyme (*Inschr. Kyme 48*). There is even (if the stone may be believed) an eclectic—Anonymus of Alexandria (*Inschr. Eph.* 789).[5]

Such philosophical inscriptions, mostly in Greek but a few in Latin, are numerous. An amateur trawl will quickly produce a couple of hundred pertinent stones. Some famous names appear—from Aristotle to Apuleius, from Calvenus Taurus to the Emperor Julian. But most inscribed philosophers,

[5] Julius Amynias was a prominent Samian, one of numerous philosophers who served as ambassadors for their cities (he is number 150 in Goulet 1989). On Menecles see J. Barnes 1990. The name of the anonymous eclectic began with a pi—hence he has been identified with the only other known eclectic philosopher, Potamo of Alexandria (Diog. Laert. 1. 21): see Runia 1988.

although they will have been local bigwigs, are philosophically obscure—hayseed Humes, to fortune and to fame unknown.[6]

II

The dominant philosophical sect of late antiquity is not mentioned as such on the stones. At least, I have not noticed any inscriptional reference to 'the Christian philosophy'. This might seem unsurprising. After all, Paul had issued a warning: 'Beware lest any man spoil you through philosophy and vain deceit' (*Col.* 2:8). And no one forgets Tertullian:

What likeness is there between a philosopher and a Christian? between a student of Greece and a student of heaven? between the business of reputation and the business of life? between the management of words and the management of deeds? (*Apol.* 46. 18)

All that a Christian needs is belief: philosophy is a useless exercise, and dangerous (*De Praescr. Haeret.* 7. 9. 13).

Tertullian's opinion of philosophy was not unique—Clement remarks that: 'Some Christians, thinking themselves naturally endowed, demand that we do not touch philosophy or dialectic and that we do not even learn physics—they demand faith, pure and simple' (*Strom.* 1. 9. 43. 1) But such anti-philosophical attitudes were heterodox among Christians, and rare.[7]

Tertullian knew that his contemporaries liked to think of Christianity as 'another philosophy' (*Apol.* 46. 18); and Clement wrote reams in order to prove that that is exactly what it was. In the fourth century, Gregory of Nazianzus denounced 'Greek' philosophy, only to laud the true philosophy of the Christians (*Or.* 4. 113. 2–5). One of his rhetorical extravaganzas begins thus: 'I shall praise the philosopher . . . For either we should practise philosophy or we should honour it, unless we are to fall wholly outside the noble and be condemned for irrationality' (*Or.* 25.1). Whereas Gregory's brother had chosen the worldly trade of the physician, he himself had decided to become a philosopher—'for as philosophy is the greatest undertaking, so it is the most difficult and not for the many' (*Or.* 7. 9).

[6] For Aristotle, see *SIG*³ 275; for Apuleius, *AE* 1916: 16; for Taurus, *FD* iii. 91; for Julian, *Inschr. Iasos 14* ('he who rules by philosophy'). As far as I know, there is no collection of 'philosophical inscriptions'. The old article by Marcus Tod (1957), which he wrote for the Festschrift of his friend and Oriel colleague Sir David Ross, is unsupplanted—for a few further references see e.g. J. Barnes 1997: 5 n. 19.

[7] See also e.g. *Strom.* 1. 1. 18. 3, 6. 11. 93. 1—together with Clement's sustained argument against the view: 1. 6. 93. 2–95. 5; cf. Méhat 1966: 322–6 and for a general survey, e.g. Wolfson 1970: 102–41.

The second-century apologists were equally sure of their philosophical credentials. Melito, addressing Marcus Aurelius, observed that 'our philosophy flourished of old among the barbarians; and it flowered among your nations during the magnificent reign of your ancestor Augustus' (*apud* Eus. *Hist. Eccl.* 4. 26. 7). Justin, who was executed on the denunciation of a pagan philosopher, had anticipated Gregory: 'In truth, philosophy is a very great possession and one most honourable to God, to whom it alone leads us and consolidates us; and truly are they holy who have devoted their minds to philosophy' (*Dial. Tryph.* 2. 1). Nor was veneration for philosophy limited to the learned among the Christians. The *Sentences* of Sextus, that most popular of early Christian texts, urges that 'in honouring a philosopher you will honour yourself' (§219). And again, engagingly: 'Do not believe slander against a philosopher' (§259).

It was unremarkable when the first Christian emperor declared that 'the Son of God confirmed that this is the supreme strength: firmness of mind together with philosophy, which is knowledge of the true and the good' (Constantine, *Or.* 15). And Constantine's contemporary, Eusebius, took the final step: our Lord and Saviour was himself a philosopher (*Dem. Evang.* 3. 6. 8).

To regard the new religion as a philosophy was not a peculiarly Christian conceit. The pagan in Minucius Felix' *Octavius* claims that the Christians are so far in agreement with the Greek philosophers that you would take them for philosophers themselves (*Oct.* 20. 1). Some Christian sectarians attached themselves to Plotinus' circle, and Plotinus treated them as renegade Platonists (see Porph. *V. Plot.* 16; Plotinus *Enn.* 2. 9). Alexander of Lycopolis, writing in about 300, records that Christianity began as a simple philosophy, and then became puffed up with metaphysics and riddled with faction (*c. Man.* 1).[8]

The triumph of Christianity fanned rather than quenched the fires of philosophy. The Christian Empire claimed to be more philosophical, and more truly philosophical, than its pagan predecessor.

III

Such reflections flatter the philosopher: to the philologist they may seem a fantasy and a confusion. To be sure, the philologist will allow, countless citizens of the Empire were happy to be described by the Greek word φιλόσοφος or by its Latin transliteration. But it should not be inferred that they thought of themselves as philosophers. That inference would be a

[8] On Alexander of Lycopolis see van der Horst 1996.

fallacy, a fallacy of equivocation. From the fact that the word 'fraise' applies to numerous items in France we do not infer that France is the land of the ruff: from the fact that φιλόσοφος applies to numerous items in the imperial world let us not infer that the Empire was an Empire of philosophers.

The word φιλόσοφος,[9] the philologist alleges, was—like most words—ambiguous. Two aspects of the alleged ambiguity are pertinent here. First, the word came to acquire a specifically Christian sense. The transference of the term from pagan thinkers to the votaries of Christ was not arbitrary; but it was a transference, and the transference gave it a new meaning. The word φιλόσοφος was true of a Christian; but Christianity was not, and was not taken to be, a philosophy. Secondly, the word came to be used as a general term of praise. Its range of application was enlarged and its content correspondingly reduced. Again, the enlargement was not arbitrary—but it imported a new sense. The word φιλόσοφος was true of Magnilla; but she was not thereby called a philosopher.[10] Aristotle, Aedesius, and Appius Alexander—each is correctly called φιλόσοφος. Only one of them was a philosopher.

I shall not deny that the word φιλόσοφος shows different 'shades of meaning' in different contexts, nor even that it possesses more senses than one. But there is no specifically Christian sense of the word, no sense which it standardly bears when applied to Christians and standardly does not bear when applied to pagans. And there is no reason to think that there is, so to speak, an 'inscriptional' sense of the word, a special sense which it standardly bears on honorific and funerary stones.

The alleged ambiguities are a modern discovery. At any rate, although antiquity had a nose for ambiguity, no ancient text (to my knowledge) suggests that the word φιλόσοφος was ambiguous—and in particular, no Christian text suggests that it has a Christian sense.[11] The modern discovery of the Christian sense—with which I shall start—depends on bad lexicography.

Here is a simple example of one type of error. In his *Symposium*, Methodius asks: 'What need is there to say that the evangelical and divine philosophy is in no way inferior to the ordinary philosophy (φιλοσοφία ἡ

[9] Here and hereafter 'the word φιλόσοφος' should generally be taken as short for 'the word φιλόσοφος and its cognates, together with *philosophus* and its cognates'.

[10] The classic study of the word φιλόσοφος is Malingrey 1961. This work contains an invaluable collection of references, particularly to Christian texts; but its methods and its inferences are flawed.

[11] Except perhaps Clem. *Strom.* 6. 7. 55. 2 (cf. 8. 67. 1)? But closer inspection shows that Clement is making a distinction not between two senses of the word φιλοσοφία but rather between two types or branches of philosophy.

ἐγκύκλιος) and culture?' (*Symp.* 8. 170). A scholar comments that 'the sense of *philosophia* here is plain—it designates profane culture by contrast to religious culture'. More precisely, in its second occurrence, the word φιλοσοφία means 'pagan philosophy', and in its first occurrence it means something completely different—namely, 'Christian philosophy' (Malingrey 1961: 182). This is evidently mistaken. And it is not the word φιλοσοφία but the phrase φιλοσοφία ἡ ἐγκύκλιος[12] which designates profane culture, or rather, non-Christian philosophy. As to the word φιλοσοφία itself, it means, both times 'philosophy'. It is churlish to rap a scholar on the knuckles for what can only be a trivial slip. But many a scholar has thus slipped, and the error is slipshod.

However that may be, a different sort of error is rather more subtle. In his *Life of Severus*, Zacharias describes Evagrius, the leader of a group of Christians in Beirut at the end of the fifth century:

He was a practical philosopher of our Lord Jesus Christ. He fasted, in one way or another, every day, and he spent the flower of his youth in the divine philosophy. He tortured his body by not sleeping, and he never bathed save one day a year . . . The great Severus came gradually to match him in practice and theory. (*V. Sev.* Kugener 1903: 56)[13]

Evagrius was exceptionally filthy; but his philosophy was not idiosyncratic. The Church historian Sozomen refers to a group of Syrian monks called the Bosci or Pasturers—because they lived like sheep, never washed, and sang hymns all day: 'This was the way in which these men philosophized' (*Hist. Eccl.* 6. 33). In the fourth century, and particularly by the Cappadocian Fathers, the solitary or monastic life was often referred to as 'philosophy'—when Basil, or either of the Gregorys, speaks of a philosopher, he usually has in mind an isolated and unworldly ascetic. And such a conception was discovered in the earliest days of the Church: James, brother of Jesus and bishop of Jerusalem, 'had in his life reached the pinnacle of philosophy and of piety'; 'he drank no wine or strong drink, he ate no meat, no razor ever touched his head, he did not oil his body, he did not bathe; and he prayed so much that his knees were as hard as a camel's' (Hegesippus, *apud* Eus. *Hist. Eccl.* 2. 23. 2, 5–6).

To return to Zacharias. He describes how the young pagan Paralios was converted to Christianity: bewildered by the evident impotence and mendacity of the pagan gods, he was urged to read the works of Gregory of Nazianzus; and having done so, 'he exclaimed: "Then let us take wing and fly to divine philosophy with the aid of the redeeming baptism." . . . He took

12 For which see scholia to Dion. Thrax, *Grammatici Graeci* 3. 1. 112. 16–20.

13 The *Life* survives only in a Syriac tradition, edited by Kugener 1903.

the monastic dress and embraced the divine philosophy' (*V. Sev.* Kugener 1903: 39). The monastic dress and divine philosophy are one. A Christian philosopher is someone who rejects pleasure and society, who renounces the barber and the bath-house, and who lives in squalor and solitude. How different from the home life of our own dear Aristotle.

What is to be concluded? To be sure—it has been argued—the rules of Greek allow the term φιλόσοφος to be applied to Evagrius and to Aristotle. But the two men are so utterly different that the word cannot be applied to them in the same sense. Aristotle was a philosopher. Evagrius was a philosopher. But Aristotle was a philosopher in the pagan sense of the word, Evagrius in the Christian. And the sentence 'Aristotle and Evagrius were both philosophers' is a pun.

This argument exemplifies the subtler sort of lexicographical error. There are several things wrong with it. The first point to notice is this: whatever the case of Evagrius may show, it cannot establish a Christian sense for the word φιλόσοφος. Damascius' pagan *Life of Isidore* is roughly contemporary with Zacharias' Christian *Life of Severus*. With Zacharias' Evagrius compare Damascius' Serapion:

> In piety and in the whole philosophy of his life he surpassed all men, except Isidore himself . . . When he grew old he very rarely left his own house; and he lived alone in a small cottage, having genuinely chosen a monastic life and dealing with his neighbours only in matters of extreme necessity. He was extraordinarily given to praying . . . He so despised wealth that he owned nothing except for two or three books . . . and he so despised bodily pleasures that from the start he gave his body only the necessities and he was undefiled by sex throughout his life. (*Suda*, s.v. Σαραπίων)[14]

We may confidently assume that Serapion rarely washed.

Eunapius was a contemporary of the Cappadocians: he assures us that his teacher Chrysanthius rarely visited the baths—implausibly adding that he always smelt clean (*VS* 502). As for philosophical monasticism, it is the subject of an essay by Dio Chrysostom—who remarks that although a 'retreat' from the world is deemed essential by many for the practice of philosophy (*Or.* 20. 11), in fact it is likely to lead to a dangerous form of lunacy (ibid. 17–18).

Dirt and the lonely road are especially associated with those quasi-philosophers, the Cynics.[15] But the Cynics were only practising what the Platonists preached. Porphyry, for example, observes as though it were a

[14] The *Life* survives only in fragments: the text I cite is divided between fr. 34 and fr. 287 in Zintzen 1967; it is part of fr. 111 in Athanassiadi 1999*a*.

[15] On monks and Cynics see Hatch 1914: 165–8 who thinks that the former derived from the latter. Julian's hostility to Cynics is of a piece with his anti-Galileanism.

banality that philosophers should retire from ordinary life and ordinary pleasures (*Abst.* 1. 36). And he cites as his proof-text a familiar page of Plato's *Theaetetus* (173e–174a). A century and a half after Porphyry, the same text was cited to the same end by Theodoretus, the Christian bishop of Cyrrhus (*Cur.* 12. 24–32).

The story demands refinement: there were different varieties of asceticism and different ways of retreating from the world; moreover, an ascetic is not necessarily a solitary, nor a solitary an ascetic. None the less, what I have said is enough to show that philosophical asceticism was no more a Christian than a pagan phenomenon. Not all pagan philosophers, and not all Christians, idealized the monkish life; and still fewer practised it.[16] But the 'practical philosophy' of Evagrius was not particularly Christian. *A fortiori*, the case of Evagrius does not establish a Christian sense for the word φιλόσοφος.

Secondly, the case of Evagrius does not establish that φιλόσοφος sometimes meant 'ascetic' or the like. Aristotle and Evagrius were utterly different in their customs and their outlook. It does not follow that the word 'philosopher' applies to them in different senses. A predicate may apply, in one and the same sense, to two utterly different subjects—as my parrot and my Pekinese are both pets, and my opinions and my clothes are both dated. (Conversely, 'right-winger' might apply in two distinct senses to Tweedledum and to Tweedledee.) When a predicate is applied to two subjects, and you wonder whether it is applied in the same sense, the question to ask is not: how alike are the subjects one to another? Rather, it is: in virtue of what features of the two subjects is the predicate applied to them?[17]

In virtue of what was the word φιλόσοφος applied to Evagrius? It is plain that his ablutionary habits were connected to his philosophizing—they were not an accidental feature of Evagrius the philosopher, in the way in which the colour of his hair was. But it does not follow that it was in virtue of his asceticism that he was called φιλόσοφος, or that the word φιλόσοφος, as applied to Evagrius, means something like 'ascetic'. For, though necessarily tied to philosophy, asceticism might be not a feature in virtue of which Evagrius was called φιλόσοφος, but rather a sign or a concomitant or a corollary of such a feature.

That this was in fact so is demonstrable. Severus, who modelled himself

[16] Note e.g. Epict. *Diss.* 4. 8. 17–20, on Euphrates, the rich and worldly Stoic (whom Epictetus none the less admired). On Euphrates and the question of the philosophical worldling see Frede 1997*a*.

[17] This is perfectly obvious. Yet numerous articles in ancient philosophy (some of them celebrated) depend on the tacit principle that a difference in nature among subjects implies a difference in sense in any common predicate.

on Evagrius, was through and through a philosopher and a teacher of philosophy—of 'the true philosophy' (*V. Sev.* Kugener 1903: 8). Indeed, 'so great was his progress in the virtues that, even before he put on the habit of a monk, he showed himself a Christian philosopher by his acts and by his knowledge' (*V. Sev.* Kugener 1903: 90). Severus was remarkable in that he had the strength of soul to pursue philosophy—both in its practical and theoretical parts—even before he turned to ascetic isolation. In other words, Severus was a philosopher, in the sense in which Evagrius was a philosopher, before he became a monk. It follows that asceticism is not a feature in virtue of which the word φιλόσοφος applied to Severus—or to Evagrius. The relation between philosophy and asceticism is like the relation between health and exercise. And just as 'healthy' does not mean 'taking exercise', so 'philosopher' does not mean 'recluse'.

There is a further nail to be hammered in. Two texts will do it. First, in his discourse *In Praise of Heron*, Gregory of Nazianzus describes how Heron decided to devote himself to a life of philosophy. After that decision, the next question was which philosophy he should espouse—'the philosophy of the outsiders or our own'. Heron 'was not seduced by the cleverness of argument on which those who philosophize according to the Greeks pride themselves'; and he chose the Christian philosophy (*Or.* 25. 4). Secondly, at the beginning of the *Dialogue with Trypho* Justin is recognized, by his dress, for what he is: 'Good morning, philosopher' (1. 1). A little later Trypho meets him, sees at once that he is a philosopher, and asks: 'Then what is your philosophy?' (1. 6). Justin explains how he had tried in turn Stoicism and Aristotelianism and Pythagoreanism and Platonism, finding them all wanting. Finally, he discovered the Christian philosophy (1. 8).

The theme of the 'choice of philosophies' was a common enough motif; and scholars have surmised that neither Gregory nor Justin was telling the strict historical truth. No matter. They portray a choice. Christianity is one of the items on offer, stocked on the same shelf as Stoicism, Epicureanism, and the rest. The choice is among philosophies, not among senses of the word 'philosophy'. Both Heron and Justin opted for one philosophy rather than another; they did not opt for one sense of the term φιλόσοφος rather than another. They left the TSB for the Banque Nationale de Paris—they did not leave the TSB to sit by the side of the Seine.[18]

[18] For the choice of philosophies see especially Lucian, *Hermot.*; also e.g. Josephus, *Vita* 10 (Josephus tried all the Jewish philosophical sects—see below, pp. 305–6; he spent some time contemplating in the desert; and he then joined the sect of the Pharisees 'which is similar to what the Greeks call Stoicism'). Note also Dionysius *apud* Eus. *Hist. Eccl.* 6. 43. 15: the schismatic Novatian claimed that he was 'enamoured of a different philosophy'—that is to say, he did not accept the orthodox Christian philosophy.

To be sure, a Christian philosopher—like a Platonist or a Pyrrhonian—might have his own ideas about the proper objects of philosophical study and the proper ways to pursue them.[19] But that does not insinuate that he was using the term φιλόσοφος in a specially Christian sense—quite the opposite.

IV

What about the 'inscriptional' sense of the word, in which it is a general term of commendation? Here an appeal might be made to a syntactical fact which I have hitherto ignored. In Greek, φιλόσοφος is now an adjective and now a noun. Perhaps the difference in syntax is matched by a difference in sense? When the word is used substantivally, then—as a rule—it means 'philosopher'. Taken adjectivally it means—as a rule—something different and less formal, something non-professional. (In English there is a difference between the noun 'philosopher' and the adjective 'philosophical'—which, according to my dictionary, means, 'calmly uncomplaining in defeat or difficulty'. Philosophers are rarely philosophical.)

The inscriptions which I have cited therefore need a more scrupulous translation. On *Inschr. Claud* 67, for example, Julius Nicetas is not styled 'philosopher, Caesarian, patriot'. The Greek has three adjectives, not three nouns: φιλόσοφον, φιλοκαίσαρα καὶ φιλόπατριν. Perhaps: 'He loved wisdom, his Emperor and his country'. In any event, there is no warrant for turning the adjective by an English noun, no warrant for making Nicetas a philosopher.

Now it is true that φιλόσοφος has both a substantival and an adjectival use. In *IG* v/1. 598, for example, it is evidently used adjectivally; and in *Inschr. Prusa* 18, where it carries the qualifying adjective 'Stoic', it is evidently a substantive. But in many cases it is difficult to determine the syntax; and often there is no correct answer to the question 'Noun or adjective?' After all, the noun is no more than a hardened adjective.[20] That being so, it will seem unlikely that the syntax has any semantic implications.

[19] Thus Alexander of Lycopolis observes that Christianity was originally a 'simple' philosophy, i.e. it consisted only of ethics (*c. Man.* 1). In the early *Didache* Christian teaching is exclusively ethical (see 1. 2); and the notion that Christianity was at first a purely ethical doctrine has proved congenial to modern Protestants (see e.g. Hatch 1914: 159–70). But, as Alexander adds, the new philosophy was not long content to remain simple.

[20] For this common Greek phenomenon see e.g. Blass and Debrunner 1931: 241, 263–4. LSJ s.v. φιλόσοφος appear to treat the adjective as a softened noun (contrast the entry for φιλόλογος).

Next, was there a 'professional' sense for the noun *φιλόσοφος*? There were professional philosophers in antiquity—private schoolmasters like Epictetus, public professors like Alexander of Aphrodisias. And such professionals, when they were recognized in imperial edicts, were designated by the term *φιλόσοφος*.[21] The noun also designates non-professionals: it designates those whose occupation was philosophy—full-time amateurs, as it were—among them, Plato and Plotinus; and it designates part-time amateurs, men of such diverse talents as Apuleius and Galen and Seneca.

It is plain that the noun *φιλόσοφος* applies in one and the same sense to Alexander and Plotinus and Galen. And in that sense it does not mean 'professional philosopher'. Does the noun also have a different sense in which it applies to Alexander but not to Plotinus or to Galen?[22] I doubt it—but in any event such an ambiguity would not be pertinent to the present argument.

Next, the adjectival use of the word: does the adjective usually convey a general commendation? (Certainly it does not mean the same as 'philosophical' in English.) Well, it demonstrably does not always have such a broad function. In *IG* v/1. 598, for example, Aurelia Oppia is 'most philosophical and modest' (*φιλοσοφωτάτην καὶ σώφρονα*): two terms of commendation, picking out two commendable features, so that *φιλόσοφος* has a specific and not a general sense. Again, in *Inschr. Ephesus* 616 *τὸν φιλόσοφον* stands alongside *τὸν ἁγνὸν καὶ δίκαιον καὶ πάσῃ ἀρετῇ κεκοσμημένον*—Appius Alexander is both a philosopher and also pious, just, and adorned with all virtue and so on. The formula which serves as a general commendation is the last in the list, *πάσῃ ἀρετῇ κεκοσμημένον*: the earlier members of the list are specific.

If the adjective *φιλόσοφος* is not a general word of commendation, is it a general word of intellectual commendation, roughly equal to 'endowed with the intellectual virtues'? I cannot prove that it is not. On the other hand, I know of no text which hints that it is. That is to say, there is no reason to think that the adjective ever means 'intellectually gung-ho'. In other words, there is nothing against the simple hypothesis that the adjective and the noun mean the same thing.

[21] The wittiest such edict was issued by Antoninus Pius *Dig*. 27. 1. 6. 2. Cf. Bowersock 1969: 340.

[22] The Supplement to LSJ, s.v. *φιλόσοφος*, suggests that the noun is perhaps used as 'an official title'. They cite *IG* ii². 791. 30 and *SEG* xxx. 159; but I cannot see any reason to find a title, let alone an official title, in these texts.

V

Byzantine professors liked to give half a dozen definitions of their subject to debutant students of philosophy (e.g. Ammon. *in Isag.* 2. 17–9. 24). One of them is etymological: philosophy is a love of wisdom. The definition is found in a hundred earlier texts, pagan and Christian. Two Latin examples:

> Philosophy is love and longing for wisdom—it strains to be where wisdom already is. Why philosophy is so called is clear—it confesses its love in its very name. (Sen. *Ep.* 89. 4)

> I beseech you, let not the philosophy of the gentiles be more honourable than our philosophy, insofar as the love of wisdom is signified by this word. (August. *c. Iul.* 4. 14. 72)[23]

The definition was frequently supplemented by an explanatory gloss: wisdom is 'knowledge of things divine and things human'. The gloss belongs to no sect or party; and it is used by Christians (e.g. Clem. Al. *Strom.* 1. 5. 30. 1) and by pagans (e.g. Sext. Emp. *Math.* 9. 13).

That is grand, but imprecise. At any rate, not 'all things divine and human' were actually studied by philosophers. Rhetoric, for example, is a thing human; yet few imperial philosophers thought that it fell within their purview. Grammar was certainly no part of philosophy—nor agriculture, nor architecture, nor medicine.

A closer characterization is provided by the standard imperial tripartition: philosophy divides into logic, physics, and ethics. Other 'divisions' are found, notably a bipartition into the theoretical and the practical. The Peripatetics denied that logic was properly a part of philosophy at all. Some philosophers rejected, or declined to study, one or more of the three parts. None the less, as Seneca put it, 'most authorities, and the best authorities, have said that philosophy has three parts' (*Ep.* 89.9).[24]

If more detail is demanded, then the best thing to say is this: you study philosophy in so far as you interest yourself in the sort of things which were discussed by Plato, by Aristotle, by Epicurus, by Chrysippus . . . Josephus likes to boast of 'our laws and traditional philosophy' (*Ap.* 2. 5. 47): in one text he distinguishes three groups 'who philosophize among the Jews', Pharisees, Sadducees, and Essenes (*BJ* 2. 8. 119, cf. 166); and in a longer passage he describes the four philosophies of the Jews (*AJ* 18. 1. 11–26). It

[23] Note that Augustine expressly says that Christian philosophy is a philosophy in the standard sense of the word.

[24] The best surviving account of the tripartite syllabus is to be found in a Christian text, Gregory the Thaumaturge, *ad Orig.* 7. 93–14. 172. On Gregory see e.g. Crouzel 1969: 12–43; Mitchell 1993: ii. 53–7.

might be thought that philosophizing, for Josephus, is nothing else than following, in one way or another, the Laws of Moses. But that would be quite wrong; for in the *Antiquities* Josephus makes it clear why he uses the term *φιλοσοφία* of the Jewish sects, a use which he evidently feels the need to justify. It is because the four groups all had views and developed theories about certain traditionally philosophical subjects—theories about the immortality of the soul, theories about causal determinism, and so on. Josephus can justly call the Sadducees philosophers; for they are concerned about issues which concerned Plato and Chrysippus.[25]

In sum, imperial citizens who styled themselves philosophers thereby declared a love of wisdom; that is to say, they claimed to study things divine and things human—or, more solidly, to study logic, physics, and ethics. And you would recognize them by the congruence between their intellectual interests and those of the great Greek masters. This is the sense in which Alexander and Plotinus were philosophers—and Justin and Origen, and Aedesius and Magnus and Menius and Magnilla.

Magnilla was not a new Aristotle. She never published a book or contributed a learned article to *Nous*. Perhaps the desert air was the best place for her fragrance. But she and her family were philosophers in our sense of the word. That is to say, they were philosophers. And the Empire teemed with such people.

[25] Note that Porphyry, *Abst.* 4. 11, refers without qualm to 'the three types of philosophy' among the Jews—and then cites Josephus on the Essenes with approval.

BIBLIOGRAPHY

Adam, J. (1938). *The Republic of Plato* (Cambridge).

Alexander, L. C. A. (1993). 'Acts and Ancient Intellectual Biography', in B. W. Winter and A. D. Clarke (eds.), *The Book of Acts in its First Century Setting*, i. *Ancient Literary Setting* (Grand Rapids, Mich., and Carlisle), 31–63.

——(1994). 'Paul and the Hellenistic Schools: The Evidence of Galen', in T. Engberg-Pedersen (ed.), *Paul in his Hellenistic Context* (Philadelphia and Edinburgh), 60–83.

——(2001). 'IPSE DIXIT: Citation of Authority in Paul and in the Jewish and Hellenistic Schools', in T. Engberg-Pedersen (ed.), *Paul Beyond the Judaism–Hellenism Divide* (Louisville, Ky.).

Alföldi, A. (1973). 'La Divinisation de César dans la politique d'Antoine et d'Octavien entre 44 et 40 avant J.C.', *Revue Numismatique*, 6th ser. 15: 99–128.

——(1975). Review of Weinstock 1971, *Gnomon*, 47: 154–79.

——(1984). *Caesariana: Gesammelte Aufsätze zur Geschichte Caesars und seiner Zeit* (Bonn).

——and Giard, J.-B. (1984). 'Guerre civile et propagande politique: L'Émission d'Octave au nom du Divos Iulios (41–40 avant J.C.)', *NAC* 13: 147–61.

Alföldy, G. (1969). *Fasti Hispanienses: Senatorische Reichsbeamte und Offiziere in den spanischen Provinzen des römischen Reiches von Augustus bis Diokletian* (Wiesbaden).

——(2000). 'Das neue Edikt des Augustus aus El Bierzo in Hispania', *ZPE* 131: 177–205.

——and Halfmann, H. M. (1973). 'Cornelius Nigrinus Curiatius Maternus, General Domitians und Rivale Trajans', *Chiron*, 3: 331–73.

Algra, K. (1997). 'Chrysippus, Carneades, Cicero: The Ethical *Divisiones* in Cicero's *Lucullus*', in B. Inwood and J. Mansfeld (eds.), *Assent and Argument: Studies in Cicero's Academic Books* (Leiden), 107–39.

——van der Horst, P. W., and Runia, D. T. (eds.) (1996). *Polyhistor: Studies in the History and Historiography of Ancient Philosophy Presented to Jaap Mansfeld on his Sixtieth Birthday* (Philosophia Antiqua, 72; Leiden).

Anderson, G. (1989). 'The *Pepaideumenos* in Action: Sophists and their Outlook in the Early Empire', *ANRW* II.33.1: 79–208.

——(1990). 'The Second Sophistic: Some Problems of Perspective', in Russell, D. A. (ed.), *Antonine Literature* (Oxford), 91–110.

——(1993). *The Second Sophistic: A Cultural Phenomenon in the Roman Empire* (London).

Annas, J. (1976). 'Was Plato a Feminist?', *Philosophy*, 51: 306–21.

——(1989). 'Cicero on Stoics and Private Property', in J. Barnes and M. T. Griffin (eds.), *Philosophia Togata* (Oxford), 151–73.

Annas, J. (1993). *The Morality of Happiness* (New York).
Anson, J. (1974). 'The Female Transvestite in Early Monasticism: The Origin and Development of a Motif', *Viator*, 5: 1–32.
Arnim, H. von (1898). *Leben und Werke des Dio von Prusa* (Berlin).
Arnim, J. von (1903–5). *Stoicorum Veterum Fragmenta*, i–iii (Leipzig).
Arrighetti, G. (1973). *Epicuro: Opere*, 2nd edn. (Turin).
Athanassiadi, P. (1991). 'The Fate of Oracles in Late Antiquity: Didyma and Delphi', *Delt. Chr. Arch. Et.* 15: 271–8.
—— (1992). *Julian: An Intellectual Biography*, 2nd edn. (London, now rewritten as *Ἰουλιανός: μιὰ βιογραφία*. Athens, 2001).
—— (1993*a*). 'Dreams, Theurgy and Freelance Divination: The Testimony of Iamblichus', *JRS* 83: 115–30.
—— (1993*b*). 'Persecution and Response in Late Paganism: The Evidence of Damascius', *JHS* 113: 1–29.
—— (1995). 'The Oecumenism of Iamblichus: Latent Knowledge and its Awakening', *JRS* 85: 244–50.
—— (1999*a*). *Damascius: The Philosophical History* (Athens).
—— (1999*b*). 'The Chaldaean Oracles: Theology and Theurgy', in P. Athanassiadi and M. Frede (eds.), *Pagan Monotheism in Late Antiquity* (Oxford), 149–83.
—— and Frede, M. (eds.). (1999) *Pagan Monotheism in Late Antiquity* (Oxford).
Atkins, E. M. (2000). 'Cicero', in C. Rowe and M. Schofield (eds.), *The Cambridge History of Greek and Roman Political Thought* (Cambridge), 477–516.
—— and Dodaro, R. D. (2001). *Augustine: Political Writings* (Cambridge).
—— and Griffin, M. T. (1991). *Cicero on Duties* (Cambridge).
Badian, E. (1986). 'The Young Betti and the Practice of History', in G. Crifò (ed.), *Costituzione Romana e crisi della repubblica* (Perugia), 73–96.
Baldwin, B. (1995). 'Roman Emperors in the Elder Pliny', *Scholia*, 4: 56–78.
Balsdon, J. P. V. D. (1962). *Roman Women, their History and Habits* (London).
Bargagli, B., and Grosso, C. (1997). *I Fasti Ostienses: Documento della storia di Ostia* (Ostia).
Barnes, J. (1989). 'Antiochus of Ascalon', in J. Barnes and M. T. Griffin (eds.), *Philosophia Togata*, i (Oxford), 51–96.
—— (1990). 'Pourquoi lire les anciens?', *Cahiers du Collège international de philosophie*, 2: 1–29
—— (1997). *Logic and the Imperial Stoa* (Philosophia Antiqua, 75; Leiden).
—— (1999). 'Roman Aristotle', in J. Barnes and M. T. Griffin (eds.), *Philosophia Togata*, ii (Oxford), 1–69.
—— and Griffin, M. T. (eds.) (1989). *Philosophia Togata*, i. *Essays on Philosophy and Roman Society* (Oxford).
—— and Griffin, M. T. (eds.) (1997). *Philosophia Togata*, ii. *Plato and Aristotle at Rome* (Oxford).
Barnes, T. D. (1971). *Tertullian: A Historical and Literary Study* (Oxford).
—— (1978). 'A Correspondent of Iamblichus', *GRBS* 19: 99–106.

Barton, T. S. (1994). *Power and Knowledge: Astrology, Physiognomics, and Medicine under the Roman Empire* (Ann Arbor).
Bauman, R. A. (1985). *Lawyers in Roman Transitional Politics* (Munich).
——(1995). 'The Death of Ulpian, the Irresistible Force and the Immovable Object', *ZRG* 112: 385–99.
Beagon, M. (1992). *Roman Nature: The Thought of Pliny the Elder* (Oxford).
——(forthcoming). *Pliny: Historia Natura Book 7. An Introduction, Translation and Commentary*.
Beard, M., North, J., and Price, S. R. F. (1999). *Religions of Rome* (Cambridge).
Bennett, J. (1997). *Trajan: Optimus Princeps* (London).
Béranger, J. (1953). 'Le Refus de pouvoir', in *Recherches sur l'aspect idéologique du principat* (Basle), 137–68.
Bidez, J., and Cumont, F. (1922). *Imperatoris Caesaris Flavii Claudii Iuliani: Epistulae, Leges, Poematia* (Paris).
Birley, A. R. (1997). *Hadrian: The Restless Emperor* (London).
——(2000). 'Senators as Generals', in G. Alföldy, B. Dobson, and W. Eck (eds.), *Kaiser, Heer und Gesellschaft in der römischen Kaiserzeit: Gedenkschrift für Eric Birley* (Stuttgart), 97–119.
Blass, F., and Debrunner, A. (1931). *Grammatik des neutestamentlichen Griechisch*, 5th edn. (Göttingen).
Bleicken, J. (1990). *Zwischen Republik und Prinzipat: Zum Charakter des zweiten Triumvirats* (Abhandlungen der Akademie der Wissenschaften in Göttingen, Philologisch-Historische Klasse, 3rd ser. 185).
——(1998). *Augustus: Eine Biographie* (Berlin).
Bloch, R. (1963). *Les Prodiges dans l'Antiquité classique* (Paris).
Blok, J. (1987). 'Sexual Asymmetry: An Historiographical Essay', in J. Blok and D. Mason (eds.), *Sexual Asymmetry: Studies in Ancient Society* (Amsterdam), 1–57.
——and Mason, D. (eds.) (1987). *Sexual Asymmetry: Studies in Ancient Society* (Amsterdam).
Boissier, G. (1897). *Cicéron et ses amis* (Paris).
Bömer, F. (1952). 'Über der Himmelserscheinung nach dem Tode Caesars', *BJ* 152: 27–40.
Bonner, G. (1984). 'The Extinction of Paganism and the Church Historian', *Journal of Ecclesiastical History*, 35: 339–57.
Bostock, D. (1990). 'The Interpretation of Plato's *Crito*', *Phronesis*, 35/1: 1–20.
Bowersock, G. W. (1969). *Greek Sophists in the Roman Empire* (Oxford).
——(ed.) (1974). *Approaches to the Second Sophistic* (University Park, Pa.).
——(1992). Review of Russell 1990, *Gnomon*, 64: 638–40.
——(1998). Review of Swain 1996, *International Journal of the Classical Tradition*, 4: 477–80.
Bowie, E. L. (1970). 'Greeks and their Past in the Second Sophistic', *P&P* 46: 3–41, reprinted with changes in M. I. Finley (ed.), *Studies in Ancient Society* (Oxford, 1974), 166–209.

Bowie, E. L. (1982). 'The Importance of Sophists', *YCS* 27: 29–59.

Brancacci, A. (1985). *Rhetorike philosophousa: Dione Cristostomo nella cultura antica e bizantina* (Rome).

Branham, R. B. (1996). 'Defacing the Currency: Diogenes' Rhetoric and the Invention of Cynicism', in R. B. Branham and M.-O. Goulet-Cazé (eds.), *The Cynics* (Berkeley, Calif.), 81–104.

—— and Goulet-Cazé, M.-O. (eds.) (1996). *The Cynics: The Cynic Movement in Antiquity and its Legacy* (Berkeley, Calif.).

Bremen, R. van (1996). *The Limits of Participation: Women and Civic Life in the Greek East in the Hellenistic and Roman Periods* (Dutch Monographs on Anc. Hist. and Arch., 15; Amsterdam).

Briscoe, J. (1973). *A Commentary on Livy, Books XXXI–XXXIII* (Oxford).

Brisson, L. (1987). 'Amélius: Vie, œuvre, doctrine'. *ANRW* II.36.2: 793–860.

Brittain, C. (2001). *Philo of Larissa: The Last of the Academic Sceptics* (Oxford).

Broughton, T. R. S. (1951). *The Magistrates of the Roman Republic*, i (New York).

Brown, P. (1972). *Religion and Society in the Age of Saint Augustine* (London).

Bruce, F. F. (1990). *The Acts of the Apostles: The Greek Text with Introduction and Commentary*, 3rd edn. (Grand Rapids, Mich.).

Brunt, P. A. (1962). Review of A. H. M. Jones, *Studies in Roman Government and Law* (1960), *CR* 76: 70–3.

—— (1971). *Italian Manpower 225 BC–AD 14* (Oxford).

—— (1975). 'Stoicism and the Principate', *PBSR* 43: 7–35.

—— (1977*a*). 'From Epictetus to Arrian', *Athen.* NS 55: 19–48.

—— (1977*b*). 'Lex de Imperio Vespasiani', *JRS* 67: 95–116.

—— (1989). 'Philosophy and Religion in the Late Republic', in J. Barnes and M. T. Griffin (eds.), *Philosophia Togata*, i. *Essays on Philosophy and Roman Society* (Oxford), 174–98.

—— (1994). 'The Bubble of the Second Sophistic', *BICS* 39: 25–52.

—— and Moore, J. M. (1967). *Res Gestae Divi Augusti* (Oxford).

Buecheler, F. (1908). 'Prosopographica', *Rhein. Mus.* NF 63: 190–6.

Bunt, C. G. E. (1947). *Gothic Painting* (London).

Burkert, W. (1962). 'Caesar und Romulus-Quirinus', *Historia*, 11: 356–76.

Butts, M. (1937). The *Crystal Cabinet: My Childhood at Salterns* (Manchester).

Cameron, A. (1966). 'The Date and Identity of Macrobius', *JRS* 56: 25–38.

—— (1977). 'Paganism and Literature in Late Fourth Century Rome', in *Christianisme et formes littéraires* (Entretiens Hardt, 23; Geneva), 1–30.

—— (1980). 'Neither Male nor Female', *G&R* NS 27: 60–7.

—— (1986). 'Redrawing the Map: Early Christian Territory after Foucault', *JRS* 76: 266–71.

—— and Kuhrt, A. (1993). *Images of Women in Antiquity*, 2nd edn. (London).

Campanile, M. D. (1999). 'La costruzione del sofista: Note sul *βίος* di Polemone', *Studi Ellenistici*, 12: 269–315.

Campbell, B. (2000). *The Roman Land-Surveyors* (Journal of Roman Studies Monographs, 9; London).

Chadwick, H. (1985). 'Augustine on Pagans and Christians: Reflections on Religious and Social Change', in D. Beales and G. Best (eds.), *History, Society and the Churches: Essays in Honour of Owen Chadwick* (Cambridge), 9–27.

Chastagnol, A. (1984). 'Sur un chapitre négligé de l'épigraphie latine: La Titulature des empereurs morts', *REL* 62: 275–87.

Chirasso Colombi, I. (1993). 'Il mestiere di Dio e suoi rischi: Riflessioni in chiave storico-religiosa intorno a *SIG*³ 760', in D. Poli (ed.), *La cultura in Cesare* (Rome), 397–426.

Christ, K. (1988). *Geschichte der römischen Kaiserzeit* (Munich; 2nd edn. 1992).

Ciferri, L. V. (1991). 'Cicero's Conception of *Iurisprudentia*', *RIDA* 3rd ser. 38: 103–19.

Clark, G. (1981). 'Roman Women', *G&R* NS 28: 193–212. Repr. with addenda in I. McAuslan and P. Walcot (eds.), *Women in Antiquity* (Greece and Rome Studies, 3; Oxford, 1996), 36–55.

——(1989). *Iamblichus: On the Pythagorean Life. Translated Texts for Historians* (Liverpool).

——(1993). *Women in Late Antiquity: Pagan and Christian Life-Styles* (Oxford).

Classen, C. J. (1962). 'Romulus in der römischen Republik', *Philologus*, 106: 174–204.

Clauss, M. (1996). '*Deus praesens*: Der römische Kaiser als Gott', *Klio*, 78: 400–33.

Clay, D. (1998). *Paradosis and Survival: Three Chapters in the History of Epicurean Philosophy* (Ann Arbor).

Cogrossi, C. (1981). 'Pietà populare e divinizzazione nel culto di Cesare del 44 a.C.', *CISA* 7: 141–60.

Coleman, J. (2000). *A History of Political Thought: From Ancient Greece to Early Christianity* (Oxford).

Colish, M. L. (1985). *The Stoic Tradition from Antiquity to the Early Middle Ages*, i (Leiden).

Combès, J. (1986–1991). *Damascius: Traité des premiers principes*, I–III (Paris).

Costa, E. (1927). *Cicerone Giureconsulto* (Bologna).

Cotton, H. M. (2000). 'Cassius Dio, Mommsen and the *quinquefascales*', *Chiron*, 30: 217–34.

Crawford, M. H. (1974). *Roman Republican Coinage* (Cambridge).

Crifó, G. (1976). 'Ulpiano: Esperienze e responsabilità del giurista', *ANRW* II.15: 708–89.

Crook, J. A. (1996). 'Political History, 30 BC to AD 14' in A. K. Bowman, E. Champlin, A. Lintott (eds.), *Cambridge Ancient History X*, 2nd edn. (Cambridge), 70–112.

Crouzel, H. (1969). *Grégoire le Thaumaturge: Remerciement à Origène* (Sources chrétiennes, 148; Paris).

Darwall-Smith, R. (1996). *Emperors and Architecture: A Study of Flavian Rome* (Collection Latomus, 195; Brussels).

Degrassi, A. (1952). *I Fasti consolari dell'impero Romano, dal 30 avanti Cristo al 613 dopo Cristo* (Rome).

Desideri, P. (1978). *Dione di Prusa: Un intellettuale greco nell' impero romano* (Florence).

De Ste Croix, G. E. M. (1954). 'Aspects of the "Great" Persecution'. *HThR* 47: 75–113.

——(1963). 'Why were the Early Christians Persecuted?', *Past and Present*, 26: 6–38.

——(1964). 'A Rejoinder' *Past and Present* 27: 28–33.

——(1981). *The Class Struggle in the Ancient Greek World* (London).

Des Places, E. (1973). *Numenius: Fragments* (Paris).

Devereux, G. (1973). 'Self-Blinding of Oidipous in Sophokles' Oidipous Tyrannos', *JHS* 93: 36–49.

Digeser, E. (2000). *The Making of a Christian Empire: Lactantius and Rome* (Ithaca, NY).

Dillon, J. (1977). *The Middle Platonists* (London).

Dodaro, R. (2000). 'Augustine's Secular City', in R. Dodaro and G. Lawless (eds.), *Augustine and his Critics: Essays in Honour of Gerald Bonner* (London and New York), 231–59.

Dodds, E. R. (1960). *Numenius and Ammonius* (Entretiens Hardt, 5; Geneva).

——(1961). 'New Light on the "Chaldaean Oracles"', *HThR* 54: 263–74.

Domenicucci, P. (1996). *Astra Caesarum: Astronomia, astrologia e catasterismo da Cesare a Domiziano* (Pisa).

Dougan, T. W., and Henry, R. M. (1934). *M. Tulli Ciceronis Tusculanarum Disputationum Libri Quinque: A Revised Text with Introduction and Commentary and a collation of Numerous MSS*, ii, containing books 3–5 (Cambridge).

Douglas, A. E. (1995). 'Form and Content in the *Tusculan Disputations*', in J. G. F. Powell (ed.), *Cicero the Philosopher* (Oxford), 197–218.

Drijvers, J. W. (1987). 'Virginity and Asceticism in Late Roman Western Elites', in J. Blok and D. Mason, *Sexual Asymmetry: Studies in Ancient Society* (Amsterdam), 241–73.

Droge, A. J., and Tabor, J. D. (1992). *A Noble Death: Suicide and Martyrdom among Christians and Jews in Antiquity* (San Francisco).

Ducos, M. (1994). 'Philosophie, littérature et droit sous le Principat', *ANRW* II.36.7: 5134–80.

Duffy, J. M. (ed.) (1992). *Michaelis Pselli: Philosophica Minora*, i (Stuttgart and Leipzig).

Dumézil, G. (1966). *La Religion Romaine Archaique* (Paris), tr. as Dumézil 1970.

——(1970). *Archaic Roman Religion* (Chicago).

Duruy, V. (1870–85). *Histoire des Romains* (Paris).

Dyck, A. (1996). *A Commentary on Cicero's De Officiis* (Ann Arbor).

Eck, W. (1970). *Senatoren von Vespasian bis Hadrian* (Munich).

——(1974). 'Beförderungskriterien innerhalb der senatorischen Laufbahn: Dargestellt an der Zeit von 69 bis 138 n. Chr.', *ANRW* II.1: 158–228 = 'Criteri

di avanzamento nella carriera senatoria (69–138 d. C.)', in *Tra epigrafia, prosopografia e archeologia: Scritti scelti, rielaborati ed aggiornati* (Rome, 1996), 27–83.
——(1982). 'Jahres- und Provinzialfasten der senatorischen Statthalter von 69/70 bis 138/139', *Chiron*, 12: 281–362.
——(1989). 'Die Gestalt Frontins in ihrer politischen und sozialen Umwelt', in Frontinus-Gesellschaft (ed.), *Sextus Iulius Frontinus, Wasserversorgung im antiken Rom*, 4th edn. (Munich), 47–62.
——(1991). 'Die italischen Legati Augusti propraetore unter Hadrian und Antoninus Pius', *Historiae Augustae-Colloquia.* Colloquium Parisinum 1990: 183–95. Macerata. = R. Frei-Stolba and M. A. Speidel (eds.), *Die Verwaltung des römischen Reiches in der Hohen Kaiserzeit*, i. 315–26 (Basle, 1998).
——(1993). 'Ein Militärdiplom traianischer Zeit aus dem pannonischen Raum', *KJ* 26: 445–50.
——(1998). *Augustus und seine Zeit* (Munich).
——(1999). *L'Italia nel'impero Romano: Stato e amministrazione in epoca imperiale* (Bari).
——(2002). *Traian: Ein Kaiser der Superlative am Beginn einer Umbruchzeit?*, Sonderbände der Antiken Welt (Mainz) 7–20.
Edwards, M. (2000). *Neoplatonic Saints: The Lives of Plotinus and Proclus by their Students* (Liverpool).
Elm, S. (1994). *'Virgins of God': The Making of Asceticism in Late Antiquity* (Oxford).
Engberg-Pedersen, T. (2000). *Paul and the Stoics* (Edinburgh).
Erler, M. (1991). '*Ἐπιτηδεύειν ἀσάφειαν*', *Cron. Erc.* 21: 83–8.
Finley, M. I. (1973). *The Ancient Economy* (London).
——(ed.) (1974). *Studies in Ancient Society* (London).
Fischel, H. A. (1946). 'Martyr and Prophet: A Study in Jewish Literature', *Jewish Quarterly Review*, 37: 265–80 and 363–86.
——(1977). *Essays in Greco-Roman and Related Talmudic Literature* (New York).
Fishwick, D. (1975). 'The Name of the Demi-God', *Historia*, 24: 624–8.
——(1987). *Imperial Cult in the Latin West* (Leiden).
Fitz, J. (1982). 'Tribuni laticlavii in Pannonien', in S. Panciera (ed.), *Epigrafia e ordine senatorio* (Rome), 319–31.
——(1993). *Die Verwaltung Pannoniens in der Römerzeit* (Budapest).
Fitzmyer, J. A. (1998). *The Acts of the Apostles* (The Anchor Bible, 31; New York).
Foerster, R. (1893). *Scriptores Physiognomonici*, i (Leipzig).
Fontanella, F (1995). 'L'interpretazione ciceroniana del culto degli eroi e delle virtù: Un contributo delle *leges de religione* alla formazione morale della *elite* repubblicana', *RSA* 107: 5–19.
Forbes-Irving, P. M. C. (1990). *Metamorphosis in Greek Myths* (Oxford).
Fowden, G. (1982). 'The Pagan Holy Man in Late Antique Society', *JHS* 102: 33–59.
Fowler, D. P. (1989). 'Lucretius and Politics', in J. Barnes and M. T. Griffin (eds.), *Philosophia Togata* (Oxford), 122–33.

Franke, T. (1991). *Die Legionslegaten der römischen Armee in der Zeit von Augustus bis Trajan*, i–ii (Bochum).

Frede, M. (1987). 'Numenius', *ANRW* II.36.2: 1034–75.

——(1997*a*). 'Euphrates of Tyre', in R. Sorabji (ed.), *Aristotle and After* (BICS Supplement, 68; London), 1–11.

——(1997*b*). 'Celsus' Attack on the Christians', in J. Barnes and M. T. Griffin (eds.), *Philosophia Togata*, ii. *Plato and Aristotle at Rome* (Oxford), 218–40.

Friedlaender, L. (1920). *Darstellungen aus der Sittengeschichte Roms in der Zeit v. Aug. bis zum Ausgang der Antonine*, i–iii, 9th edn. by G. Wissowa (Leipzig).

Frier, B. W. (1985). *The Rise of the Roman Jurists* (Princeton).

Gager, J. G. (1972). *Moses in Greco-Roman Paganism* (SBLMS, 16, Nashville, Ten.).

Galpérine, M.-C. (1987). *Damascius: Des Premiers Principes* (Lagrasse).

Gardner, J. F. (1986). *Women in Roman Law and Society* (London and Sydney).

——(1993). *Being a Roman Citizen* (London).

Garland, R. (1995). *The Eye of the Beholder: Deformity and Disability in the Graeco-Roman World* (London).

Garnsey, P. (1970). *Social Status and Legal Privilege in the Roman Empire* (Oxford).

Garzetti, A. (1950). *Nerva* (Rome).

——(1974). *From Tiberius to the Antonines: A History of the Roman Empire, AD 14–192* (London).

Gee, E. (2000). *Ovid, Aratus and Augustus: Astronomy in Ovid's Fasti* (Cambridge).

Gigante, Marcello (1995). *Philodemus in Italy: The Books from Herculaneum*, tr. D. Obbink (Ann Arbor).

Girardet, K. M. (1990). 'Die Entmachung des Konsulates im Übergang von der Republik zur Monarchie und die Rechtsgrundlagen des augusteischen Prinzipates', in W. Görler and S. Koster (eds.), *Pratum Saraviense* (Stuttgart), 89–126.

——(2000). 'Imperium "Maius": Politische und verfassungsrechtliche Aspekte', in A. Giovannini (ed.), *La Révolution romaine après Ronald Syme: Bilans et perspectives* (Entretiens Hardt, 46; Geneva), 167–227.

Gleason, M. W. (1995). *Making Men: Sophists and Self-Presentation in Ancient Rome* (Princeton).

Goldbacher, A. (1898). *S. Aurelii Augustini Hipponensis Episcopi Epistulae*, ii (Corpus Scriptorum Ecclesiasticorum Latinorum, 34/2; Vienna).

Goldin, J. (1965). 'A Philosophical Session in a Tannaite Academy', *Traditio*, 21: 1–21; repr. in H. A. Fischel (ed.), *Essays in Greco-Roman and Related Talmudic Literature* (New York, 1977), 366–86.

Goodman, M. (1994). *Mission and Conversion: Proselytizing in the Religious History of the Roman Empire* (Oxford).

Görler, W. (1995). 'Silencing the Troublemaker: *De Legibus* 1. 39 and the Continuity of Cicero's Scepticism', in J. G. F. Powell (ed.), *Cicero the Philosopher* (Oxford), 85–113.

Goulet, R. (1989). *Dictionnaire des philosophes antiques*, i (Paris).

Grégoire, H., and Kugener, M.-A. (1930). *Marc le Diacre, Vie de Porphyre* (Paris).

Greenidge, A. H. J. (1901). *Roman Public Life* (London, repr. New York, 1970).

Griffin, M. T. (1971). Review of Bowersock 1969, *JRS* 61: 278–80.

——(1976). *Seneca: A Philosopher in Politics* (Oxford).

——(1984). *Nero: The End of a Dynasty* (London).

——(1986). 'Philosophy, Cato, and Roman Suicide', *G&R* 33: 64–77, 192–202.

——(1988). 'Philosophy for Statesmen: Cicero and Seneca', in H. W. Schmidt and P. Wülfring (eds.), *Antike Denken—moderne Schule: Beiträge zu den ant. Grundlagen unseres Denkens* (Gymnasium Beih. 9; Heidelberg and Zurich), 133–50.

——(1989). 'Philosophy, Politics, and Politicians at Rome', in J. Barnes and M. T. Griffin (eds.), *Philosophia Togata* (Oxford), 1–37.

—— and Atkins, E. M. (1991). *Cicero on Duties* (Cambridge).

——(1994). 'Claudius in the Judgement of the Next Half-Century', in V. M. Strocka (ed.), *Die Regierungszeit des Kaisers Claudius* (41–54N. Chr.): *Umbruch oder Episode?* (Mainz), 307–16.

——(1995*a*). 'Tacitus, Tiberius and the Principate', in I. Malkin and Z. W. Rubinsohn (eds.), *Leaders and Masses in the Roman World: Studies in Honor of Zvi Yavetz* (Leiden) 33–57.

——(1995*b*). 'Philosophical Badinage in Cicero's Letters', in J. G. F. Powell (ed.), *Cicero the Philosopher* (Oxford), 325–46.

——(1996). 'Cynicism and the Romans: Attraction and Repulsion', in R. B. Branham and M.-O. Goulet-Cazé (eds.), *The Cynics: The Cynic Movement in Antiquity and its Legacy* (Berkeley, Calif.), 190–204.

——(1997). 'The Composition of the *Academica*: Motives and Versions', in B. Inwood and J. Mansfeld (eds.), *Assent and Argument: Studies in Cicero's Academic Books* (Leiden), 1–35.

——(1997*b*). 'The Senate's Story', *JRS* 77: 249–63.

——(2000). *Nerva to Hadrian* (Cambridge Ancient History, xi, 2nd edn. Cambridge), 84–131.

Grilli, A. (1971). 'Il piano degli scritti filosofici di Cicerone', *Rivista Critica di Storia della Filosofia*, 26: 302–5.

——(1990). 'Data e senso nel *De Legibus* di Cicerone', *PP* 45: 175–87.

——(1995). 'Cicero e la speranza d'una costituzione', *ACUSD* 31: 55–63.

Grmek, M. D. (1989). *Diseases in the Ancient Greek World*, tr. M. and L. Muellner (Baltimore and London).

Gualandi, G. (1963). *Legislazione imperiale e giurisprudenza*, i–ii (Milan).

Gurval, R. A. (1997). 'Caesar's Comet: The Politics and Poetics of an Augustan Myth', *MAAR* 42: 39–71.

Gwynne, A. (1926). *Roman Education from Cicero to Quintilian* (Oxford).

Hackl, K. (1997). 'Der Zivilprozess des frühen Prinzipats in den Provinzen', *ZRG* 114: 141–59.

Hadot, I. (1978). *Le Problème du Néoplatonisme Alexandrin: Hiéroclès et Simplicius* (Paris).

Hadot, P. (1996). '"Porphyre et Victorinus": Questions et hypothèses', *Res Orientales*, 9: 115–25.

Hadot, P. (1998). *The Inner Citadel: The Meditations of Marcus Aurelius*, tr. M. Chase (Cambridge, Mass.).

Hagendahl, H. (1967). *Augustine and the Latin Classics*, i–ii (Göteburg).

Hahn, J. (1989). *Der Philosoph und die Gesellschaft* (Heidelberger Althistorische Beiträge und Epigraphische Studien, 7; repr. as *Der Philosoph und die Gesellschaft: Sebstverständnis, öffentliches Auftreten und populäre Erwartungen in der hohen Kaiserzeit*; Stuttgart).

Hammond, M. M. (1933). *The Augustan Principate in Theory and Practice during the Julio-Claudian Period* (Cambridge, Mass.).

Hankinson, R. J. (1987). 'Causes and Empiricism: A Problem in the Interpretation of Later Greek Medical Method', *Phronesis*, 32: 329–48.

Hanson, V. D. (1989). *The Western Way of War: Infantry Style in Classical Greece* (London).

Harkins, P. W., and Riese, W. (eds.) (1963). *Galen: On the Passions and Errors of the Soul* (Columbus, Ohio).

Harl, M. (1982). 'Origène et les interprétations grecques de l' "obscurité" biblique', *VC* 36: 334–71.

Harnack, A. von (ed.) (1916). *Porphyrus 'Gegen die Christen'* (Abh. der Preuss. Akademie der Wissenschaften. Phil.-hist. Kl. Nr. 1, Berlin).

Harrison, S. J. (2000). *Apuleius: A Latin Sophist* (Oxford).

Harte, V. (1999). 'Conflicting Values in Plato's *Crito*', *Archiv für Geschichte der Philosophie*, 81/2: 117–47.

Hatch, E. (1914). *The Influence of Greek Ideas and Usages upon the Christian Church* (London).

Heck, E. (1966). *Die Bezeugung von Ciceros Schrift De re publica* (Hildesheim).

Hemelrijk, E. (1987). 'Women's Demonstrations in Republican Rome', in J. Blok and D. Mason (eds.), *Sexual Asymmetry: Studies in Ancient Society* (Amsterdam), 217–40.

——(1999). *Matrona Docta: Educated Women in the Roman Elite from Cornelia to Julia Domna* (London).

Hense, O. (ed.) (1905). *Musonii Rufi Reliquiae* (Leipzig).

Hershbell, J. (1989). 'The Stoicism of Epictetus: Twentieth Century Perspectives', *ANRW* II.36.3: 2148–63.

Heuss, A. (1964). *Römische Geschichte*, ii (Brunswick).

Hickson, F. V. (1993). *Roman Prayer Language: Livy and the Aeneid of Vergil* (Stuttgart).

Hirzel, R. (1883). *Untersuchungen zu Ciceros Philosophischen Schriften*, iii. *Academica priora, Tusculanae Disputationes* (Leipzig).

Hock, R. F. (1980). *The Social Context of Paul's Ministry: Tentmaking and Apostleship* (Philadelphia).

Holford-Strevens, L. (1988). *Aulus Gellius* (London).
——(1997). 'Favorinus: The Man of Paradoxes', in J. Barnes and M. T. Griffin (eds.), *Philosophia Togata*, ii. *Plato and Aristotle at Rome* (Oxford), 188–217.
Honoré, T. (1982). *Ulpian* (Oxford); 2nd edn. (2002) *Ulpian: Pioneer of Human Rights*.
——(1994). *Emperors and Lawyers*, 2nd edn. (Oxford).
Huisman, H. (1956). *Augustinus' Briefwisseling met Nectarius* (Amsterdam).
Hume, D. (1985). *Essays Moral, Political and Literary*. ed. E. Miller (Indianapolis).
Jocelyn, H. D. (1988). 'Romulus and the *di genitales* (Ennius, *Annales* 110–111 Skutsch)', in J. Diggle, J. B. Hall, and H. D. Jocelyn (eds.), *Studies in Latin Literature and its Tradition in Honour of C. O. Brink* (Cambridge), 39–65.
Johnson, P. (1988). *Intellectuals* (London).
Joll, J. (1960). *Intellectuals in Politics* (New York).
Jones, A. H. M. (1951). 'The *Imperium* of Augustus', *JRS* 41: 112–19 = A. H. M. Jones 1968.
——(1964). *The Later Roman Empire 284–602*, i (Oxford).
——(1968). *Roman Government and Law* (New York), 3–17.
——(1970). *Augustus* (New York and London).
Jones, C. P. (1970). 'Sura and Senecio', *JRS* 60: 98–104.
——(1971). *Plutarch and Rome* (Oxford).
——(1972). 'Two Friends of Plutarch', *BCH* 96: 263–7.
——(1973). 'The Date of Dio of Prusa's Alexandrian Oration', *Historia*, 22: 302–9.
——(1978). *The Roman World of Dio Chrysostom* (Cambridge, Mass.).
——and Bowersock, G. (1970). *Philostratus: Life of Apollonius*. (Harmondsworth).
Jones, H. S. (1934). 'The Princeps' in S. A. Cook, F. E. Adcock and M. P. Charlesworth (eds.), *Cambridge Ancient History*, x (Cambridge), 127–58.
Kajanto, I. (1981) 'Fortuna', *ANRW* II.17.1: 502–58.
Kalligas, P. (1991). *Porphyry: On the Life of Plotinus Modern Greek and Greek* (Athens).
Kaster, R. A. (1995). *C. Suetonius Tranquillus: De Grammaticis et Rhetoribus* (Oxford).
Kayser, C. L. (1870–1). *Flavii Philostrati Opera Auctiora* (Leipzig).
Kempshall, M. (2001). '*De Republica* I.39 in Medieval and Renaissance Political Thought', in J. A. North and J. G. F. Powell (eds.), *Cicero's Republic* (London).
Kidd, I. G. (1955). 'The Relation of Stoic Intermediates to the *summum bonum* with Reference to Change in the Stoa', *CQ* NS 5: 181–94.
——(1988). *Posidonius*, ii. *The Commentary* (Cambridge).
Kierdorf, W. (1986). '"*Funus*" und "*consecratio*": Zu Terminologie und Ablauf der römischen Kaiserapotheose', *Chiron*, 16: 43–69.
Kolbe, W. (1931). 'Von der Republik zur Monarchie', in *Aus Roms Zeitwende* (Das Erbe der Alten, 2nd ser. 2, 20: 37–65.
Kraut, R. (1984). *Socrates and the State* (Princeton).
Kroll, F. W. (1902). *Syriani in Metaphysica Commentaria* (Berlin).

Krueger, D. (1996). 'The Bawdy and Society: The Shamelessness of Diogenes in Roman Imperial Culture', in R. Branham and M.-O. Goulet-Cazé, (eds.), *The Cynics: The Cynic Movement in Antiquity and its Legacy* (Berkeley, Calif.), 222–39.

Kugener, M.-A. (1903). 'Zacharias: Vie de Sévère', *Patrologia Orientalis*, ii/1: 7–115.

Kunkel, W. (1967). *Herkunft und soziale Stellung der römischen Juristen*, ii (Graz).

Kurke, L. (1990). 'Pindar's Sixth *Pythian* and the Tradition of Advice Poetry', *TAPA* 120: 85–107.

Lambot, D. C. (1950). *Sancti Aurelii Augustini Hipponensis Episcopi Sermones Selecti Duodeviginti* (Utrecht and Brussels).

Lane, M. S. (1998). 'Argument and Agreement in Plato's *Crito*', *History of Political Thought*, 19/3: 313–30.

Langslow, D. (2000). *Medical Latin in the Roman Empire* (Oxford).

La Penna, A. (1988). 'Brevi considerazioni sulla divinizzazione degli eroi e sul canone degli eroi divinizzati', in D. Porte and J.-P. Néraudau (eds.), *Hommages à Henri Le Bonniec: Res sacrae* (Brussels), 275–87.

Laurenti, R. (1986). 'Musonio, maestro di Epitteto', *ANRW* II.36.3: 2105–46.

Lebek, W. D. (1970). *Verba Prisca* (Göttingen).

Lefkowitz, M. R. (1990). 'Should Women Receive a Separate Education?', *New Literary History: A Journal of Theory and Interpretation* 21/4: *Papers from the Commonwealth Center for Literary and Cultural Change*, 799–815.

——(1993) 'Influential Women', in A. Cameron and A. Kuhrt (eds.), *Images of Women in Antiquity*, 2nd edn. (London), 49–64.

——and Fant, M. B. (1992). *Women's Life in Greece and Rome: A Source Book in Translation*, 2nd edn. (London).

Lenel, O. (1889). *Palingenesia Iuris Civilis*, i–ii (Leipzig).

Lepelley, C. (1979–81). *Les Cités de l'Afrique Romaine en Bas-Empire*, i–ii (Études Augustiniennes; Paris).

Leuze, O. (1905). 'Metellus Caecatus', *Philol.* 18: 195–215.

Levick, B. (1978). '*Concordia* at Rome', in R. A. Carson and C. M. Kraay (eds.), *Essays Presented to Humphrey Sutherland* (London), 217–33.

——(1983). 'The *Senatus Consultum* from Larinum', *JRS* 73: 97–115.

——(1990). *Claudius* (London).

Lewis, S. (1839). *Women's Mission*, 2nd edn. (London).

Liou-Gille, B. (1988). 'Funérailles *in urbe* et divinisation, les funérailles de César', in D. Porte and J.-P. Néraudau (eds.), *Hommages à Henri Le Bonniec: Res sacrae* (Brussels), 288–93.

Lloyd, G. E. R. (1962). 'Left and Right in Greek Philosophy', *JHS* 82: 56–66.

Locke, J. (1988). *Two Treatises of Government*, ed. P. Laslett (Cambridge).

Long, A. A. (1983). 'Arius Didymus and the Exposition of Stoic Ethics', in W. W. Fortenbaugh (ed.), *On Stoic and Peripatetic Ethics: The Work of Arius Didymus* (New Brunswick, NJ), 41–65.

——and Sedley, D. N. (1987). *The Hellenistic Philosophers*, i (Cambridge).

Luterbacher, F. (1904). *Der Prodigienglaube und Prodigienstil der Römer: Eine hist.-phil. Abhandlung* (Burgdorf; repr. Darmstadt 1967).

Luz, M. (1983). 'Eleazar's Second Speech on Masada and its Literary Precedents', *Rheinisches Museum,* 126: 25–43.

McAuslan, I., and Walcot, P. (eds.) (1996). *Women in Antiquity* (Greece and Rome Studies, 3; Oxford).

MacBain, B. (1982). *Prodigy and Expiation: A Study in Religion and Politics in Republican Rome* (Collection Latomus, 177; Brussels), 126–35.

MacKendrick, P. L. (1989). *The Philosophical Books of Cicero* (London).

MacMullen, R. (1980). 'Women in Public in the Roman Empire', *Historia,* 28: 208–18.

Malcovati, E. (1969). *Imperatoris Caesaris Augusti Operum Fragmentae*, 5th edn. (Turin).

Malcovati, H. (1956). *Oratorum Romanorum Fragmenta liberae rei publicae* (Turin).

Malherbe, A. J. (1977). *The Cynic Epistles* (SBLSBS 12; Missoula, Mo.).

Malingrey, A.-M. (1961). *'Philosophia': Étude d'un groupe de mots dans la littérature grecque des présocratiques au IVe siècle après J.C.* (Paris).

Malitz, J. (1988). 'Philosophie und Politik im frühen Prinzipat', in H. W. Schmidt and P. Wülfring (eds.), *Antike Denken—moderne Schule: Beiträge zu den ant. Grundlagen unseres Denkens* (Gymnasium Beih. 9; Heidelberg and Zurich), 151–79.

Maltby, R. (1991). *A Lexicon of Ancient Etymology* (Leeds).

Mansfeld, J. (1994). *Prolegomena: Questions to be Settled before the Study of an Author or a Text* (Philosophia Antiqua, 61; Leiden).

Markus. R. A. (1974). 'Paganism, Christianity and the Latin Classics' in J. W. Binns (ed.), *Latin Literature of the Fourth Century* (London), 1–21.

Marrou, H. I. (1956). *History of Education in Antiquity*, tr. H. Lamb (New York).

Mason, H. J. (1974). *Greek Terms for Roman Institutions: A Lexicon and Analysis* (Toronto).

Matthews, J. (1970). 'The Historical Setting of the "Carmen contra Paganos" (Cod. Par. Lat. 8084)', *Historia*, 19: 464–79.

May, J. R. (1988) *Trials of Character: The Eloquence of Ciceronian Ethos* (London).

Méhat, A. (1966). *Étude sur les 'Stromates' de Clément d'Alexandrie* (Paris).

Mehl, A. (1974). *Tacitus über Kaiser Claudius: Die Ereignisse am Hof. Stud. et Testim. Ant.*, 16 (Munich).

Ménage, G. (1984). *The History of Women Philosophers* (*Historia Mulierum Philosopharum* transl. B. H. Zedler (New York and London).

Menichetti, M. (1995). *Quoius forma virtutei parisuma fuit: Ciste prenestine e cultura di Roma medio-repubblicana* (Arch. Perusina, 12; Rome).

Mette, H. J. (1986–7). 'Philon von Larisa und Antiochus von Askalon', *Lustrum*, 28–9: 9–63.

Michel, J. (1956). 'Sur les origines du "ius gentium" ', *RIDA* 3rd ser. 3: 313–48.

Millar, F. (1963). 'The Fiscus in the First Two Centuries', *JRS* 53: 29–42.

Millar, F. (1965) 'Epictetus and the Imperial Court', *JRS* 55: 141–8.

——(1973). 'Triumvirate and Principate', *JRS* 63: 50–67 also in H. M. Cotton and G. M. Rogers (eds.), *Rome, the Greek World and the East I: The Roman Republic and the Augustan Revolution* (North Carolina, 2002), 241–70.

——(1984). 'Condemnation to Hard Labour in the Roman Empire, from the Julio-Claudians to Constantine', *PBSR* 52: 124–47.

——(1986). 'A New Approach to the Roman Jurists', *JRS* 76: 272–80.

——(1990). 'The Roman *Coloniae* of the Near East: A Study of Cultural Relations', in H. Solin and M. Kajava (eds.), *Roman Eastern Policy and Other Studies in Roman History* (Helsinki), 7–58.

——(1993). *The Roman Near East, 31 BC–AD 337* (Cambridge, Mass.).

——(1998). *The Crowd in the Late Roman Republic* (Ann Arbor).

——(1999). 'The Greek East and Roman Law; the Dossier of M. Cn. Licinius Rufinus', *JRS* 89: 90–108.

——(2000). 'The First Revolution: Imperator Caesar, 36–28 BC', in A. Giovannini (ed.), *La Révolution romaine après Ronald Syme: Bilans et perspectives* (Entretiens Hardt, 46; Geneva), 1–30.

Mitchell, S. (1993). *Anatolia: Land, Men and Gods in Asia Minor* (Oxford).

Moles, J. L. (1978). 'The Career and Conversion of Dio Chrysostom', *JHS* 98: 79–100.

Momigliano, A. (1975). *Alien Wisdom* (Cambridge).

——(1977). 'Popular Religious Beliefs and the Later Roman Historians', in *Essays in Ancient and Modern Historiography* (Oxford), 141–59 (= *Studies in Church History*, 8 (1971): 1–18).

Mommsen, T. (1887). *Römisches Staatsrecht*, i–iii, 3rd edn. (Leipzig).

——(1898). 'Der Zinswucher des Marcus Brutus', *Hermes*, 24: 145–50.

Münsterberg, R. (1915). 'Die Münzen der Sophisten', *NumZeit* 8: 119–24.

Murray, A. (2000). *Suicide in the Middle Ages*, ii. *The Curse on Self-Murder* (Oxford).

Murray, O. (1967). Review of B. Grenzheuser (1964). *Kaiser und Senat in der Zeit von Nero bis Nerva*, Münster, in *JRS* 57: 280–1.

Nisbet, R. (1939). *Cicero: De Domo Sua* (Oxford).

Nörr, D. (1973). 'Iurisperitus sacerdos', in E. von Caemerer, J. H. Kaiser, G. Kegel, W. Mueller-Freienfels, and H. J. Wolff (eds.), *Xenion: Festschrift für P. J. Zepos* (Athens), 555–72.

——(1976). 'Der Jurist im Kreis der Intellektuellen: Mitspieler oder Aussenseiter? (Gellius, Noctes Atticae 16.10)', in D. Medicus and H. H. Seiler (eds.), *Festschrift für Max Kaser zum 70. Geburtstag* (Munich), 57–90.

——(1983). 'Zu einem fast vergessenen Konstitutionentyp, interloqui de plano', *Studi in onore di Cesare Sanfilippo* (Milan), 521–43.

North, J. A. (1975). '*Praesens Divus*', *JRS* 65: 171–7.

Nussbaum, M. C. (1994). *The Therapy of Desire: Theory and Practice in Hellenistic Ethics* (Princeton).

——(1997). 'Kant and Stoic Cosmopolitanism', in J. Bohmann and M. Lutz-Bachmann (eds.), *Perpetual Peace: Essays on Kant's Cosmopolitan Ideal* (Cambridge, Mass.), 25–58.

——(2000). 'Duties of Justice, Duties of Material Aid: Cicero's Problematic Legacy', *Journal of Political Philosophy*, 8: 176–206.

——(2002). 'Musonius Rufus: Stoic, Platonist, and Roman', in M. Nussbaum and J. Sihvola (eds.), *The Sleep of Reason: Erotic Experience and Sexual Ethics in Ancient Greece and Rome* (Chicago).

O'Donnell, J. (1980). 'Augustine's Classical Readings', *Recherches Augustiniennes*, 15: 144–75.

Ogilvie, R. M. (1965). *A Commentary on Livy Books I–IV* (Oxford).

Oliphant, M. (1865–6). *Miss Marjoribanks* (London).

Oliver, J. H. (1975). 'The Empress Plotina and the Second Thymelic Synod', *Historia*, 24: 125–8.

——(1989). *Greek Constitutions of Early Roman Emperors from Inscriptions and Papyri* (Mem. Amer. Philos. Soc. 178; Philadelphia).

O'Meara, D. J. (ed.) (1989). *Michaelis Pselli: Philosophica Minora*, ii (Leipzig).

——(1989). *Pythagoras Revived* (Oxford).

Ooteghem, J. (1967). *Les Caecilii Metelli de la République* (Namur).

Orwell, G. (1970). *Collected Essays, Journalism and Letters*, i (Harmondsworth).

Overing, J. (1986). 'Men Control Women? The "Catch-22" in the Analysis of Gender', *Journ. Mor. and Soc. Stud.* 1: 135–56.

Peachin, M. (1996). *Iudex Vice Caesaris: Deputy Emperors and the Administration of Justice during the Principate* (Stuttgart).

Pelham, H. F. (1911). 'The "Imperium" of Augustus', in F. Haverfield (ed.), *Essays by Henry Francis Pelham* (Oxford), 60–88.

Pflaum, H.-G. (1960–1). *Les Carrières procuratoriennes équestres sous le Haut-Empire romain*, i–ii (Paris).

Picard, G.-C. (1990). 'Le Monument qui Réconforta Neron', *Compt. Rend. de l'Acad. des Inscr. et Belles Lettres* (Jan.–Mar.): 659–66.

Pleket, H. W. (1969). *Epigraph*, ii: *Texts on the Social History of the Greek World* (Leiden).

Pohlenz, M. (1964). *Die Stoa: Geschichte einer geistigen Bewegung*, i–ii, 3rd edn. (Göttingen).

Pomeroy, S. (1975). *Goddesses, Whores, Wives, and Slaves: Women in Classical Antiquity* (New York).

Powell, J. G. F. (1994). 'The *rector rei publicae* of Cicero's *De Republica*', *Scripta Classica Israelica*, 13: 19–29.

——(ed.) (1995). *Cicero the Philosopher* (Oxford).

——(1996). 'Second Thoughts on the Dream of Scipio', *Proceedings of the Leeds International Seminar*, 9: 13–27.

Premerstein, A. von (1937). *Vom Werden und Wesen des Prinzipats* (Abhandlungen der bayerische Akademie der Wissenschaften, philologisch-historische Klasse, NF 15; Berlin).

Price, S. R. F. (1984*a*). *Rituals and Power: The Roman Imperial Cult in Asia Minor* (Cambridge).
——(1984*b*). 'Gods and Emperors: The Greek Language of the Roman Imperial Cult', *JHS* 104: 79–95.
——(1987). 'From Noble Funerals to Divine Cult: The Consecration of Roman Emperors', in D. Cannadine and S. R. F. Price (eds.), *Rituals of Royalty* (Cambridge), 56–105.
Rajak, T. (1997). 'Dying for the Law: The Martyr's Portrait', in M. J. Edwards and S. Swain (eds.), *Portraits: Biographical Representation in the Greek and Latin Literature of the Roman Empire* (Oxford), 39–67.
——and Noy, D. (1993). '*Archisynagogoi*: Office, Title and Social Status in the Greco-Jewish Synagogue', *JRS* 83: 75–93.
Ramsey, J. T., and Licht, A. L. (1997). *The Comet of 44 BC and Caesar's Funeral Games* (Atlanta, Ga.).
Rawski, C. H. (1991). *Petrarch's Remedies for Fortune Fair and Foul*, i (Indiana City).
Rawson, E. (1971). 'Prodigy Lists and the Use of the Annales Maximi', *CQ* 21: 158–69.
——(1985). *Intellectual Life in the Late Roman Republic* (London).
Raz, J. (1986). *The Morality of Freedom* (Oxford).
Reimer, I. R. (1995). *Women in the Acts of the Apostles: A Feminist Liberation Perspective* (Minneapolis).
Reinhardt, T. (2000). 'Rhetoric in the Fourth Academy', *CQ* 50: 531–47.
Rhodes, P. J. (1981). *A Commentary on the* Athenaion Politeia (Oxford).
Riccobono, S. (1941). *Fontes Iuris Romani Anteiustinianae*, i. *Leges* (Florence).
Rich, J. W., and Williams, J. H. C. (1999). '*Leges et Iura P.R. restituit*: A New Aureus of Octavian and the Settlement of 28–27 BC', *Numismatic Chronicle*, 159: 171–213.
Richardson, J. S. (1998). 'Old Statutes Never Die: A Brief History of Abrogation', in M. Austin, J. Harries, and C. Smith (eds.), *Modus Operandi: Essays in Honour of Geoffrey Rickman* (London), 47–62.
Rives, J. (1995). 'Human Sacrifice among Pagans and Christians', *JRS* 85: 65–85.
Rosenberger, V. (1988). *Gesähmte Götter: Das Prodigienwesen der römischen Republik* (Stuttgart).
Rubincam, C. (1992). 'The Nomenclature of Julius Caesar and the Later Augustus in the Triumviral Period', *Historia*, 41: 88–103.
Rudd, N. (1998). *Cicero: The Republic and the Laws* (Oxford).
Runia, D. T. (1988). 'Philosophical Heresiography: Evidence in Two Ephesian Inscriptions', *ZPE* 72: 241–2.
Russell, D. A. (ed.) (1990). *Antonine Literature* (Oxford).
Rutherford, R. B. (1989). *The Meditations of Marcus Aurelius: A Study* (Oxford).
Saffrey, H. D., and Westerink, L. G. (1968) *Proclus: Théologie Platonicienne*, i (Paris).
Salmann, K. (ed.) (1997). *Handbuch der lateinischen Literatur der Antike*, iv. *Die*

Literatur des Umbruchs: Von der römischen zur christlichen Literatur, 117 bis 284 n. Chr. (Munich).
Sandnes, K. O. (1993). 'Paul and Socrates: The Aim of Paul's Areopagus Speech', *Journal for the Study of the New Testament*, 50: 13–26.
Scarcia, R. (1991). '*Fragmentum Agrippinae*: Ipotesi di un ricupero (et un riscontro shakespeariano)', *GIF* 43: 243–63.
Schermaier, M. J. (1993). 'Ulpian als wahrer Philosoph: Notizen zum selbstverständnis eines römischen Juristen', in M. J. Schermaier and Z. Vegh (eds.), *Ars boni et aequi: Festschrift für W. Waldstein zum 65. Geburtstag* (Stuttgart), 303–22.
Schiller, A. (1971). 'Custom in Classical Roman Law', in *An American Experience in Roman Law* (Göttingen), 41–55.
Schmidt, H. W., and Wülfring, P. (eds.) (1988). *Antike Denken—moderne Schule: Beiträge zu den ant. Grundlagen unseres Denkens* (Gymnasium Beih. 9; Heidelberg and Zurich).
Schmitz, T. (1997). *Bildung und Macht. Zur sozialen und politischen Funktion der zweiten Sophistik in der griechischen Welt der Kaiserzeit* (Zetemata, 97; Munich).
Schofield, M. (1991). *The Stoic Idea of the City* (Cambridge; reissued Chicago, 1999).
——(1995). 'Cicero's Definition of *Res Publica*', in J. G. F. Powell (ed.), *Cicero the Philosopher* (Oxford), 63–84.
Schwarte, K. H. (1979). 'Trajans Regierungsbeginn und der "Agricola" des Tacitus', *BJ* 179: 139–76.
Schwartz, D. R. (1990). *Agrippa i* (Text und Studien zum antiken Judentum, 23; Tübingen).
Schwering, W. (1914–15). '*Deus* und *divus*', *Indogermanische Forschungen*, 34: 1–44.
Scott, K. (1941). 'The *sidus Iulium* and the Apotheosis of Caesar', *CP* 36: 257–72.
Shackleton Bailey, D. R. (1977). *Cicero: Epistulae ad Familiares*, i. *62–47* BC (Cambridge).
Shaw, G. (1995). *Theurgy and the Soul* (University Park, Pa.).
Sherwin-White, A. N. (1952). 'The Early Persecutions and Roman Law Again', *JTS* 3: 199–213.
——(1964). 'Why were the Early Christians Persecuted? An Amendment', *Past and Present*, 27: 23–7.
——(1966). *The Letters of Pliny* (Oxford).
Sihler, A. L. (1995). *New Comparative Grammar of Greek and Latin* (Oxford).
Simmons, A. J. (1979). *Moral Principles and Political Obligations* (Princeton).
Skutsch, O. (1985). *The Annals of Quintus Ennius* (Oxford).
Slings, S. R. (1995). 'Protreptic in Ancient Theories of Philosophical Literature', in J. G. J. Abbenes, S. R. Slings, and I. Sluiter (eds.), *Greek Literary Theory after Aristotle: A Collection of Papers in Honour of D. M. Schenkeveld* (Amsterdam), 173–92.
——(1999). *Plato: Clitophon. Edited with Introduction, Translation and Commentary* (Cambridge).

Smith, M. F. (1996). *The Philosophical Inscription of Diogenes of Oinoanda* (Vienna).
——(1998). 'Excavations at Oinoanda 1997: The New Epicurean texts', *AS* 48: 125–70.
Smith, R. R. R. (1998). 'Cultural Choice and Political Identity in Honorific Portrait Statues in the Greek East in the Second Century AD', *JRS* 88: 56–93.
——(1999). Review of Zanker 1995, *Gnomon*, 71: 448–57.
Sorabji, R. (ed.) (1997). *Aristotle and After* (BICS Supplement 68; London).
——(2000). *Emotion and Peace of Mind: From Stoic Agitation to Christian Temptation* (Oxford).
Southern, P. (1998). *Augustus* (London).
Spengel, L. (1854). *Rhetores Graeci*, ii (Leipzig).
Staden, H. von (1997). 'Galen and the "Second Sophistic"', in R. Sorabji (ed.), *Aristotle and After* (BICS Supplement, 68; London), 33–54.
Stein, P. (1978). 'The Place of Servius Sulpicius Rufus in the Development of Roman Legal Science', in *Festschrift F. Wieacker* (Göttingen), 175–84.
Steinby, E. M. (ed.) (1993). *Lexicon Topographicum Urbis Romae*, i (Rome).
Stern, M. (ed.) (1974). *Greek and Latin Authors on Jews and Judaism*, i–ii (Jerusalem).
Stowers, S. K. (1984). 'Social Status, Public Speaking, and Private Teaching: The Circumstances of Paul's Preaching Activity', *Novum Testamentum*, 26/1: 59–82.
——(2001). 'Does Pauline Christianity Resemble a Hellenistic Philosophy?', in T. Engberg-Pedersen (ed.), *Paul Beyond the Judaism–Hellenism Divide* (Louisville, Ky.), 89–102.
Swain, S. (1990). 'Plutarch's Lives of Cicero, Cato, and Brutus', *Hermes*, 118: 192–203.
——(1996). *Hellenism and Empire* (Oxford).
——(1997). 'Plutarch, Plato, Athens, and Rome', in J. Barnes and M. T. Griffin (eds.), *Philosophia Togata*, ii (Oxford), 165–87.
Syme, R. (1939). *The Roman Revolution* (Oxford).
——(1958). *Tacitus*, i–ii (Oxford).
——(1970). 'Three Jurists', *Bonner Historia-Augusta Colloquium 1968/9* (Bonn), 309–23 = *Roman Papers*, ii (Oxford, 1979), 790–804.
——(1971). 'Hadrian in Moesia', in R. Syme, *Danubian Papers* (Bucharest), 204–12.
——(1972). 'Lawyers in Government: The Case of Ulpian', *Proc. Am. Philos. Soc.* 116: 406–9 = *Roman Papers*, iii (Oxford, 1984), 863–8.
——(1980). 'Fiction about Roman Jurists', *ZRG* 97: 78–104 = *Roman Papers*, iii (Oxford, 1984), 1393–414.
——(1988). *Roman Papers V*, ed. A. R. Birley (Oxford).
Tardieu, M. (1996). 'Recherches sur la formation de l'Apocalypse de Zostrien et les sources de Marius Victorinus', *Res Orientales*, 9: 7–114.
Tarrant, H. (1993). *Thrasyllan Platonism* (Ithaca, NY, and London).
Taylor, L. R. (1931). *The Divinity of the Roman Emperor* (Middletown, Conn.).

Temporini, H. (1978). *Die Frauen am Hof Trajans: Ein Beitrag zum Stellung der Augustae im Prinzipat* (Berlin and New York).

Thesleff, H. (1965). *The Pythagorean Texts from the Hellenistic Period* (Åbo).

Thomas, P. J. (1998). 'Alternative Paradigm for Roman Law', *RIDA* 3rd ser. 45: 647–57.

Tod, M. N. (1957). 'Sidelights on Greek Philosophers', *JHS* 77: 132–41.

Toohey, P. (1984). 'Politics, Prejudice, and the Trojan Genealogies: Varro, Hyginus, and Horace', *Arethusa*, 17: 5–28.

Trapp, M. B. (1997). *Maximus of Tyre: Orationes* (Oxford).

Trombley, F. R. (1993). *Hellenic Religion and Christianization c. 370–529*, i (Leiden).

Turpin, W. (1999). '*Formula*, *Cognitio* and Proceedings *Extra Ordinem*', *RIDA* 46: 489–574.

van den Hout, M. P. J. (1999). *A Commentary on the Letters of M. Cornelius Fronto* (Leiden).

van der Horst, P. W. (1996). '"A Simple Philosophy": Alexander of Lycopolis on Christianity', in K. Algra, P. W. van der Horst, and D. T. Runia (eds.), *Polyhistor: Studies in the History and Historiography of Ancient Philosophy Presented to Jaap Mansfeld on his Sixtieth Birthday* (Philosophia Antiqua, 72; Leiden) 313–29.

Vanderspoel, J. (1999). 'Correspondence and Correspondents of Julius Julianus', *Byzantion*, 69: 396–478.

Van der Waerdt, P. A. (1994). 'Philosophical Influence on Roman Jurisprudence? The Case of Stoicism and Natural Law', *ANRW* II.36.7: 4851–900.

van Weddingen, R.-E. (1957). *Favonii Elogii Disputatio de Somnio Scipionis* (Collection Latomus, 27; Brussels).

Versnel, H. S. (1987). 'Wife and Helpmeet: Women of Ancient Athens in an Anthropological Perspective', in J. Blok and D. Mason (eds.), *Sexual Asymmetry: Studies in Ancient Society* (Amsterdam), 59–86.

Vidman, L. (1982). *Fasti Ostienses*, ii (Prague).

Vlastos, G. (1983). 'The Socratic Elenchus', *Oxford Studies in Ancient Philosophy*, 1: 27–58.

Vretska, K. (1976). *Sallust de Catilinae Coniuratione* (Heidelberg).

Wachsmuth, C. (1871). *Commentatio de Stobaei eclogis* (Göttingen).

Wallace-Hadrill, A. (1982). '*Civilis Princeps*: Between Citizen and King', *JRS* 72: 32–48.

Wallmann, P. (1988). *Triumviri Rei Publicae Constituendae: Untersuchungen zur politischen Propaganda im Zweiten Triumvirat* (Frankfurt).

Walzer, R. (1949). *Galen on Jews and Christians* (London).

Watson, A. (1974). *Law Making in the Later Roman Republic* (Oxford).

——(1985). *The Digest of Justinian: Latin Text Edited by Theodor Mommsen with the Aid of Paul Krueger. English Translation Edited by Alan Watson*, i–iv (Philadelphia).

Weinstock, S. (1971). *Divus Julius* (Oxford).
Weiss, P. (1999). 'Ein Diplom des Antoninus Pius für Moesia Inferior von Dez. 145/Dez. 146', *ZPE* 124: 279–86.
Weiss, R. (1998). *Socrates Dissatisfied: An Analysis of Plato's Crito* (Oxford).
Westerink, L. G. (1973). *The Greek Commentators on Plato's Phaedo*, i (Amsterdam).
White, S. A. (1995). 'Cicero and the Therapists', in J. G. F. Powell (ed.), *Cicero the Philosopher* (Oxford), 219–46.
Wilamowitz-Moellendorff, U. von (1925). Review of André Boulanger, *Aelius Aristide et la Sophistique dans la province d'Asie au IIe siècle de notre ère*, *Litteris* 2: 126, repr. in *Kleine Schriften*, 3 (1969): 421.
Winterbottom, M. (1974). *The Elder Seneca*, i. *Controversiae* i–vi (Cambridge, Mass., and London).
Wiseman, T. P. (1974). 'Legendary Genealogies in Late Republican Rome', *G&R* 21: 153–64.
——(1979). *Clio's Cosmetics* (Totowa, NJ).
——(2000). 'Liber: Myth, Drama and Ideology in Republican Rome', in C. Bruun (ed.), *The Roman Middle Republic: Politics, Religion, and Historiography c.400–133 BC. Papers from a Conference at the Inst. Rom. Finlandiae, Sept. 11–12, 1998, Acta Inst. Rom. Finlandiae* 23 (Rome), 265–99.
Wistrand, E. (1987). *Felicitas Imperatoria* (Gothenburg).
Wolfram, S. (1985). 'Divorce in England: 1700–1857', *Oxford Journal of Legal Studies*, 5: 155–86.
Wolfson, H. A. (1970). *The Philosophy of the Church Fathers*, 3rd edn. (Cambridge, Mass.).
Woolf, V. (1929). *A Room of One's Own* (London).
——(1938). *Three Guineas* (repr. 1943; London).
——(1976). *Moments of Being: Unpublished Autobiographical Writings of Virginia Woolf*, ed. J. Schulkind (London).
Woozley, A. D. (1979). *Law and Obedience: The Argument of Plato's Crito* (London).
Wörrle, M. (1988). *Stadt und Fest im kaiserzeitlichen Kleinasien* (Munich).
Yakobson, A., and Cotton, H. M. (1985). 'Caligula's *Recusatio Imperii*', *Historia*, 34: 497–503.
Zanker, P. (1995). *Die Maske des Sokrates: Das Bild des Intellektuellen in der antiken Kunst* (Munich). English tr., *The Mask of Socrates: The Image of the Intellectual in Antiquity* (Sather Classical Lectures; Berkeley, Calif.).
Zeller, E., and Mondolfo, R. (1961). *La filosofia dei Greci nel suo Sviluppo Storico* vi (Florence).
Ziegler, K. (1949). *Plutarchos von Chaironeia* (Stuttgart = *RE* 21/1 (1951): 636–962).
——(1958). *M. Tulli Ciceronis De Re Publica*, 4th edn. (Leipzig).
Zintzen, C. (1967). *Damascii vitae Isidori reliquiae* (Hildesheim).

INDEX OF ANCIENT NAMES

INDEX OF MODERN AUTHORS

GENERAL INDEX

DATE DUE

Printed in USA